Baetica Felix

Baetica Felix

PEOPLE AND PROSPERITY IN SOUTHERN SPAIN FROM CAESAR TO SEPTIMIUS SEVERUS

EVAN W. HALEY

UNIVERSITY OF TEXAS PRESS

Austin

This book has been supported by an endowment dedicated to classics and the ancient world and funded by the Areté Foundation; the Gladys Krieble Delmas Foundation; the Dougherty Foundation; the James R. Dougherty, Jr. Foundation; the Rachael and Ben Vaughan Foundation; and the National Endowment for the Humanities. The endowment has also benefited from gifts by Mark and Jo Ann Finley, Lucy Shoe Meritt, the late Anne Byrd Nalle, and other individual donors.

LIBRARY OF CONGRESS CATALOGING-IN-PUBLICATION DATA

Haley, Evan W.
Baetica felix : people and prosperity in southern Spain from Caesar to Septimius Severus / Evan W. Haley. — 1st ed.
p.   cm.
Includes bibliographical references and index.
ISBN: 0292722265.
1. Andalusia (Spain)—Economic conditions.   2. Andalusia (Spain)—Social conditions.   3. Land settlement—Spain—Andalusia—History—To 1500.
4. Social structure—Spain—Andalusia—History—To 1500.   5. Andalusia (Spain)—Civilization—Roman influences.   I. Title.
HC387.A64 H35   2003
330.9366—dc21   2002011488

To Dorothy Geyer Haley and Frederick Thomas Haley

※

Contents

List of Illustrations

Acknowledgments

Various institutions and persons have supported me during the preparation of this book. The German Archaeological Institute in Madrid under its directors Professor Dr. Hermanfrid Schubart and Professor Dr. Thilo Ulbert extended unlimited hospitality and access to its library. The staff of the interlibrary lending office of Mills Library at McMaster University deserves special thanks for its help. I wish to thank *Phoenix*, journal of the Classical Association of Canada, for permission to reproduce material that I published in volume 50 (1996). For suggestions, fruitful discussion, and offprints, I am grateful to Géza Alföldy (Heidelberg), Juan Manuel Abascal (Alicante), José Beltrán (Sevilla), Michael Blech (Madrid), José Ramón Carrillo (Córdoba), Patrice Cressier (Madrid), Antonio Caballos (Sevilla), Jonathan Edmondson (Toronto), Garrett Fagan (Penn State), Helena Gimeno (Madrid), Patrick Le Roux (Paris), Juan Francisco Rodríguez Neila (Córdoba), Enrique Melchor (Córdoba), Reg Ripton (Hamilton), Encarnación Serrano (Málaga), and Armin Stylow (Munich).

Many other friends, as well as family and in-laws, have given support and encouragement. My deepest appreciation goes to Professor Robert C. Knapp (California) for his constant advice and encouragement at different stages of the manuscript. My wife Sabine and daughter Charlotte have helped me keep my sense of humor throughout.

Abbreviations

AAA = *Anuario Arqueológico de Andalucía*
AAC = *Anales de Arqueología Cordobesa*
AE = *L'Année Epigraphique*
AEA = *Archivo Español de Arqueología*
AJPh = *American Journal of Philology*
AncSoc = *Ancient Society*
ANRW = *Aufstieg und Niedergang der Römischen Welt*
AntJ = *The Antiquaries Journal*
BCAR = *Bullettino della Commissione Archeologica Comunale di Roma*
BJ = *Bonner Jahrbücher*
BMC = H. Mattingly, *Coins of the Roman Empire in the British Museum,* vol. 3, *Nerva to Hadrian* (London, 1936)
BRAC = *Boletín de la Real Academia de Córdoba*
BRAH = *Boletín de la Real Academia de Historia*
Bronces = *Los bronces romanos en España* (Madrid, 1990)
BSEAA = *Boletín del Seminario de Arte y Arqueología de la Universidad de Valladolid*
CB = *Classical Bulletin*
CCG = *Cahiers du Centre G. Glotz*
CIL = *Corpus Inscriptionum Latinarum*
CIL II ^{2}/5 = A. U. Stylow et al., *Corpus Inscriptionum Latinarum: Editio altera,* vol. 2, part 5: *Conventus Astigitanus* (Berlin, 1998)
CIL II ^{2}/7 = A. U. Stylow et al., *Corpus Inscriptionum Latinarum: Editio altera,* vol. 2, part 7: *Conventus Cordubensis* (Berlin, 1995)

CILA 2 = J. González Fernández, *Corpus de Inscripciones Latinas de Andalucía*, vol. 2, *Sevilla*, book 1: *La Vega (Hispalis)* (Seville, 1991)

CILA 2, 3 = J. González Fernández, *Corpus de Inscripciones Latinas de Andalucía*, vol. 2, *Sevilla*, book 3: *La Campiña* (Seville, 1996)

CILA 6 = C. González Román and J. Mangas Manjarrés, *Corpus de Inscripciones Latinas de Andalucía*, vol. 3, *Jaén*, book 1 (Seville, 1991)

Coll. = *Mosaicarum et Romanarum Legum Collatio*, in *FIRA²* II, 543–589

CP = *Classical Philology*

CPAM = *Cuadernos de Prehistoria y Arqueología de la Universidad Autónoma de Madrid*

C.Th. = *Codex Theodosianus*

DE = E. de Ruggiero, ed., *Dizionario epigrafico di antichità romane* (Rome, 1895–)

Dig. = *Iustiniani Digesta*

ERBC = A. M. Canto, *Epigrafía Romana de la Beturia Céltica* (Madrid, 1997)

ES = *Epigraphische Studien*

FIRA² = S. Riccobono et al., *Fontes Iuris Romani Anteiustiniani*, 3 vols. (Florence, 1940–1943)

FlorIlib = *Florentia Iliberritana*

HAE = *Hispania Antiqua Epigraphica*

HAnt = *Hispania Antiqua. Revista de Historia Antigua*

HEp = *Hispania Epigraphica* (Madrid)

I.Eph. = H. Wankel et al., *Die Inschriften von Ephesos* (Bonn, 1979–)

IG = *Inscriptiones Graecae*

ILS = *Inscriptiones Latinae Selectae*

IRCádiz = J. González, *Inscripciones romanas de la provincia de Cádiz* (Cádiz, 1982)

JRA = *Journal of Roman Archaeology*

JRS = *Journal of Roman Studies*

MBAH = *Münstersche Beiträge zur Antiken Handelsgeschichte*

MCV = *Mélanges de la Casa de Velázquez*

MDAI(M) = *Mitteilungen des deutschen archäologischen Instituts (Madrider Abteilung)*

MEFRA = *Mélanges d'archéologie et d'histoire de l'Ecole française de Rome, Antiquité*

MHA = *Memorias de Historia Antigua*

MRR 2 = T.R.S. Broughton, *The Magistrates of the Roman Republic*, vol. 2 (New York, 1952)

NAH = *Noticiario Arqueológico Hispánico*

OLD = *Oxford Latin Dictionary*

PBSR = *Papers of the British School at Rome*

PIR² = *Prosopographia Imperii Romani*, 2d ed. (1933 –)

RAN = *Revue archéologique de Narbonnaise*

REA = *Revue des Etudes Anciennes*

Roman Statutes = M. H. Crawford et al., eds., *Roman Statutes* (London, 1996)

SHHA = *Studia Historica. Historia Antigua* (Salamanca)

TLL = *Thesaurus Linguae Latinae* (Leipzig, 1900 –)

ZPE = *Zeitschrift für Papyrologie und Epigraphik*

A note on epigraphic conventions: A letter or group of letters followed by parentheses indicates the abbreviation of a name or word. A letter or group of letters followed by square brackets indicates a letter or letters missing in the inscription. For the sake of clarity and uniformity, I have generally, except for quotations from inscriptions, left parentheses and square brackets empty—e.g., P(   ) or R[   ]—in the absence of secure indications as to the number of abbreviated or missing letters.

※

Glossary of Technical Terms

aedes Augusti, free-standing or attached temple/enclosure devoted to the imperial cult.

aedificia (pl.), buildings and outliers erected on rural properties.

aerarium (Saturni), public treasury and archives.

ager, rural territory of a *municipium* or *colonia.*

ager publicus, public or state-owned land.

annona, public grain supply, by extension the bureau responsible for supplying the city of Rome and the Roman army with grains and other foodstuffs.

apparitores (pl.), usually freedmen assistants to Roman magistrates.

arbores (pl.), upright supports for a wine- or oil-press.

calles publici (pl.), cattle or sheep paths for transhumant herds.

coloni (pl.), tenants involved in farming or in manufacturing.

colonia/coloniae, a native or greenfield community with a Roman constitution, all or some of whose inhabitants were Roman citizens.

conventus, a juridical assize district.

conventus civium Romanorum, an informal grouping of Roman citizens resident in non-Roman provincial communities.

decurionales (pl.), town councilors and their families.

deductiones (pl.), settlements of veterans in Roman colonies.

defrutum, unfermented grape juice (must).

diffusores olearii (pl.), suppliers of olive oil contractually engaged with the Roman authorities.

dignitas, the esteem or honor that flows from officeholding or the eligibility to hold office or serve as a local or imperial juror.

dolia (pl.), food-storage jars.

domini navium (pl.), shipbuilders and owners.

domus Augusta, imperial household.

ducenarii (pl.), freeborn Romans with a minimum wealth of 200,000 sesterces eligible to serve as imperial jurors.

duovir, chief magistrate of a *municipium* or *colonia.*

eques/equites, an equestrian or knight, the second-ranking aristocratic order in ancient Rome, marked by a qualification of free birth, moral probity, and the possession of a minimum wealth of 400,000 sesterces.

familiae (pl.), slave and/or freedman households.

figlina/figlinae, a pottery devoted to the manufacture of utilitarian objects ranging from finewares to construction materials such as bricks and tiles.

fiscus, lit. "basket," the imperial treasury or treasury of a provincial governor.

flamen, a priest devoted to one particular deity; in the Principate, dedicated to the imperial cult.

fundus, an agricultural estate.

garum, salted fish sauce or paste.

honestus, see s.v. *vir honestus.*

imbrices (pl.), semi-circular roof tiles.

imperium, power of command.

incolae (pl.), resident aliens domiciled in a *municipium* or *colonia.*

ingenui (pl.), freeborn persons.

iudices (pl.), jurors.

ius Latii, the "Latin right," which assimilated at law peregrines to the status of Roman citizens in their communities, and which gave the Roman citizenship to local officeholders.

Kalendarium Vegetianum, a collection of agricultural properties originally in the possession of the senatorial Valerii Vegeti, which, through inheritance or confiscation, passed into imperial control by c. A.D. 160 and henceforth was managed by an imperial *procurator.*

laterculi (pl.), small bricks.

legatus Augusti propraetore, senatorial governor of an imperial province.

liberta, a female ex-slave.

locupletes (pl.), wealthy or prosperous landowners.

mercenarii (pl.), wage or salaried workers in the Greco-Roman world.

metallum, mine or mining area.

munera (pl.), uncompensated civic duties involving the provision of labor, services, or money.

munera patrimoniorum (pl.), obligations, mostly financial, connected with the possession of land.

municipium/municipia, a native community endowed with a Roman constitution.

navicularius, a ship owner.

negotia (pl.), business or commercial activities or undertakings.

negotiator/negotiatores, a trader or merchant.

nomina (pl.), the "family" or clan name of Romans.

officinator, a master potter.

oppidum, a fortified or semi-fortified indigenous community, frequently placed on high ground or a prominence.

opus caementicium (or simply *caementicium*), mortared rubble or concrete.

opus signinum, waterproof concrete/cement.

opus spicatum, pavement laid with small bricks, arranged in a herringbone pattern.

opus tessellatum, a mosaic pavement.

ordo/ordines, social and legal rank or estate, marked by qualifications of birth and wealth. In a more specialized sense, a local town council.

originarius, citizen of a community (from *origo,* or "birthplace").

pagus, a rural administrative (fiscal) district.

pars fructuaria, portion of a farm or villa devoted to the processing of agricultural products.

pars urbana, the residential portion of a farm or villa.

patrimonium Caesaris, private property of the emperor.

plebs, slave, ex-slave, or freeborn persons ineligible to serve as a local town councilor or juror.

portoria (pl.), import and export duties.

possessores (pl.), Roman landowners or owners of other productive facilities.

potestas, power or control exercised by the head of a household.

praefurnium, door or opening to a kiln combustion chamber through which combustibles are admitted.

procurator, administrator or official, especially concerned with finances.

publicani (pl.), persons acting in association who are devoted to the collection of taxes or leasing of mines/lands.

putei (pl.), grain-storing silos.

res privata, property of the emperor obtained through confiscation.

sacerdos, a priest or priestess.

scriptura libraria, inscriptional letter forms marked by a gracile shape and serifs.

sevir Augustalis, member of a corporate body of rich freedmen and the free-born below the rank of decurions. Six of them constituted annual boards of priests devoted to certain aspects of emperor worship.

societas, an association, of varying duration, of two or more individuals (*socii*) for the purposes of business and/or production.

sportulae (pl.), gifts or handouts in kind or in cash.

stercilinum, large-scale manure pit.

tegulae (pl.), flanged roof-tiles.

terra sigillata (or simply *sigillata*), plain or decorated red-slip ceramics.

tituli picti (pl.), painted inscriptions.

vicus, in an urban context, a neighborhood; in a rural one, a small town or village not enjoying the status of a *colonia* or *municipium*.

vilicus, the slave manager/foreman of a farm or other productive facility.

vir honestus (or simply *honestus*)/*viri honesti,* a person of free birth, moral probity, and eligible as a local juror or above.

vir idoneus/viri idonei, see s.v. *vir honestus*.

※

Baetica Felix

✳

Introduction

This book is a social and economic history of the Roman province of Baetica from Augustus to the Severan emperors. It represents also a contribution to the complex debate over the nature of the Roman economy. Those reflections on the Roman economy published in recent years that have helped to frame this study conceptually include the essays of Whittaker, Parkins, and others in Parkins' *Roman Urbanism,* as well as works by Harris, Jongman, and Pleket.[1] They touch on, among other things, the problems of the role of the (consumer?) city, the nature of exchange, the primitiveness versus modernity of the ancient economy, consumption, labor, and the conceptualization of the ancient economy. A summary of the historical debate on the nature of the Roman and ancient economy in general, extending from the primitivist-modernist opposition of Bücher and Meyer, the substantivist position of Polanyi and his school, the legacy of Moses Finley and genesis of the "New Orthodoxy," and the tenets of the school of Gramsci represented by Carandini, Schiavone, and others, is neatly laid out by Molina Vidal in his study of trading contacts between Hispania Citerior and Italy in the late Republican and early imperial periods.[2] Also worth careful study is Neville Morley's *Metropolis and Hinterland.*[3] That book summarizes exhaustively the history of investigation into, and theoretical approaches to, the ancient economy in general, and Roman economy in specific. Morley propounds the "New Orthodoxy" and argues that within the constraints of a preindustrial economy, Rome did witness some growth in the central period of its history.

To what degree the needs of the central state in the form of taxes or the needs of the city of Rome and army in the shape of foodstuffs and supplies were responsible for this undoubted growth is a controversial matter. Noneconomic or only indirectly economic factors may have been, in part, at work in Hispania. A principal argument in this book is that Rome's bestowal of municipal and colonial status—but particularly the former—in Further Spain and in the province of Baetica that emerged from it under Augustus also generated economic growth for a variety of reasons, not least of which were the extraordinary financial demands—social in origin as much as economic—that municipalization imposed on the elite members of new *municipia,* in addition to potential elite members of Baetican communities.

Cui bono? Whom did the Roman economy benefit? Both critics and advocates of the "New Orthodoxy" hold that the mass of the population during the Principate lived at or just above subsistence.[4] This notion is part of the widespread conception that the Roman economy during the Principate was underdeveloped. Proponents of this view argue with bravura: even classical economic analysis is brought in to argue that the imperial period saw little or no gain in labor productivity—certainly not enough to matter to the mass of the population. No evidence shows a rise in real per capita Gross Domestic Product during the Principate, and return on capital investment was stymied in part by a considerable number of slaves living at subsistence, and overall by lack of demand.[5] The old minimalist versus maximalist debate is now eclipsed: the Roman economy was productive, on the whole, to a marvelous degree; was sophisticated in many respects; and generated complex patterns of commerce.[6] A common assumption is that the wealth of the Roman world created splendid urban centers and urban-based elites, whose affluence rested on the "sufferings of the low-in-status."[7] City-dwelling landowners siphoned off the resources of the town's territory and peasantry, chiefly in the form of rents, unequally imposed taxes, and grain requisitions.[8] With limited resources and capacity for growth, Roman society came to a peculiar form of accommodation by which social inequalities and wealth disparity were largely immutable. Possibilities for social mobility existed but were restricted largely to freedmen and their descendants. Even the *apparitores,* adjutants to senatorial magistrates, who were frequently freeborn but of sub-decurional status, owed their social mobility to their relationship with, and access to, the powerful.[9] They were also a minute percentage of the total Roman population.[10]

A notable exception to the prevailing view is that of Engels, whose optimistic estimate of an average peasant surplus of 50 percent is based on what is, on the face of it, an inapposite use of a passage from Aristotle to describe the situation of peasants in the Roman imperial period.[11] L. A. Thompson, drawing on the testimony of authors such as Strabo and Pliny the Elder, underscores the anachronistic notion of development versus underdevelopment as applied to antiquity. In terms of ancient, elite values, a province such as Baetica stands as developed: the main yardstick here is the proliferation of city-units and their sophistication. But even Thompson speaks of the essential exploitative nature of the Pax Romana, by which local elites used the provincial peasantry to satisfy their material wants; and he can characterize Roman society in the western provinces as marked by a widening "social and economic distance between the local aristocracy and the exploited peasant masses."[12] Harl, in his survey of coinage in the Roman world, expresses a certain skepticism about the underdevelopment model and envisages the common use of coins as a medium of exchange even in rural contexts, but, in the end, he writes in general terms only about the "wealthy" or "richer" versus "humbler" or "poorer" elements in society.[13] Did most peasants in southern Hispania have only a minimum of disposable income? Who are the peasants in Baetica? This book has as its central aim the elucidation of a variant of the "New Orthodoxy," namely not only that the Roman world witnessed growth in the later Republic and early Principate, but also that in the province of Baetica, economic growth benefited the mass of the nonslave and ex-slave population in the form of income growth and increase in nonliquid wealth. A principal tenet of this study is that nonsenators, nonequestrians, and nondecurions in Hispania Ulterior Baetica created wealth both for themselves and for their social superiors.

This book first attempts to sketch in outline the material impact of Rome on Baetica in the form of the pattern of rural settlement and production. The spread of Roman-style rural settlement in Baetica during the early Principate is a physical manifestation of the generalized growth that the Roman economy experienced from c. 50 B.C. to A.D. 200. And rural settlement along Roman lines in Baetica was complemented by the progressive inten-

sification of production. Rural settlement and production are intercon-
nected problems that cannot be fully understood in isolation. This book
will elucidate both phenomena in detail.

Second, this study will tackle the related questions of who built these
new settlements, who benefited from this production, and why. The core
argument of this book is that rural landowners and tenants not only represent the senatorial, equestrian, or decurional orders in Baetica but also include a broad "middle stratum,"[14] the freeborn component of which can be
assigned the shorthand label of the municipal juror class, that is, those persons — including *viri honesti* outside the *ordo* (described below) and the
descendants of freedmen — whose birth, moral repute, and property qualification, ranging from a modest 5,000 sesterces to the ducenarian census of
200,000 sesterces, permitted them to serve as local jurors in noncapital
cases.[15] It is best to write "middle stratum" because no contemporary
scholar invokes a "middle class," that is to say, a clearly defined intermediate group in the Roman world with independent economic resources or social standing.[16] Modern scholars generally will only go so far as to categorize persons of free birth below the level of decurions as heterogeneous in
composition and sizable in number.[17] A principal aim of this study is to jus-
tify the invocation, if only in a heuristic manner, of the expression "middle
stratum" or, alternatively, "middle layer" in connection with the society of
Baetica in the early and middle Principate.[18] This book's concern is with
wealth and income and their distribution: from this perspective, the
"middle stratum" in Baetica ought to encompass both the freeborn and ex-
slaves, and refer indiscriminately to individuals with property ranging in
value from 5,000 to 200,000 sesterces. In this sense, it would be perfectly
legitimate to speak of middle-income earners in the early Roman Empire.
But the Romans did not think in terms of the "middle class," "stratum" or
"sort," or even of "middle-income earners" — hence the emphasis in this
study is on *honesti*, whose membership extended beyond decurions and
local magistrates. Let another scholar be the torch-bearer for Harris' interesting reorganization of the society of the Roman world into three social
classes, namely those who were politically active and whose wealth came
from the labor of slaves or other dependents; a "separate" class of those
who, with a modicum of land or other resources, such as a shop, and relying on their own labor, succeeded in earning an independent survival, but
whose political power was slight; and a third class of *mercenarii*, dependent labor, and almost all slaves.[19] Chapter Six will devote some words to

the problematic nature of Harris' scheme. Is this to deny the economic importance and potentially sizable number of prosperous freedmen in Hispania? Not at all. But freedmen in Hispania are a comparatively well-known phenomenon.[20] By comparison, *viri honesti* outside the *ordo* are scholarly *terra incognita*.

What does the expression "vir honestus" mean in the context of Baetica? To anticipate the more detailed discussion in Chapter Seven, the Lex Irnitana of the late first century A.D. makes it clear that at Irni (Molino del Postero, El Saucejo, Sevilla province), and probably throughout most of Baetica, *viri idonei* (= *viri honesti*) were any freeborn males who possessed a minimum census of 5,000 sesterces (see Map 1). The unassailable and highly radical conclusion follows that *viri honesti* throughout Baetica, on the standard estimation of an average 6 percent return on capital, were those with a yearly income that could be as low as approximately 300 sesterces, whether imputed or in coin, a figure that is roughly 2.6 times the estimated minimum subsistence income in the Roman world during the first two centuries A.D. These persons, and prosperous freedmen as well, are the particular beneficiaries of the generalized growth that the Roman world experienced during the Principate, growth that is nowhere more manifest than in the province of Baetica. And it is vital to emphasize, in the most forceful terms possible, that the municipal "juror class" includes *honestae feminae*, that is, those women *possessores* and tenants whose wealth was on a par with or even, on occasion, exceeded that of *decurionales* (decurions and their families). The numbers of these reputable and wealthy women are appreciable, as will become manifest in any cursory look at the names of Baetican olive-oil producers and merchants. The municipal "juror class" obviously includes local *iudices* or jurors, whose wealth fell short of that required for entry into local town councils, and it also encompasses *honesti* possessing the wealth required of decurions but who remained outside the *ordo*. When I speak of *honesti* outside the *ordo*, I am referring to "middle stratum" males who did not become decurions or local magistrates.

The upper social and economic strata of the Roman Empire were defined through statute and fixed by custom, but they were not closed, immutable castes. The Roman economy during the early Principate was a generator of social mobility that elevated countless ex-slaves and their descendants into the upper strata of Roman society. The "juror class" of Baetica embodies, therefore, both Romanized freeborn natives and descendants of Italian settlers, as well as the offspring of ex-slaves. The emphasis

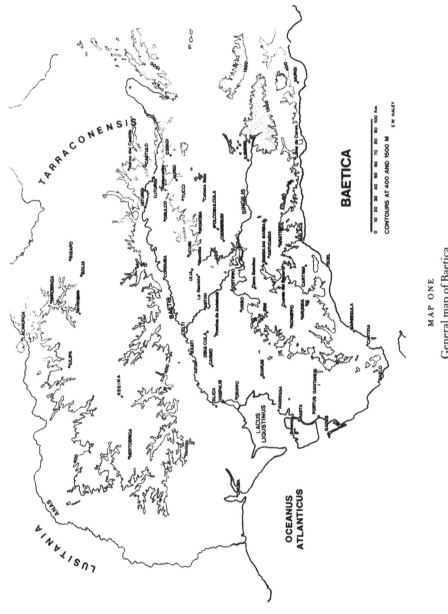

MAP ONE

General map of Baetica

on income distribution may allow us to gauge the effects of Roman economic growth at the microscopic, provincial level of individuals and groups of persons in the communities and countryside of a core province of the Roman Empire during the early Principate. The focus on total wealth and, more importantly, income may permit the use of modern concepts of economic growth and analysis without side-stepping or dispensing altogether with the Romans' own self-conscious division of their society into the dichotomous categories of *honesti* and *plebs*. But even the seemingly innocuous notion of the "middle stratum" or of middle-income earners will not carry conviction unless it can be argued that the aforementioned grouping of freeborn persons represented a substantial proportion of the total population of Baetica during the early Principate.

It is, unfortunately, impossible to know with exactitude what percentage of the provincial population the aforementioned grouping represents. As a working hypothesis, though, it may be reasonable to posit a component in Baetica of prosperous freeborn females, decurions, potential and serving municipal *iudices* with a sub-decurional census — the latter defined as those possessing a capital worth of between 5,000 and 20,000/25,000 sesterces, and *honesti* possessing the decurional census, but who remained outside the *ordo*, which comprised up to 25 percent of the total number of that province's inhabitants. The picture of the socioeconomic structure of Baetica's population in the earlier Principate that emerges in this study is thus at considerable variance with contemporary estimations of the makeup of the population in the Roman Empire as a whole. It is worth stating plainly, at this point, that Baetica during the reign of Trajan possessed a grand total of something in the order of 225–275 *municipia* and *coloniae*, each one of which on average possessed no more than roughly 1,000 to 3,000 free inhabitants and whose decurions alone, therefore, represented a substantial proportion of the total adult male population — certainly larger than the 2 percent posited for Africa by Duncan-Jones, and more in the order of 6 to 8 percent of the adult male population.[21] Le Roux, certainly, takes Irni to be the average example of many Baetican communities in terms of number of inhabitants, and estimates a total population in that *municipium* of 1,500 to 2,000 individuals, out of which decurions constituted at most 5 percent of the dwellers.[22] On the hypothesis of a maximum of 2,000 inhabitants in that community, it is thus possible to envisage up to 500 men, women, and children there who were *honesti* and *honestae*. As a preliminary point, the aforementioned group of males who were qualified to serve as local councilors and magistrates but who escaped this activity (*honesti* outside the *ordo*) also requires some elaboration.

To be sure, Garnsey has signaled the existence of this latter category of persons on the basis of the jurists as well as epigraphical evidence from North Africa and Asia Minor.[23] It is likely, therefore, that a number of the Baetican *negotiatores* and *possessores* named or implied in the sources fall into that broad spectrum of persons whose census ranged from the 5,000 sesterces that we know from the Lex Irnitana was necessary for service as a municipal *iudex* to the 200,000 to 400,000 sesterces that, during the Principate, defined an individual as eligible for two of the (eventually) five panels of jurors serving at Rome.[24] The merchants/shippers named in position beta in *tituli picti,* or painted inscriptions, of Dressel 20 oil-bearing amphoras, about whom more below, invariably possessed a capital worth in excess of 5,000 sesterces, and probably, in most cases, met the 20,000–25,000 sesterces census minimum posited by Le Roux, with great insight, as necessary for entry into the local *ordo* in most Baetican communities.[25] Le Roux's figure, be it duly noted, is in line with Alföldy's estimate of a minimum decurional census of 20,000 sesterces in the small African *municipia* during the early Principate.[26] A fortiori, those freeborn traders involved in the supply of staples to the city of Rome fall into the category of *honesti* outside the *ordo,* as their activity provided them immunity from civic *munera* (lit. "burdens")—uncompensated provisions of labor, services, or money. This immunity will have, as a practical matter, extended to freedom from service as local councilors and magistrates.

The preceding points require elaboration. Kruse was right to roundly criticize the author of this book for his defense of the notion of a "middling class" in the Roman world against the view of Alföldy, who posits the dichotomy of the three aristocratic *ordines,* that is, senators, equestrians, and decurions on the one hand, and the *plebs* below on the other, of various categories and attainments.[27] The defect of this writer's argument was its lack of terminological and conceptual precision. The cumulative evidence suggests that *honesti* and/or freeborn *possessores* outside local *ordines decurionum* in Hispania, and Baetica specifically, existed in appreciable numbers during the Principate. It is desirable to add, as it were, to Alföldy's model of Roman society, first, the horizontal category of *honesti* who were capable of serving as decurions but who remained outside the *ordo,* and second, those *viri idonei,* in the language of the Lex Irnitana, possessing a sub-decurional census, who made up, in substantial part, the ranks of jurors in

Baetican communities. Le Roux makes the fine observation that it is precisely from this group of jurors that future decurions could be recruited.[28] Mackie, following Garnsey (1970), acknowledges the conceptual possibility and actuality of *honesti* who were not decurions, but she is wrong, in my judgment, to categorically assert that local *ordines* in Spain, albeit of small size, "tended to embrace all resident citizens of social importance."[29] The main problem is terminological, and it is on terminology, above all, that we must not get hung up. The Spanish inscriptions, to be sure, make a distinction between the *plebs* on one side and the *ordo* on the other.[30] It is this language, one may judge, that led Mackie to conclude that the evidence for *honesti* outside the *ordo* is slight. This is to ignore Garnsey's very point that the terms *decuriones* and *ordo*—for him coextensive—could, in the jurists and in the inscriptions, be "regarded as representative of a wider group, composed of those with matching dignitas and honor in the community."[31] It is precisely to this wider group that the Lex Irnitana makes explicit and unmistakable reference, as we shall see in Chapter Seven. To her credit, however, Mackie—a tough- and fair-minded scholar—noted the technically accurate distinction between *honesti* and *plebs,* citing Pliny (*Ep.* 10.79.3), a lawyer whose testimony on this point may surely be taken as definitive. F. Jacques and J. Scheid write, on the basis of Pliny (*Ep.* 9.5), that the "opposition la plus féconde" in Roman society was that between *honesti* and *plebs.*[32] In this connection, Woolf's suggestion that villa owners in the territory of the Ambiani in Picardy constituted a class that extended beyond a hundred or so decurial families is welcome as an analogous argument to that of this book, as is his notion of broad elite strata in many Gallic societies.[33] Less helpful, perhaps, is the same author's dualistic vision of emergent divides during the first century A.D. in Gaul between the "rich" and the "poor."[34]

This study will go beyond a survey and analysis of the interlocking phenomena of settlement patterns, production, and social-juridical groups in Baetica in its attempt to identify explicitly those persons who prospered from the agricultural and mineral wealth of the province. As a practical matter, this entails the identification of Baetican landowners, tenants, and traders.[35] In numerous instances they can be shown to be one and the same persons. And, mostly on the basis of nomenclature, it will be desirable to categorize *possessores* and traders in terms of juridical and social status. All of this will entail detailed prosopographical exposition, but the undertaking is necessary in order to substantiate the claim that *honesti* outside the

ordo represented a substantial component of the Baetican population during the early Principate. It may be mainly the vagaries of the documentation
that promote the notion that traders were an independent category of the
Roman population, somehow divorced from the prevailing landowning
mentality of the Romans.[36] But it is also possible to agree with Whittaker,
echoing Finley, that the very rich senatorial elite, while maintaining a general interest in gain, was not directly involved in entrepreneurial capital
profit.[37] On the other hand, it is also possible that the aforementioned
scholars apply too loosely the terms "wealthy landowners" or "elite landowners," and, in consequence, deny the more or less direct participation in
negotia by any and all substantial Roman landowners and/or tenants, in
general, below the level of senatorials. A typical statement in this regard is
that of Harris, who notes that in the western empire, "merchants seldom
seem to have possessed even curial status."[38] The question remains, to be
tackled, among others, by this book: Who are Roman traders in the West?
In this regard, it may be pertinent, however briefly, to address the question
of the "typicality" of Trimalchio.

The question of traders and their identity raises large issues concerning
the population and socioeconomy of Baetica from c. 50 B.C. to A.D. 200.
This book will not shy away from these larger problems. But its conclusions
and implications may be relevant for other areas and provinces of the Roman world, particularly the western and central portions. Thus the experience of Baetica in the early Principate may serve as a test case applicable to
certain "core" parts of the empire, such as coastal Tarraconensis, Narbonensis, Italy, and proconsular Africa. The nature and importance of trade
to, within, and from Baetica will also be a subject of concern in this study.
It therefore will not be possible to address the more general question of the
importance of trade in the Roman world, that is, to what degree trade was
tied or administered and to what degree it represented the play of the free
market and the forces of unfettered supply and demand. But it may be pertinent to spell out some assumptions concerning the Roman economy that
underlie many of this book's conclusions. For example, it assumes the essential soundness of the view, albeit debatable in certain of its details, that
much, if not most, long-distance seaborne trade in the Roman Empire, at
least in its western portions, from the reign of Claudius on, was stimulated
by the state for the various purposes of the supply of the *plebs* of Rome
or the army.[39] Wickham has made the same point, in his review of *Società
Romana e Impero Tardoantico III,* that the extent and scale of commercial-

ization—he has in mind African olive oil—depended "in the last analysis on the presence of a state that needed to move goods for its own ends," and that the role of the state was, above all, to push a few products such as oil and pottery from the level of intraregional commerce to a truly pan-Mediterranean plane.[40] Computer simulations modeling the distribution of various commodities, including olive oil, wine, and fish sauces, according to transportation costs and the location of centers of production suggest nonmarket or redistributive mechanisms at work in the diffusion of Baetican olive oil and fish sauce in the Roman West.[41] More problematic, it seems, is Whittaker's insistence that much long-distance trade represents the efforts of senatorials and equestrians to supply their slave *familiae* and clients in the *urbs* and environs from their own properties.[42] In the case of the Baetican olive-oil export, the preceding notion is questionable, because the painted inscriptions on oil-bearing Dressel 20 amphoras reveal a host of traders, many of whom are named and discussed in Chapter Six, dealing in the oil of named, mostly unrelated tenants and/or landowners who are not obvious senatorials or equestrians. To salvage Whittaker's thesis in the case of the oil trade would be to assume to the point of special pleading that the names of *possessores* and/or tenants on the amphoras represent, for the most part, the tenants of absentee senatorial or equestrian proprietors, and that proposition goes beyond, and even against, the available evidence.[43]

Be that as it may, private individuals still thereby became wealthy, not least through the commerce and sale of supplementary cargoes whose distribution may have been subsidized by the transport, partly at the behest of the Roman state, of high-density, high-value cargoes in the form of precious and semi-precious metals or indispensable cargoes such as grain.[44] It is worth stating plainly at this point that Harris has arguably misunderstood the terms of the debate on Roman trade in driving a hard and fast distinction between the "redistributive" economy and the "market" with regard to the supply of the city of Rome.[45] The presence of concessions and incentives to traders and *domini navium* who entered into specific, contractual relations with the *fiscus,* as Sirks reminds us, from at the least the reign of Claudius onward[46] plainly means that a substantial number of private traders and *possessores* were not responding to pure market forces in deciding to participate in the supply of the *plebs* and *urbs.* The same criticism may fairly be leveled against Paterson, who characterizes the Roman economy during the early Principate as a free-market one, without taking into account the factor of transport subsidies, whether direct or indirect.[47]

Temin is similarly silent on nonmarket factors at work in the supply of the city of Rome and the army during the early Roman Empire.[48] In addition, it remains possible to disagree with Remesal's assertion that olive oil came to Rome from the reign of Augustus onward as a tributary item.[49] But the lamentable reality is that it is not possible to disprove Remesal's thesis; at the same time, though, Liou and Tchernia are surely justified to insist that the names of *mercatores* painted on the sides of Baetican olive-oil containers—about which much more below—represent "les noms des commerçants qui ont acheté les amphores et leur contenu et en assurent l'exportation."[50] A premise of this book is that the Roman economy in the West during the Principate represents a "subsidized market economy," for want of a neater expression or term.

This study does not pretend to be exhaustive in the detailing, rehearsing, and exposition of every published item of archaeological interest in Hispania Ulterior Baetica. Nor does this book aim to supersede Thouvenot's monumental study of Baetica published in 1940. With the astounding explosion in archaeological survey, sondages, and emergency and systematic excavation within the confines of the province of Baetica since 1975, such an undertaking would be impossible. And it shall not be possible to adduce all the evidence for Baetican commodities in the Roman world outside Baetica. Nonetheless, this study will attempt to treat, if only summarily, most aspects of the production of goods and staples in Baetica within the period chosen. In that sense, part of the book's purpose is to complement and update the detailed overview of Baetican and Spanish production in Blázquez's study of the economy of Roman Spain, published in the late 1970s, and in the book on the economy of southern Spain under the Antonines, virtually unknown outside Spain, by Sánchez León.[51] The reader will find, accordingly, detailed discussions of many facets of the economy and society of Baetica from the end of the Republic to the Severan dynasty in this book. The goal of this exercise, though, is to be as rigorously selective, accurate, and fair in the exposition of that detailed evidence, mainly archaeological and epigraphical, as is necessary to construct a model of the genesis and distribution of wealth and its relation to social mobility in Baetica that bears an approximate resemblance to the truth.

The first five chapters of the book will provide a diachronic overview of the political and administrative context for wealth creation in Further Spain between c. 50 B.C. and c. A.D. 200. They will also allude to the results of published archaeological surveys in Baetica and outline the physical impact of the Roman peace on Baetica in terms of the settlement pattern. And they will examine the general circumstances and specific forms of economic activity that enabled thousands of known and unknown Baetici from the late Republican period through the end of the Antonine period to enter into the ranks of senators, equestrians, and *honesti,* whether those in the *ordo decurionum* or those remaining outside town councils.[52] Chapter Six will identify all those explicitly attested Baetican senators, equestrians, decurionals, *honestae,* and *honesti* outside the *ordo,* including possible local jurors, who can be directly or indirectly connected with *negotia* and/or specific wealth-making activity. Chapter Seven will consider the nature of economic growth in Baetica from the late Republican through late Antonine period from a theoretical perspective. And the same chapter will discuss in more detail the genesis and nature of the municipal "juror class" in the province. This chapter develops the hypothesis that the Roman peace elevated, in social and economic terms, not only those Baetici who pursued senatorial, equestrian, or decurional careers, but also *viri honesti* and *feminae honestae* in general. An eighth and final chapter sets out the principal conclusions of the study.

CHAPTER ONE

Rural Settlement and Production in Baetica, c. 50 B.C.–27 B.C.

Change and continuity in the Baetican settlement of the land, sources of income, and the varying degrees to which the inhabitants of Baetica profited from the Pax Romana are the themes of this and subsequent chapters. I shall explore the social and economic transformation of Further Spain and the future province of Baetica from the late Republican period to the end of the Antonine dynasty. A brief examination, however, of the historical and administrative development of Further Spain and the future province of Hispania Ulterior Baetica will provide a context in which to understand the socioeconomic development of the province.

It seems appropriate to emphasize at the outset that Further Spain was a military province throughout the later Republican and triumviral periods. The province was essentially an arena for triumph- and ovation-hunting Roman governors and lieutenants in the period from 133 to c. 80 B.C. and again in the triumviral era; and it was the setting of Roman civil conflict between c. 80 and 45 B.C. Tax collection and the administration of justice were concerns of the governor and his staff, but these were of secondary importance, whether through circumstance or design. Nevertheless, it can be argued that Italian and Roman emigrants to Further Spain had an influence on the economic development of the future province that went beyond their actual numbers.

History and Administration on the Eve of the Civil Wars

In 55, under the Lex Trebonia, Pompey received command of Spain for five years and ruled it through legates.[1] The names of two of Pompey's legates in Spain are known: L. Afranius and M. Petreius. In 49 Cn. Calpurnius Piso (Frugi?) served as *proquaestor* in Further Spain.[2] In 49, or at some point during the next six years, Gades became a *municipium*.[3] At the outbreak of civil war in 49, Afranius and Petreius commanded troops at Ilerda (Lleida), while M. Terentius Varro was in command of Ulterior. Many excellent studies contribute to our knowledge of the vicissitudes of the war in Spain from 49 to 45, and it would be otiose to rehearse all of them in detail here.[4] When Varro surrendered, Caesar replaced him with Q. Cassius Longinus, who ruled *propraetore;* Longinus had served as quaestor in Further Spain in 52.[5] Longinus' rapacity occasioned an assassination plot among his own men, and conflict broke out between his supporters and his enemies in the province. The governor of Citerior replaced Longinus with C. Trebonius in 47. Exploiting Pompeian sentiments in the legions in Ulterior who had expelled Trebonius, Cn. Pompeius and his brother Sextus installed themselves in the valley of the Baetis by the end of winter 46. Caesar defeated Pompeian forces at Ategua in February and at Munda in March 45, and ended organized Pompeian resistance in Ulterior by capturing Urso and other towns by June of that year. C. Carrinas, a legate(?), was sent to Further Spain to fight Sextus Pompeius' guerilla campaign in the balance of the year.[6] 45 and/or the following year saw Caesar's organization of several colonies in the valley of the Baetis. We know with certainty that Urso (Osuna) and Hispalis (Sevilla) were two of these newly established colonies.[7] Other possible Caesarian colonies are Hasta (Mesas de Asta, Jerez de la Frontera, Cádiz province), Itucci (Cortijo de las Vírgenes?, Córdoba province), and Ucubi (Espejo).[8] Scholars tend to view these colonial establishments as the imposition of Roman-style communities and colonists in native communities that had been friendly to the Pompeians, and as foundations that would serve a useful strategic and administrative role in maintaining Roman security and other interests in southern Ulterior.[9]

Scholarship is divided on the question of the numbers of Roman and Italian settlers in the future province of Baetica during the late Republic, with some, like Fear, who emphasize their relatively restricted numbers, and others, like Gabba, Richardson, and Marín Díaz, who see a more numerous presence of Romans and Italians in Ulterior by c. 45 B.C.[10] The more recent arguments in this debate are those of Fear, who suggests that the *legio Vernacula* may have been raised from native Spaniards, much like the *legio Alaudae* of Caesar in Gaul, during the 50s, in a period of instability and under pressing circumstances.[11] The latter scholar, too, suggests that at most two legions (the *legio Quinta* and, subsequently, one "facta ex colonis" fighting for the younger Pompey [*BHisp.* 7.4]), of roughly 4,000 men each, would have been raised in Hispania Ulterior from *cives Romani* during the period of the Civil Wars, and that these two units may have had, in part, overlapping personnel. All this, however, is seemingly to ignore the compelling points made by Brunt, that the Pompeian legions in Spain consisted in part of resident (Roman) citizens and that the *legio Vernacula* similarly was composed of "Romanized natives, perhaps partly of Italian descent."[12] Certainly, the epithet of the legion is no bar to Brunt's thesis.[13] More recently, M. Downs has alerted us to the possibility of widespread hybridity and biculturalism in the populations of centers such as Italica, Corduba, and Gades by the first century B.C.[14] The two legions raised in Ulterior in the period of the Civil Wars may indeed remain in court, ultimately, as possible evidence for Italian or Roman emigrants to the Iberian peninsula in the pre-Caesarian period. A remarkable bronze inscription, which came to light at Elche, the ancient Ilici, in the course of construction work in 1996, offers possible evidence for the presence of the descendants of Italians in Hispania Ulterior in the late Republican period.[15] The inscription is a list of ten veterans allotted centuriated land in the territory of the *colonia* Iulia Augusta Ilicitana; the document is probably contemporary with the foundation of the colony itself, which may be as early as 29 B.C.[16] Each of the veterans is allotted 13 *iugera* of land—a local census minimum perhaps? Three of the recipients are from Icosium in North Africa, one is from Praeneste, and a fifth recipient is from Vibo Valentia in Calabria. Five of the veterans, though, are from Spain, and of their number, four are from Ulterior. Lucius Aemilius L.f., enrolled in the Horatia tribe, is from Ulia (Montemayor), Publius Horatius P.f., enrolled in the Quirina tribe, is from Malaca, Caius Marius C.f., enrolled in the Veturia tribe, is from Corduba, and Lucius Fabius L.f., enrolled in the Galeria tribe, is from Aurelia Carissa (Cortijo de Carija, Bornos, Cádiz province). A fifth veteran is designated as a "Balearicus," that is, he came from the Balearic islands. It should be noted that the first four veterans are from that area of the future province of Baetica where scholars surmise the greatest concentration of Roman and Italian emigrants in the Republican period.

On the likely assumption that the cadastral inscription dates as early as 29 B.C., it might be further supposed that the veterans were enrolled from twenty to twenty-five years earlier, that is, that they were present in Ulterior precisely in the period of the Civil Wars and their prelude. On the other hand, the possibility at least ought to be raised that the aforementioned veterans were native Hispani who received the citizenship upon enrollment in the legions.

The literary sources and the testimony of Ibero-Roman coinage would seem to offer unproblematic evidence for more named Romans and Italians in southern Spain before 44 B.C.[17] The best known from the literary sources are Vibius Pac(c)iaecus and his son L. Vibius Pac(c)iaecus.[18] The former was a landowner, probably in Carteia or its environs, who sheltered M. Licinius Crassus in 85 B.C., when the latter fled from the Marians at Rome.[19] His son was a partisan of Caesar in the early 40s.[20] A close analysis of their nomenclature shows that the *Vibii Pac(c)iaeci hispanienses* were originally from Campania, or perhaps the Marsic territory. The suggestion seems plausible, furthermore, that their ancestors, having served in allied contingents in Hispania, were among the very earliest Italic settlers at Carteia, where Vibii show up as Republican-era moneyers.[21] Without doubt, many of the moneyers named on Republican issues from mints in Ulterior are Romans or Italians or their descendants. One recent commentator, nevertheless, identifies implicitly as a native who has adopted a Roman nomen the aedile Lucius Aemilius, attested on *asses* of Obulco dating between c. 120 and 90 B.C., while categorizing Aemilius' colleague, M. Iunius, named on the same issues, as an Italian.[22] The underlying argument here is based on onomastics, or the study of names: the possession of "strictly" Roman or Latin nomina by magistrates in Ulterior during the later Republican period may be, to a large extent, the result of native elites assuming the nomina of Roman magistrates active in the province, whereas "Italic" *gentilicia* point to immigrants and their descendants.[23] Without doubt, this kind of onomastic borrowing involving Roman or Latin nomina occurred in Ulterior and elsewhere in the later Republican period.[24] But it seems hazardous to take this phenomenon as a general principle that will explain the specific example of the first-named moneyer at Obulco. It remains possible that we are dealing, in the case of Aemilius, with a Roman or Italian or his descendant at Obulco. The idea that the aedile M. Iunius was an Italian or descendant need not strain belief: on one accounting, 36 percent of the more than seventy names found in the coin legends from Ulterior are manifestly Oscan, Samnite, and Etruscan; this points with virtual certainty to members of families coming from Italy and not the native clientele of high-profile Romans.[25] Exceptional non-numismatic inscriptional testimony from the *oppidum ignotum* situated at La Rambla in Córdoba province does, indeed, reveal an Italian immigrant or the descendant of one serving as a local magistrate in the late Republican period. An inscription, dated 49 B.C., records the construction of a gate at the *oppidum* by the indigenous "decemvir maxs(umus)" (sic) Binsnes, son of Vercello, and by the aedile M(arcus) Coranus Acrini f(ilius) Alpis. The latter was possibly a non-Roman citizen of central Italian extraction.[26] What conclusions are to be drawn from all this? It is difficult to say. Though it may remain an exaggeration to speak of a "massive" presence of Italians and Romans in Ulterior before c. 44 B.C., it might be accurate to think in terms of a significant or influential presence, particularly after factoring in the offspring and descendants of mixed unions.[27] One expression of that influence seems to be in the realm of coinage itself. Chaves Tristán, though agnostic with respect to the number of Italians in southern Spain during the Republican period, nevertheless emphasizes their role in the inception, typology, metrology, and mint emplacement of local bronze coinage in Ulterior.[28]

What remains uncontroversial is the importance of *conventus civium Romanorum,* or informal communities of Romans and Italians, in the mostly native, larger communities of Ulterior throughout the Republican period.[29] Explicit testimony attests to their existence at Hispalis and at Corduba.[30] Fear emphasizes their weight in the events at Corduba of 49–48; and he suggests that they had no formal role—or even, necessarily, influence—in the governing of those communities in which they were situated. The Roman citizens belonging to these *conventus* would have been, for the most part, urban dwellers. Factors inhibiting the large-scale settlement of Romans and Italians in the countryside of southern Spain before the rule of Augustus will have included the general instability of the province and the desire of time-served peasant soldiers to return to Italy.[31]

But, as a practical matter, the direction of affairs in large areas of the future province would have been in the hands of mining-related *societates,* or companies, some, but not all, of whose members would have been Italians. As an illustration of the preceding point may be cited the *servitus viae,* or right-of-way, imposed by the *societas Sisaponensis* on the road (camino del Pretorio) leading from Corduba to ore-rich areas of the Sierra Morena in the vicinity of Almadén. The servitude was effected at some point during the second half of the first century B.C., perhaps at the same time that Corduba was elevated to the status of *colonia civium Romanorum*.[32] The important point here is that the *societas* would have been responsible for the embellishment and upkeep of the road and associated infrastructure, such as bridges, culverts, and embankments. It is possible to envisage that the *societas* would have been composed of both Roman and Italian settlers on the one hand, and native Spaniards on the other. It may well be the case that a relatively restricted number of Romans and Italians occupied the more senior managerial and technical posts in the company; but, at the same time, it is likely that a broader penumbra of Romans, Italians, and their descendants settled in the larger towns of the province, enjoyed the proceeds of mining through their ownership of shares in this and other *societates,* or otherwise benefited from the ancillary activities of the processing and distribution of the metal.[33]

The administration of Ulterior between Caesar's assassination and 27 B.C. is obscure. Relevant details on the situation from 44 to 40 are easily found in Broughton and do not need to be rehearsed here.[34] From 39 to 27, both Spanish provinces were under the control of a succession of single governors of proconsular(?) rank.[35] González, furthermore, seems persuasive in arguing that M. Petrucidius M.f. served as *legatus propraetore* in Ulterior not in 45 B.C. but during the reign of Augustus.[36] Petrucidius is attested on brick stamps from Carteia, Ilipa Ilia, Hasta, Italica, and Siarum.[37]

Settlement

In general terms, it may be desirable to outline here and elsewhere in a broadly summary fashion the spatial and geographical contexts in which the pre-Roman and Roman inhabitants of the province of Baetica exploited their environment to satisfy not only their own needs and wants, but also the demands, chiefly in the form of taxation and foodstuffs, of the central Roman administration. At a less abstract, but practical, level, it may also be fruitful to establish the general contexts and specific settings in which named and unnamed senatorial, equestrian, and local elites, in addition to slaves, freedmen, and the nonelite freeborn, pursued various economic interests. Such an inquiry will serve as a means of determining, as much as possible, specific sources of wealth and social mobility in Baetica from the late Republican period to the early Severan period.

From c. 133 through the end of the Augustan period, the population in most areas of the province was mainly confined to towns and to fortified *oppida*.[38] To be sure, the inhabitants—both elite and nonelite—of these towns and *oppida* exploited surrounding land without establishing residences on it. But it is certain that the level of exploitation was less intensive than was to be the case in a landscape dominated from the late Augustan and Julio-Claudian periods onward by dispersed Catonian-Varronian villa establishments.[39] Native settlement in isolated farmsteads undoubtedly existed, but it is virtually unknown in terms of systematic archaeological exploration.[40] The relatively small number of Republican- and triumviral-era Roman *aedificia* in the lower Guadalquivir valley and possible late Republican- and triumviral-era rural establishments along the Mediterranean littoral may have been settled by both Italian emigrants (*Hispanienses*) and acculturated natives (*Hispani*).

Production and Trade

Trade in Further Spain between c. 200 and 27 B.C. was essentially adventitious. The ancient Phoenician cities of the Mediterranean and Atlantic coasts continued to be important sources in the western Mediterranean of processed-fish products, transported mainly in Maña C2b and C2c amphoras, and ceramics of the so-called red-varnish Kouass type.[41] Molina Vidal insists that Italian wine in Hispania during the last two centuries B.C. is ultimately the consequence of the rise of the slave mode of production organized according to the norms of the Catonian and Varronian villa, and that this Italian product exploited new "markets" in the western Mediterranean—markets that reflected not only the imported tastes of Italian soldiers, administrators, and traders in Hispania, but also the tastes of Romanizing and Hellenizing natives.[42] Perhaps he is right. But Wickham may also be justified to suggest that the success of Italian wine producers in the first century B.C. in Gaul, Spain, and the city of Rome may simply derive from the fact that there was no other major supplier of wine to be found anywhere else in the Roman West outside of Italy.[43] In this regard, it would not make much sense to explain the presence of a great deal of Italian wine in Hispania as the outcome of "free market" competition between rival suppliers. And even Molina Vidal suggests that ships laden with Italian wine for Carthago Nova returned to Italy carrying precious metals[44]—commodities that will have acted to subsidize the transport of wine to Spain.

The literary and documentary sources provide isolated bits of information and hints concerning production, trade, and the sources of wealth in late Republican and triumviral Hispania Ulterior. The main factor that impedes our capacity to identify the specific agents and beneficiaries of profit-making or subsistence economic activities during these periods in Further Spain is the terrible silence of the epigraphical sources. Indeed, it is not until the reign of Augustus that the quantity and quality of inscriptional evidence of all kinds becomes appreciable. This silence extends to inscriptions of all sorts on *instrumentum domesticum,* or inscribed artifacts of a utilitarian nature, such as pottery, ingots, bricks, and glass. The Vibii Pac(c)iaeci, mentioned above, were undoubtedly substantial landowners, probably in the vicinity of Carteia, during the first century B.C., but it is impossible to ascertain their precise source(s) of wealth. It is a pity that we are in no position to gauge the exact sources of wealth of those three Roman *equites* from Hasta who joined forces with Caesar before the battle of Munda.[45]

Chapter 76 of the colonial charter of Urso (Osuna, Seville province) prohibits tileries of greater than a certain size within the *oppidum* or built-up portion of the *colonia.* Fear argues persuasively, following d'Ors, that the provision of the Lex was aimed at preventing the erection of buildings exceeding a certain size, structures that could have posed a fire hazard to the other buildings of the town itself.[46] It is obvious that at Urso, as early as 44 B.C., certain individuals were devoting a portion of their resources to the production of tiles and other ceramics for the colonists, but their identities and actual potteries remain unknown. The clause of the Lex also makes certain reference to the owner(s) of illegal *figlinae* who will find their unsanctioned installations and property expropriated by the colony's magistrates ("qui habuerit, it[a] aedificium isque locus publicus colon(iae) Iul(iae) esto"). As a general proposition, it may be ventured, mainly on the basis of the archaeological evidence, that the surplus agricultural production of late Republican and triumviral Ulterior, with the exceptions of fish sauce and metals, was directed mainly to the satisfaction of the Roman garrison in Hispania and Ulterior in particular, rather than destined for exportation.[47]

CEREALS

The most important stuff in the life of ancient man was bread. A variety of sources show the importance of cereals cultivation in late Republican Further Spain. Pompeius' legate in Further Spain, Marcus Terentius Varro, sent grain from Ulterior to Petreius and Afranius, in addition to the Pompeians in Massilia (Caes. *B Civ.* 2.18.1–3); and he extracted 120,000 *modii* (1 *modius* = 6.55 kilograms) of grain from the inhabitants of Ulterior in 49 (*B Civ.* 2.18.4). This latter figure may seem impressive in isolation but pales besides the 160,000 *modii* capacity of the forty or so subterranean grain-storage pits alone at the Caserío del Gramalejo, mentioned below, in Córdoba province. Dio notes that Caesar turned his attention to Ategua because he had learned there was an abundance of grain there (43.33.2). Where was grain cultivated with special intensity in this period and later? The answer may be found, in part, through survey archaeology. In a survey area of roughly 215 square kilometers in the region of Fuentes de Andalucía (Sevilla), Fernández Caro has identified two broad areas corresponding to different soil and hydrological regimes. One area represents a continuation of the escarpment on which sits Carmona to the west, and is marked, in general, by tertiary soils characterized by a high content of gravel and sands, subject to inundation in the winter. The second, corresponding to the southern portion, generally speaking, of the survey area, represents the vega of the Corbones River. The soil of this latter area is quaternary and marked by black earth and clays, particularly suitable for grain growing, in antiquity as now. The dispersion of rural settlements in the Roman period is conspicuously shaped by the different regimes described above. On the terrace are few Roman sites—some of them undoubtedly exploited the more fertile, lower-lying soil to the south, while others were probably involved in a mixed regime of hunting-gathering and animal husbandry. The region of the campiña to the south was marked, during the Julio-Claudian and later periods, by a generalized dispersion of second- and third-order sites, not far distant from each other, which were devoted to cereals cultivation sufficient to offer a profitable return.[48]

Some explanation of terminology is necessary at this juncture. First-order sites are those which present in their surface scatters or assemblages not only a wide spectrum of utilitarian and fine ceramics, but also constructive and decorative elements, such as marble revetment plaques, mosaics, painted stucco, columns, and capitals. In brief, first-order sites possess elements pointing to a *pars urbana* representing the residence of an owner, tenant, or *vilicus*. Second-order sites are those which disclose surface scatters or other diagnostic elements, such as the remains of basins or mills/presses, that point to the strictly agricultural function of the site. Such sites, upon excavation, may or may not reveal a discrete residential section. Second-order sites may show constructive elements, such as dressed stones, but are otherwise lacking in those decorative elements, specified above, that suggest a luxurious or semiluxurious *pars urbana*. Third-order sites are those whose surface scatters are generally restricted to bricks, tiles, or common ceramics, that is, diagnostic elements that do not per se suggest the existence of the residential function of a structure or structures. Third-order sites are also those which, through their location or relative poverty of surface remains, stand, in many instances, in an obvious or possible relation of dependency vis-à-vis nearby first- or second-order sites. The term "villa" is to be avoided whenever possible precisely because many, if not most, first-order sites in Baetica were, in their earliest phase(s), relatively simple structures with outliers, which only in the course of their occupation and activity assumed the characteristics appropriate to a residential villa, such as luxurious appointments, including mosaics, and bath complexes.[49]

Archaeological survey and excavations, too, have revealed numerous places in Baetica where grain-storing silos, or *putei*, are present. They represent an efficient means of storing cereals whose utilization goes back into the Neolithic period. There are, for example, campaniform silos in the municipal districts of Castro del Río (Caserío del Gramalejo) and Córdoba (Cortijo Nuevo de la Silera), ranging in capacity from 35 to 68 cubic meters and capable of storing from 27,000 to 53,000 kilograms, respectively, of grain.[50] There will have been a minimum of forty *putei* at the Caserío del Gramalejo with a total storage capacity of 160,000 *modii* of grain, while the ten *putei* of the Cortijo Nuevo de la Silera will have been able to accommodate over 77,000 *modii* of grain. These capacities sound impressive, and they are, but it should be borne in mind that Varro, describing similar structures in Hispania Citerior, records that they were capable of storing grain for up to fifty years free of deterioration.[51] In this light, we might be better advised to see the structures in both Hispania Ulterior and Citerior as bunkers against bad harvests, as native Hispani sought to alleviate the consequences of slim yields by storing surpluses gained from bountiful crops. Alternatively, the large quantities of grain stored and preserved in these silos or *putei* would have enabled the growers to meet both their own needs as well as predictable or ad hoc demands of the Roman authorities in the form of rents or requisitions. Numerous silos, furthermore, have come to light in the hinterland of Ategua: Santa Cruz (Córdoba), Cerro de la Ventosilla, Cerro del Agua, and Cortijo de Valdepeñas. Silos in large numbers have been discovered at La Rambla (Córdoba). Other places in Córdoba province at which silos appear are Cortijo Trinidades, Cortijo del Carrascal, and Cortijo del Toril. Near the mouth of the Guadalquivir are two campaniform silos at Montegil de Buenavista, a Roman rural settlement immediately to the south of the marisma del Cuervo in the municipal district of Jerez de la Frontera.[52] In Roman times, the rural settlement at Montegil de Buenavista lay next to the navigable *Lacus Ligustinus.* The two silos had their narrow mouths closed with flat stones and ranged in depth from 1 to 1.5 meters, and from 0.80 to 1.00 meters in width. The archaeologists note oral reports of up to ten silos discovered in the course of agricultural work at the site. It emerges that the middle and lower Guadalquivir river valley was already in the late Iberian and Republican periods the setting for widespread cereals cultivation.

OLIVE OIL

The evidence for the large-scale exportation from Hispania during the Principate of olives and olive oil is overwhelming. Many Baetici and non-Baetici alike became rich from oil production and export. Evidence exists for the presence of olive groves in the province as early as the Caesarian period. The anonymous author of the *Bellum Hispaniense* notes the deaths of Caesar's foragers in an olive grove ("in oliveto") near Soricaria (27.1). At this early period, however, there is no evidence to suggest that the olives and oil produced from this and similar Baetican groves would have been destined for anything other than local or regional consumption. For instance, there is no site in southern Spain that reveals the production of amphoras destined for the storage and transport of olive oil dating earlier than the later reign of Augustus. Is this all that is to be said on this subject? Perhaps not. One well-informed archaeologist suggests that certain amphora fragments from the Roman encampment Lomba do Canho (Arganil), in central Portugal, are identifiable as the earliest examples on record of form 24 (= Oberaden 83 = Dressel 25 = type A) olive-oil containers.[53] If this were the case, then the evidence from the Lomba do Canho would represent Baetican olive-oil containers of possibly late triumviral date or from the first years of Augustus' reign. The containers, on this reconstruction, would still confirm the proposition that Baetican oil production, if not destined for consumption within the future area of the province of Baetica, was transported to centers of consumption within the confines of the Iberian peninsula. In any event, the only certainly identifiable amphora carrying olive oil in Hispania before the very late triumviral period or early reign of

Augustus is of non-Spanish origin. Various sites in Hispania Ulterior reveal the importation, to the end of the late Republic, of Italian amphoras corresponding to Peacock and Williams class 1 (= Baldacci I or Brindisini) containers. The sites in Ulterior that show the importation, albeit probably not in great quantity, of these oil-bearing amphoras of south Italian, more specifically Apulian and Calabrian, origin include Carteia, La Loma (Chipiona, Cádiz), Baelo, Gades, and Chões de Alpompé (Santarém, Portugal).[54]

WINE

A number of late Republican and triumviral issues emanating from Baetican mints portray a bunch of grapes. These include coins from Acinippo, Orippo (Torre de los Herberos, Dos Hermanas, Sevilla province), Osset (Cerro de la Chavoya, San Juan de Aznalfarache, Sevilla province), Baesippo (Castillo de Santiago[?], Barbate, Cádiz province), Ulia, Arva, and Turri Regina (= Regina [Los Paredones, Casas de Reina, Badajoz province]).[55] The issues suggest the existence of some degree of cultivation of the vine, though the scale of the production of wine is unknown. Presumably the wine was locally or regionally consumed. It is likely, for example, that the wine or *defrutum* amphoras (Haltern 70 and smaller variants) discovered at the Roman fort at Lomba do Canho, 2 kilometers northeast of Arganil (Coimbra) in present-day Portugal, have a south Spanish origin; the fort dates probably from the late 60s to possibly as late as the first years of Augustus' rule, more specifically from 27 to 25 B.C.[56] On the other hand, the notion is problematic that Dressel 1 C amphoras, produced in the Bay of Cádiz during the second half of the first century B.C., were destined for the bottling and transport of wine.[57] It is just as likely that the containers were used to transport locally produced fish sauces.[58]

FISH SAUCE

There is considerable evidence for the production and commerce of salted fish, *garum*, and associated products in Further Spain during the late Republican and triumviral periods. Some of this production was exported. The main outlines of this activity are clear.[59] The main prerequisites were fish, salt, fresh water, and labor. As far as we can tell, the production and commerce of fish sauce in this period were in the hands of native Spaniards. The Bay of Cádiz, in particular, is flush with sites devoted to the production of fish sauces and the containers that carried them.[60] Salteries were located in both urban and extra-urban contexts. The impressive scale of urban fish-sauce manufacture is brought out in excavations in the urban core of Cádiz. The excavations have revealed the remains of a fish-sauce installation located on the southern side of the smallest of the three islands that in antiquity comprised the Gaditane archipelago, namely the island of Erytheia (alternatively "Afrodisias" or "Insula Iunonis").[61] The site of the installation in antiquity was very near the canal that separated Erytheia from the larger island, Kotinoussa, facing it. The excavators discovered twenty-six basins, as well as a central patio with canalization and a cistern; fish preparation for salting took place in this central area. The purpose of the canals in the patio seems to have been to draw rainwater into the cisterns. The excavators surmise the existence of an equal number of basins, not excavated, on the other side of the patio. The installation seems to have been constructed in the first century B.C. and abandoned at the beginning of the fifth century A.D.

MINING

The most notable economic activity in the province during the late Republican and triumviral periods, aside from subsistence and above-subsistence agriculture for local or regional markets, was one that reflects neither the tied nor the market economy, namely mining. The mines of Hispania Ulterior represented a combination of state-owned installations leased out, through the *locatio censoria,* to *societates publicanorum,* individuals, and small-scale, private *societates* on the one hand, and privately owned mines on the other hand.[62] The best known of these *societates publicanorum* was the *societas Sisaponensis,* which held the cinnabar and mercury franchise centered at Sisapo (La Bienvenida, Córdoba province) near modern Almadén.[63] From Pliny the Elder we learn that in his day, the *metallum Antonianum* and *metallum Samariense* were farmed out by the Roman state, sc. the *aerarium;*[64] the mines began their existence, possibly already in the late Republican period, as private holdings, as their names disclose.

It would be interesting to know what proportion of those who profited from mining were Romanizing natives and what proportion were Italian immigrants. Posidonius, referring to the period at the end of the second and beginning of the first centuries B.C., observed that Iberians exploited private copper and silver mines in Turdetania.[65] All of the available evidence suggests that mining, at the level both of extraction/processing and of the carrying trade in metals, was an activity open to both natives and non-natives. The situation in Baetica during the first century B.C. would thus stand in contrast with mining around Carthago Nova during the second and early first centuries B.C., which seems to have been largely the affair of Italian immigrants and/or their freedmen and descendants. The ability to identify the beneficiaries of mining and metallurgical activity in Hispania Ulterior during the late Republican and triumviral periods is stymied by two factors: the first is the lower number of ingots securely provenanced to the mines of the Sierra Morena and elsewhere compared to the larger number from the area of New Carthage; and the second is the relatively smaller number of individuals and small-scale *societates* named on the ingots. To a larger extent than in the mines around New Carthage, the mines of Ulterior in this period seem to have been exploited by larger-scale *societates publicanorum*. It is a notorious fact that only one Italian with exclusive interests in the mines of the region is named on the ingots from the mines of the Sierra Morena in Ulterior.[66] Sources of information other than ingots or inscriptions on the ingots themselves, consequently, are crucial to reconstructing the production and distribution of metals from Ulterior during the late Republican and triumviral eras. It is, for example, to the evidence of coinage that we turn to reconstruct the probable routes by which metals mined from the eastern and central Sierra Morena reached their ports of embarkation during the later Republican era. The presence along the way of fractional bronze issues of Castulo, Obulco, Malaca, and to some extent Ulia and Corduba stands, on this accounting, as the vestige of an important traffic of mule- and donkey-trains carrying metals from the Sierra Morena to Malaca. The animals and their drivers took the ancient Iberian route from Castulo to Malaca, running through the campiñas of Jaén and Córdoba, and eventually turning south after its junction with the Corduba-Malaca road at Monturque.[67]

Even if, as suggested above, the Roman and Italian presence prior to c. 45 B.C. in southern Spain was not massive, the Roman impact on mining may have been more than minimal, particularly in the sphere of ore-processing centers. Emergency excavations, occasioned by the construction of the Madrid-Sevilla gas pipeline, have revealed a planned, urbanized center in the Sierra Morena at Valderrepisa (Ciudad Real), active c. 150–50, devoted to the refining of ore from local mines.[68] The center possesses wide, parallel streets, a broad, open central square, and a carefully laid-out drainage system. It is difficult to see in this place anything less than the impact of skilled Roman or Italian technical personnel. Their subsistence needs would presumably have been met by native farmers of the region.

One aspect of rural production in Baetica that goes unmentioned in Domergue's repertorium of mines in the Iberian peninsula is local, small-scale mining and metallurgical activity devoted to the satisfaction of the demand for utilitarian objects, chiefly in the form of tools and nails. As systematic excavation in the countryside of Andalusia is virtually in its infancy, there is not a great deal of material to illuminate what was probably a widespread phenomenon. Stray site reports suggest the ubiquity of this activity, which extended from Republican times through the later Empire. The second-order site "Las Viñas," situated on the right bank of the Salado River, 700 meters north of the village of Zamoranos in southeastern Córdoba province, reveals fragments of red ochre, which may have emanated from known workings on a nearby hill.[69] Leiva Briones and Madruga Flores suggest that the same source may have supplied the red ochre found in the prehistoric settlement "La Fuente del Río" at Cabra. From the second-order, unexcavated site Los López, situated in the municipal district of Carcabuey, comes not only evidence of olive-oil production, but also iron and copper slag. Carrillo Díaz-Pines notes the proximity of worked copper ore deposits, and suggests that Los López was dedicated not only to agricultural production but to metallurgical activities as well.[70] Gallic and Spanish *terra sigillata,* Republican *denarii,* and a La Tène II *fibula* suggest an occupation of the site from Republican times through at least the second century A.D. Investigators identify four out of a total of 115 rural sites in the "Depresión de Ronda," situated in the northwestern portion of Málaga province, devoted to metallurgy in Roman times. Two of the sites are in immediate proximity to the iron mines at Malaver, mines that were worked at the beginning of the twentieth century. Two further sites, which the authors describe as smaller in extension, are situated next to less rich iron deposits and served, in the authors' estimation, as sources for the manufacture of iron implements designed for the needs of the sites themselves.[71] It would be interesting to know if the kind of rural or urban production outlined above was tied into larger exchange networks. The market for the products, whether utilitarian or ornamental, certainly existed in Baetica. One indication that iron or other metal implements ultimately became items of exchange comes in the form of an inscription of possibly high imperial date from Hispalis, which names the ironmonger (*negotiator ferrarius*)

Frutonius Brocchus. From his cognomen, it may be fairly surmised that he was freeborn; and he was of some distinction as well, since he possessed the formal status of *incola* or resident alien in that riverine metropolis.[72]

The settlement Horno del Castillo (Guarromán) in Jaén province may be a further example of a small-scale operation, in this instance devoted to the washing and smelting of ore. The site is situated in the valley of the Guadiel River, an affluent of the Guadalquivir, which in antiquity was probably part of the *saltus Castulonensis.* The following comments derive from the preliminary site report and analysis.[73]

Emergency excavations revealed a Roman settlement with three phases, extending from the mid-first century B.C. to the fourth century A.D. The earliest settlement, corresponding to phase one, evidently had its inception c. 50 B.C., to judge from the ceramics evidence, and seems to have centered on the highest point in the area, namely the Cerro Castillejo. The Civil Wars of the late Republican and triumviral periods apparently interrupted the life of the settlement in its earliest phase, not represented by any surviving structures. The cerro yields up remains of cisterns, canals, and habitations, connected with the processing of ore, which represent phase two in the activity of the settlement. The structures on the cerro seem to have had their inception in the early first century A.D., from the presence of Italian and Gallic *terra sigillata.* The excavators ascribe to phase three the construction of new habitations and structures associated with the processing of ore, including a well-preserved smelting oven in the southern portion of the site. The new settlement was on lower ground south of the Cerro Castillejo. Excavations in this area have disclosed a Roman house with foundations of dressed stone on which rose adobe walls in a wooden frame. Two of the partially excavated three rooms of the house had a pavement of mortar. One of the rooms seems to have served as a storeroom and contains remains of *dolia* crushed by the collapse of the roof. The roof seems to have been covered by unflanged tiles and not *tegulae.* The habitations also produced various types of domestic common ceramics, lamps, and African red-slip ware. The circular oven, roughly 4 meters in diameter, seems to date to the third phase, that is, from the second half of the second or early third century A.D. The excavators suggest a reduction in the scale of operations between the second and the third phase—certainly the structures of the Cerro Castillejo seem to have been completely abandoned, and the excavators envisage at most several "families" working the site in its third and final phase. The material evidence of both phases two and three, but particularly the latter, is certainly not consonant with individuals or families living at or near subsistence, and suggests instead a metallurgical installation that was open to the outside world. In any case, the presence of *dolia* in phase three of the site suggests that those inhabiting it engaged in a combination of smelting and subsistence agricultural activities.

CHAPTER TWO

Baetica Pacata

Recent survey work in southern Spain has revealed a proliferation of rural settlements in Baetica from Augustus' reign onward.
This and the remaining chapters will seek to explain this settlement activity. The exposition and analysis will concentrate on
the *conventus Astigitanus,* the southern *conventus Cordubensis,*
and the southeastern *conventus Hispalensis* for the simple reason
that it is in these portions of Baetica, representing ancient assize
districts, that modern survey archaeology and excavation have
been practiced with the greatest frequency and intensity since the
early 1970s (see Map 2).

The expansion and intensification of settlement, particularly rural, relate to a variety of factors external to the Iberian
peninsula, as well as those which reflect the internal dynamics of
Baetican society. A point of extreme methodological delicacy in
all that follows is the relationship of the settlement pattern and
the character of individual sites to the make-up of Baetican society. A rural first- through third-order site will not, for example,
reveal in an explicit fashion whether the inhabitants are tenants
or *possessores.* But the examination of the overall settlement pattern and its relationship to urban centers may provide the means
to make more or less secure inferences about the social positions
of those exploiting rural sites. It is the conviction of this author
that an analysis of all the evidence, archaeological, epigraphical,

MAP TWO
Approximate *conventus* boundaries of Baetica

and literary, suggests that agricultural tenancy in Baetica from Augustus to the first of the Severan emperors was a comparative rarity, the exceptional presence of which was dictated largely by the apparent lack of dispersed landholding by Baetican elites and by the relatively constrained sizes of most Baetican municipal territories. I return to this subject below.

History and Administration

The date of the creation of Hispania Ulterior Baetica is a vexing question. On the other hand, for those who enjoy puzzles, the exposition of the evidence may be pleasing. To begin with, Cassius Dio is certainly wrong to state that in 27 B.C., Augustus organized Hispania into three provinces (53.12.4–5). For some time after 27, an undivided Hispania Ulterior was under the control of an imperial legate. From 27 to 22(?), Publius Carisius was *legatus propraetore* of Ulterior.[1] L. Sestius P.f. Quirinalis Albinianus was consular legate of Ulterior from 22(?) to 19(?).[2] Alföldy puts the *legatio* of Q. Acutius Faienanus over Lusitania between 19 and 1 B.C.; nevertheless, Stylow has demonstrated that Faienanus was active sometime from the Flavian era to the first two decades of the second century.[3] Dio has his partisans, including Albertini, though Alföldy, drawing on Syme, offers powerful arguments for putting the division of Ulterior into Baetica and Lusitania in c. 16–13 B.C., and specifically, closer to the latter date.[4] This would coincide with, and partly explain, Augustus' presence in Spain in these years. The provincial division in this interval would also account for the reduction of the Spanish garrison from six to four legions and its placement under the unified command of the governor of Nearer Spain by c. 13 B.C. at the latest.[5] Most commentators have subsequently accepted Alföldy's dating of the creation of the province of Baetica.[6] Mackie, however, holds, on uncertain grounds, that the province of Baetica came into being in 25 B.C., and suggests that Tingi and the twelve triumviral-Augustan colonies in Mauretania, including Zulil, were attached administratively to the new province at that time.[7] In any case, the testimony of Pliny the Elder suggests that the main lines of the province of Lusitania were established by 12 B.C., the year of Agrippa's death (4.118: "Agrippa has recorded that Lusitania along with Asturia and Gallaecia extends 540 miles in length and 536 miles in breadth").

There is also the problem of an adjustment in the eastern boundary of the new province of Baetica after c. 13 B.C. The difficulty here is that Pliny offers diverse figures for the east-west dimensions of Baetica: he chides both Agrippa and Augustus for offering the mistaken figure of 475 miles for the length of Baetica. The reference is to Agrippa's geographical survey and map of the world, unfinished at his death and completed by Augustus. Pliny, writing in the mid-first century A.D., notes that "now the length of Baetica is 250 miles from the boundary of the town of Castulo to Gades, and 25 miles more from the shore of Murgi" (3.17). It is difficult to know, therefore, what Alföldy means when he suggests that the eastern adjustment in the boundary of Baetica could have occurred anytime between 27 and 2 B.C.[8] The significance of the latter date is that a number of milestones, erected between January 1 and February 5, 2 B.C., announce various distances on the *Via Augusta* from the *Ianus Augustus* on the Baetis—a monument that marked the eastern boundary of Baetica—to Ocean at Gades.[9] The case would be a good one that the erection of the milestones in Baetica was timed deliberately to coincide with the erection of an altar to Augustus toward another extremity of ocean on the banks of the Middle Elbe by L. Domitius Ahenobarbus.[10] The milestones represent a likely ante quem for the reorganization of Baetica. A literal interpretation of Pliny would seem to support a date of 2 B.C. for the eastern boundary realignment, as it is probably in that year that Augustus completed the work on Agrippa's map, displayed in the Porticus Vipsania.[11] It is surprising to find a modern scholar concurring with Pliny's jejeune criticism of Agrippa and Augustus' map-making efforts:[12] On the above accounting, it looks like Agrippa and Augustus were, in fact, reckoning correctly with a maximum provincial breadth of 475 miles up until, and probably including part of, the year 2 B.C. That is to say, Baetica at its creation in c. 13 B.C. had an east-west extension of 475 miles. The motive for the contraction of the eastern boundary of Baetica to a line west of Castulo may be connected with the desire of Augustus to place the *saltus Castulonensis* and its mineral resources under imperial control.

No certain evidence reveals the identities of the governors and their staff of the new province under Augustus. In the Conobaria oath of 5-3 B.C. to Augustus, his sons Gaius and Lucius Caesar, and grandson Agrippa, it is a fair surmise that the P. Petronius P.f. T[   ] and M. Alfius G.f. Laches are the proconsul and quaestor or *legatus propraetore,* respectively, of the province of Baetica.[13] Apart from these two, the first proconsul of Baetica on record is the otherwise unknown Aulus Cottia, commemorated by his daughter in Rome in an inscription of Augustan or even Tiberian date.[14] In the light of this uncertainty, it is possible that the *legatus propraetore* M. Petrucidius, mentioned in Chapter One, served under some unknown proconsul of the province between c. 13 B.C. and A.D. 14.

ILS 103 represents a statue base set up in the Forum Augustum shortly after the receipt of the title *pater patriae* by Augustus on February 5, 2 B.C., as Alföldy argues, and is the first documentary or literary reference to the province of Baetica.[15] The inscription records the gift of some sort of object—possibly an *effigies provinciae*—made out of 100 pounds of gold by Hispania Ulterior Baetica to Imperator Caesar Augustus *pater patriae* "quod beneficio eius et perpetua cura provincia pacata est" ("because through his beneficence and perpetual care the province had been pacified"). Alföldy argues that the purpose of the dedication was to honor the conferment of the title *pater patriae* on Augustus; but perhaps it would not be excessively speculative to see in the dedication the gratitude also of the new province to the emperor for his pacification of the province, which inter alia involved the definitive delimitation of provincial boundaries. Dessau probably went too far in suggesting that it was precisely in 2 B.C. that Augustus turned the province over to senatorial control. What does seem to emerge with increasing clarity is that the erection of milestones in Baetica from New Year's Day to February 5, 2 B.C., and the consecration of the Forum Augustum in Rome in the first half of 2 B.C. were designed to be simultaneous and to advertise the princeps' universal dominion. Be that as it may, the rule of Augustus marks a watershed in the history of Hispania Ulterior, and particularly of that portion of the province which became Baetica.

The status of Baetica as a senatorial province was unaltered subsequently save for three relatively brief episodes. The first occurred in 122/123, when Hadrian was in Spain. At that time, it looks as if he installed the consular C. Iulius M.f. Proculus, his *comes,* as an imperial legate of Baetica *extra ordinem.* Hadrian's action may have been prompted by the unanticipated death of the serving proconsular governor. During the 170s, the province was disturbed by certain Mauri, and Baetica and Hispania Citerior were folded into one unified province under the *legatus Augusti propraetore* C. Aufidius C.f. Victorinus.[16] Again, during the mid-third century, but before c. 285, the administration of senatorial proconsuls was interrupted — it is uncertain for how long — by imperial legates of praetorian rank.[17]

The important thing about Augustus' reign is that it would have brought the first extended period of peace and stability that Ulterior, and later Baetica, had enjoyed since the 50s B.C. That peace is the first important factor in understanding the rise of numerous wealthy Hispani and Hispanienses during the Principate. The second factor is the interlocking element of increasing demand for staples on the part of the central power, coupled with the relatively easy navigability of the Baetis and the prodigious fertility of the Baetis valley and adjoining areas in Baetica.

In administrative terms, another phenomenon of the reign of Augustus, and of the preceding triumviral and Caesarian periods, that is both important and remarkably obscure is the widespread elevation of Spanish communities to Roman legal status. Aside from the likelihood that a sizable number of communities received such promotions in the aforementioned periods, there is, unfortunately, hardly any unanimity as to the actual status these communities received — aside from the secure instances of Roman *coloniae* such as Astigi and Tucci — or whether certain towns thought to have been elevated to Roman status did, in fact, receive Roman-style constitutions. Fear trenchantly argued that the possession of a title in the name of a town is no guaranty that that town actually possessed Roman status.[18] Moreover, there is lasting controversy as to whether certain towns were *municipia civium Romanorum,* Latin *municipia,* or Latin colonies, or even whether the category of *municipia civium Romanorum* ever existed in Spain.[19] Many of those persons and families whom we know gained the Roman citizenship at the end of the first century B.C. and during the early first century A.D. may have gained that citizenship on the basis of individual and not corporate grants of citizenship.[20] One enduring aspect of the Augustan reform of Spain and Baetica is the creation of the *pagus,* or fiscal district, which constituted an administrative intermediary between the rural productive unit(s) (*fundus*) and town (*civitas*). The institution of the *quadragesima Galliarum,* or two-and-a-half percent customs-dues, probably dates to the reign of Augustus, and its Spanish counterpart, the *XXXX Hispaniarum,* is likely a contemporary development.[21]

Settlement

The Caesarian, triumviral, and Augustan establishment of *coloniae* and *municipia* throughout the province, but principally in the lowlands of the Guadalquivir valley, nevertheless produced widespread rural settlement in the form of isolated farmsteads. These were virtually ex novo foundations in a countryside that had been largely devoid of habitation. It is difficult to know what form these early, Roman-style establishments took or even whether they were permanently inhabited throughout the year. In many contexts, these establishments would have been substantial masonry-built structures, as seems to have been the case in the *ager* of Carmo;[22] in other instances they may have reflected native constructive techniques, employing adobe walls on stone foundations. Durán and Padilla suggest that the veterans settled at Astigi during Augustus' reign lived, for the most part, in the *oppidum* and utilized flimsy temporary huts on their land. It is surely an exaggeration, though, to posit, as does Sáez, a massive transfer of land and landholding from natives to Romans and Italians from Caesar's rule through the end of the reign of Augustus, and to link the appearance of villas in southern Spain exclusively with this non-Baetican element.[23] It must be borne in mind that many of the time-served veteran colonists in Baetica settled in the later first century B.C. were native Hispani, as well as

Gauls from Narbonensis and Italians. It is certainly misleading, though, to speak of the upper Guadalquivir valley as extraneous to the currents of Romano-Italic acculturation during the triumviral and Augustan periods. Evidence to the contrary is the adoption, adaptation, and construction of Italic-inspired funerary monuments in Caesarian and Augustan *coloniae* and *municipia* in the area of modern Jaén province; these communities include the *colonia* Salaria (Úbeda), the *colonia* Augusta Gemella Tucci (Martos), Castulo (Cortijos de Sta. Eufemia y de Yanguas, Linares), Iliturgi (Maquiz, Mengíbar), and Ossigi (Cerro Alcalá, Mancha Real). Blending central and northern Italian prototypes with indigenous traditions, including the use of Iberian-style animal protomes, these free-standing monuments, which sometimes incorporated the sculptural representations of the commemorated, responded to the tastes of Romano-Italic immigrants and their descendants, in addition to acculturated natives.[24]

A more or less complete accounting, even in summary fashion, of changes in the settlement pattern during the Augustan period (and before) in Baetica would also have to indicate the movement of population in urban contexts. Thus in the southwestern portions of Baeturia Celtica corresponding to eastern Seville and western Huelva provinces, in the period from Julius Caesar to Augustus, it is possible to detect the movement, perhaps forced, of native inhabitants from pre-Roman communities into artificial urban foundations. Such is the case of the pre-Roman *oppida* at the Cerro del Castillo de las Peñas de Aroche and El Castillo de la Solana del Torrejón into the new and nearby centers at Fuente Seca (Arucci?) and San Mamés, the latter place corresponding to Turobriga.[25] A similar phenomenon, about which more will be said below, is discernible in the northern part of Baeturia Celtica during the earlier Julio-Claudian period, affecting centers such as Lacimurga, Nertobriga, and Mirobriga.

Production and Trade

All the documentary and archaeological evidence points to an increase in Spanish and Baetican exports to Rome, Italy, and the army during the reign of Augustus. It is impossible to quantify the increase from the preceding triumviral and Republican periods. The following summarizes the main points about the nature of production and export from Baetica to Rome and elsewhere in the Roman world during Augustus' reign. As in the previous chapter, the survey begins with the components of the Mediterranean triad of cereals, olive oil, and wine and proceeds to other goods and staples.

The archaeological evidence exists in Baetica for substantial cereals production during the early Principate. If Lacort Navarro is correct in his analysis, then large-scale, Roman-era grain-storage structures exist in the Cortijo de Las Cuevas, situated within the municipal district of Castro del Río. The structures are located on the right bank of the arroyo Carchena, and situated approximately 200 meters from that watercourse. They occupy an area of roughly 10,000 square meters. Next to the structures was discovered a grain millstone 1.35 meters in diameter and 40 centimeters thick. All but one of the structures consist of a series of semi-subterranean chambers of rectangular plan, built of *opus caementicium,* with barrel-vaulted roofs. The exterior dimensions of these structures vary: the largest is 9.5 meters long and 4.3 meters wide; the smallest is 5 meters long and 2.90 meters wide. All of the aforementioned structures apparently possess a uniform height of roughly 2.5 meters.[26] But the largest structure, and one that is apparently distinct in function from the aforementioned ones, is a cryptoporticus 32.5 meters long, 3.1 meters wide, and 3.3 meters high, with two lateral openings or windows. Lacort dates the structures, including the cryptoporticus, from the end of the first century B.C. to c. A.D. 50. The structures are generally equidistant from Ucubi, Ulia, Ipagrum (Cerro del Castillo, Aguilar de la Frontera), and Munda (Cerro de las Camorras[?], La Lentejuela). Lacort suggests that the structures served the Roman authorities as granaries destined to supply the *urbs.* Lacort sees the grain as either *frumentum mancipale* from *ager publicus*—that is, grain owed the state in the form of rent-in-kind from the lessees of the public land—or as grain purchased by the *annona* in the form of *frumentum emptum.*[27]

Archaeological evidence of an indirect kind suggests also that there was substantial grain-growing in the central valley of the Guadalquivir during the reign of Augustus and later. That evidence consists of the remains of grain mills. For instance, *metae* and at least one *catillus* of considerable dimensions, belonging to animal-drawn mills, have been found at four sites in the vicinity of Palma del Río.[28] The *meta* corresponds to the lower, fixed element of a mill, while the *catillus* represents the upper, movable part. Much of the grain grown in the middle valley of the Guadalquivir would have reached the principal city of this region, namely Corduba. It would have arrived at the provincial capital by means of the Roman road connecting Iliberri and upper Singilis valley with Corduba and the middle stretches of the Baetis. This road, the so-called Vereda de Granada, already alluded to in the *Bellum Hispaniense* (6.1–3), assumed Roman characteristics in the Augustan period in the form of paving and bridge construction. The road passed through prime grain-growing areas of the eastern campiña of Córdoba, including the territories of the Roman towns of Iponoba, Ipsca, Castro del Río (Roman name unknown), and Ategua.

OLIVE OIL

It is late in Augustus' reign that shipwreck evidence suggests the first hint of olive-oil exportation from Baetica to Rome and elsewhere. The first securely datable instance of a shipwreck with a substantial cargo of early forms of the Dressel 20 known to this author is the *Capo Graziano C* (Italy) wreck of c. A.D. 1–10(?). Parker describes its "main" cargo as olive-oil containers, similar to an amphora from the contemporary La Longarina deposit of Ostia, and therefore dating to the first decade of the common era.[29] One wreck, *Le Secanion* off of Juan-les-Pins, dated as early as c. 10 B.C. and as late as c. A.D. 40, is reported to have contained one "early" Dressel 20 amphora;[30] the container may well have formed part of the ship's stores and thus not represent an item of exportation. Other early wrecks, also found off the southern coast of France, that evidently carried multiple Dressel 20 amphoras include the *Sud-Lavezzi B* of A.D. 10–30 and the *Jarre* of c. A.D. 10–50(?).[31] The chronology of the very earliest proto-Dressel 20 consignments is perfectly in line with the theory that Baetican olive-oil exportation was, from the beginning, under the indirect supervision of the prefect of the *annona,* whose administration may have officially begun in A.D. 6. One knowledgeable investigator of olive cultivation in antiquity, citing the common (and fallacious) view that a new olive tree took up to two decades to bear a significant fruit, notes that in Roman times, most trees were grown from cuttings, slips, or grafts and not from seed, and that such plants could begin to produce, under good conditions, "substantial" fruit within five to eight years.[32] It is obvious that the settled conditions in Baetica produced by Augustus provided more than enough time to promote the deliberate cultivation of olive plantations that were sufficiently extensive for surplus production and export.

WINE

Strabo refers to the export of wine from Turdetania, that is, Baetica (3.2.6). It is worth emphasizing anew that Strabo is probably referring to exports as late as the latter part of Augustus' reign or beginning of Tiberius'. Meticulous site excavation in Andalusia is beginning to reveal places where the vine was cultivated and processed into wine as early as Augustus' reign. The roster of localities where this activity took place includes the first-order rural complex on the Loma de Ceres (Molvízar-Granada), not far to the north-northwest of Los Matagallares. The excavated portions correspond to the *pars fructuaria* of a Roman villa and a dump for wasters of fine and utilitarian ceramics, including amphoras. The presence of Campanian B, *terra sigillata italica,* and thin-walled ceramics suggests an inception of the structure and outliers in the Augustan period. Dressel 2–4 containers for transporting wine were produced at or near the installation at the Loma de Ceres (about which more below). Meticulous excavation outside Hispania reveals the destination of some of the wine produced here or elsewhere. Excavations at Colchester in 1970 revealed seven Dressel 2–4 amphoras, dated by stratigraphic context from A.D. 43 to 60/61, that the excavator suggests transported Baetican wine.[33]

Boiled wine, or must (*defrutum*), was bottled and transported from southern Spain to the northwestern provinces of the Empire and elsewhere from at least c. 30 B.C. onward.[34] The product was carried in the characteristic Haltern 70 amphoras, remains of which appear in shipwrecks dating from the early first to the early second century A.D. The same container type also transported olives preserved in *defrutum.* The varieties of grape grown in Baetica during the late Republic and Principate were varied, and include the Amineae, Coccolobis, Bumasti, Numisianae, Duracinae, and Purpureae.[35]

FISH SAUCE

An important number of fish-sauce amphora-producing centers in the province began their activity in the reign of Augustus. Again, without being doctrinaire on the matter, it is possible to link this renewed activity with the diversification and intensification of Baetican exports to the army and the *urbs,* under the general cover of the prefecture of the *annona.* One of the better-known amphora-producing complexes having its inception in Augustus' reign is that called Venta del Carmen (Casa de Postas) in the munic-ipal district of Los Barrios in the Bay of Algeciras. Emergency excavations revealed the existence of at least two amphora ovens at the site.[36] The best-preserved oven has a diameter of just under 4 meters. Before the ovens are a series of partially excavated rooms given over, in all probability, to some stages in the manufacture of amphoras and other objects, including com-mon ceramics, *tegulae, imbrices,* and bricks, including *semilateres* and *spi-catum.* Connected to the complex was a subterranean canal built of am-phora remains and *tegulae;* excavation has been completed on 22 meters of the canal's length. The canal supplied water obtained from nearby wells for various aspects in the preparation of the clay and materials to be fired at the site. The pottery was active between the reign of Augustus and the end of the first century A.D., when production came to an abrupt halt for some un-known reason. At that later date the ovens were filled in with ceramics re-mains and other debris.[37] The installation produced Dressel 7–11, Dressel 14, Beltrán II A 1 and II B amphoras, the latter in smaller quantities rep-resenting the initial stages of that container's production. The site also represents the first confirmed production center in Baetica of Haltern 70 *defrutum*-containing amphoras. Dressel 28 amphora remains at Venta del Carmen allegedly represent importations. A number of fragments, cor-responding to Dressel 14 and probably Beltrán II A containers, bear the stamp CNPFCR and variants.[38]

Other amphora-producing centers devoted to the manufacture of containers for the transport of fish sauce that have their certain or likely inception in the reign of Augustus include those at the Loma de Ceres (Molvízar, Granada province) mentioned above, Carranque (Málaga), Haza Honda (Málaga), Fontanar (Chiclana de la Frontera), Jarana or Villanueva (Puerto Real), Puente Melchor (Puerto Real), Las Canteras (Puerto Real), El Gallinero (Puerto Real), El Almendral (Puerto Real), Los Tercios (El Puerto de Santa María), and Orippo (Torre de los Herberos, Dos Hermanas).[39] This is an impressive proportion of the more than four score amphora-producing sites known through survey or excavation, and doubly so given that most of these sites' inception dates are unknown.

TEXTILES

Strabo, in a possible allusion to exports in his own day (i.e., the later Au-gustan and early Tiberian periods), refers to the export of wool from Tur-detania (3.2.6). The high frequency with which loom weights figure among published site scatters and in the assemblages of ceramics produced by rural *figlinae* suggests also that weaving was a widespread activity, probably as early as the reign of Augustus, throughout the countryside in Baetica.

ANIMAL HUSBANDRY

The literary sources complement the archaeological evidence for animal husbandry, specifically cattle raising, in the lower portion of the Guadalquivir valley, which in antiquity was dominated by the *Lacus Ligustinus*. The *Lacus Ligustinus,* into which the Baetis flowed, was a virtual inland sea at high water, and only after antiquity silted up to form the so-called Marismas. Strabo (3.2.4), in a statement that may derive from one of his late Republican sources but is applicable, in all likelihood, to the Augustan period and later, refers explicitly to the dangers posed by flood and ebb tides affecting the *Lacus Ligustinus.* He mentions cattle that have crossed over to islands in the *Lacus* and that have been engulfed by the flood or, alternatively, perished while they attempted to swim back to dry land. Otherwise, as Strabo notes, the cows have learned to wait out the flood and to walk back to dry land on an ebb tide.

Analysis

It is not easy to be sure of the precise reasons for the quickening of Baetican exports during the reign of Augustus. Surely Augustus' establishment of the prefecture of the *annona* is a factor. The accurate reading of Pompeius Trogus, as preserved in Justin (44.1.5), shows that grain was touted as an important export to Italy from Spain in the Augustan period—an export that, along with precious and semi-precious metals, will have acted to subsidize the transport of other commodities, including fish sauce and oil.[40] Indeed, Justin, in his epitome, writes that Spain produced enough food not only for itself but also for Rome and Italy: the items include grain, wine, honey, and oil. Strabo claims the export from Turdetania of grain in large quantities (3.2.6). Of course, much of this grain may have been shipped to Rome in the form of tax- or rent-in-kind. Was olive oil imported under the direct control of the *annona* as early as Augustus' reign? Probably not. But the competence of the *praefectus annonae,* in addition to the general supervision of Rome's markets, surely extended beyond grain importation and distribution, to a more general care for the import of oil and other staples in quantities sufficient to meet Rome's needs.[41] The prefect of the *annona* may have exercised a general control over the prices of foodstuffs, including olive oil. The precise means by which he did so are unclear, at least until the reign of Claudius, when incentives for persons involved in the grain trade to Rome may well have acted as a prop for the subsidized or semi-subsidized importation of oil and other staples. In the Augustan period and during the reign of Tiberius, the transport of high-density and high-value metals from southern Spain also will probably have acted to subsidize the transport costs, and hence to encourage the export of staples such as olive oil and wine. Strabo and Pompeius Trogus make statements that are just as likely to be reflective of imperial ideology as normative descriptions of reality. Of course, there is no way of testing quantitatively their statements that Spain, and Baetica in particular, exported "large" quantities of foodstuffs and staples during the reign of Augustus.

Why, then, do Strabo and Pompeius Trogus single out Spain and Baetica for special praise with respect to their productivity and exports? The answer may lie in the identity of the first incumbent of the prefecture of the *annona* during Augustus' reign. That individual is C. Turranius Gracilis, of Gaditane origin. Turranius, on the most likely reconstruction of his career, probably entered office in A.D. 8.[42] Strabo, and possibly Pompeius Trogus, may well be indirectly praising the prefect of the *annona* by lauding the fertility and value to the *annona,* overall, of his *patria.* This solution has also the implication of dating Strabo's *laudes Hispaniae* to the latter part of Augustus' reign or the beginning of Tiberius', a supposition that is in line with his comments about the vicissitudes in the organization and administration of Baetica (and the other provinces and prefectures) during Augustus' reign (17.3.25).

Also a likely—if banal—reason for an increase in Spanish exports at the end of the first century B.C. is the resumption of more or less peaceful and stable conditions throughout most of the Mediterranean basin under the Augustan regime. It may be possible to identify other factors. Perhaps Chic García is right to suggest that the release of the treasury of the Ptolemies in the early part of Octavian-Augustus' rule stimulated demand in the central and western Mediterranean.[43] The archaeological and epigraphical record certainly shows a rise in the number of rural establishments, the embellishment and expansion of certain urban centers, and the beginnings of the widespread use of inscriptions to honor the living and commemorate the dead during Augustus' long rule.[44] Not all of this construction and production will have been powered by external demand during Augustus' reign:

the preferences of Baetican consumers are hinted at by the imitation of Italian *sigillata* at or near Celti (Peñaflor), beginning in the last decades of the first century B.C. and extending until about A.D. 50.[45] And it is possible to adduce an ideological basis for the embellishment of certain urban centers in the form of temples and precincts serving the imperial cult.[46] The human catalysts for this surge in agricultural production and export were undoubtedly, in the main, Italian and Roman emigrants to southern Spain and their descendants, particularly those clustered in Caesarian, triumviral, and Augustan colonies in the area. Italian and other settlers at Astigi, for example, probably played an important role in the beginnings of large-scale olive-oil processing there. The predilection during the pre-Claudian period of many time-served soldiers and their immediate descendants at Astigi (and, presumably, at other centers subjected to colonial *deductiones,* such as Hispalis and Corduba) to reside in the town would have been fomented by oleiculture, with its less-intensive labor requirements and generally steady returns.[47]

CHAPTER THREE

The Julio-Claudian Experience

History and Administration

Broad changes affecting Baetica and Spain as a whole from the latter part of Augustus' rule to the death of Nero include not only Augustus' definitive organization of Tarraconensis, Lusitania, and Baetica, but also the formal articulation of the *conventus* system and imperial cult. A number of commentators emphasize the initiative of the provincials in matters such as monumental building, local coinage, and worship of the emperor and the *domus Augusta*.[1] The emperor and his agents were not passive, though, in matters affecting the provincials' identification with the ruling power, and positively fostered loyalty. This is made clear by the crucial evidence of the oath of allegiance to Augustus, his sons Gaius and Lucius Caesar, and his grandson M. Agrippa, taken by the inhabitants of Conobaria between 6/5 and 3/2 B.C., and presumably on a widespread basis throughout the province, at a time when Tiberius, in exile on Rhodes with both the tribunician power and probably the *imperium,* posed a potential military threat to Augustus; by the promulgation of instructions for honoring Germanicus and later Drusus; and by the publication in various places of the decree of the senate referring to the trial and death of Cn. Piso pater in A.D. 20.[2] The pace, furthermore, of the elevation of peregrine communities to Roman status slackens considerably from the preceding periods. Only one such enfranchisement stands more or less securely on record during the Julio-Claudian period, namely Claudius' conferment of municipal status on Baelo, probably in the early 40s.[3]

Settlement

The pace of new rural settlement from the death of Augustus to the reign of Vitellius is very uneven when compared with that of the Caesarian-triumviral-Augustan periods. It is in broad areas of the province, nevertheless, that survey and sondages reveal the first permanent, Roman-style rural construction during the Julio-Claudian period. Conspicuous in this regard is the hilly and mountainous swath between the Guadalquivir River and the Mediterranean known as the penibético, especially low-lying intermontane areas such as the so-called depresión de Antequera and the Vega of Granada.[4] And a number of rural, Roman-style *aedificia* in the upper Guadalquivir valley seem to have their inception precisely at some point in the period from late in the reign of Augustus to c. A.D. 50 or slightly later. The presence of various forms of Gallic *sigillata* in numerous sites of the aforementioned areas and the complete or near complete absence of Italian *sigillata* or late Campanian ware and its imitations provide a definite terminus a quo of the reigns of Tiberius through Claudius for many rural settlements in the penibético and in the campiñas of Sevilla, Córdoba, and Jaén provinces. Any rectangular farmstead in the Baetican countryside is a manifestation of Romano-Italic influence, and its appearance in both the lower and upper Guadalquivir valley, in the Augustan and Julio-Claudian periods, disproves the conventional view that Roman villa construction only appears in the upper Guadalquivir valley from the second half of the first century A.D. onward.[5] Nevertheless, the presence of Campanian A, B, or C wares and Dressel 1 amphoras at many sites in the campiñas of the middle Guadalquivir valley shows that material Romanization, if not Roman-style building, was present already in the late Republican, triumviral, and Augustan periods. The foregoing observation certainly seems to hold true even for the survey area around Fuentes de Andalucía in the province of Sevilla.[6]

Romano-Italic house forms in this period were varied. The prevailing Roman type of construction in Baetica may have been the Vitruvian single-story farmhouse with a central court or simple peristyle — a type that Gorges terms the "villa-bloc à péristyle."[7] But many areas of the penibético at intermediate elevations (300–650 meters) and in the northern portion of the province manifest in the Julio-Claudian period, and even earlier, a peculiar type of quadrangular edifice alluded to above, possessing ashlar or polygonal masonry bases, ground plans of 100 to 500 square meters, a tripartite interior arrangement marked by a central corridor, earthen floors, and at least one upper story. Moret categorizes these suburban and rural structures as "maisons fortes" with Italian antecedents, inspired also by privately owned Punic and Phoenician towers.[8] The available archaeological data shows that in no manner are these "maisons fortes" Iberian in origin.[9] They reflect instead Romanized and Romanizing native elites and/or Italian colonists and their descendants in search of an architectural form that satisfied the functional demands of increasingly olive-based agriculture and the need to advertise increasing personal wealth and status according to Roman norms.

The concentration of these structures in the campiñas of Córdoba and Jaén provinces may reflect the intensity of archaeological survey in the aforementioned areas, but they do seem to be more exceptional in other areas, save for the mining region of La Serena in the extreme northerly portion of Baetica. Their presence in the latter area allegedly has nothing to do with civilian settlement or veteran *deductiones*. One commentator suggests that the "recintos-torres" in that area were occupied by two vexillations from *legio Prima, IIII Macedonica* and *X Gemina*.[10] On Garcia-Bellido's reconstruction, the troops were engaged in the extraction of ore from lead mines in the area during the period immediately after the conclusion of Agrippa's Cantabrian campaigns in 19 B.C. She may be right; but in the meantime, there seems no obvious connection with the military of one well-excavated "maison-forte" in the region, namely the structure at Esparragosa de Lares. It is a structure with a tripartite interior arrangement with overall dimensions of 14 by 15 meters, and it seems to have been occupied in the first half of the first century A.D., according to its excavators.[11] And Ortiz Romero suggests, based in part on the results of the excavation of one "torre," namely that called "Hijovejo," that the "torres" in La Serena date to the Sertorian wars.[12] Ortiz Romero sees them as housing garrisons intended to protect this zone of mining. They were allegedly the creations of Metellus, proconsul in Further Spain during the 70s, constructed for the purpose of protecting both the lead and silver deposits of La Serena and the colony at Metellinum.

Moreover, archaeologists describe the site El Esparragoso II, in the municipal district of Montellano in southeast Sevilla province, as a large rectangular structure, measuring 20 by 25 meters, of which only the foundations of walls remain. Within the structure are three divisions, delimited again by walls for which only foundations remain.[13] The preceding description seems to be that of a "maison forte," with the ceramics evidence at the site indicating an early Flavian construction. And there is the "maison forte" "El Tesorillo," situated in the vicinity of Teba (Málaga province), well distant from the campiñas.[14] Be that as it may, the "maison forte" type of rural *aedificium* ceased to be built after the early Flavian era, and it seems to have been completely abandoned as a form of habitat, albeit a temporary one, as Moret alleges in the majority of cases, by the middle of the second century.

Some areas of Baetica show settlement and building activity that must have equaled or exceeded the pace of similar phenomena during the Augustan period. In this category would be the area of Montellano (Sevilla province) and the campiña of Sevilla surveyed by Oria Segura et al. and Ruiz Delgado, respectively. Indeed, it is during the period from A.D. 14 to 68 that survey and excavation point to the construction, throughout many areas of the province, of the first permanent rural structures along Roman lines. Urban development is not the subject of this study, and Keay offers a useful survey of changes to Baetican towns in the Augustan and Julio-Claudian periods, including building in towns as diverse as Gades, Carmo, Italica, Obulco, Baelo, Anticaria, Iliturgi Forum Iulium, Lacippo, Aratispi, and Munigua.[15] At Onuba (modern Huelva), Roman-style construction, including a structure with dressed stones and moldings, as well as structures associable with the storage areas of its port, seems to date from the latter part of Claudius' reign.[16] It is harder, on the other hand, to detect positive signs of much new building or alteration of pre-existing habitations during the latter part of Nero's reign. Without much exaggeration, it may be possible to speak of Nero's reign as a period of the doldrums in Baetica. Indeed, one knowledgeable commentator has characterized the latter period of Nero's reign as a period of "crisis" in Baetican commerce, noting also a sharp reduction at the same time of coinage in circulation in the Río Tinto mining region.[17] The point about the Río Tinto region is borne out time and time again in site and local studies throughout the Iberian peninsula that show that Neronian coinage is totally absent.[18] The cessation of Roman

military activity associated with the annexation of Mauretania and its os-
tensible consequence, about which more below, in the form of the more or
less sudden end of activity in a number of pottery-producing complexes
connected with the production of fish-sauce containers is a harbinger of
Neronian stagnation in Baetica. The termination of the local minting of
small-denomination coinage in various cities of Baetica under Gaius and
early in Claudius' reign may also have had negative repercussions on settlement and economic activity in Baetica. A Neronian "recession" in Baetica
is attributable, in brief, to a dip in demand for Baetican staples and a temporary decrease in liquidity.

In the *conventus Astigitanus,* pre-Flavian rural first- through third-order
establishments along Vitruvian lines predominate in the northwestern,
north-central and northeastern lowland portions of the *conventus,* which
include the territory of the Caesarian colony Urso and the Augustan colony
Astigi.[19] The first-order site at the Cortijo de la Lámpara is an important
manifestation of Claudian-era rural construction in the north-central area
of the *conventus.*[20] The following remarks derive from the detailed but preliminary excavation report of Morena López. The site is situated 1.5 kilometers northeast of Montilla. Roadwork of the early 1990s necessitated the
emergency excavation of that portion of the site in immediate danger of
being obliterated. The excavated portion seems to correspond to the *pars
rustica* of this villa establishment. It is possible to classify this as a first-
order site, from the discovery there in the 1930s of a fragment of a bronze
statue of Bacchus and an acephalous marble statue of Diana the Hunter.
Initial work in connection with road construction also seems to have unearthed remains of *opus tessellatum* pavements. The excavation did disclose
a series of north-south and east-west aligned wall foundations. The foundations consist partly of small or medium-sized, irregularly-shaped stones,
although some of the rocks have been partially dressed. At sporadic intervals there are set dressed limestone blocks. The smaller stones are set either
horizontally in regular courses or in a herringbone pattern. The stones
were joined with "tierra" (i.e., clay?) and packed with bits of rubble, *tegulae,*
and bricks, reminiscent of the construction techniques of the second-order
site at the Cortijo de la Cancha in Málaga province described below. The
walls evidently served as foundations for various rooms, the precise functions of which are unknown. In sector B of the excavation, two basins were
unearthed, in addition to a portion of what seems to have been a larger one.
The basins are composed of mortared rubble; one possesses quarter-round

molding at its bottom and the other an *opus signinum* (moisture-proof cement) bottom. The walls of both basins are lined with mortar. The excavation also yielded painted Iberian ceramics, Italian *sigillata,* Gallic *sigillata* in abundance, *sigillata hispanica,* African *sigillata,* thin-walled ware, common ceramics, glass fragments, lamp fragments, imitation red-slip ware produced during the Julio-Claudian period in the central Guadalquivir valley ("tipo Peñaflor"), iron nails, and bone remains. In addition to late imperial bronzes, the site also produced a coin of colonia Patricia and a possible *as* of Carbula. There is no material that predates the turn of the era. The excavators suggest a foundation date of the villa toward the mid-first century A.D.; certainly the excavated material leaves open an initial date of c. 40–50, if not slightly earlier. The basins belong to a reconstruction of the villa of the late third or early fourth century A.D. The excavators suggest that the function of the reconstructed section of the villa was the processing of the olive. If so, then we are left in the dark as to the economic basis of the establishment in its earliest phase(s). But it is evident on the basis of the range of finished goods from outside, in addition to the coins discovered at the site, that the settlement was open, from its inception, to the wider world. Consequently, it does not seem reasonable to exclude the possibility that oil, or perhaps a combination of oleiculture and arable, underpinned the settlement's activity in the mid-first century and later. Such a hypothesis would certainly be in line with the foundation of a number of Dressel 20-producing *figlinae* along the Singilis and Baetis rivers during the reign of Claudius. The idea deserves serious consideration that the reign of Claudius had a greater material impact on Baetica, as a whole, than did that of Augustus.

In the pre-Flavian period, the eastern and southern portions of the district—mainly upland areas in excess of 400 meters elevation—saw, for the most part, widely dispersed Iberian *oppida* and smaller, quadrangular recintos (or *turres,* in the traditional nomenclature). The latter structures are not Iberian survivals at all but utilitarian "maisons fortes," based on Italian prototypes, built by Roman settlers and acculturated natives in the early imperial period. There are, to be sure, exceptional areas, such as the "depresión de Antequera" and the Vega of Granada, where pre-Flavian, Roman-style rural *aedificia* do show up in the archaeological record. Immediately to the north of the urban center of Anticaria (Antequera), the semi-urban villa "La Estación" seems to have had its inception in the Julio-Claudian period, to judge from the ceramics recovered at the site of this establishment, which eventually included baths and mosaics.[21] The first-order site at the Cerro del Batán, located 8 kilometers northwest of Antequera, similarly seems to have had its inception in the Julio-Claudian period, to judge from the recovery at the place of thin-walled ceramics and Gallic *sigillata*.[22] There is also the second-order farmstead at the Cortijo del Canal, situated on the right bank of the Río Cubillas, 14.5 kilometers northwest of Granada, which seems to have a Tiberian or Claudian inception and to show no previous signs of habitation or other use.[23] In the extreme western part of the Vega of Granada, there is also the first-order villa establishment at the "Llanos de Plines." The aforementioned establishment seems to have a late Augustan or Tiberian inception, to judge from the *terra sigillata italica, gallica,* and thin-walled pottery found there.[24] Pre-Flavian Roman first- through third-order sites also begin to appear in the upper Guadalquivir valley in the territories of communities such as Ossigi, Iliturgi, and even in the vicinity of Sosontigi. The latter place is situated in a zone of ecological transition between the Andalusian plain and the mountainous country of the penibético.

All the same, the policy of Caesar and Augustus seems to have favored the juridical promotion of lowland cities in the valley of the Baetis and Singilis, such as Hispalis, Urso, Astigi, Corduba, Ucubi, Obulco, and Tucci, as a means of defining and maintaining Rome's political and military control over the core areas of the province.[25] That this desire for control and consolidation extended to the upper Guadalquivir region and the ore-rich areas there, including the *saltus Castulonensis,* should cause no surprise, particularly when it is remembered that it is this area of Baetica that was transferred to Tarraconensis, probably in or about 2 B.C. Juridical promotion and rural settlement went hand in hand at Astigi, while the state ignored the stipendiary, peregrine towns of most of the *conventus Astigitanus,* whose inhabitants, living for the most part in native *oppida,* worked the largely unsettled land to produce tribute and to provide for subsistence needs. Moreover, local elites in these stipendiary towns during the Julio-Claudian era are inconspicuous in our sources. Of thirty-one inscriptionally attested magistrates in former peregrine communities of the *conventus,* only one appears in a pre-Flavian text.[26] No Baetican inscription of pre-Flavian date names an explicitly designated town councilor. Of forty-one instances of euergetism in the province in which the value of the benefaction is recorded, not one is datable before the Flavian epoch.[27] So far as is known to this author, there exists only one dated and uncosted example of euergetism from the *conventus Astigitanus* of pre-Flavian date. It is telling that the gift—a statue of the emperor Claudius—donated in A.D. 46 not by a local magistrate or senator but by Optatus, freedman of Reburrus, was mediated by the local senate of Ipsca, acting as "recipient and guardian" of the benefaction.[28] It is also a sign of the political dependency and immaturity of stipendiary communities in Baetica and elsewhere in Hispania that they sought relations of *hospitium* with the older communities of the peninsula endowed with colonial or municipal status.[29] It is remarkable that such *hospitium* agreements virtually cease to be contracted by the Flavian era, only to reappear in Tarraconensis during the later second century.[30]

The picture is similar in the southeastern *conventus Hispalensis*. Pre-Flavian Roman first- through third-order settlements tend to be a phenomenon of lower-lying areas within the plain of Andalusia. But even some of these may have been built on land that was either occupied or exploited in some way in the Augustan or pre-Augustan period. The remains in the Cortijo de Miraflores, situated 2.5 kilometers northeast of the medieval wall of Sevilla close to a Roman road leading out in a northeasterly direction from Hispalis, are a case in point. Emergency excavations in anticipation of the construction of a park led to the discovery of the remnants of a portion of the *pars rustica* of what seems to have been a first-order site. Its excavators connect the installation with the supply of the Roman population of Hispalis.[31] The remains correspond to a storage area with abundant *dolia* protected by stout walls and roofs covered with tiles. The ceramics and amphora remains suggest the habitation of the site from some point during the second century B.C. onward, with the semi-subterranean storage building proper being erected around the middle of the first century A.D. The structure seems to have been abandoned at the end of the first or beginning of the second century A.D., due to a possible shift in the course of the Arroyo del Tagarete, which flows northward into the Guadalquivir. But not too much, perhaps, ought to be read into the remains of the rural establishment in the Cortijo de Miraflores, the function of which could have been pre-eminently directed, as indicated above, toward the supply of the immediately nearby population of Hispalis, and not toward the processing and funneling of staples for export.

There exists more certain evidence for Roman first-order villas with inceptions in the Julio-Claudian period in the vicinity of Dos Hermanas. An example is the first-order site in the Hacienda de Doña Ana; in antiquity, the place would have lain squarely within the territory of Orippo (Torre de los Herberos, Cortijo de Tige, Dos Hermanas, Sevilla province).[32] The place yields one possible fragment of *terra sigillata italica,* more abundant south Gallic *sigillata* fragments, abundant remains of Spanish *sigillata,* and African red-slip finewares. The ceramics remains suggest the beginning of occupation at this site in the later Julio-Claudian period. The site also produces fragments of marble, *opus signinum,* bricks, *laterculi,* tiles, amphoras, common ceramics (including *dolia*), and apparently the remains of a substantial, animal-drawn grain mill.[33] The first-order villa site "Corchuela II," situated in the extreme northwest portion of the Finca de Doña Ana, also in the municipal district of Dos Hermanas, shows unmistakable indications of having a Julio-Claudian inception from the recovery at the site of fragments of Gallic *sigillata,* a fragment of a Haltern 70 wine must container, and the handle of a Beltrán II B fish-sauce container of Gaditanian production.[34] The upland areas of the extreme southeastern corner of the *conventus Hispalensis* generally shared, on the other hand, in the settlement boom of the Flavian era.

The coastal and southernmost areas of the province, for the most part within the *conventus Gaditanus,* reveal many first- through third-order rural settlements, excluding amphora-producing centers, with an initial construction phase in the Julio-Claudian period or even earlier. These sites in Cádiz province include El Santiscal (Arcos de la Frontera), Fuente de la Salud (El Cuervo), La Isleta (El Cuervo), Haza de la Torre (El Cuervo), La ·Torre (El Cuervo), Romanina Alta (El Cuervo), Olivar de los Valencianos (Puerto Real), and Casa de la Pintada (Puerto de Santa María), with an inception as early as the Augustan period on the basis of the discovery of Italian *sigillata* there.[35] One of the more compelling first-order sites in Cádiz province is the villa "Puente Grande," of which extensive portions of the *pars urbana* were excavated in 1998. The villa is situated immediately to the south of the urban center of Los Barrios in the Bay of Algeciras. Roadwork necessitated the excavation of this sprawling complex. Its first phase, of which only the stumps of walls survive, seems to date to the latter part of Augustus' rule or the earliest part of Tiberius' reign. This first phase is datable through the presence of Italian *sigillata,* the absence of Campanian and painted Iberian pottery, and the position of the first walls of the structure immediately beneath those of the second phase, or so-called phase IB, of the villa. This second phase was marked by an amplification of the surface area and complexity of the villa and is distinguished by the presence of *terra sigillata gallica, hispanica, clara* A, lamp fragments, glass, *tegulae, imbrices,* and metal fragments. To this second phase, with an inception in the reign of Claudius, also belong the remains of what seems to be a *castellum aquae* supplying water to the site and the remains of a large *natatio,* lined with waterproof cement and measuring 12 by 5 meters.[36] The villa at Los Barrios shows occupation until the late fifth century A.D. First-through third-order sites with a Julio-Claudian or earlier inception in Málaga province include those at La Hacienda de Manguarra y San José (Cártama) and Las Torres (San Pedro de Alcántara).[37] In Granada province, the first-order site at the Loma de Ceres (Molvízar) evidently possesses an Augustan inception, as mentioned already in Chapter Two in connection with wine production in Baetica.

The areas of the province in the Sierra Morena and north to the provincial confines of Lusitania and Tarraconensis remain, for the most part, archaeological *terra incognita.* This is the area known in antiquity as Baeturia.[38] Published archaeological survey for these areas remains practically unknown, although individual *oppida* and conspicuous sites in their territories have received some attention. Such is the case of Mellaria (Cerro Masatrigo, Fuenteobejuna, Córdoba province) and its environs, Mirobriga (Cerro del Cabezo, Capilla, Badajoz province), Regina (Los Paredones, Casas de Reina, Badajoz province), and Sisapo (La Bienvenida, Ciudad Real).[39] Nevertheless, meticulous excavation would surely show considerable rural settlement and construction activity during the Julio-Claudian period in the territories of *municipia* such as Iulipa, Ugultunia, and Nertobriga, that is, in those parts of Baeturia Celtica in which native communities may have received Roman-style constitutions as early as Augustus' reign. This putative settlement activity would be in line with the rural epigraphy of many of these communities: numerous inscriptions, revealing slaves, ex-slaves, and *ingenui,* are of Julio-Claudian date. It may be worth noting in this context that it is precisely during the early Julio-Claudian period that a number of smaller native *oppida* tended to be abandoned in favor of those communities which had received Roman municipal institutions, such as Metellinum, Lacimurga, Nertobriga, Mirobriga, and Fornacis.[40]

Production and Trade

The quantity and quality of the sources illuminating production and trade increase substantially during the Julio-Claudian period in Baetica. One

important reason is the upswing in the frequency of epigraphic commemoration and inscription, reflecting a variety of motives, including religious
dedications, the honoring of local, provincial, and imperial notables, and
funerary commemorations. The importation and production of transport
amphoras and finewares also allows the closer dating of shipwrecks and sites
on land. On a variety of levels, it is possible to discern changes in native
tastes in matters affecting habitation, production, and the requirements and
possibilities of daily living, including an increasing preference for Roman-
style ceramics and nourishment. The Julio-Claudian period in Baetica sees,
in brief, the first really widespread implantation of the villa system and a
corresponding increase of regular agricultural surpluses.

CEREALS

Cassius Dio records, under the year A.D. 44, that Umbonius Silo, governor
of Baetica, was expelled from the senate because he had not sent sufficient
grain to the troops in Mauretania (60.24.5). In addition, it looks as though
some grain was reaching Rome in the form of rent on *ager publicus.* It is
possible to infer this from an inscription of A.D. 49 from the territory of
Ostippo (Estepa), which records the restoration and renewal of boundaries
of *agri decumani* (tithe lands) while Claudius was censor.[41] The grain from
the environs of Ostippo might represent *frumentum mancipale* in the form
of a tithe arising from the lease of this public land by grain farmers.[42] In the
picture that emerged in the previous chapter, the middle Guadalquivir
valley was a prime cereals-growing region of Baetica. An inscription from
Ulia, dating to the reign of Tiberius, reinforces this picture. It is an honorary inscription attesting the *duovir* and *praefectus C. Caesaris* P. Aelius
P.f. Fabianus. The same stone that contains his *cursus* also bears fragmentary lines whose surviving portion seems to record the magistrate's allevia-
tion of the price of grain: "municip[es] quod annon[a ipsos levaverit
donum dant]."[43] Grain grown in Baetica during the Julio-Claudian era was
probably locally and regionally consumed for the most part, rather than exported. Nevertheless, it remains possible that the grain cultivated and
milled at the first-order site at the Finca de Doña Ana, mentioned above,
was, in part, exported during the Julio-Claudian era. The villa was situated
close to the *Lacus Ligustinus,* and grain grown here could have been easily
shipped to Italy. Pliny the Elder may well have had the *Lacus Ligustinus* in
mind when he wrote about the agricultural richness of Spain—including
grain—in those parts bordering the sea (*HN* 37.203). Grain exportation

seems all the more plausible from his other references to the return on seed of Baetican grain (18.95), its weight per *modius* (18.66–67), and the abundance of grain crops in that province from the intercultivation of olive trees (17.94).

OLIVE OIL

The evidence for substantial olive-oil production in Baetica becomes plentiful for the Julio-Claudian period. It is now clear that olives were cultivated and processed in an area extending beyond the fluvially bound triangular area with Hispalis, Corduba, and Astigi at its extremities. Already in this period, large areas of the Andalusian Cordillera saw olive cultivation and oil processing. In the "Subbética Cordobesa," an area including the ancient territories of Cisimbrium, Iliturgicola (Cerro de las Cabezas, Fuente Tójar, Córdoba province), and the region of modern Priego, there have come to light the remains of approximately eighteen olive presses in fifteen sites that were active in the later Julio-Claudian through Severan periods.[44] The most remarkable installation in this region—without parallel to date in Hispania—at the Cerro Lucerico (Cerro de las Estacas, Fuente Tójar) reveals the remains of six olive-oil presses in the same oilery. The oilery, which began operation at some point in the second third of the first century A.D., engaged in the large-scale processing of oil, possibly destined for export.[45] Not far to the north-northwest of Iponoba (Cerro Minguillar, Baena, Córdoba province) and within its tributary territory, the Loma del Juncal reveals the remains of a cylindrical oil-press counterweight and two cisterns, at least one of which may have served as a *lacus,* or repository of oil.[46] The best-preserved oilery in Andalusia is associated with the Roman settlement (first-order site?) El Gallumbar, situated 4.5 kilometers southwest of Antequera in the Andalusian Cordillera.[47] The ceramics evidence suggests the inception of the site in the middle Julio-Claudian period—more precisely, late in the reign of Tiberius or early in Claudius'. The singular interest of the place derives from the fact that the three main processes associated with the production of olive oil are found at the site, namely the preparation of olives through the extraction of water or amurca and the pitting of the fruit; its pressing; and the subsequent decanting and purification through settling into basins and *dolia,* or large clay containers. Its excavators suggest that the (eventually) first-order site "La Estación," mentioned above, a semi-urban rural establishment on the northern outskirts of Anticaria situated on a gentle slope overlooking, and in immediate proximity to, the Vega of Antequera, was devoted to olive-oil production.[48] Emergency excavations have revealed a portion of the *pars fructuaria* of a first-order site at Cuevas del Becerro in Málaga province.[49] The villa is situated next to the Arroyo de las Cuevas in a fertile valley between the Sierra de Viján to the north and the Sierra de los Merinos to the south, and it lies astride a natural avenue of communications—used as a royal transhumance route in modern times—between the "Depresión de Ronda" to the west and the valley of the Guadalhorce to the east. Infrared spectrographic analysis of the contents of three *dolia* found at the site confirms the sterified remains of olive oil; a basin lined with *opus signinum* that adjoined the area of storage had up to 10,000 liters capacity. Ceramic remains at the site suggest an inception in the Claudian-Neronian period, with the productive portion of the villa active at least until the early fourth century. The excavators suggest that the production of the villa was destined for regional consumption, at a minimum.

The reign of Claudius represents a watershed in the economic history of Baetica, particularly for the region along the Singilis (Genil) River. This impression stems from a consideration of the initial dates of oil-bearing amphora-producing installations in the province. Chic García's catalogue of *figlinae* along the Guadalquivir and Genil has a relative value at best, from the fact that his dating of potteries does not depend on the results of systematic excavations, but on the chronology established for Dressel 20 stamps arising from excavation and stray finds elsewhere than Hispania. With this caveat in mind, it is worth looking at his dating of *figlinae* along the Baetis and Singilis rivers. Chic García identifies, with some certainty, sixteen *figlinae* along the middle stretch of the Guadalquivir.[50] Of this number, he assigns confident initial and terminal dates to seven installations. To only two does he assign origins before c. A.D. 50: Villaseca (*figlina Caeraria*), beginning possibly in the reign of Augustus, and La Dehesilla, with an inception possibly in the latter part of Tiberius' reign.[51] Along the length of the Genil, Chic García identifies a total of sixteen amphora-producing workshops.[52] Of this number, he is able to assign chronological termini to eight installations. Of this latter number, three may be confidently assigned an initial date of the mid-first century A.D.: Las Delicias, Las Animas, and Casilla de Tarancón.[53] It is highly significant that of the twenty-five more or less certain *figlinae* identified by the same scholar along the lower Guadalquivir between Peñaflor and Coria del Río, only one (Villar Tesoro) is assigned an inception of the mid-first century A.D., whereas not one installation is given a terminus a quo before Claudius' reign.[54] The chronology of the Dressel 20-producing *figlinae* showing the prominence of the Genil in terms of the Claudian-era inception of potteries is thus in line with the survey data for rural sites, which show an upsurge in construction in Astigi's territory during the Julio-Claudian period—more specifically, in the reign of Claudius.[55]

The Julio-Claudian era represents a period of significant wine exportation from Baetica. Columella refers to his paternal uncle's practice of sheltering vines, which were in the area of Ceret (Jerez de la Frontera), with palm fronds against the east wind and the sun's heat. Columella's uncle would have been active in the reigns of Tiberius and Claudius. Columella, furthermore, makes an unequivocal allusion to the exportation in his own day (that is, the A.D. 60s) of wine from Baetica to Rome and Latium (1 pref. 20). The same author elsewhere refers to the vintage in the coastal regions of Baetica ("in Baetica maritimis regionibus," 11.2.60).

A Dressel 9 amphora from the Castra Praetoria in Rome bears the painted consular date "Ti. Caesare V. cos." and the designation "Gaditanum" (*CIL* XV 4570). Dressel, the *CIL* editor, was unsure whether the container—reused in any event—was utilized anew to carry wine or oil. In the end, Zevi discounted the likelihood that the amphora carried wine on re-use; the latter scholar thinks it strange that a *garum* container should have been used to transport wine.[56] Sealey, on the other hand, is an enthusiastic proponent of the possibility that the container from Rome did carry wine.[57] And it may be the case that Sealey was right to suggest that seven Dressel 2–4 amphoras from his 1970 excavation at Colchester carried wine from Baetica. Indeed, Dressel 2–4 amphora production in Baetica receives archaeological confirmation in the form of the containers identified as such and produced at or near the Roman wine- and fish-sauce-producing first-order(?) villa and adjoining *pars fructuaria* at the Loma de Ceres in coastal Málaga province.[58] Baetican wine in the Julio-Claudian period and somewhat later was bottled and transported in the flat-bottomed Dressel 28 amphora; the container shows up in the *Port-Vendres II* wreck of the early A.D. 40s, and its excavators left open the receptacles' Baetican origins.[59] The putative Baetican origin of the Dressel 28s from the wreck could be affirmed, but not demonstrated, by the discovery in the Castra Praetoria of a Dressel 28 container bearing in its *tituli picti* the names of the south Spanish merchants Auli Atinii.[60] Those commentators who have rendered a positive judgment on the nature of the contents carried by Dressel 28s are unanimous in seeing it as a wine container.[61] Dressel 28 amphora remains do show up at the amphora-producing facility at Venta del Carmen near Algeciras, but the installation's excavators suggested that they may be importations.[62]

The Baetican production of Dressel 28 wine-bearing containers is now definitely established through the discovery of a substantial amphora-producing installation in Hispalis. The pottery, discovered beneath the Hospital de las Cinco Llagas de Sevilla, now the seat of the Andalusian parliament, was active from c. A.D. 50 to the end of the third century A.D. and manufactured a variety of amphoras, common ceramics, and construction materials.[63] In its first phase, extending from the Claudian era to the end of the first century A.D., the installation produced and fired in abundance Dressel 28 containers, in addition to Dressel 20s, Haltern 70s, and Beltrán II A and possibly II B amphoras. An additional—and exceptional—hint at the social status of Baetican wine producers is provided by the painted inscriptions on a well-preserved Haltern 70 amphora, recovered in an ancient underwater amphora and ceramics dumping ground at Port-la-Nautique (Aude).[64] This place corresponds to the ancient port of Narbo Martius. The amphora, recovered with other amphora fragments of possibly earlier Julio-Claudian date, bears the horizontal inscription at the base of the neck FIRMI VALERIOR(um). Perpendicular to the aforementioned inscription and running parallel to the right handle of the container is the painted name, in the genitive, of a certain Aelius Fuscus. The amphora is conceivably the product of Firmus, slave of certain Valerii, while Aelius Fuscus is the producer of the wine or must contained in the receptacle. The name Aelius Fuscus smacks of a Baetican of decurional (or higher) rank, who profited from the cultivation and processing of the vine.

HONEY

Honey was produced in, and exported from, Baetica in quantity, according to Strabo (3.2.6) and Justin (44.1.5). An inscription of first century A.D. date from the Sierra Morena north of Corduba refers to the lease of bee hives ("Alvari locum") in the *ager publicus coloniae* by a certain L. Valerius C.f. Kapito for the sake of apiculture.[65] Lead tokens (*tesserae*) bearing the marks L.HER, P.C., A.N., M.C, N.L, DE L, L.ANI (or L.ANT), and C.AN. that were discovered in the Guadalquivir valley refer to proprietors of mule trains who were involved in the transport of bee hives from pasture to pasture and in the delivery of the honey from its point of production to point of embarkation in Baetica.[66] Three of the tokens depict mules on their obverse and bees on their reverse. The interpretation of the marks is difficult, but it is possible to conjecture the activity of a certain L(ucius) Her(renius), as well as a C(aius) An(nius) and L(ucius) An(n)i(us) or L(ucius) Ant(   ). And Van Nostrand notes, citing Pliny (*HN* 11.8), that wax was also a product of apiculture and the object of trade.[67]

FISH SAUCE

Abundant testimony for Baetican fish-sauce production and commerce during the Julio-Claudian period is at hand. At this point it is appropriate to raise certain questions vital in assessing the contribution of salteries and fish-sauce production to wealth creation. These include the scale of the operations, their organization, and the persons involved with production and commerce. There is no magic number of salting vats that marks a distinction between large- and small-scale operations. The large-scale urban salteries at Baelo may have been, in part, municipally owned and leased to individuals or associations. Some salteries were built in proximity to, and in obvious conjunction with, first- or second-order establishments. One certain instance is the first-order site Las Torres, in the vicinity of San Pedro de Alcántara (Málaga province). Las Torres discloses baths, mosaics, sculpture, and an unspecified number of salting vats.[68] Another clear example is the first-order settlement-saltery combination at El Faro (Torrox, Málaga).[69] A rural settlement situated 2.5 kilometers north of Fuengirola (ancient Suel), and obliterated in the course of modern road construction, reveals the remains of *garum* vats lined with waterproof cement along with amphora fragments.[70] The villa, on the arroyo de Pajares, is located relatively close to the sea. In San Luis de Sabinillas, 6 kilometers north of Fuengirola, there exists a first-order site with mosaics in conjunction with salting vats.[71] It is difficult to see the processing of fish into various products as anything but the main source of income for the owners of such operations. Moreover, in many instances, there is a clear combination of fish-product amphora production and the production of the fish sauce. Such is the case at the Finca El Secretario in Fuengirola. The site, active in the Flavian period and later, discloses five ovens that apparently fired Beltrán II A and Dressel 30 amphoras.[72] The ovens, moreover, seem to have fired the transport containers for fish sauce produced on site in eight basins.[73] But it is

evidently the case also, on occasion, that a single amphora-producing installation could serve more than one fish-sauce-producing center, a situation analogous to the relationship between oil-amphora *figlinae* and a
multiplicity of clients served by single oil-amphora-producing centers in
Baetica. And the evidence suggests that a number of fish-sauce and fish-
sauce amphora-producing centers were owned or leased by an association
or associations. Stamps from Rinconcillo and Baelo that read S. C. G. and
S. CET may indicate the existence of a *societas cetariorum Gaditanorum* in
Baetica, active as early as the Julio-Claudian period.[74] Presumably, the production of many smaller-scale fish-sauce producers was sold to itinerant or
local traders for local/regional consumption or for export.

It is from the stamps impressed on the amphoras and the *tituli* on their
bodies that we glean details about the identities of those who produced
fish sauces, commercialized the product, and manufactured the containers
used to transport it. The names of the proprietors and/or lessees of fish-
sauce installations are remarkably elusive. The names and initials found
on the stamps of fish-sauce amphoras refer, following the analogy of the
Dressel 20 containers, to the proprietors, lessees, and/or *officinatores* of
the amphora-producing installations themselves. Broadly put, they seem
to refer to *societates,* individual *socii,* or unaffiliated individuals. Some
stamps both refer to a *societas* and name an *officinator*/potter, as, for example, those found at Baelo bearing the elements SCG and OP.M.LUCR.[75]
The stamps, in general, seem to refer to both freedmen and the freeborn.
Other amphora-workshop proprietors and/or *officinatores* include L(ucius)
OC(tavius) CAES(ius), named on a Dressel 9 container from the Castra
Praetoria, and a certain C(aius) FUF(icius) ANT(onius), or, on the likelier
reading of the cognomen, AVITUS, whose name is stamped on fish-sauce
and wine amphoras from Alcalá del Río, Vienne, and Geneva.[76] It is an ar-
resting but unverifiable suggestion that the P(   ) FLAC[CUS] found
in a stamp on a Dressel 12 amphora from Augst may be no less than a relative of L. Pomponius Flaccus, consul in A.D. 17 and friend of Tiberius (Suet.
Tib. 42.1).[77] The truth of the matter may be this: Flac(cus) is, if not connected with the family of Tiberius' friend, an *honestus vir,* to judge from his
cognomen, and of likely Baetican origins.

It is from the *tituli picti* that we learn the names of fish-sauce producers
and merchants. The main problem for our understanding is the poor survival rate of painted inscriptions on the amphoras themselves. It is a rare
container that combines the designation of the product, the name(s) of the

merchant(s), and the name or initials of the producer. Such is the case for a well-preserved Dressel 8 container recovered in dragging operations at Port-la-Nautique (Aude), one of the ancient harbors of Narbo Martius (Narbonne).[78] The amphora reveals its contents as "G(ari) f(los)," the merchants as the QQ. Caecilii, and the producer as a certain L.C.F. The QQ. Caecilii were active probably in the reign of Tiberius, and were involved also with the commerce of Baetican oil and possibly metals.[79]

In exceptional circumstances, a combination of different amphoras and their stamps and *tituli picti* permits the reconstruction of the relationship between amphora manufacturers and the merchants of the products contained within them. Such is the case of several stamps on fish-sauce amphora fragments found at Olivar de los Valencianos at Puerto Real in the Bay of Cádiz. The stamps read AA.AT.D and AA.AT.M., and reveal a *societas* of amphora manufacturers familiar from other containers used to transport olive oil, fish sauce, and possibly wine.[80] The *tituli* of the latter containers show this association, that of the Auli Atinii, in their capacity as merchants.[81] The material from the Olivar de los Valencianos shows that the same family acted as both amphora manufacturers and merchants, a vertical arrangement that is apparent in certain instances related to the manufacture and distribution of Baetican olive oil. Producers of Spanish fish sauce named in the *tituli picti* include Domesticus, Cornelia, and a certain Vitalis.[82] Domesticus, be it duly noted, was a producer in the vicinity of Malaca, but otherwise we cannot exclude utterly the possibility that some of the producers named on Spanish fish-sauce containers may be from Lusitania or Tarraconensis.[83]

A number of fish-sauce merchants on record as being active during the Julio-Claudian period were also likely or certain freeborn persons. The *Cala Rossano* wreck on Ventotene (Pontine Islands) dates to c. A.D. 1–50(?) and held a mixed cargo of amphoras, tin ingots, and round wooden boxes. The amphoras were mainly Baetican(?) Dressel 7–11 types and bore painted inscriptions on the neck. The summary of the wreck notes that several of the amphoras bore the name C. Annius Senecio, whom Parker identifies tout court as a merchant.[84] The aforementioned name is not that of a freedman and should act as a corrective to any inclination to view fish-sauce merchants as essentially ex-slaves.[85] Senecio also is an obvious Spaniard, from the near-exclusive concentration of the cognomen in Hispania. A Dressel 9 container of south Spanish origin of possibly the first half of the first century A.D. found at Augst names the fish-sauce trader L. Sempronius

Fuscus.[86] Fuscus is evidently freeborn, though Martin-Kilcher goes too far in suggesting a possible relationship with either the prefect of the *cohors Baetica* M. Sempronius Fuscus or the proconsul of Baetica under Vespasian, Sempronius Fuscus. In any case, Senecio and Fuscus are members of an emerging middle stratum in Baetica during the Julio-Claudian period, an expanding component of the province's population that obviously counted the processing, transport, and sale of fish products among its sources of wealth.

It is remarkable that a number of Baetican fish-sauce amphora-producing installations show a definite cessation or hiatus in their activity at the end of the reign of Claudius or during the period after c. A.D. 54, but before the inception of the Flavian era. The installation at Haza Honda, situated roughly 3.5 kilometers west of the urban center of Málaga, had an inception during Augustus' reign but ended its activity in the later Julio-Claudian period.[87] The amphora-producing installation in the Huerta del Rincón (Torremolinos) had an inception in c. A.D. 25, but shows a break in activity c. A.D. 50 and a resumption of manufacture at some point during the second half of the first century — on the finewares evidence, possibly in the Flavian period.[88] If its excavators can be believed on this point, the fish-sauce amphora-producing facility "El Gallinero," at Puerto Real in the Bay of Cádiz, had an even shorter life, extending from late in the reign of Augustus to A.D. 25,[89] but the ceramics evidence certainly leaves open a terminal date during the reign of Claudius.[90] The sudden cessation or hiatus of activity at these and other sites, including Toscanos (Málaga province), El Rinconcillo (Cádiz province), and Buena Vista (El Puerto de Santa María, Cádiz province), along the Atlantic and Mediterranean littorals may be associable with the completion of the Roman annexation of Mauretania under Claudius.[91]

ANIMAL HUSBANDRY

Columella provides precious testimony for sheep-raising in Baetica during the Julio-Claudian period. He records with open pride his uncle Marcus Columella's cross-breeding of domestic Spanish animals and African ones from neighboring Mauretania, and, subsequently, the breeding of the lambs so produced with imported ewes, namely the Tarentine strain. The result, according to Columella, was a finer sort of wool, which was obviously destined for the market (7.2.4–5). Columella in the same passage also mentions as noteworthy the black and dark brown sheep raised at Corduba and the high price they commanded: no evidence of subsistence husbandry here. Martial praises in four places Baetican sheep and the natural golden color of their wool, making clear that it was available in Rome (9.61.3–4, 12.63.4–5, 12.65.5, 12.98.1–2). *Lacernae Baeticae,* or Baetican woolen cloaks, must have been an item available to Romans in the *urbs* of Martial's day (14.133). Juvenal also describes garments made from the naturally golden wool of Baetican sheep in a passage that suggests their exportation in his day (12.40–43).[92] Although both Martial and Juvenal wrote in the post-Julio-Claudian period, it is likely that Baetican wool and finished wool products were a feature of the Julio-Claudian era as well.

MINING

Changes in the organization of Spanish mining include the increasing ownership of the mines by the state from the later first century B.C. onward. The most notorious instance of the transfer of mines from private to state ownership is that of Sextus Marius in A.D. 33, discussed in Chapter Six. Mines belonging to the state were initially farmed out, on senatorial authority, to individuals, to small-scale *societates,* and to *societates publicanorum,* passing, by the reign of Domitian, into the control of the *fiscus.* The best-known *societas publicanorum,* mentioned already in Chapter One, was the *societas Sisaponensis,* which continued its activity into the Julio-Claudian period. A first-century inscription from Corduba points to the activity of a "societas aerar(iarum fodinarum <Cordubensium>)" that farmed the rights to copper mining north of the provincial capital.[93] There was also the "S(ocietas) C(astulonensis?)," active in the eastern Sierra Morena and perhaps in the Roman-era open-air gold mine near Granada at the Hoyo de la Campana. Domergue suggests that the "Soc(ietas) Vesc(   )," attested on an ingot of the first quarter of the first century A.D. from the *Cabrera 4* shipwreck, was active in lead-silver mining in Baetica.[94] There is also the "S(ocietas) C(   ) E(   ) L(   )," active at some point during the first century A.D. The existence of this company came to light through the discovery at Campanario (Badajoz province) of a lead ingot stamped with the initials of this mining-related association of *publicani.*[95] Campanario is situated in the metal-rich area of La Serena in the eastern part of Badajoz province. On the other hand, a lead ingot from New Carthage bearing the name of the colonia Augusta Firma (Astigi) proves that that colony, and possibly other communities as well, owned mines in the province, at least during the early Principate.[96] It is easily within the realm of possibility that the small foundries of Julio-Claudian date that studded the western section of the intramural area of Astigi (about which more in Chapter Four) were involved with the transformation of ore into ingots and other objects.

Against this larger organizational backdrop, it is possible to reconstruct, with a fair degree of accuracy, the details of the production and commercialization of lead as it existed by the reign of Tiberius. From the evidence of the lead ingots themselves and the various stamped and inscribed inscriptions they bear, Domergue suggests a complex scheme in which wholesale merchants ("Grossistes") collected ingots stamped with the names of their producers at the point of production and marked them with their own names in the form of molded stamps. The same merchants then arranged for the transport of these ingots from the mines of the Sierra Morena to the Baetis, whereupon they were floated on small river craft downstream to Hispalis, where presumably they were taken over by other merchants who counterstamped the ingots with their names and incised the weight of the ingots. The latter merchants arranged for the transport of the ingots to Rome and Italy.[97]

The evidence of certain lead ingots, meanwhile, suggests alternative arrangements, by which a *mercator* collected ingots at their point of production and subsequently entrusted them to a *navicularius* for transportation overseas.[98] Still other ingots, such as those from the *Sud-Lavezzi B* wreck of the A.D. 20s, suggest a third scheme in which the same individual acted as collector-purchaser of the ingots and as their transporter overseas.[99] It is, sadly, not possible to extend the discussion concerning the production and distribution of lead ingots to that of copper, due to the absence of intelligible inscriptions on the ingots themselves.

Unlike the names of a number of olive-oil merchants of Baetican origin or of those who possess a trading connection with the province, the names of these producers and merchants do not appear anywhere but on the ingots themselves, though the claim has been advanced of a connection between Q. Aelius Satullus, a putative exploiter of mines in the vicinity of Munigua, named on a lead ingot of the *Cabrera 5* wreck, and the Aelii of Munigua.[100] The claim remains unsubstantiated. And although it is possible to hazard guesses as to the juridical status of these producers and traders, it is otherwise impossible to get a sense of their relative social standing in Baetica. But one thing is clear: the wealth of some of these merchants must have been substantial. A salient case in point is the freeborn M. Licinius M.f. Ausua, who counterstamped the lead ingots of at least five different producers(?) from the *Cabrera 4* wreck of A.D. 1–25.[101] Ausua's nomenclature suggests a possible Baetican origin—more specifically, in the northern, more celticized portion of the province.

It remains to mention Domergue's postulate of a broad shift in elite investment from mining to agriculture in Baetica during the late Republican and early imperial periods.[102] Such a shift stands to reason: one important factor certainly was the increasing state ownership and control of the mines during the Julio-Claudian period. On the other hand, Domergue in 1972 could point to no certain instance in which it was possible to identify a family or individual from Baetica whose interests demonstrably shifted from mining to agriculture in the period c. 100 B.C. to c. A.D. 100. This particular silence of the sources has not changed. And it may be relevant that the *mercenarii* who figure prominently in the epigraphy of mining areas of Baetica such as the Río Tinto or the central and eastern Sierra Morena do not, except in one possible instance, seem to have been born in Baetica. The possible exception comes in the form of a fragmentary epitaph, found on a gravestone in the Río Tinto mining area, of an unknown "[– – –]pensis," whose *origo* may correspond to Ilipa (Alcalá del Río) in Baetica.[103] Moreover, those handfuls of Baetican producers and merchants who do show up on ingots of late Augustan through Flavian date appear to have their origin in Baetica Celtica or Turdula, that is, north of the Baetis. In other words, it is apparent that during the early Principate, the free or freeborn of the agricultural core of Baetica south and east of the Guadalquivir did not find opportunities for enrichment in the mines and mining to be as attractive as did immigrants from the remainder of the Iberian peninsula, including Lusitania and the Meseta, or native Celts or Turduli from the northern portions of the province. The argument, to be sure, is partly one from silence, but the epigraphy of the province is sufficiently abundant and representative to have attested Baeticans from the *conventus Gaditanus, Astigitanus,* southeastern *Hispalensis,* and southern *Cordubensis* involved in mining, below the level of a large-scale owner such as Sextus Marius, had they existed in any significant numbers during the early Principate. Contemporary and future archaeological discoveries will modify but not substantially overturn this picture. Thus recent unpublished archaeological survey in the territory of Munigua, situated north of the Guadalquivir River, shows that iron-smelting was a widespread nonurban activity during the first and second centuries A.D. The settings for this metallurgical activity were modest rural "houses" and not the kind of elaborate villa establishments one associates with large-scale oleiculture or viti-culture.[104] Although explicit epigraphical testimony is lacking, it looks to be the case that a substantial proportion of Munigua's free, freed, and slave population, elites and middle-stratum persons alike, derived their wealth from the processing of metals rather than from a more direct involvement in mining or agriculture. Syme was wrong, it appears, to put mining and fish-sauce production on an equal footing with viticulture and, more importantly, oleiculture as sources of aristocratic (sc. senatorial) wealth in Baetica during the Principate.[105] The discussion of senatorial and non-senatorial wealth in Chapter Six will demonstrate the overwhelming im-portance of oleiculture and the associated manufacture of oil-bearing amphoras as a source of Baetican wealth from the Flavian period onward.

CHAPTER FOUR

The Flavian Impact:
The Evidence Surveyed

The purpose of this and the following chapter is to document the explosion of rural settlement in Baetica during the period c. A.D. 70–150, and to argue that the new first- through third-order rural establishments are connected with both the Flavian municipal policy affecting Spain and the demands of the *annona* and other interests for Baetican goods and staples. The essential argument of these two chapters is this: As a result of the Flavian municipalization of Spain, financial demands on local elites and potential elites increased, arising from an augmented tribute and from the need to maintain one's census rating, to seek and hold local office, to meet increased indirect taxes (in the case of those who had achieved Roman citizenship), to pay for building programs, and to engage in socially competitive benefactions. And because landowning was the most common and secure means of wealth in the Roman world—one that met with the greatest approbation in the Roman scale of values (see, e.g., Columella 1 *pref.*)—local elites and members of the middle stratum in Baetica during the Flavian epoch and later turned to the intensive exploitation of private property centered on permanently inhabited farmsteads, not only to meet expenses but also to advertise their acceptance of and assimilation into the Roman order. The argument will be set forth that after a relatively brief period of adjustment, local elites and those in the middle stratum were successful in meeting these various financial demands simply due to steady or increasing external demand for Baetican agricultural staples and products—a demand that the Baeticans were able to meet precisely through the expansion and intensification of rural settlement and agricultural infrastructure in Baetica. External demand for Baetican products was the primary, though not exclusive, motor for the elevation of freeborn plebeians and the offspring of ex-slaves into the ranks of local *honesti,* both within and outside town councils.

History and Administration

The bestowal of the *ius Latii* to communities throughout the Iberian peninsula constitutes the main episode of administrative interest and reform in Spain and Baetica during the Flavian era. The motives for and date of the conferral of the Latin right continues to be a matter of debate, with some scholars suggesting the years A.D. 70/71 and others the years A.D. 73/74, when Vespasian and Titus were joint censors.[1] I will defer a discussion of the socioeconomic implications of the promulgation of the *ius Latii* and associated Flavian municipal law to Chapter Six. Otherwise, looking beyond the Flavian period, Baetica mainly intersects with the annals of imperial history up to the invasions of the Mauri during the 170s in connection with the notorious trials of several proconsuls of the province and their accomplices at the end of the first and beginning of the second century A.D., and the presence of Hadrian in the early 120s. The certain and possible proconsuls facing charges of extortion were Baebius Massa in 93, possibly Pomponius Gallus Didius Rufus in 97(?), and Caecilius Classicus, condemned posthumously, in 100 or 101.[2] Birley argues that Hadrian did indeed journey to Baetica after his sojourn in Tarraco in early 123, but that he avoided his native Italica, as Dio explicitly states.[3] The notice in the *Historia Augusta* (*HA Had.* 12.7) of Hadrian's suppression of a revolt of the Mauri and the subsequent vote of thanksgiving by the senate seems incomprehensible to a modern historian unless we assume that Hadrian was in nearby Baetica when the reports of a disturbance in Mauretania reached the emperor.[4] Baetica was subject to disruptions in 171–172 and again in 177 from Mauri. The invaders managed to besiege Singili(a?) Barba and to threaten Italica.[5] Archaeological evidence also shows that mining operations in the Río Tinto region of western Baetica were interrupted during the 170s.[6] The ceramics evidence seems to point to a disjuncture at about this time, as the majority of thin-walled and *sigillata* ware in the Río Tinto region dates to between A.D. 75 and 175, with some material dating as late as the end of the third century.[7] After defeating Clodius Albinus at Lugdunum in early 197, Septimius Severus executed a number of Albinus' supporters in Gaul and Hispania and confiscated their property.[8] Just how many Baetican notables were affected is unknown, but it does seem to be the case that a number of properties in Baetica were confiscated. The question of Severan confiscations in Baetica will return in Chapters Six and Seven in connection with Mummius Secundinus and the ownership of certain Baetican amphora-producing workshops. For further details of provincial and municipal administration in Baetica from c. 50 B.C. to c. A.D. 200 that go unmentioned in this book—and they are many—various modern discussions, indicated in the notes, are illuminating.[9]

Settlement

Intensive and extensive survey in almost all parts of the province reveals a second, high peak of rural settlement and building activity beginning in the early Flavian period. The telltale ceramic evidence consists of Spanish *sigillata* and the earliest forms of African red-slip fineware, and, conversely, the total or near complete absence of Gallic *sigillata* and thin-walled finewares. It is in the middle and upper Guadalquivir valley and in upland areas of the penibético that the Flavian rural settlement explosion is most apparent. In these areas, the majority of identifiable settlements have their inception during the second half of the first century—more specifically, during the Flavian epoch. But a substantial proportion of rural establishments in areas of the lower Guadalquivir and along the Mediterranean littoral in portions of the *conventus Gaditanus* and southern *conventus Hispalensis* have their inception also in the Flavian epoch. At the same time, many rural settlements took on the characteristics of Roman building for the first time. It is essential, at this juncture, to emphasize the substantial proportion of rural sites in regions as diverse as the area of Atalayuelas (Jaén province), Palma del Río, southeastern Córdoba province, Fuentes de Andalucía, and the watersheds of the Aguas Blancas and Fardes rivers (Granada province) that have their inception in the second half of the first century A.D.—more specifically, on a close consideration of the material evidence, from the Flavian era on.[10] A recent study of ceramics production in and near the theoretical territory of Ipolcobulcula (Carcabuey, Córdoba province) shows that only one rural site (Sierra Leones II) can be shown to have been inhabited before c. A.D. 50, while fully eighteen sites have their inception after c. 50, and most of them, at that, probably in the Flavian period.[11] All three likely first-order farmsteads identified in an area immediately to the southeast of the Laguna de Fuente de Piedra in the northwestern part of Málaga province have a Flavian inception; they lay probably in the northwestern portion of the territory of the municipium Flavium Liberum Singiliense, that is, Singili(a?) Barba (El Castillón, Málaga province).[12] Immediately to the west and northwest of the Laguna is the municipal district of Sierra de Yeguas (Málaga province). In the pre-Flavian period, the population in this area was confined to hilltop *oppida;* only in the Flavian era is there a dispersal of the population into first- through third-order Roman-style rural habitations.[13]

The best known of these habitations with a Flavian inception is the first-order site on the Cerro Sánchez at Sierra de Yeguas. Emergency excavations of the site in 1988 revealed what seems to be a portion of the *pars rustica* of this rural establishment. The earliest finewares, on the published data, are various forms of Spanish *sigillata.*[14] Marble fragments, stucco, and painted mortar point to the existence of a *pars urbana.* The agricultural activity of this villa site is revealed by the discovery of the bottom of at least one basin lined with *opus signinum,* olive seeds, barleycorns, and remains of transport and storage containers.

Immediately to the north of the Sierra de Peñarrubia in Málaga province, in an area of rolling hills punctuated by surface streams and subterranean water sources, is the villa site at the Cerro del Capitán.[15] Like so many imperial-era Roman first- through third-order sites, this rural establishment possessed excellent visual control over the surrounding countryside, is situated on a hill dominating its immediate environs, and is close to sources of water, most patently in the form of an arroyo of the same name that bounds the cerro to the east and south. Intensive surface survey reveals the presence of Roman-era common ceramics, including remains of *dolia,* in addition to *terra sigillata hispanica*—the latter represented by both decorated and undecorated forms, with a chronology clustering in the second century A.D. The inception of the villa, according to the archaeologists, cannot precede the early second century by much; it is evident from the testimony of the surface ceramics alone that the villa has a Flavian inception.[16] On the southeast side of the hill atop which sits the villa establishment are the remains of substantial limestone blocks, which probably belonged to the structure of the villa itself, in addition to the remains of an olive-oil installation in the form of a mill devoted to the separation of the flesh of the fruit from its pits. The meticulously excavated villa and outliers at El Ruedo (Almedinilla, Córdoba province) possess a Flavian inception and show, through the discovery of various structures associated with the pressing, decantation, and storage of olives and olive oil, the presence of this crucial agricultural activity from the Flavian period on in a more remote, inland area of the hilly and mountainous swath between the Guadalquivir River and the Mediterranean.[17]

Even along the Mediterranean littoral of the *conventus Gaditanus,* there are first- through third-order sites that do not have their inception until the later first century A.D. A salient case-in-point is the first-order villa of Auta Riogordo in Málaga province. The villa eventually came to be embellished with mosaics in the later Principate, and was inhabited until the fifth century. The excavators date the first phase of the villa to the end of the first century A.D. from the presence of numerous forms of *terra sigillata hispanica* and *sigillata clara* A; conversely, the site shows not one sherd of Italian or Gallic *sigillata.*[18] And Corduba itself, where we ought to reckon with a Roman and Italian presence as early as the second century B.C., shows new villa sites springing up in its immediate vicinity during the Flavian period. A dramatic example is the villa discovered in the course of the excavations of the late imperial palace at Cercadilla. The villa is situated 700 meters from the northwest wall of Corduba, and has its inception at the very end of the first century A.D. In its first phase, the villa was endowed with an oilery. The excavated portion of the villa in its first phase belongs to the *pars rustica* of this suburban settlement, but fragments of stucco, *opera sectilia* (shaped tiles of colored stone or marble), and marble architectonic fragments have been recovered that also correspond to the *pars urbana* of the first phase of the villa.[19]

Numerous Baetican communities undertook new building in the Flavian era. This activity ranged from the reconstruction of the civic center as at Iponoba, Iliberri, and Iliturgicola, or the extension of a pre-existing *oppidum* as at Atalayuelas, a possible Flavian *municipium,* to the construction of a new town altogether as at Sabora (Cortijo del Carrascal, Cañete la Real, Málaga province), Ipolcobulcula, and Olaurum (Lora de Estepa).[20] One well-informed commentator emphasizes the desire of the Saborenses to move their hilltop *oppidum* to the plain below on economic, not political, grounds; that is, they wanted to be closer to their fields and to the Roman road network, "and hence [to] other urban centers in the region and especially their markets."[21] A similar phenomenon is in evidence at Aratispi (Cauche el Viejo, Málaga province) in the *conventus Astigitanus* on the other side of the Sierra del Torcal from Singili(a?) Barba and Anticaria. There is clear evidence for the abandonment or reconversion to utilitarian use of the hilltop *oppidum* at Aratispi during the Flavian period, and for the transfer of the inhabited portion of the town to a lower-lying saddle in the ridge at the end of which Aratispi is situated. In any event, Perdiguero López identifies signs of destruction or of the toppling of structures within and outside of the southern wall of the *oppidum* at Aratispi in the late first century A.D. He also records remains of structures, African *sigillata,* and coins of the later Empire in the level ground just below, and to the north of, the hill on which the pre-Roman and early Roman *oppidum* of Aratispi is situated. He conjectures, rightly it seems, that Aratispi was subjected to the same kind of urban relocation as is evident at Sabora.[22]

At some point in the second half of the first or early second century, a cryptoporticus, measuring 37.5 by 6.25 meters and oriented in a north-south direction, was constructed at the hilltop *oppidum* at Monturque (Córdoba province);[23] the place is possibly the site of ancient Spalis, and was certainly a Flavian *municipium.*[24] The cryptoporticus and adjoining cisterns served as the substructure for some kind of public edifice, to judge from the remains of a Corinthian capital and a column base, one meter in diameter, found in the fill of the cryptoporticus. Keay suggests that the public space was a forum complex.[25] Celti saw the construction of a forum complex, including a possible *aedes Augusti,* at "some time around the third quarter of the 1st c. A.D."[26] The Flavian *municipium* of Arva was embellished with a new bath complex built during the Flavian epoch.[27]

There is certain evidence, furthermore, that during the Flavian period, a number of *oppida* experienced a decrease in surface area as structures fell into disuse or were abandoned altogether. The complementary phenomenon during the same period is pronounced rural "drift." For instance, the maximum inhabited area of the *oppidum* at the Cabeza Baja de Encina Hermosa was 9 hectares. By the end of the Flavian era, the occupied surface area of the *oppidum* had decreased to approximately 2.5 hectares.[28] The best explanation for this process would be the dispersal of the *oppidum*'s inhabitants into rural first- through third-order settlements in the environs of the Cabeza Baja. A similar process of denucleation is clearly evident in the

Cerros de San Pedro in the territory of ancient Obulcula (La Monclova). The highest hill of the Cerros de San Pedro shows signs of being an Iberian *oppidum* of substantial dimensions that was totally abandoned by the Flavian period, in favor of isolated first- through third-order rural settlements in the lowlands around it.[29] Torremorana is another Iberian *oppidum* that shows signs of total or near-total abandonment by the later first century A.D. Torremorana is situated in the municipal district of Baena, roughly 5 kilometers northeast of the latter place, and rests at an elevation of 688 meters. The fortified *oppidum* had a surface area of 5 hectares.[30] Murillo Redondo and others suggest the abandonment of the site by the early first century A.D., although a quadrangular structure at the highest point of the hilltop community, built of large prismatic blocks and measuring 21 by 20 meters, sounds like the description of a "maison forte." If that were the case, then we might suppose the presence of an isolated habitation at the site of the former *oppidum* well into the first century A.D. The crucial fact about Torremorana remains that the place yields up, on the published accounts, Iberian ceramics and Campanian ware, but no *sigillata,* a definite pointer to the cessation of habitation there after the third quarter of the first century A.D.[31]

The decrease in the occupied area of certain *oppida,* and in some instances their complete abandonment, coheres with the apparent fact that it is during the Flavian period that a substantial proportion of the province's population began to live permanently on rural estates, or *fundi.* This process evidently began even before the Flavian period in the case of Torremorana, but it remains possible that some of the inhabitants of Torremorana dispersed into the substantial *oppidum* at the Cerro de "El Molinillo." The latter place is located 4 kilometers to the northeast of Torremorana and 11 kilometers northeast of Baena. The Cerro de "El Molinillo" consists of a substantial meseta, immediately to the south of the Guadajoz River, with a total surface area of between 12 and 15 hectares.[32] The site shows signs of continuous occupation from the final Bronze Age to the Visigothic period. The place is profuse in surface ceramics, including Campanian ware, common ceramics, thin-walled ware, amphoras, loom weights, *dolia,* Italian, Gallic, and Spanish *sigillata,* and African red-slip. In the southwestern corner of the meseta are the remains of a basin lined with *opus signinum.* The place also discloses *tegulae,* dressed stones, remains of mosaics, and grain mills. At the base of the meseta, agricultural work revealed the remains of an ancient pottery. The site also yields marble revetment plaques, glass, and coins. Morena López suggests the existence of some sort of public building from the reutilization of large limestone paving slabs in the late Roman necropolis to the north of the hill. Some have categorized the place as a *vicus* from the putative absence of epigraphy; the problems with this view will become clearer below,[33] but it seems more appropriate to conceive of this *oppidum* as another Iberian town that received the Latin right under Vespasian. It is the certain evidence for a population on the meseta itself during the Principate and later that prompts the idea that some of the former inhabitants of Torremorana may have migrated to the *oppidum/municipium ignotum* at the Cerro de "El Molinillo." Does this mean that the movement of persons from smaller *oppida* into the larger ones in Baetica describes the majority of instances of intraregional movement in the early Principate? Not at all. But we need to nuance our examination of denucleation, recognizing the urban and rural aspects of the phenomenon. For our purposes, it is settlement in the countryside that will command our attention. The increase in rural establishments from the reign of Augustus to the end of the Flavian period throughout Baetica contrasts vividly with the decline in rural settlement and parallel increase in nucleation in Achaia during the late Hellenistic and early Roman eras, as summarized by Alcock.[34]

Efforts to establish the site hierarchies of *oppida,* whether walled or unwalled, are confused and confusing. Scholars, in general, see the simultaneous settlement of larger and smaller *oppida* as reflective of a pre-Roman state of dependency tying smaller centers with larger ones, such as Obulco. In this view, under the Romans, and particularly from the widespread concession of the Latin right during the early Flavian period on, the smaller *oppida* served as centers of exchange for a suddenly proliferating number of rural establishments, or villas, surrounding them. While larger centers in the campiñas of Córdoba and Jaén were endowed already with colonial status or, with the advent of the Flavians, with municipal status, the smaller *oppida* fell into the category of *vicus* or *pagus.* There remain severe problems with such a reconstruction of site hierarchy, particularly in the penibético and upper Guadalquivir valley. A *pagus* is an administrative district that served the purposes of tax and tribute assessment and collection.[35] A *pagus* in Baetica is never, in any context, a discretely definable locality or place such as an *oppidum.* Furthermore, there is only one example in Baetica of an epigraphically attested *vicus* known to this author outside of larger, urban contexts. The *vicus Forensis* and *vicus Hispanus* of Corduba come immediately to mind as examples of urban *vici*.[36] The exception is disclosed by an altar found in the Ermita de la Magdalena o del Templaero at Puebla de Alcocer in Badajoz province. In antiquity, this place may have lain within the territory of Mirobriga at a point almost in the northernmost tip of the province of Baetica. The altar measures 124.5 by 72 by 59 centimeters and consists of a votive dedication to Ceres on behalf of certain unnamed *vicani* by L. Iulius L.f. Afer.[37] Thus "smaller" *oppida* such as Torrebenzalá, Cabeza Baja de la Encina Hermosa, or Atalayuelas in Jaén province could never have been termed *pagi* during the Principate, as a number of scholars have alleged.[38] And it is hardly likely that they would have been termed *vici*.[39] Independent evidence shows that Torrebenzalá is the *municipium* of Batora, which probably gained municipal status under the Flavians.[40] Epigraphic evidence from the site of the hilltop *oppidum* Atalayuelas, as fragmentary as it is, suggests that it, too, was probably a Flavian *municipium*.[41]

Scholars note, inter alia, the apparent reduction of the inhabited area of the *oppidum* at the Cabeza Baja de la Encina Hermosa during the Principate as evidence that this place was a *vicus* or a *pagus*. But a similar diminution in size is also in evidence at Iponoba, not far to the northwest; and the Cabeza Baja, where a number of inscriptions, now lost, were reported in the early twentieth century, was also most likely the site of an unknown Flavian *municipium*. There is no certain evidence for the existence of agricultural "villages" in Baetica, at least south and east of the Guadalquivir in the area of the subbético, during the Principate.[42] Alleged villages may reflect nothing more than unknown *municipia* or complex first-order sites with numerous *aedificia* and outliers. A quick glance at, for example, Tovar's catalogue of Baetican toponyms shows that many place names are in search of a site with which to be attached. Extensive settlements such as the Cabeza Baja, "El Molinillo," or the Cerro Boyero, the latter with a surface area of 16 hectares and showing Roman imperial habitation, are perfect candidates as the potential recipients of such toponyms.[43] That archaeologist is on shaky ground, therefore, who categorically asserts that extensive and intensive surveys suggest that secondary sites or nonurban agglomerations "were more common [in Baetica] than is generally supposed."[44] The inscriptions of the province of Baetica are sufficiently numerous and informative to reveal the existence of named villages or *vici* had they existed in most areas; we can rely on the argument from silence in this case, and conclude that named, nonurban agricultural agglomerations, at least in the southern portions of the province, simply did not exist during the Principate in any appreciable numbers. The story is far different in the case of mining-associated villages, as the examples of El Centenillo and other mines show.[45]

The one explicit indication of the size of elite or proto-elite landholding in Baetica during the Principate comes from Jaén province. An inscription of possibly mid-second-century A.D. date from the Flavian *municipium* Aurgi records the donation by the *IIvir bis* and "pontufex [sic] perpet(uus)" Caius Sempronius C.f. Gal(eria) Sempronianus and his daughter Sempronia Fusca Vibia Anicilla of baths, an aqueduct, and 300 *acnuae* of woodland for their operation; an *acnua* is equivalent to a square *actus,* a unit of surface area 120 Roman feet on a side that is a core element of centuriation.[46] The *acnua* certainly does not refer to a pre-Roman, Turdetanian system of land measurement, as Keay has suggested.[47] Ulpian's *forma censualis* (*Dig.* 50.15.4), showing that landowners normally reckoned in terms of *iugera* for fiscal purposes, is perfectly in line with the evidence of Aurgi, as a *iugerum* was simply two conjoined *actus quadratus* or *acnuae.* Obviously, the extent of landholding by the decurional at Aurgi exceeded the 150 *iugera* donated to that town. Otherwise, estimates of the sizes of *fundi* in Baetica remain more or less informed guesswork; such is the case of Didierjean's estimate of average site areas of 246 hectares in the Aljarafe region west and northwest of Sevilla.[48] To be sure, Blázquez believes that landholding in Baetica during the Principate was marked by widespread small- and medium-sized properties, arguing against the existence of latifundism in the province.[49] Blázquez does not quantify his supposition, but, by way of hypothesis, it might be reasonable to start with the assumption, based on the results of surface surveys to date, that Baetican *honesti,* in or outside the *ordo,* possessed, on average, *fundi* with a surface area in the range of 200 to 500 hectares. Remesal is right, it would seem, on a priori grounds to argue against widespread latifundism in the province, at least south of the Guadalquivir, from the existence of numerous *municipia* whose town councils would have required a substantial number of landowners to fill their ranks. One final point: there are absolutely no secure grounds for thinking that the territories of Baetican towns other than *coloniae* were ever subjected to *limitatio* or, in more conventional terms, centuriation.[50] Thus the suggestion that rural settlements in the area of Torredelcampo and Atalayuelas (Fuerte del Rey) in Jaén province were situated in *fundi* of 25 and 50 hectares, respectively, resulting from centuriation,[51] is lacking in any documentary or archaeological basis.

Site surveys are consistent in suggesting a leveling-off or drop in the number of sites, either new or those continuing preexisting settlement, in the period c. A.D. 150 through the end of the fourth century. Indeed, many Baetican rural sites, particularly second- and third-order sites, suggest abandonment in the second half of the second century from the absence of telltale finewares in their surface and excavated assemblages. To be sure, some of this may be the result of the consolidation of property, about which more in Chapter Seven, but much of the change may be more apparent than real, due to the failure, for reasons as yet unknown, of many sites to register African fineware after the putative cessation of Baetican *sigillata* production in c. A.D. 160.[52] The sites in question may simply have not been receiving African fineware. Recent work, though, suggests the continuation of Baetican *sigillata* production after the aforementioned date in the form of late Baetican *sigillata* whose existence and typology is only now beginning to be recognized and established.[53] This ware, also referred to as Roman fine common ware, seems to have been inspired by contemporary African fineware. Conversely, there is relatively little evidence of appreciable numbers of new first- through third-order rural establishments in Baetica in the period c. A.D. 150 and later. In many areas of the province, though, there is definite evidence for the fourth and fifth centuries of a drop-off in total number of rural settlements, coupled with evidence of the decay of urbanized *oppida*.

A cautionary illustration of the problem is provided, once again, by the *oppidum* at the Cabeza Baja de la Encina Hermosa in southwestern Jaén province. This was an Ibero-Roman *oppidum* that probably received the Latin right under the Flavians, but whose ancient name is unknown. The *oppidum* was allegedly abandoned after c. A.D. 130–150, but such an early date is surely incorrect: a fragment of a paleo-Christian sarcophagus, dating c. 315–335, was discovered in the necropolis immediately south of the town, and one of the weights excavated in a *taberna* of the *oppidum* seems to be late imperial.[54] The Cabeza Baja has yielded no African *sigillata,* and it seems prudent, therefore, to leave open the possibility that many first- through third-order sites in the *conventus Astigitanus* and elsewhere that are devoid of African fineware continued to be inhabited and exploited during the later imperial period.

There is no warrant, furthermore, for believing that a class of peasants in Baetica—whether owners or tenants—had permanent habitations that have utterly perished from the archaeological record, as Garnsey and Saller would generalize from the case of peninsular Italy. They state in no uncertain terms that the "normal 'small site'" occupied by farmers throughout the Roman world has a relatively sophisticated construction "inappropriate to a basic peasant cottage," and that its owner farmed an estate of 50 to 80 *iugera* (or 12.5 to 20 hectares).[55] There is no first- through third-order site of whatever surface area on any *fundus* that is undetectable in the archaeological record in Baetica, save for the accidents of surface visibility, such as vegetation, or postdepositional surface disturbance, such as sedimentation through flooding or erosion. Nor is there any first- through third-order site that has completely vanished, save for the accidents of modern construction, farming, or natural phenomena, such as the shifting of river beds.[56] The Roman farmstead at the Cortijo de la Cancha in western Málaga province is an illustration of the preceding point.[57] The Cortijo de La Cancha is situated on the south bank of the arroyo de Montecorto on the southern slopes of the Sierra de Malaver. As its excavators note, the site was identified as Roman already in a survey of 1989. Impending road construction motivated the emergency excavation of the site. Investigators describe a spot consisting of a gentle incline, marked by compact clay in which cereals are grown today. The existence of superficial accumulations of stone was a telltale sign that a man-made structure existed at the place. Excavation revealed the remains of the foundations of what may have been a modest Roman rural habitation. The foundations are partly gone, due to plowing. Only in those sections of the foundations that are best conserved is it possible to discern the use of reinforcing bases composed of what seems to be a single layer of squared or semi-squared stones, arranged in file. These reinforcing stones are set in those places in the foundation that are subject to the greatest strain and load, such as corners. The foundations were also packed with bits of *tegulae, imbrices,* and bricks. The foundations describe a quadrangular enclosed space, approximately 13 by 13.5 meters.[58] A transverse wall separates this space from a second, incompletely excavated one. The site also yields up fragments of painted stucco, bits of mortar, and *opus signinum*—the latter a sure sign of the existence at the site of a basin or basins. And the place, for all its structural simplicity, also discloses at least one coin—an *as*(?) of Hadrian—in addition to thirty-one fragments of Spanish *sigillata,* some of it decorated. Bits of slag at the site also indicate the working of iron ore from the Sierra de Malaver, a peculiarity noted at several other sites in the area, as mentioned above in Chapter One. Its excavators suggest that this farmstead was based on a mixed economic regime, involving arable, animal husbandry, and metal extraction and metalworking, at least for local use. The farmstead's location in a river valley also leaves open the possibility of the exploitation of orchards. The excavators note the existence of surface remains of Roman date at a level spot, 100 meters south of the excavated structure. Their descriptions are vague, so the possibility cannot be utterly ruled out that the excavated structures correspond to the *pars fructuaria* of a more complex rural establishment. But even if this were the case, then surely the original point about the visibility and durability of rural habitations in Baetica stands, because there is no warrant for believing that this site, dating from the Flavian period, is anything other than the construction of a *municeps* of Acinippo or, perhaps, of neighboring Lacilbula. And more to the point: this author knows of no wholly or partially excavated and published second- or third-order Roman-era site in all of Baetica that displays a ground plan and structures simpler than those at the Cortijo de la Cancha.

In a similar vein, and more briefly, the house corresponding to phase three of the Roman settlement and foundry at the Horno del Castillejo (Guarromán) in Jaén province also provides truly striking confirmation of the truth that permanent habitations and utilitarian structures in Baetica were not, on any informed accounting, simple structures of perishable materials that have utterly vanished from the archaeological record. Here, as we saw in Chapter One, the house possessed a foundation of dressed stones atop which were erected adobe walls in wooden frames. Two of the three partially excavated rooms of the house show floors made of mortar. Put more directly still: permanent structures in the province invariably possessed stone foundations and floors of various characteristics that, save for accidents of nature or deliberate destruction, have left more or less substantial vestiges. Garnsey and Saller's idea that lowly Roman peasants lived in nonstone "basic peasant" cottages that have completely vanished does not match observable reality on the ground in Baetica.

Production and Trade

Stray bits of information from the literary and nonliterary documentary sources illustrate aspects of the agricultural and other production of Baetica in the Flavian period and later. As usual, the archaeological and material evidence provides the fullest picture of production and trade. The interpretation of the material evidence, however, is not always straightforward.

This latter point will become clear in the following sections, particularly that dealing with Baetican olive-oil production and exports.

Pliny (*HN* 18.66) mentions the importation, in his day, of Baetican grain. And Silius Italicus, writing under Domitian, refers to the grain-bearing regions of the Baetis valley (3.403). Even the documentary evidence of the Lex Irnitana suggests the importance of cereals cultivation and viticulture at Irni, where otherwise the evidence of archaeology is mute. The drafter(s) of the Lex Irnitana (chs. K and 92) make provisions for the suspension of business at Irni twice a year for a maximum of thirty days at a time for the purposes of attending to the grain harvest and, subsequently, to the vintage. Le Gall believes that the vintage at Irni would have occurred in late August. That such provisions are not merely tralatitious from earlier Italian laws is suggested by Suetonius' notice (*Aug.* 35.3) that individual senators—but not the senate as a whole—were authorized to take only one such *vacatio*, in September or October. The implication of Suetonius' notice is that the senate by the reign of Augustus was no longer concerned with the grain harvest, which would have occurred much earlier than September or October.[59] A certain Pius, an "Aug(usti) N(ostri) verna" and "Dispensator [frumen]t(i) Mancip(alis)," may have been involved in collecting the rent-in-kind of grain from lessees of imperial property in Baetica at some point during the mid-second century A.D.[60] Moreover, the precise nature of Sextus Iulius Possessor's charges as equestrian *adiutor praefecti annonae* under the *divi fratres* continues to be a source of debate, but if it is correct to see in his task "transferenda solamina" the emergency shipment of grain in times of shortage, then Possessor will have been involved in the transport of Baetican cereals.[61] To where exactly this grain will have been shipped is unknown, and, aside from the statement of Pliny cited above, there exists no evidence for the exportation of Baetican grain to Rome after the Flavian period.

On the other hand, the epigraphical sources show considerable grain production in the province during the high Principate—production destined for the inhabitants of Baetica itself. For instance, an inscription of uncertain reading from Ucubi (Espejo) records certain benefactions by an individual whose name is not preserved. The benefactions included the gift of 150,000 *denarii* or 600,000 sesterces worth of grain to Ucubi.[62] Melchor Gil dates this benefaction to the second half of the second or third century, and, taking 10 to 12.5 *denarii* as the price of a *modius* of grain in times of scarcity during the second century in North Africa, suggests that with 600,000 sesterces, the benefactor at Ucubi gave between 12,000 and 15,000 *modii* of grain to the community. This quantity of grain would have fed a population of approximately 1,000 persons for roughly three months.[63] Another inscription, evidently from Anticaria, records the distribution, at some point during the second half of the second or first half of the third century A.D., of grain from an unknown *sevir Augustalis* to the "cives et incolae" of that community.[64] A fragmentary statue base of a certain "Sera[nus]"(?), of the second half of the second or beginning of the third century A.D. from Oducia (Lora la Vieja), records his gift of grain to the "municipes et incolae" of that town.[65] It may be worth observing that these three indirect attestations of grain-growing show up in the portion of Baetica where a priori we would expect that activity to have been most intense, namely in the broad and fertile areas of the middle Guadalquivir valley and the "depresión de Antequera."[66] And yet, the discovery and excavation of sixteen silos of fairly substantial dimensions in the immediate vicinity of the villa at El Ruedo in the hilly portion of southeastern Córdoba province shows the ubiquity of grain-growing in Baetica, although we might suppose that the silos at El Ruedo, dating from the first through third centuries A.D., were destined for the storage of grain meant to serve only the owners and dependents of the villa establishment there.[67] However, the most important source of elite and proto-elite wealth in the province during the Flavian and subsequent eras seems to have been the growing and processing of the olive.

OLIVE OIL

Martial favorably compares olive oil from Corduba with that from Venafrum and Istria (12.63) and describes the hair of Baetis as wreathed with a crown of olive (12.98). So, too, Pliny notes that Istria and Baetica, in general, compete on equal terms behind Venafrum in the quality of olive oil (*HN* 15.8). Otherwise, we depend on the archaeological evidence, including the testimony of oil-bearing amphoras, to show in vivid detail the preeminent role that oil played within the Mediterranean triad of cereals, olive oil, and wine as sources of elite and middle-stratum wealth in Baetica during the Flavian and post-Flavian periods.

The archaeological testimony for olive-oil production and commerce becomes abundant in the Flavian period and thereafter. Not all *fundi* producing olives would have possessed facilities for processing the olive into oil, and, conversely, not all installations devoted to the production and bottling of oil would have been annexes of olive plantations. Chic García provides a *catalogue raisonné* of amphora-producing sites along the Baetis and its main tributary, the Singilis, and it would be otiose to reproduce his results here fully. Put briefly, the installations, close to a hundred in total, cluster along the Baetis between Ilipa and slightly downstream of Corduba, while along the Singilis they are situated downstream of Astigi to the confluence of the Genil with the Guadalquivir. Most identifiable *figlinae* are situated relatively close to substantial Roman villa sites, to which the potteries would have been attached. The more pressing logic of the installations' emplacement is simply this: the massive amphoras they produced were filled at or near their point of manufacture in places that were closest to the sources of the oil, to navigable stretches of the Baetis and the Singilis, and to clay deposits.[68] There is, as yet, no compelling archaeological proof for the view that only about one in five of the *figlinae* possessed kilns, and that the empty containers were transported to select depots or *portus,* where they were filled.[69] The suggestion is better-founded that shallow-draft vessels or barges collected the amphoras—which when filled would have weighed in the order of 100 kilograms—and then brought them to Hispalis, whence larger, ocean-going ships transported the containers and their contents to Ostia and elsewhere. In this context, it is worth noting that the word *portus* may, on occasion, refer to river jetties, dikes, and dams situated at intervals along the Baetis.[70] The function of these *portus* would have been to regulate the current and the level of the water in the river, with a view to enhancing its navigability. It is precisely this hydraulic activity to which Philostratus refers in his description of Baetica. The sophist, in his *Life of Apollonius,* describes the province as the best of lands in the Roman world, rich in cities, pastures, controlled watercourses, and all sorts of crops, including, presumably, grain.[71] The alternative reading of the term *portus,* as a "deposit" or "storage-place" (sc. of olive oil), controlled by the *fiscus,*[72] smacks of special pleading.

There is also a growing body of evidence for olive-oil production and the associated manufacture of oil-bearing containers along the Mediterranean coast of Baetica and along the Guadalete River in Cádiz province. The pottery installation and associated first- or second-order establishment at Huerta del Rincón (Torremolinos) in Málaga province has yielded remains of an olive-oil press; the same complex produced Dressel 20 oil-bearing containers, one of which bears the mark of the proprietor(?) CLICM.[73] Dressel 20 containers were also produced at Almayate Bajo (Finca de Manganeto) at the mouth of the Vélez River in Málaga province, and possibly at the pottery found below the calle Carretería in the city of Málaga.[74] In coastal Almería province, there exists evidence for Dressel 20 production at the Loma de Cabriles in the vicinity of Guardias Viejas (El Ejido), the port of ancient Murgi.[75]

The stamps and painted inscriptions on olive-oil containers are an invaluable archive of hundreds of individuals connected with the production and distribution of oil, as well as the manufacture of the amphoras that transported the product. A principal concern of Chapter Six will be the utilization of the documentary evidence from the amphoras themselves as a means of identifying Baetican elites and middle-stratum persons who profited from olive oil. The interpretation of the stamps and *tituli picti* is anything but straightforward, however. The *tituli picti* and stamps, the latter usually in relief within rectangular cartouches, appear, for the most part, on the handles and shoulders of the amphoras, which are the globular Dressel 20 containers, superseded by the smaller Dressel 23 amphoras in the course of the third century (see Fig. 1). In point of strict accuracy, let me make clear that the first true Dressel 20 containers do not appear until the reign of Claudius and are preceded both by the morphologically dissimilar type A oil-bearing amphora (equivalent to the Oberaden 83 container), produced in the reign of Augustus before the turn of the era, and by the type B container, which sees production from the first decade of the first century A.D. until probably the end of Tiberius' rule.[76]

The stamps fall into three main categories.[77] There are stamps that name free persons, usually indicated by the initials of the *tria nomina,* and sometimes by more or less abbreviated elements of the same. At times the stamps indicate persons operating in association, such as fellow freedmen, free siblings, fathers and sons, or unrelated freeborn individuals. The second broad category of stamps refers to the names of places of amphora production, whether pottery-making complexes, estates, or individual workshops. The third major type of stamp designates a potter by his given name, followed in some cases by the letter *F* for "F(ecit)." In other cases, three categories combine in two stamps, one bearing elements of the *tria nomina* plus the name of the pottery works, and the other stamp bearing a slave

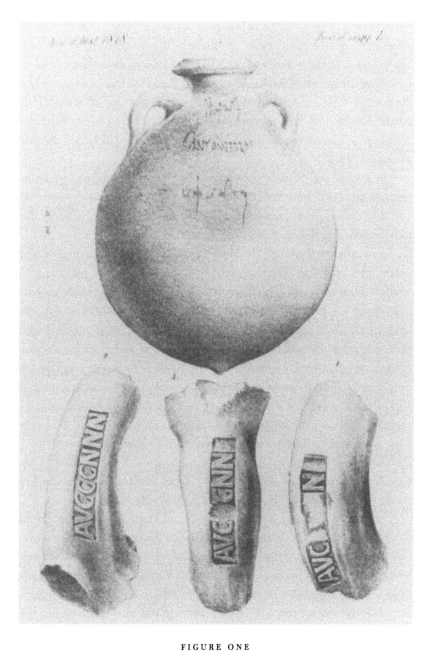

FIGURE ONE

Dressel 20 amphora showing position of *tituli picti* and handle stamps
(from H. Dressel, "Ricerche sul Monte Testaccio," *Annali dell'Instituto
di Correspondenza Archeologica* [1878], pl. L

name followed by the letter *F* for "F(ecit)." More exceptionally, it is also possible for the three basic categories of stamp to combine into one stamp, containing the *tria nomina*, the name of the pottery, and a slave name.

The interpretation of the stamps is highly controversial. Nevertheless, the view that sees the names in the stamps as those of the proprietors of the amphora works, accompanied in exceptional cases by the names of the workshop managers and, somewhat more frequently, by the names of slaves, seems a compelling one.[78] As a practical matter, the stamps may have served to differentiate the owners of different lots of amphoras fired en masse at a common kiln.[79] And it may be possible to detect in certain of the names, by the second century, the operation of leasing and sub-leasing arrangements embodied in the various *locatio-conductio* contracts joining landowners with lessees and the lessees, in turn, with their own workshop managers, in a situation similar to that which seems to have characterized Italian red-slip fineware production.[80] Leasing rather than ownership could help to explain the fact that stamps bearing the names of certain individuals begin to appear in profusion in widely scattered *figlinae* during the second century. And, on general principles, it should be expected that *figlinae* and any associated estates could and did change ownership or lessees on occasion. A change of ownership may have been the fate of the *figlina Virginensia* (Villar de Brenes or Puerto el Barco) in the late Antonine period.[81]

The developed *tituli picti* of the period from roughly A.D. 110 to 190 consist of five components; Dressel referred to them using the letters *alpha, beta, gamma, delta,* and *epsilon*.[82] Dressel component alpha, painted on the neck of the amphora, refers to the empty weight of the amphora in pounds. Dressel component beta, appearing on the upper shoulder of the amphora, represents the name(s), in the genitive, of the merchant(s) or shipper(s) of the oil—sometimes, but not invariably, the same individual(s). The number in Dressel component gamma, on the lower part of the shoulder, indicates the weight of the oil.[83] The elements of Dressel component delta, written to the right of beta, next to the handle, and in an oblique position relative to the aforementioned components, do not follow a standard order, nor do they appear in every *titulus*. And it is crucial to note that simple versions of the delta component appear as early as the reign of Claudius. The elements in Dressel component delta variously refer to the name of the agent acting on behalf of a buyer whose responsibility it is to test the quality and weight of the contents,[84] as well as indicate the district in which the transaction took place. They also refer to a name that probably represents the name of the proprietor or the tenant of the oil-producing estate, and another designation, derived from the name of the producing estate, that indicates the product. It is worth underscoring at this point the strong possibility that not all estate owners or tenants will have had the means to press oil, and may have, instead, sold olives to estates that did possess the means to do so.[85] The elements in the delta component can also on occasion include a number, which may indicate the number of amphoras filled with oil from a particular estate. The delta inscription sometimes indicates the name of the person who weighed the amphora and its contents. A number of second-century delta *tituli* record the names of the eponymous consuls.[86] Many delta inscriptions of the second century show at the beginning of the first or second line an *R* crossed by a horizontal bar.[87] Most investigators see here an abbreviation for the word "r(ecensitum, -a)" and a reference to some sort of official tallying or recording of the amphora's contents.[88] Finally, Dressel component epsilon does not appear on all Dressel 20s; it represents a number that may be a control number used by the Roman authorities.

Worth more detailed consideration is the activity of the persons named in Dressel component beta. Independent epigraphical evidence refers to the persons named in Dressel component beta as *navicularii, mercatores olei Hispani ex Baetica,* or *diffusores olearii ex Baetica.*[89] Furthermore, a fragment from the first book of the *Regulae* by the Antonine jurist Scaevola refers to "mercatores olearii."[90] Scholars tend to dissociate *navicularii* or ship operators from merchants, strictly speaking, although *navicularii* could and did act simultaneously as ship operators and merchants. Otherwise, do these different designations indicate diverse functions? The matter is not simple. The arguments, though, seem persuasive that consider *mercatores, negotiatores,* or *diffusores olearii,* aside from those who acted as both *navicularii* and merchants, as having essentially the same functions.[91] Moreover, the majority of these individuals, from the close study of their names, came from the province of Baetica. And all of these merchants and shippers seem to have operated on the basis of a contract with the prefecture of the *annona* in order to supply the city of Rome and the army.[92] Their cooperation with the *annona* in any case is clear from a remarkable series of bronze seals and seal impressions from Rome and Ostia that name persons whom the independent inscriptional evidence puts indiscriminately in the category of *mercatores, negotiatores, diffusores,* and even one oil *negotiatrix* from Baetica. The function of the seals, of standard size and design, may have been to demarcate areas in Ostian and Roman warehouses allocated to oil traders by the *annona*.[93]

It may well be the case that all those *navicularii* and *negotiatores* who entered into a formal, contractual relationship with the *annona* enjoyed exemption, possibly from some point during the reign of Trajan, and certainly by Hadrian's rule, from *munera publica,* including service on embassies. The critical evidence is the testimony of the Severan jurist Callistratus in book 1 of *De cognitionibus:* "Negotiatores, qui annonam urbis adiuvant, item navicularii, qui annonae urbis serviunt, immunitatem a muneribus publicis consequuntur, quamdiu in eiusmodi actu sunt" (*Dig.* 50.6.6.3: "Traders and shippers who aid and serve the food supply of the city of Rome shall obtain immunity from public burdens as long as they are engaged in the same activity"). Sirks, it seems, is justified in ascribing the regulation to Trajan.[94] More uncertain is the contention by Herz of the existence of traders supplying Rome's free market who received immunities from the state in the absence of a contract with the *annona*.[95] Both Herz and Sirks, however, see in the phrase "negotiatores, qui annonam urbis adiuvant" a reference to those supplying both grain and oil, as well as other staples, to the city of Rome.[96] And another critical point is that traders were a priori nondecurions, precisely because they could enjoy exemptions from liturgies, whereas decurions could not.[97] The names of freeborn persons in Dressel component beta, consequently, represent *honesti viri,* or persons of repute, not enrolled in local town councils in Baetica during the Principate. The incentives, existing probably from Trajan's reign onward, to independent oil traders to supply Rome and the army must have entailed that the authorities had at their disposal means to check those traders who were eligible for benefits, including immunity from civic *munera.* The detailed notations on the Dressel 20 amphoras referred to the growers of the olives, the estates from which the processed oil originated, its weight, the weight of the container, the name of the trader, and the district in which the acquisition and testing of oil consignments took place. The notations must have enabled the authorities to confirm the investment of all parties concerned—in terms of the mandated investment of a major part of their fortunes, including oil produced or acquired—in order to extend benefits to those who met the imperially mandated criteria for immunity. The role of the *tituli picti,* and particularly of the delta inscription—the increasing complexity of which by the second century is well noted—was likely in part to identify and confirm those traders and shippers eligible for benefits. A letter of Hadrian and a rescript of Marcus Aurelius and Lucius Verus show that there were wealthy persons (*locupletes*) fraudulently claiming exemption from local *munera* on the basis of their alleged involvement in shipping—either directly or through investing the larger part of their property.[98] All the foregoing is an argument against those who would see the export of Spanish olive oil as a purely "commercial" matter with "no state involvement."[99] And it is not an endorsement of the view that postulates that the persons named in the genitive in Dressel inscription delta represent *publicani*. It is my opinion that Baetican oil was not a tributary item. It is a fair assertion that tribute from Baetica, from the reign of Vespasian onward, came in the form of money taxes.[100]

There is a further dimension to the involvement of the freeborn in the supply of the *annona* and the consequent immunities deriving from that service. It was noted above that decurions, as such, were ineligible for these immunities. It is no accident that so few Baetican merchants or shippers connected with the supply of the *annona* can be identified as decurions or local magistrates. This situation stands in notable contrast to the Gallic, German, and Danubian provinces, where the inscriptions do reveal town councilors and local magistrates acting as traders and shippers.[101] The difference is this: the curial merchants of the northwestern provinces were not linked with the supply of the *annona,* and instead served regional commercial demands and networks not directly connected with the Roman state. The clear implication is that merchants from Baetica or those connected with staples from that province destined for Rome and the army did stand in a relatively privileged position vis-à-vis provincials from other parts of the Empire. It is also worth stating, in passing, that it shows a lack of awareness of the full dimensions of the debate concerning the identities of oil traders and their relationship with the *annona* to assert categorically that *mercatores, negotiatores,* and *diffusores olearii* were engaged in private *negotia,* while *navicularii* transported products that were solely the property of the *annona.*[102]

But it is a telling indication of the centrality of landed property as the essential basis of elite wealth that an exemption from *munera* for these shipowners, operators, and merchants, in addition to not encompassing the *munera patrimoniorum* (obligations linked to landholding), did not extend to the responsibility of guardianship.[103] The importance of the latter *munus,* at first a *munus privatum* and then *publicum* in the form of the *tutela dativa* (guardianship assigned by a magistrate), is underscored by

Saller's demographic simulations, which suggest that up to a third of all "upper-class" Romans had lost their fathers by puberty, and that a further third were bereft of their fathers by the age of 25.[104]

Silius Italicus, writing during the Flavian epoch, connects poetically the town of Nabrissa Veneria (Lebrija, Sevilla province) with the vine (3.393–395); perhaps the town and its territory were producing wine for export in the poet's day. In any case, archaeological evidence shows that the production and export of wine continued in Baetica during the Flavian period and later. Signal testimony for this activity is the first-order rural site on the Loma de Ceres (Molvízar-Granada). The site has an Augustan inception, but various African *sigillata* (A, C, D, and Hayes 197) and late common ceramics suggest that the villa and its producing installations continued functioning throughout the fourth century. The excavations also yielded coins of Caracalla through Herennius Etruscus.[105] The remains of three vats, the vestiges of a press, *dolia* in situ in an area corresponding to a *cella vinaria*, an area for crushing grapes, and the remains of Dressel 2–4 and 30 amphoras produced on site point to the large-scale production of wine for export, at least on a regional scale, from the late first century A.D. onward. The discovery of fragments, in quantity, of Dressel 7–11, 14, 18, and Beltrán II A and II B amphoras, traditionally associated with the storage and transport of fish sauces and related products, leads the excavators to suggest that they were sent to other centers, where they were in demand for the bottling of fish sauces, or, alternatively, that they were used for transporting wine. The foregoing presumption derives from the discovery of two basins, lined with *opus signinum,* that evidently were designed for fish-sauce production but that, in the estimation of the site's excavators, would have produced a quantity of product inferior to the capacity indicated by the number and variety of fish-product containers found at the site.[106]

Our understanding of Baetican wine production and possible export in the later Empire requires significant modification from the results of the excavations of a kiln and associated structures at the place called Los Matagallares, situated 2 kilometers northwest of Salobreña (Granada), not far inland from the Mediterranean coast.[107] The complex, consisting of two rooms and the kiln, was a dependency of a nearby, unexcavated villa. The site also reveals bricks belonging to a now-destroyed kiln and two areas immediately adjoining the preserved rooms that were used to discard wasters. Spanish and African *sigillata,* lamps corresponding to Dragen-dorff form 28, and coins suggest that the workshop was active during the third and fourth centuries A.D. The workshop produced common ceramics, construction materials — chiefly *tegulae,* bricks (including small bricks destined for *opus spicatum* flooring), and amphoras. There are five identifiable amphora types. The complex produced Gauloise 4 containers, previously known in connection with the export of Narbonensian wine from the first through third centuries A.D. In Gaul itself, the container ceased to be produced, so far as is known, in the first decades of the third century A.D. The center also produced Dressel 14 fish-sauce amphoras. A stamp on a surviving fragment of a Dressel 14 container from Los Matagallares reads IAN, and may refer to a producer/trader "Ian(uarius)," possessing a name with a certain servile air. The workshop also produced Dressel 30 wine-bearing amphoras. It made Almagro 50 and 51c containers as well, used to carry fish-sauce products. Both the Loma de Ceres, discussed above, and Los Matagallares, but particularly the latter place, would have been much closer to the Mediterranean coastline than they are today, due to extensive silting at the mouth of the Guadalfeo River. There is also the testimony of the amphora-producing installation Puente Melchor at Puerto Real in Cádiz province. Its excavators underscore an increase in the quantities of amphoras devoted to the transport of wine from the late second century A.D. onward in the form of the Gauloise 4–Dressel 30 hybrid and, beginning in the early fourth century, the Beltrán 68 wine-bearing container.[108] Richardson's allegation that Baetican wine production trailed off entirely in the second half of the first century A.D. is simply incorrect.[109]

FISH SAUCE

The participation of the *principes* in the production of fish sauce is certain from their attestation in a *titulus pictus* on a fragment of a Dressel 7–11 amphora. The fragment, from Fos-sur-mer, refers to fish sauce made from the mackerel ("scomb[ri] flos"), distributed by Iunius Cilo, and produced "[e]x of(ficina) Augg(ustorum)."[110] The emperors involved may be Vespasian and Titus; but Curtis' alternative idea that the container had a long life, and was re-used in the reigns of Marcus Aurelius and Lucius Verus, is strained.[111] The recent suggestion that the emperors involved may have been Nerva and Trajan is more believable.[112] The surmise would be a wise one, moreover, that the emperor(s) involved came into possession of a particular fish-sauce-producing property or properties through inheritance or confiscation. The senatorial Cornelii Pusiones from Portus Gaditanus may have been the proprietors of the fish-sauce amphora-producing installation at the Cortijo del Tesorillo (Jerez de la Frontera), about which more in Chapter Six.

It is during the Flavian period that the fish-sauce amphora-producing installation at the Huerta del Rincón (Torremolinos) in Málaga province resumed its activity after a hiatus that began late in the reign of Claudius.[113] During the period of resumed activity, the installation manufactured Beltrán II A and II B, Beltrán III, IV A and B (= Dressel 14), Dressel 20 and 23, and Beltrán VI (= Dressel 17 and 28) amphoras, extending its activity into the later Empire. It may be relevant, furthermore, that during the first phase of the pottery's activity, corresponding to the period of c. A.D. 25 to 50, only one oven seems to have been in service, whereas in the second phase, beginning, as suggested above, in the Flavian era, two ovens were functioning in the firing of amphoras, and a third, contemporary kiln seems to have been devoted exclusively to the production of stoppers for the containers. The enlargement of the area for storing amphoras also is a feature of this second phase in the installation's activity. Otherwise, just two installations seem to have their inception within the Flavian era: the atelier in the Finca de Manganeto (Almayate Bajo), and the pottery at the Finca El Secretario (Fuengirola). Both sites are in Málaga province.[114]

Baetican fish sauce met the demands of both external consumers and those within the province itself. Emergency excavations at Ecija show this internal demand in a vivid way. Excavations at no. 9 of the Plaza de Puerta Cerrada, near the western gate of the modern town, uncovered portions of a *domus*.[115] The *domus* seems to have been part of a concerted program of urban reconstruction in the western part of the urban core of Astigi during the earlier second century A.D. This portion of the colony's *oppidum* had formerly been the site of an artisanal quarter, to judge from the discovery in this area of small foundries active in the Julio-Claudian period. The excavations disclosed the remains of walls and their foundations, associable with the *domus*. Fragments of Beltrán II B amphoras were used extensively as constructive materials in the beddings and walls themselves. They were used in lieu of bricks or stone in a region notoriously lacking in quarries. More than fifteen amphora fragments, corresponding to the necks and mouths of the recipients, were found embedded in the base of the wall and in the wall itself. The wall seems to have been rebuilt in the last third of the second century, while the bedding of the wall, containing the majority of amphora fragments, seems to predate the reconstructed wall, possibly by a generation or so. It is the inspired hypothesis of the excavator that the *domus* belonged to an importer of fish sauce, who utilized the empty containers resulting from his trade for the partial (re)construction of his *domus*. The suggestion is that the merchant was active from roughly c. A.D. 150 to the end of the second century. One of the amphora fragments built into the wall bears a barely legible *titulus pictus* that may reveal the initials of the merchant "C.L.L.A." Otherwise, the epigraphical sources name one explicitly designated trader of Baetican fish-sauce products during the Flavian and later periods. P. Clodius Athenio was "negotians salsarius" and a *quinquennalis* of the *corpus negotiantium Malacitanorum* in Rome, possibly during the 140s A.D.[116] He may be the same person as a certain P. Clodius . . . .io, named in an honorary inscription to Valeria Lucilla, the wife of L. Valerius L.f. Quir(ina) Proculus, the prefect of the *annona* and of Egypt, among other charges.[117] Proculus was prefect of the *annona* in 144. If Hübner is right, following Velázquez, to restore the fragmentary name in the inscription from Malaca as "[Athen]io," then we would have further evidence for the close involvement of the *annona* with Baetican traders supplying the city of Rome with staples besides olive oil in the first half of the second century A.D. There is no warrant, furthermore, for assuming that Athenio represented the fish salters of Malaca tout court;[118] it is more likely, on a prima facie reading of the epitaph that attests him, that he was an officer of a corpus of fellow *negotiatores* of fish-sauce products, active in the export trade from southern Spain to Rome and elsewhere. It is a common assumption, moreover, that the Asian(?) and Syrian merchants represented in a second-century A.D. Greek inscription from Malaca were involved in the export of fish products.[119] It may well be the case, however, that their involvement in exporting Baetican fish sauce was complemented by their importation of Aegean wine to southern Hispania.[120]

SALT

There is compelling indirect evidence for the production and commerce of salt, at a local and regional level, in wide areas of Baetica during the Principate. It is possible, for instance, that the roads passing by, and emanating from, the brackish Laguna Salada or Laguna de Fuente Piedra in Málaga province served to transport salt produced from the lake. The Roman first-through third-order sites that cluster around the laguna, most with a Flavian inception, were conceivably dedicated to the production of both olive oil

and salt. Moreover, the sites seem to have also been involved in animal husbandry and the preservation of meat. In this connection, it is possible that
the numerous quarter- and half-round bricks from many of the sites that
show evidence of having belonged to ovens were involved in the accelerated
curing of the meat through its exposure to high heat.[121]

POTTERY

The evidence for non-olive-oil and fish-sauce amphora pottery manufacture and brick and tile production in Baetica is abundant but dispersed.
This section represents an attempt to survey the better-known and published production sites. Many potteries await systematic excavation or have
been destroyed through modern construction. The latter fate probably
befell an alleged pottery at El Tejar, situated just over 3 kilometers south of
Benamejí in Córdoba province. At the Cerro Barrero, modern construction revealed wall remains, possibly some structures of *opus caementicium*,
tegulae, common ceramics, fragments of amphoras, and *sigillata*. The summary description of the site identifies the place as a Roman pottery.[122] The
best-known pottery installations, in some senses, are those which produced
the globular Dressel 20 and 23 oil-bearing containers. But it is notable that
most of the centers producing oil amphoras also produced a wide variety of
utilitarian ceramics, as well as construction materials. And not all identifiable *figlinae* along the Guadalquivir or its main tributary, the Genil, produced amphoras.

It is possible to identify a multiplicity of installations that produced not
only oil-bearing containers but other items as well. At Remolino, 3 kilometers east-northeast of Palma del Río, on the left bank of the Guadalquivir, a
workshop produced not only Dressel 20 amphoras but also *tegulae* and
dolia, as well as other unspecified ceramics.[123] At Las Delicias, on the right
bank of the Genil 4 kilometers downstream of Ecija, a *figlina*, situated
250 meters from the villa of which it was a dependency, produced not only
Dressel 20 containers, but also *tegulae*, bricks, and, among other items,
earthenware tubs with holes at the bottom. The tubs had a utilitarian function of serving either as seedbeds or for the transport of cuttings and shoots,
and an aesthetic function as planting pots for ornamentals.[124] Jashemski
discusses similar planting pots from Italy, and elsewhere in the Roman
world apart from Spain.[125] The complex at Las Delicias was active from
c. A.D. 50 to c. A.D. 250.[126] The amphora-producing site at Alcotrista, on the
right bank of the Genil, located 8.5 kilometers downstream of Ecija, pro-

duced amphoras, *tegulae,* bricks, and other items, including imitations of Campanian(?) and painted Roman-era Iberian ware. The life of this workshop extends probably from the late Augustan or Tiberian period to the end of the second century A.D. An inception at the very end of the reign of Augustus would make the installation contemporaneous with the beginnings of the large-scale export of Baetican olive oil to Rome and elsewhere. At a site on the outskirts of Peñaflor(?) named Embarcadero, Bonsor discovered the remains of a kiln that produced common ceramics.[127] The expression "common ceramics" here, as elsewhere, designates ceramics intended for the storage, preparation, and serving of food. The *figlina* at Azanaque-Castillejo, 4.5 kilometers upstream of Arva, on the left bank of the Baetis, produced not only amphoras, but also earthenware basins, bricks, and tile. Meticulous excavations here in 1993 exposed two circular kilns and remains of not only Dressel 20 amphoras, but also common ceramics, *imbrices,* bricks, and *laterculi,* all presumably fired at the site.[128] The two ovens seem to have commenced their operations in the mid-second century A.D. Chic García connects this installation and the adjoining villa, of which it formed a part, with the Aelii Optati discussed in Chapter Six.[129] At El Tejillo or Tejarillo are the remains of five circular kilns with a central pillar. This complex, situated 3.4 kilometers downstream of Arva on the right bank of the Baetis, produced not only Dressel 20 and 23 amphoras, but also bricks, tiles, *dolia,* and bowls.[130] Chic García suggests the proprietor of the pottery resided in the "villa rustica" Manuel Recuero, upstream from the site. A site called Valdevacas, situated 2.3 kilometers downstream from Villanueva del Río, on the right bank of the Guadalquivir, produced, it seems, bricks, amphoras, *dolia,* and other, unspecified ceramics. One kilometer from the aforementioned place is a second-order site revealing dressed stones, tiles, bricks, and remains of both common ceramics and *sigillata*—the aforementioned two sites would seem to be yet further examples of the typical configuration of a rural settlement proximate to a kiln that it controlled.[131]

What are the larger implications of all this information? All of the places mentioned above show that proprietors and lessees of potteries not only could have profited from olive-oil exportation, but also could have served the needs of rural and urban sites in the vicinity of their installations. It may be reasonable to conjecture that oil-amphora production and bottling occupied most of the period corresponding to the sailing season in the Mediterranean, on the principle that olive oil would not have been stored for lengthy periods, while during the off-season the production of household utilitarian ceramics and construction materials produced further employment and proceeds.

Investigators have published a preliminary but detailed report of three pottery-producing installations in the municipal districts of Priego de Córdoba and Fuente Tójar.[132] Unlike the *figlinae* described above, they did not produce oil-bearing amphoras. But they do illustrate with clarity the widespread opportunities for wealth creation and moneymaking that the Flavian reforms in Baetica brought in their train. The three sites—Fuente Barea, Tejar de Genilla, and Todosaires—are all situated in upland areas rich in clay deposits, rainfall, and wood, and are well connected with a thick array of Roman rural and urban settlements. The ceramics evidence from Fuente Barea shows its Flavian inception, and the other two potteries probably are also Flavian in origin. The three potteries were active in the production of *tegulae, imbrices,* bricks, loom weights, and common ceramics, including *dolia,* intended for storage and domestic use. All three sites have been studied on the basis of the superficial remains of the kilns and their wasters, and not on the basis of excavation. They were all probably dependencies of a nearby first- through third-order settlement. The surveyors suggest that Iliturgicola would have met much of its need for construction materials from the *figlina* at Todosaires, 2.5 kilometers to the west-southwest, and that, similarly, Ipolcobulcula could have been supplied by Tejar de Genilla. Only Fuente Barea would have most likely supplied the needs of rural settlements alone—but at a critical time in the history of the province: the workshop sprang into existence during the rural settlement and building boom of the Flavian period, supplying rurally based customers with building materials.

Recent agricultural work reveals the existence of a pottery complex at La Alcantarilla, a farm just over 1.5 kilometers to the east of Carcabuey.[133] Camacho and Lara describe an installation including a well-preserved rectangular oven with a central combustion chamber and corridor. The indistinct remains of what seems to be a second oven are situated in its immediate vicinity. The pottery functioned, on the evidence of *terra sigillata hispanica* recovered at the site, from the Flavian era to some indeterminate point between c. A.D. 150 and 200. The site reveals no Italian or Gallic *sigillata.* The main and specialized production of the pottery seems to have consisted of a wide range of common ceramics destined for the preparation, serving, and storage of food. In addition, the complex produced *dolia* and construction materials, including *tegulae, imbrices, lateres,* and *laterculi.* Three kilometers to the east-northeast of Carcabuey and 1.5 kilometers to the northeast of La Alcantarilla is the workshop, described above, at Tejar de Genilla. Both La Alcantarilla and Tejar de Genilla manufactured ceramics and construction materials for the *oppidum* at Ipolcobulcula, as well as for the first- through third-order rural sites in the territory of that *municipium.* In the absence of any major stream, the pottery at La Alcantarilla, as well as that at Tejar de Genilla, would have depended for the distribution of its products on the secondary road connecting Málaga province with mining areas in Jaén province running along the valleys of the Anzur and Zagrilla rivers and passing near or through Carcabuey. Camacho and Lara suggest that the common ceramics produced at La Alcantarilla would have found a market in the entire Priego-Alcaudete basin, as well as in the immediate area of Carcabuey.

Other, similar installations with activity extending from the Claudian or Flavian periods onward have come to light in the penibético. To them I now turn. One of the more significant modern discoveries is the installation called "El Tejar," situated in the vicinity of the urban center of Lucena on the right bank of the river of the same name.[134] Its inception and activity are emblematic of the changes occurring throughout Baetica during the Flavian epoch. Excavators have identified here a number of ovens and an attached service/storage structure, measuring 30.5 meters in length and 8.20 meters in width. It is divided into two areas by a row, along its long side, of pillars, each one of which is constructed of bricks and stones. The area may have had the purpose of storing the vessels before and after firing. Off of the area, and apparently in line with it, is a row of four elliptical or trapezoidal ovens, in each of which the *praefurnium,* combustion chamber, and firing platform are preserved. To the west of this complex are two — and perhaps three — additional ovens, which are off-axis with respect to the four aforementioned kilns. Excavation also revealed the remains of still another oven of indeterminate type, in addition to the remains of adobe structures. The installation produced a wide variety of common ceramics destined for the preparation, cooking, serving, and storage of food and agricultural products, including containers for storing liquids. The ovens also fired construction material, such as bricks, *tegulae,* and *imbrices.* The excavation awaits thorough publication, but the ceramics evidence suggests an inception of the mid-first century A.D. and activity extending into the second half of the second century. An installation of this size was obviously serving the needs of more than a single rural settlement.

Emergency excavation occasioned by the construction of the Antequera-Málaga freeway resulted in the discovery of a pottery-producing center situated on the south bank of the Guadalhorce River at a spot called La Casería de la Mancha.[135] The place is located approximately 5 kilometers north-northeast of Anticaria (modern Antequera). Only one of the trenches revealed the remains of a structure: the lower part of a wall made of irregular stones joined with mortar, resting on the north bank of the river. Soundings on the south bank of the Guadalhorce, opposite the aforementioned structure, revealed a pottery dump, which points, on the suggestion of the excavators, to the production in this spot of building materials — presumably bricks and *tegulae*—as well as various forms of utilitarian and domestic common ceramics. Finewares are relatively scarce at the site, and it is worthy of mention that African finewares are totally absent. The pottery would have supplied the needs of a *fundus*, of which it formed a part, and possibly of neighboring *fundi* in an area of the Vega de Antequera, which is rich in Roman-era rural settlements.

As a result of modern construction, the well-preserved remains of two kilns and a portion of a third have been discovered in Cuevas del Becerro in Málaga province.[136] Both of the well-preserved ovens conserve their *praefurnium,* and consist of circular structures 2.5 meters in diameter. The kilns seem to have had a direct connection with the first-order, olive-oil-producing complex discovered at Cuevas del Becerro. Although the kilns are only preliminarily published, it is evident that they produced a combination of construction materials and common ceramics.[137]

Romero Moragas has published the remains of a villa(?) and adjoining *figlina* that produced storage and kitchen common ceramics, including *dolia* and *dolia* lids.[138] The site is in the Cortijo del Río on the right bank of the Corbones River, and within the municipal boundary of Marchena. Beltrán Lloris records the discovery at the site of an oval oven, active from the end of the first to the third century A.D.[139] Approximately 400 meters to the west of the pottery, on a hill, are walls of *opus caementicium* that seem to have formed rectangular enclosures and that apparently represent basins of some sort. In the immediate vicinity of the aforementioned concrete construction appear two bell-shaped stone mills, which correspond to the bottom, fixed portion of an animal-drawn grain mill. Unspecified Roman-era ceramics cover the entire hill on which the *caementicium* and mills rest. Romero Moragas suggests that the pottery would have served the needs of the farmstead(?) atop the hill, but it is important to note that the Corbones was navigable at this point in antiquity — at least by rafts or barges; it seems just as likely that the products of the *figlina* were dispersed beyond the *fundus* on which they were produced.

There are also the remains of a ceramics-producing installation at the Cerro Alcaide, situated 3.4 kilometers east-northeast of Casabermeja on the north bank of the Guadalmedina River in Málaga province. The place produces abundant pottery wasters that show the production of *tegulae, imbrices,* bricks, *dolia,* loom weights, and possibly various forms of common ceramics. The spot also reveals a rock of unspecified dimensions with four rectangular cuts, which the authors suggest may have served as a base for a potter's wheel. They also note the presence at the site of slag, marble, and various forms of Spanish and African *sigillata,* as well as the remains of a cistern of mortared rubble. From the site description, it seems that this pottery had a Flavian inception and provided for the needs in construction elements and common ceramics of the villa to which it would have been attached, as well as, possibly, of nearby first- through third-order sites.[140] The discovery at the site of a number of coins, including a *sestertius* of Trajan, an *as* of indeterminate but high imperial date, and a post-353/354 nummus certainly would be in line with the presence at the Cerro Alcaide of a first-order settlement with continuous habitation from the late first through the fourth century A.D.[141]

Torrox-Costa in Málaga province discloses two ovens that formed part of a pottery that produced common ceramics and *dolia,* in addition to amphoras. One of the ovens was circular with a central passageway and lateral supporting walls; the other was circular with a central supporting column. The pottery was active during the first century A.D.[142] Vélez Málaga yields a circular adobe oven with a combustion chamber having a central passageway and lateral walls. In the vicinity of the oven were discovered construction materials — small rectangular and rhomboidal bricks — and fragments of common ceramics presumably fired at the site.[143] The oven is situated between the Almachar and Iznate rivers — affluents of the Benamargosa — and stands in an area of fertile bottom land. The two aforementioned potteries were presumably serving a clientele that extended beyond their owners or tenants. Ovens firing common ceramics and construction materials in Málaga province also include those found at Bobadilla, at Campillos in the Cortijo de las Monjas, and at Peñarrubia.[144] The installations in these three places have so far not been the object of systematic excavation or publication.

To sum up so far: Archaeological survey and excavation of the 1980s and 1990s has revealed evidence of ceramics installations whose production of construction materials and common ceramics had a local and regional distribution, directed to either urban centers, rural sites, or both. Such is prominently the case of three pottery-producing installations in the municipal districts of Priego de Córdoba and Fuente Tójar. Most of these potteries had their inception in the Flavian era and functioned during the second century. It is a pity we are in no position to identify their proprietors, since the material produced in all three is unstamped. It is possible to say, however, that all or most of the potteries were somehow dependencies of rural habitations, whose owners or tenants were therefore in a position to derive much or most of their income from the products of the workshops. It is appropriate at this point to raise the possibility, as has one contemporary investigator, that Baetican decurionals frequently exploited clay beds on their properties to supply urban building projects.[145] This putative activity would be in line with senatorial and equestrian landowners profiting from brick production on their properties in the environs of Rome. It is to be hoped that someday, further archaeological work and prompt publication will make such a link in Baetica patent.

It is certain that *terra sigillata* was produced in at least seven centers in Baetica during the Principate. During reconditioning work of the patio of a church in Alameda (Málaga province), fragments of *sigillata* came to light that display sure signs of being wasters from a pottery at the site.[146] The fragments of decorated and undecorated *sigillata* present deformations associated with a too-rapid contraction of the clays and imperfections in the glaze due to misfiring. The chronology of the production is hard to pin down, but a late Claudian-Neronian inception seems plausible. Red-slip fineware also seems to have been produced at the *oppidum ignotum* situated near Teba (Málaga province). The aptly named "La Fábrica" next to the Cortijo del Tajo seems to have been the site of *sigillata* manufacture, in addition to common ceramics for cooking and service. The site yields both undecorated and decorated forms. It also produces fragments of molds, as well as one stamp—on an unspecified form—that reads OF P(   ).[147] Both plain and decorated *sigillata,* in addition to common ceramics, began to be produced at Singili(a?) Barba at some point during the second half of the first century A.D.[148] The manufacture of *sigillata* ceased relatively early at this site (early second century), possibly as a result of the arrival in quantity of cheaper African finewares. To date, the names of only two proprietors or potters stand on record from Singili(a?), namely a certain L.M.F. and TITVS OPPIVS. The latter is known at Isturgi, and it is possible either that he set up a small branch workshop at Singili(a?) or that he sold molds to be produced bearing his name by an independent potter. *Sigillata* was produced at Anticaria, located 7 kilometers to the east of Singili(a?) Barba. Excavations of Roman baths at Antequera revealed the remains of *sigillata* used as fill, associated with late Roman construction, in a drainage ramp outside the western wall of the large *frigidarium*. The lot of over 200 fragments evidently came from a dump associated with the pottery production in the environs of the baths. The material included seven mold fragments, as well as decorated and undecorated forms. The atelier producing *sigillata* at Anticaria was active during the second half of the first century A.D.[149]

The *sigillata* produced in the modern province of Málaga enjoyed a distribution that went beyond the towns and territories in which the finewares-producing potteries were situated. The ceramics traveled beyond the depression of Antequera, reaching the campiñas of Córdoba and Sevilla and even as far as the Mediterranean coast, where red-slip ware from Anticaria has been identified in the Roman villa of Sabinilla (Benalmádena, Málaga province).[150] The system of roads that united Corduba and Castulo with Malaca facilitated the overland distribution of *sigillata* ware. Anticaria was a particularly important junction where the roads from Astigi and Corduba converged and through which ran the west-east running roads from Acinippo and Arunda that led to Iliberri. *Sigillata* was produced in the environs of Iliberri at Cartuja, though apparently in smaller quantity compared to the common ceramics produced there.[151] The remains of a second center of *sigillata* production at Iliberri have come to light in the Albaicín district of the town.[152] Isturgi (Andújar) was the most substantial place of *sigillata* production in Baetica during the Principate, at a site called Los Villares, immediately to the east of the town on the north bank of the Baetis. The red-slip ware produced there shows the greatest variety of forms and the greatest geographical spread, reaching throughout Baetica, into Lusitania and Tarraconensis, and even into western North Africa. Much of the output of Isturgi's workshops was signed, but only, save for a few cases, with the bare initials of the proprietors and/or *officinatores*, making it impossible to connect any of the names on the fineware with those found in the epigraphy of that town.[153] The widespread diffusion of locally and externally produced *sigillata* fineware suggests the existence of a sophisticated Baetican clientele, as well as the intersection of consumers whose incomes were adequate for the mass purchase of these finewares and economies of scale in the production of the ceramics themselves, which reduced their unit price to the point where they became mass-market items. And just as real is the cultural revolution, of sorts, that the widespread manufacture and consumption of red-slip finewares in Baetica represents. For it is precisely at the end of the Julio-Claudian period and the beginning of the Flavian era that the manufacture and use of painted Iberian-style ceramics vanishes completely in the province.

Price, finally, has argued that several early imperial blown vessel forms concentrated in Baetica and southern Lusitania may reflect the presence of a glassmaking center in southern Iberia, active in the late first and early second centuries A.D.[154] The basis of the inference is both the concentration of certain forms in these areas and peculiarities of design. Curchin has suggested that the manufacture of glass in Baetica may have been in the control of local elites—(by which he means freeborn ones);[155] but it is difficult to envisage this activity as providing for more than a relatively constricted circle of persons or families. No certain published or unpublished glass workshop has to date come to light in southern Spain, although one is alleged to have existed at the Venta del Carmen pottery in the Bay of Algeciras.[156] The name of at least one manufacturer of likely Spanish glass is known—a certain AUG(   ), whose name is stamped on the bottom of two *unguentarii* from La Peña de la Sal (ARVA) and one from Alcolea del Río (CANANIA).[157]

The circle of owners or leaseholders of pottery-producing installations in Baetica probably included both ex-slaves and the freeborn. The ceramics are not, unfortunately, eloquent on this point. The abbreviated *tria nomina* that appear on *sigillata* produced at Isturgi and elsewhere in Baetica no doubt refer frequently to freeborn, municipal elites and members of the middle stratum. An analogous situation obtained in the production and commercialization of red-slip finewares produced in the environs of Tritium Magallum (Tricio) in the Ebro river valley. There it is possible to identify the freeborn members of an elite family of the *gens* Mamilia who owned or leased the means to produce *sigillata*—their activity may extend throughout much of the second century A.D.[158] In Baetica, there is

"P(ublius) Rocius Cleant(h)us Iponobensis," an *originarius* of Iponoba, whose name appears stamped on a *dolium* fragment from the environs of that Flavian *municipium*.[159] Cleant(h)us was a freedman, to judge from his Greek cognomen, and his appearance in the *dolium* stamp suggests that he was the proprietor of the unidentified workshop producing utilitarian ceramics in the environs of Iponoba.

QUARRIES

Quarries must have been a substantial source of wealth and economic activity in Baetica. Numerous quarries have been identified in the *conventus Astigitanus, Gaditanus,* and *Hispalensis.* Igabrum (Cabra, Córdoba province) stands out due to the exploitation and commerce in its vicinity of so-called mármol rojo de Cabra.[160] The stone from the Sierra de Cabra is not marble, strictly speaking, but a limestone capable of a high polish and displaying a characteristic reddish-pink color. The stone found widespread use from the Flavian period onward for epigraphic monuments: it shows up in Igabrum, Iponoba, Cisimbrium, Ipsca (Cortijo bajo de Iscar, Baena), Corduba, Anticaria, Priego (ancient name unknown), and Lucena (ancient name unknown). Sculpture using the stone has been found in Córdoba, Nueva Carteya, Puente Genil, and Lucena. The stone also found use for columns, such as at the villa Fuente de las Piedras at Cabra and at the Cortijo de Iscar, and for millstones. Who owned and exploited the valuable sources of this stone? Although direct evidence is lacking, Segura Arista suggests that the quarries in the vicinity of Igabrum were municipally owned, and perhaps were leased, in part, to private interests.

Large-grained white marble from the Sierra de Mijas and the eastern part of the Sierra Blanca in Málaga province was used from the Tiberio-Claudian period, and particularly from the Flavian period on, in architectonic elements, sculpture, and inscriptions in Cartima, Malaca, Suel, Barbesula(?), Alhaurín el Grande, Singili(a?) Barba, Benalmádena-Costa (villa de Erasa), Lacippo (despoblado de Alechipe), Teba, Caviclum (Torrox-Costa), and Nescania (Cortijo de Escaña, Valle de Abdalajís), until the third century.[161] The quarries may have been in the possession of a neighboring city—such as Suel or Cartima—which leased them out to individuals. Canto, on the other hand, holds that the family of the Fabii exploited the limestone quarries of the Sierra de Mijas, and principally those of the Sierra de Antequera, in their capacity as *occupatores,* and that they leased the rights to the quarries from the senate. She bases her conclusions largely on an inscription from Nescania of approximately mid-second-century A.D. date in which a certain Fabia Restituta is recorded as giving cash handouts to the decurions of Nescania, and 10 *denarii* to each of the *servi stationarii*. The latter group she interprets as slave laborers in the local quarries operated by Restituta and family.[162] It does remain possible to argue, however, that the *servi stationarii* were owned by Nescania and staffed a *statio* of the public post.[163]

The *Pagus Marmorarius* near modern Almadén de la Plata, situated 55 kilometers north-northeast of Sevilla, was the scene of marble-quarrying during the early Principate.[164] The quarries are located in the Sierra de los Covachos. The idea that the quarries were under imperial control remains unsubstantiated, and derives, in part, from the existence at Italica of a *statio serrariorum Augustorum,* or workshop of marble-working and distribution under imperial control.[165]

It is worth noting, finally, that Baetican marble does not seem to have been exported outside the province in any quantity.[166]

MINING

By the later first century A.D., an indeterminate number of mines were owned and operated by the *fiscus.* The exploitation of these mines in Hispania was both direct and indirect. The latter method is best known by the mines at Vipasca in neighboring Lusitania, in which small-scale concessionaires contracted directly with the *fiscus* through imperial procurators.[167] A similar regime must have existed at the mines of the Río Tinto region in western Baetica.[168] The evidence of the *Saintes-Maries-de-la-Mer 1* wreck shows in a clear fashion the state ownership of mines by the Flavian period.[169] This wreck, likely of the Flavian era, yielded ninety-nine lead ingots produced, in part, by a certain L. Flavius Verucla, who evidently leased a silver-lead mine or mines from the *fiscus,* from the fact that most of the ingots found in the wreck are counterstamped IMP CAES. Verucla's cognomen points to his indigenous origins, according to Long and Domergue, who postulate that Verucla received Roman citizenship as a result of the Flavian concession of the *ius Latii* to Hispania. The matter is not certain. Nevertheless, the ingots of the wreck show that Verucla was a concessionaire of the *fiscus.* Fifteen of the ingots are also cold-stamped with the name of a certain EROS, who, it is surmised, was a *socius* of Verucla. The fact that only eight ingots bear the molded name of L. Flavius Verucla prompts the hypothesis that Verucla, faced with a shortage of ingots from his own stock, purchased at least ninety-one ingots from other producers in order to meet the imperially required rent for his leased mine(s). Some small-scale mines and mining operations, however, may have remained in private hands after c. A.D. 70. In this category might belong a lead ingot of the second half of the first century A.D. from the mine "Terreras" in the vicinity of Alcaracejos (Córdoba province) and stamped C.P.T.T. CAENICORUM. The ingot was the product of four members of the Caenici, who, it is alleged, owned their own mine(s) in the Sierra Morena during this period.[170]

ANIMAL HUSBANDRY

A number of sites in Baetica display evidence of large-scale animal husbandry in the Julio-Claudian and Flavian periods. El Arenoso, for example, is a third-order(?) site in the municipal district of Dos Hermanas, and is roughly 9 kilometers southwest of Orippo.[171] The site is distinguished by a roughly circular cavity 30 meters in diameter and 3 to 4 meters deep. The cavity corresponds to a *stercilinum,* a type of agricultural fixture described by the Gaditanus Columella (1.6.21–22). Columella writes that it is desirable for a *possessor* to have two manure pits, one for keeping fresh manure for a year, and the other from which old manure is to be extracted. They should be built in the manner of fishponds with sloping bottoms ("more piscinarum devexum leni clivo"). The detail about two pits seems more prescriptive than normative. Another site to reveal a *locum concavum* is Santa María de Medinilla I.[172] The place is located in the municipal district of Dos Hermanas, 6.25 kilometers south-southwest of Orippo, and is situated on a hill forming the western rim of the cañada, or transhumance path, through which the arroyo de El Hornillo runs. The site has a surface area of roughly 0.5 hectare, and at its center at the crest of the hill is a mound, off of which to the northwest is a *locum concavum* approximately 40 meters in diameter and roughly 4 meters deep. The site can be characterized as a first-order one from the presence of *sigillata,* common ceramics, superficial wall remains, and, most importantly, fragments of marble revetment plaques, which would have adorned the *pars urbana* of the settlement. Despite the recovery at the site of an *as* of Irippo of Augustan date, Escacena and Padilla suggest its Flavian inception.

To the southeast of the aforementioned sites ringing the *Lacus Ligustinus* are a number of first- through third-order rural establishments that, on circumstantial grounds, can be plausibly connected with animal husbandry. The sites are located in the so-called sierras sevillanas in the area of Montellano. They are located in a region that is not conspicuous for the richness of its soils, and the rural habitations do not have easy access to the main routes in Baetica. They are sites that sit astride modern, short-range transhumance routes linking essentially the lowland areas of the marismas with the higher elevations of the sierra. Conspicuous as likely centers of animal pasturage in antiquity are the rural establishments of Vega de Lopera, Palancar, El Bollo III, Haldúas, Ruchenilla, Loma Vélez, and Alhorín I and IV, situated in an area where animal pasturage has always played an important role.[173]

There is no explicit literary or epigraphical testimony for long-distance transhumance in Baetica in the form of *calles publici*.[174] Nevertheless, indirect evidence of transhumance may exist in the form of an altar inscribed on two faces from Baños de Sierra Elvira, near Atarfe in Granada province.[175] One face of the altar gives the titulature of Domitian, while the other inscribed face of this badly damaged stone reads "– – –]NIS.C.P." A number of possible expansions of the partly abbreviated inscription have been offered, including "finis Coloniae Publicae," "finis Callis Publici," and "finis Campo Publico." On balance, the reading "finis Callis Publici" may be the preferable one. The stone could possibly have functioned as a marker separating imperial property and a *callis;* on this interpretation, the stone would have been set up in order to ward off incursions onto the imperial property by the herds and their tenders.[176] In support of the reading "finis Callis Publici," it may be worth noting the presence, near Baños de Sierra Elvira, of a stretch of an early modern and modern royal transhumance route, running in a northwest-to-southeast direction from Pinos Puente to Baños and in an easterly direction from Baños to Albolote.

There may be another kind of indirect archaeological evidence for widespread animal husbandry and possible transhumance in Baetica, namely surface scatters of common ceramics, bricks, *tegulae,* and other simple constructive elements placed well away from first- or second-order sites but in an obvious relation with them. These remains could, in some instances, correspond to corrals, enclosures, stables, and other kinds of structure and/or shelter associable with either stationary animal husbandry or transhumance. It may be plausible to identify these kinds of scatter in Ponsich's survey areas of Alcalá del Río, Lora del Río, and Sanlúcar de Barrameda.[177] Sánchez-Corriendo's suggestion that the sites at Puerto Hostal Blanco and Ventorro de Juanillín in the municipal district of Guillena, situated astride the Roman(?) road leading from Guillena to Badajoz, actually constituted corrals and rest stations for transhumant herds rather than farms, strictly speaking, is the kind of tantalizing suggestion that urgently requires verification through the meticulous excavation of sites, which may turn out, after all, to be Roman-era farms in which pasturage was a minimal or even a nonexistent component.[178] Ponsich, to be certain, on several occasions, has alleged the existence of long-distance transhumance routes linking the marismas south of Hispalis with the Sierra Morena.[179] He envisages transhumant herds moving both west and east of the Guadalquivir, and having as their ultimate summer destination the Sierra Morena in the area of Setefilla, north of Lora del Río. The main problem with Ponsich's argument is the chronology of the archaeological evidence, consisting mainly of proto-historic orientalizing and Iberian tombs marking the way. The evidence for long-distance transhumance in this part of Baetica during the Roman era remains absent.

Finally, the scale of animal husbandry and pasturage in Baetica during the high Principate is hinted at in a rescript of Hadrian, of uncertain date, addressed to the provincial council of Baetica. The council had sought guidance from the emperor on punishing rustling. The emperor essentially replied that the severity of punishment depends on the gravity and frequency of the rustling.[180] The sources, unfortunately, do not specify the kinds of animal involved. It seems that Baetican elites and members of the provincial middle stratum profited from animal husbandry in ways both legitimate and nefarious.

CHAPTER FIVE

✖

The Flavian Impact:
An Analysis

The purpose of this chapter is to put the abundant data set out in the previous sections into a larger perspective. Vespasian promulgated the Latin right throughout the Spanish provinces in 73–74, and from that period on, scores of communities in Baetica became *municipia* in name and provisionally in function.[1] Scholarship is unanimous in positing as the essential component of the *ius Latii* the ability of local elites to become Roman citizens through the holding of a civic magistracy. The Flavian municipalization of Baetica and elsewhere also enhanced the importance of local town councils, from the ranks of which magistrates were elected.[2] Furthermore, chapters 82–83 of the Lex Irnitana refer clearly to the rural installations and property of *privati* in the territory of that Flavian *municipium*. The essential argument is this: these *privati* were mainly local elites and middle-stratum persons at Irni and elsewhere throughout Baetica.

The new rural foundations in the *conventus Astigitanus* and elsewhere, aside from sharing a similar chronology, are of generally uniform size, employ the same materials and building techniques, and exhibit unassuming residential space and adornment in the Flavian period. But these new rural dwellings were no simple peasant cottages, as is shown by, for example, the villa "El Ruedo" (Almedinilla, Córdoba province). In its earliest, Flavian phase, it consisted of a series of rooms surrounding a patio, with painted stucco walls, brick floors, and a brick-lined drainage canal.[3] It is not until the second century that some rural dwellings begin to be embellished with mosaics, and to exhibit clearly differentiated residential and work spaces. The initial period of the first-order site "Casa del Mitra," situated 2.2 kilometers northwest of Cabra (ancient Igabrum), dates to the Flavian era, when the structure possessed a single story and consisted of a series of rooms surrounding a central, colonnaded patio. In the central portion of the patio, and open to the air, was a basin supplied with water from a lead pipe leading from the west side of the structure. At some point in the later Empire—probably in the later third century—the patio and rooms on the south and east sides were substantially modified. In these rooms were laid four geometric mosaics, which, on stylistic grounds, can be generally dated to the third and fourth centuries A.D.[4]

A certain prosperity is similarly apparent in "maisons fortes," the habitation of which continues into the Flavian period. A case in point is the pre-Flavian *turris* of possibly late Republican construction at the Cerro del Espino (Torredelcampo), 2.5 kilometers to the west-northwest of Atalayuelas. During the evidently more expansive economic conditions of the Flavian period, it underwent two successive alterations, which saw an outer fortification circuit leveled to form a platform for rooms. Rooms and work areas also spilled out beyond the central tower in the Flavian era. Structures and features associated with this second building phase include two basins lined with waterproof cement, stucco painted in red, black, and yellow, Spanish *sigillata,* terracotta lamps from Isturgi, thin-walled ceramics, coarseware, *dolia,* and roof tiles. Native construction techniques are also apparent in the Flavian rebuilding of what was evidently a large farmstead, such as the use of adobe walls and earthen floors or pavements consisting simply of closely set pebbles.[5]

The economic regime in most areas of the *conventus Astigitanus* affected by expanded settlement seems to have been one of mixed farming and pastoralism. Archaeological and epigraphical evidence suggests that grain, olives, and the vine were cultivated, sometimes in combination. It is a virtual certainty that many areas of the *conventus* were tied, in some way, to olive-oil exports to Rome and the army. The regions most profoundly affected by the intensification in rural settlement were, for the most part, outside the main region devoted to the production and export of olive oil, which extended from Hispalis to Astigi to Corduba and was closely tied to the Guadalquivir and lower Genil rivers. Indeed, many of the new Flavian farmsteads were situated in marginal upland areas of the *conventus* and elsewhere.

A sure sign of agricultural intensification in these areas is the proliferation of hydraulic cisterns in rural sites, such as are revealed in the municipal districts of Baena and Castro del Río.[6] It may seem a banal point, but one worth underscoring all the same, that similar cisterns simply are not a feature, so far as this author knows, of pre-Roman or late Iberian settlements in the future area of Baetica. But there is abundant evidence for olive-oil production in these areas, as explained in Chapter Three. In a vivid case, three unexcavated Roman rural sites lie close to each other to the southeast of the Laguna de Fuente Piedra in the northwest portion of Málaga province.[7] It is evident from the ceramics evidence that all three sites—La Torquilla, El Torquillo, and Los Corrales—have a Flavian inception. All three are likely first-order sites, and one of them, Los Corrales, produces evidence of an oilery in the form of two quadrangular stones used to anchor the *arbores* of an oil press. Some of this oil production may well have been exported. The new rural settlements also would have owed their inception and prosperity to the demand for agricultural commodities and goods generated by the towns of the *conventus Astigitanus,* as well as those located outside the *conventus* in the valley of the Guadalquivir. Furthermore, the new foundations were integrated into the Roman economy by market exchanges—the ubiquity of imported finewares alone exemplifies this point[8]—and not simply by the claims of rents and taxes.

"Market exchanges" means in this discussion the coming together in urban and rural settings of the *conventus Astigitanus* and elsewhere of persons "with goods to sell or money for purchases irrespective of their social relationships," following the definition of Greene.[9] The areas under consideration were certainly monetized, as the discovery of coins in rural and urban locations shows; and to the use of money in the form of coin we may add the use of chits, notes of exchange, and credit.[10] The wholesale modern ransacking of rural sites, especially by amateur archaeologists armed with metal detectors, has ensured the impossibility of generating studies of local coinage circulation patterns on the basis of casual coin loss, but controlled excavations do afford a glimpse at the variety and volume of coinage in use in Baetica during the Principate. Emergency excavations of a portion of the imperial-era necropolis at Gades revealed incineration and mixed incineration and inhumation tombs of the Julio-Claudian and Flavian and later periods, respectively.[11] The incineration burials of the Julio-Claudian era were endowed with mostly robbed-out grave goods, including coins — mainly Gaditane emissions and *asses*, representing local imitations of the period A.D. 45–54. All of the coins had been demonetized by being gouged with a sharp object on their obverses or reverses before deposition as part of the grave goods. These coins represent over 40 percent of the just over 100 coins recovered from an excavated area of 500 square meters. The second major group of coins consists of *asses* and *quadrantes* of the reigns of Vespasian and Domitian, with a preponderance of coins from the reign of the latter emperor. These coins show no evidence of demonetization through their defacement.[12]

It is a reasonable assumption, moreover, that Vespasian augmented the Spanish tribute.[13] Elites and proto-elites in both newly promoted Flavian *municipia* and the older Caesarian or Augustan colonies and *municipia* not exempt from tribute confronted this added fiscal burden. At the same time, elites and would-be elites in the new *municipia* of Baetica faced additional financial pressures. On top of meeting the property qualification for entrance to the *ordo* and holding magistracies, decurions and magistrates would have had to make certain out-of-pocket expenditures as part of their routine duties. New Roman citizens *per honorem*, that is, those who had obtained the Roman franchise through the tenure of a local magistracy, faced the necessity of paying indirect taxes in the form of the *vicesima hereditatium* (5 percent inheritance tax) and *vicesima libertatis* (5 percent manumission tax).[14] The establishment, possibly during the reign of Vespasian, of the cult of the divinized emperors at a province-wide level entailed added expenditures for local elites.[15]

The archaeological and epigraphical record displays other kinds of increased expenditure by local elites and proto-elites in the Flavian period and later. Local elites in newly municipalized communities began to employ marble for inscribed monuments, for sculpture, and as a building material, instead of less costly limestone or granite. The Flavian era also saw an upsurge in local benefactions — part of them building projects — as the more well-to-do reinforced their claims to pre-eminence.[16] Melchor notes that building euergetism reached its peak during the Flavian epoch, and that the proportion of all datable building benefactions is greatest in this period.[17] And worth emphasis is the fact that acts of euergetism — whether *ob honorem* or otherwise—show a remarkable uniformity in terms of their frequency throughout the four *conventus* of the province during the Flavian period that demonstrates a rapid and widespread assimilation of Greco-Roman values on the part both of elites within local *ordines decurionum* and of those remaining aloof from service as local councilors and magistrates.[18] For the latter, local benefactions would have been repaid not in the coin of local officeholding or decurional status, but in the currency of social prestige and posthumous recognition. Montenegro certainly underscores the contemporary financial difficulties of Flavian towns deriving from substantial outlays devoted to building projects, and the role of private initiative therefore will have increased in importance from the relatively shaky nature of public finances.[19] The concern of the Saborenses, as evidenced by their petition of A.D. 77 to Vespasian, to maintain, if not augment, their local revenues on the eve of the relocation of their *oppidum* to the plain below should be seen in this light.[20] Munigua's contemporary indebtedness to the tax collector Servilius Pollio may have derived from local building projects, including a monumental sanctuary in the center of that town's *oppidum*.[21] On a more negative note, Baetica was probably subject to sporadic *indictiones,* or supplementary requisitions of products-in-kind, under Domitian.[22]

All in all, the cumulative cash and other outlays of local elites in the *conventus Astigitanus* and elsewhere during the Flavian era can be reckoned as nothing less than appreciable. From where else would their income derive if not from agricultural interests and activities, supplemented or complemented by quarrying, pottery production, mining, involvement in public contracts, leasing of productive public lands or buildings, rent or sale of urban or rural possessions, animal husbandry, money-lending, or involvement with money-changers?[23] The new rural settlements of the Flavian era may be best understood, therefore, as primarily the creations of decurions, local magistrates, aspirants to office and the *ordo* (including freedmen through their sons), and *honesti* outside the *ordo,* whose numbers include individuals whose census rating debarred them from the *ordo* but who staffed municipal juries. It is clear that these groups channeled much of their wealth into socially as well as politically competitive expenditure, on top of meeting the tax demands of the Roman state. It is also clear that decisions regarding investment in intensified agricultural production would have been made in the secure knowledge of the large scale and predictability of external demand for the products of their *fundi.* A prop of this book is the conviction that much Baetican grain and, more importantly, olive oil, fish products, and wine were purchased by the state or by private *merca- tores* for distribution and sale outside Hispania. State and private purchase of grain, oil, and other staples and commodities would have represented the principal means by which cash and credits entered Baetica in the Julio-Claudian and later periods. The human agents of this monetization of the province will have included the certain and possible *diffusores olearii* M. Cassius Sempronianus, M. Iulius Hermesianus, and P. Mussidius Sempro-nianus, attested at Canania(?), Astigi, and Irni, respectively.[24]

Changes in the overall settlement pattern of the *conventus Astigitanus* and elsewhere in Baetica are not the only reflection of the responses of elites and proto-elites in the province to the new demands imposed on them dur-ing the Flavian era and later. The intensification of agricultural production during the Flavian era and an increasing emphasis on olive oil in the urban and rural economy also emerge in the archaeological record of individual sites in the province not already mentioned in the section above on olive-oil production. At least a portion of the hilltop at Aratispi was given over in the Flavian era to an oilery of substantial dimensions. The oilery, with an inception in the later first century, is situated on the southern edge of the Cerro de Cauche el Viejo.[25] The oilery was built into partially recon-structed Ibero-Roman habitations. The site seems to have been destroyed by fire in the second half of the second century A.D. I identify the cause of this destruction below. The area around the oilery is strewn with fragments of Dressel 20 amphoras, one of which bears the mark BELVRS, which is as-sociable with a *figlina* in the vicinity of Palma del Río. Perdiguero empha-sizes the solid construction of the oilery's pavement and suggests that the press beam would have been over 6 meters in length. The excavator is right, in my judgment, to suggest that the oil produced by this installation was ex-ported, and he raises the interesting possibility that the Dressel 20 am-phoras were transported empty to this place from the middle Guadalquivir valley. The installation of an oilery in the very urban center of Aratispi re-flects both the desire and the need to raise revenues, whether public or pri-vate, in this *municipium* during the Flavian epoch.

The first-order site Cuesta del Espino in the municipal territory of mod-ern Posadas in Córdoba province will serve as an illustration of the intensi-fication of production in a rural context within the *conventus Cordubensis*.[26] The site is located 2.3 kilometers west of Posadas on the north bank of the Guadalquivir River. In antiquity, it is likely that Cuesta del Espino lay on or very near the banks of the Baetis in the *territorium* of Detumo. The site was subject to emergency excavations in the late 1980s. The excavations revealed that the rural establishment at Cuesta del Espino falls into three phases. Phase one is represented by a structure of dressed rectangular stones with a pavement composed of *opus latericium,* in addition to certain other wall remains. The chronology of the phase one vestiges falls within the first half of the first century A.D. At some point during the second half of the first century A.D.—most likely at the beginning of the Flavian period, from the near-total absence of Italian and Gallic *sigillata* from the site—the structures described above were leveled and covered by a layer of earth as a means of forming a flat surface for new construction, corresponding to phase two of the site.[27] The area was subsequently paved with *opus signinum,* and there was built a large hallway with trenchlike projections on either side into which were set large *dolia.* This hallway formed part of a storage area whose walls even were lined with *opus signinum.* The *dolia* were clearly designed for the storage of olive oil. Excavations revealed numerous Dressel 20 amphora fragments, one of which bears the stamp AGRICOLAE, a *figlina* proprietor(?) and/or amphora producer known elsewhere. Márquez Moreno also discovered a well-preserved clay funnel used to fill the oil amphoras at the site itself.[28] It is important to emphasize that the excavated area of this first-order site, corresponding to the *pars rustica,* was devoted to olive-oil production even before c. A.D. 50–70. Márquez Moreno suggests that the original structure paved in *opus latericium,* incorporating a small outlet at its base, was designed to store olives, which by their weight produced oil that was drained off through the small opening. The crucial point here is that the scale most likely of the production, and certainly of the facilities, for the storage of oil were significantly expanded in the construction of the second, probably Flavian, phase. Phase three is represented by the limestone base of a column that was set above the level of the previous storage area. At some point during the second century, the storage area was leveled and sealed with a cap of earth, just as in the transition from the first to the second phase. It appears that this portion of the villa establishment was given over to purely residential purposes—of which the column base is the sole remaining testimony—from a utilitarian function in the course of this century. Because of the removal of archaeological layers in post-antique and modern agricultural activity around the site, all other traces of this first-order villa establishment have disappeared. There are, however, remains of *opus caementicium* basin(s) at the site that may have been used for grain storage from the absence of quarter-round interior base moldings. The last-mentioned feature would be expected in the case of a water basin, according to Márquez Moreno.

In parallel with the increased production of olive oil throughout the province during the Flavian epoch was an increase in the number of installations devoted to the manufacture and firing of oil-bearing amphoras. For instance, it is worth highlighting the three ovens detected by geomagnetic survey and sondages at Arva in 1991.[29] All three ovens correspond to type Ia of Cuomo di Caprio, that is, circular structures with a central pillar supporting the floor of the firing chamber. The diameter of one of the kilns of sondage II varies between 5 and 5.20 meters, which is a large dimension indeed. Amphora remains from the first oven of sondage I suggest a construction date in the Flavian or Trajanic eras. All three ovens, probably contemporaneous, are situated between the monumental center of Arva and the Baetis.

So far, much of the discussion has centered on changes in the valley of the Guadalquivir and the penibético. The reason is simple: it is in this region that the majority of surface surveys and excavations have taken place. Nevertheless, the changes that are canvassed in this study occurred on a province-wide scale. An exceptional glimpse at the effects of the Flavian municipalization of Baetica in the more thinly urbanized northern part of the province — specifically in the northern portion of the *conventus Cordubensis*— can be seen in the construction of a Roman farmstead and associated dam at Torretejada in the municipal district of Belalcázar (Córdoba province).[30] The site, resting at an altitude of 500 meters, is located one kilometer north of Casas de Torretejada. The dam collected water from the arroyo de Torretejada, a tributary of the río Guadamatilla, an affluent of the Zújar.[31] The following discussion of the site and its context derives from the observations of Romero Corral. The dam is 38 meters long and reaches a maximum height of 2.5 meters; the structure is constructed of *opus caementicium*. The dam and farmstead are situated in an area traditionally devoted to growing cereals and cultivating orchards. Next to the villa are two cisterns lined with *opus signinum*. In geological terms, the site is located on the batholith of "Los Pedroches." The lithic base on which the dam is constructed is composed of carbonaceous culm, formed of black and dark gray shale mixed with gravel roughly one centimeter wide. The dam is located next to a zone of contact between the shale and the igneous rock of the granite batholith. The *alveus* or reservoir of the dam lay above the granite, which is impermeable. This location allowed the dam to collect water immediately before the point of generalized permeability through the shale. The soil of the area is sandy, with a low content of organic materials, and slightly acidic. The soils of "Los Pedroches" are marked by an advanced state of decomposition of the underlying granite, resulting in a soil that is easy to work, and that is, by the standards of the soils of the northern part of the province of Córdoba, relatively fertile. The productivity of the soil increases today, as obviously it did in antiquity, through irrigation. The farmstead is distant from the two main Roman north-south axes of communication, namely the *Via Corduba-Sisapo* to the east and the *Via Corduba-Emerita* to the west.

The link between the site and the wider world seems to have been provided by a secondary road, running west-east, 2 kilometers to the south of Torretejada. This road joined the two larger aforementioned *viae*.[32] To the south of this secondary road, and at a distance from the road roughly equal to that which separates Torretejada from it, are two more Roman farmsteads whose chronology resembles that of the establishment at Torretejada, that is, from the second half of the first century through the third century A.D. The farmstead at Torretejada is situated relatively close to the putative *oppidum* of Baedro. Baedro evidently received the Latin right and municipal status in the Flavian period, and it is to this same epoch that the farmstead at Torretejada — or at least the construction of the dam — probably dates.[33] The municipal center of Baedro may have received the surplus production of the rural estate centered at Torretejada. Other, multiple points of demand for the products of the farm may be conjectured to be the various mining installations and communities in this portion of the Sierra Morena. The likely focus on cereals-growing by this rural installation and others in the region is underscored by the recovery in various parts of this portion of Baetica of an astonishing range of well-preserved agricultural implements — ninety-two in all — on display in the local museum at Torrecampo (Córdoba), a place that in antiquity lay just to the southeast of Solia (Majadalaiglesia).[34] The tools point to the working of soil for a variety of activities, including arboriculture, viticulture, and cereals cultivation. All of this varied activity in the Baetican countryside during the Flavian period and later is best attributed to local elites and middle-stratum persons. The case has been made above that the countryside was increasingly their place of principal residence in this and subsequent periods. But it is possible to refine this picture of rural drift. To that end, the discussion now turns to further considerations of the question of where elites and sub-elites lived in Baetica from c. A.D. 70 onward.

�֍

We can link the names of beneficiaries of external and internal demand for Baetican staples with specific rural establishments in the first two centuries A.D. It is possible thus to lodge polite disagreement with commentators when they write that we do not know the names of Baetican villa owners during the Principate.[35] Inscribed herms provide the best evidence of the names and identities of Baetican villa owners. The first-order site Cortijo de Chirino, situated between the Cortijo "El Sotillo" and the Arroyo del Salado in the municipal district of Ecija, yields a herm of possible mid-first century A.D. date, which is dedicated "Caciae n(ostrae)" by a certain "L(ucius) Sempronius Su[avi]s."[36] Cacia was evidently the *domina* of this rural establishment, which reveals a head of a Bacchus statue, in addition to *tegulae,* bricks, and finewares. The Cortijo de Vieco, located 5.5 kilometers south of Cañete de las Torres, yields a herm inscribed "Rufo n(ostro)" and set up by "Princeps dispens(ator)."[37] This site, which corresponds to a rural establishment,[38] had as its *dominus* a certain Rufus around the middle of the first century A.D. The Cortijo de Consuegra, situated 2 kilometers northeast of Lantejuela near the Cerro de la Camorra, produces a herm dedicated "Afrae n(ostrae)" by "Turpio l(ibertus)" and a certain "Vespicia," possibly a slave.[39] The *domina* Afra was honored through the herm in the first half of the second century A.D. The first-order site Los Castellones in the valley of the Guadalhorce near Campillos in Málaga province yields a herm of the second half of the first or first half of the second century inscribed "Ti(berio) Sempronio C(ai) f(ilio) Prisco" by an unknown dedicant.[40] The freeborn Priscus was obviously the *dominus* of this substantial rural establishment, whose remains include walls, a cistern, at least one Tuscan-order capital, *laterculi,* dressed stones, *tegulae, sigillata,* common ceramics, the remains of a terracotta lamp, and coins.[41] There is also a villa in the vicinity of Bobadilla in Málaga province that produced mosaics and a herm that is inscribed "C(aio) Sempronio Gal(eria tribu) Pulverino," set up by a certain "Arvero Nigri f(ilius)." As in the case of the preceding herms, it seems certain that we have here attested the *dominus* of the first-order site in the vicinity of Bobadilla by the name of Caius Sempronius Pulverinus, a Roman citizen enrolled in the Galeria tribe, who is recorded in an inscription of the first half of the second century A.D.[42]

In the first half of the twentieth century, the first-order villa "La Estación" at Antequera yielded up the funerary stone of "Licinia Logas, Osquensis."[43] Licinia Logas was an *originarius* of neighboring Osqua (El Cerro del León or Huerta de Solana near Villanueva de la Concepción), and may very well have been the proprietor at some point during the second or early third centuries A.D. of this splendid suburban villa. It is likely, on any accounting, that from the Flavian period onward, the aforementioned persons, as well as other rural *possessores* and/or tenants, lived permanently on their *fundi*. At this juncture, it is apposite to mention the revelatory case of Obulco (Porcuna). In the San Benito section of the town, O. Arteaga has uncovered an extensive portion of the ancient city consisting of Roman peristyle houses, of triumviral-Augustan date, with access from broad, paved streets.[44] Commentators are at a loss to explain the gradual abandonment of these sumptuous structures from the late Julio-Claudian period through the end of the first century A.D.[45] The desertion of these structures surely reflects the growing preference of the local elites to live in rural *fundi* from the Flavian period on.

A closer examination of the *oppidum* at the Cerro Cabeza Baja (Encina Hermosa) in southwestern Jaén province suggests the same process at work as is discernible at Obulco during the later first century A.D.[46] A detailed description of the place is worthwhile at this point. The Cerro consists of an elongated meseta running in a northwest-to-southwest direction, with a maximum height of 810 meters. To the west and east it is bounded by the arroyos of Chiclana and Piedra, respectively, both tributaries of the right bank of the San Juan River. The Cerro sits in the middle reaches of the valley of the San Juan River, which flows west into the Guadajoz. The valley is bounded to the south by the Sierras de San Pedro and La Camuña, to the north by the Sierras Ahillos and La Grana, to the east by the Sierra Morenita and Marroquí, and is contained in the west by the Sierra Caniles, through which the San Juan flows. Erosional deposition today permits the plantation of orchards next to the river, while intermediate elevations (between 600 and 800 meters) are devoted to a mixed regime of olives and cereals. Elevations above 800 meters are marked by natural vegetation (encinas and monte bajo), exploited by herds of sheep and goat.

The maximum habitable area of the meseta is 9 hectares, with the major building remains situated on the upper part of the hill. The site has suffered from clandestine archaeological activity that has revealed, among other things, *tegulae, imbrices,* and various kinds of pavement, including *opus signinum* and *opus spicatum.* Furtive digs have also yielded an olive mill and a flat stone, measuring 1.4 by 0.8 meters, which served as a surface for mashing olives and extracting their pits. The initial phase of the *oppidum* is difficult to date, in part due to the unsatisfactory nature of the excavation reports. The meseta seems to have been encircled by a fortification wall and marked by a quadrangular construction in the southwest portion of the hill, composed of a surviving course of large blocks. Late Iberian pottery and Campanian ware found at the site leave open the possibility, according to the excavators, that the *oppidum* may have been settled initially as late as the second century B.C. Roman-style construction, including a thermal establishment, at the Cabeza Baja does seem to date from the Flavian era. This transformation of the *oppidum,* so reminiscent of contemporary changes elsewhere in Baetica, seems also to have been accompanied by a diminution of the inhabited area of the meseta to 2.5 hectares. The decrease in the inhabited space of the *oppidum* reflects the transformation of the meseta from an *oppidum* whose inhabitants exploited the surrounding—and generally empty—countryside, to a local market or central place serving as a primary exchange center for a more thickly settled countryside. We await a more comprehensive publication of the survey in the region immediately to the west of the Cabeza Baja undertaken by Montilla Pérez (1987). The survey suggests clearly the inception of Roman-style rural habitats only in the second half of the first century A.D. The likely enhanced role of the *oppidum* as a center of exchange in the Flavian and subsequent eras is patent through the discovery there in excavations of the 1980s of a series of rooms off of a porticoed street that the excavators dub *tabernae.* In cut A-2, the archaeologists found fragments of *dolia,* various forms of *sigillata,* terracotta lamps, bronze vessels, a terracotta figurine, and coins—both of silver and of base metal—in addition to various pruning and tree-cutting tools. It looks as though the local economy in Roman times was devoted, in part, to orchards, just as it is today. But that is not all. An antiquarian from nearby Alcalá la Real by the name of Fernando Montijano excavated in the late nineteenth century a structure at the top of the cerro 15 meters in length and 4.33 meters wide.[47] This structure, in turn, was divided into four rooms. Montijano discovered a great variety of utilitarian and nonutilitarian objects: black and white marble weights, some with bronze handles; a bronze uncial weight; door fittings; iron candelabra; and clay and metal measures.

The likely importance of the *oppidum* as a center of exchange is certainly underscored by the discovery there of the weights and measures. Many towns in Baetica during the Principate served as administrative and religious centers, with facilities for market exchange and some other activities, such as fulling. These towns served as political centers for a widely dispersed population. It is strange that scholars speak of Baetica as a heavily urbanized province when, upon closer examination, it is clear that most "towns" in the province by the late Flavian era were monumental settings for the deliberations of the local council and assembly, the pursuit of piety toward the gods and *domus Augusta,* and the provision of services, and only secondarily served as a place of residence.[48] The preceding observation holds for both towns in the valley of the Guadalquivir and those in the highlands of the Sierra Morena and the penibético, such as the *oppidum ignotum* at the Cabeza Baja. Scholars familiar with Arva, situated on the right bank of the Baetis in the middle Guadalquivir valley, characterize the urban center of the *municipium*—and other places like it that were raised to municipal rank by Vespasian—as restricted in surface area and serving primarily as the administrative center for a fundamentally rural population dispersed in villas and more modest establishments.[49] The first- through third-order sites that survey reveals in abundance in the *territoria* of Baetican *civitates* were, in the main, the property and residences of the better-off *plebs* and *honesti viri* and *honestae feminae. Honesti viri* and *honestae feminae* include, as a matter of course, those individuals whose census rating extended from the 5,000-sesterces minimum required for service as a local juror at Irni to the minimum necessary for service as a decurion or magistrate in many Baetican settings—most likely 20,000 to 25,000 sesterces, as posited by Le Roux.

The *territorium* of the *municipium Flavium*(?) *Obulculense* situated at La Monclova will illustrate the preceding point perfectly. Surface survey in the environs of Fuentes de Andalucía, undertaken by J. F. Fernández Caro (1985; 1992), revealed a minimum of seventy-four rural first- through third-order sites settled from c. A.D. 50 to at least the middle of the following century. Fernández Caro surveyed an area of roughly 215 square kilometers that falls in substantial or complete measure within the territory of Obulcula. But the area that he surveyed represents, at best, approximately 70 percent of the total surface area of roughly 300 square kilometers, corresponding to Obulcula's tributary territory. It is easily within the realm of possibility—on the principle of the underrepresentation of even intensive survey—that Obulcula's territory would reveal a greater number of Roman sites than revealed by Fernández Caro's survey for a total of a minimum of 125 rural sites.

What would have been the size of Obulcula's *ordo decurionum* during the Flavian era and subsequently? Probably not much more or less than sixty-three decurions—the figure that is precisely specified as the size of Irni's *ordo* in A.D. 91. It is inconceivable that Obulcula's approximately sixty-three de-curions, in addition to an unspecified number of nondecurional *iudices*—say, twenty, at least—are not identifiable as the *possessores* and/or tenant leaseholders of the hypothetical 125+ first- through third-order sites and as-sociated *fundi* that would have clustered in Obulcula's *territorium*. But the preceding crude estimation still means that close to half of the rural *fundi* could have been in the possession of or leased by freedmen, *honesti* out-side the *ordo*, and the *honestae feminae* who are virtually a given from the names of *possessores* and tenants of Dressel inscription delta in the Dressel 20 amphoras. We have to suppose that a significant proportion of the pop-ulation of Obulcula lived in its *ager* from the fact that the surface area of Obulcula, at 2.6 hectares, is negligible.[50] It is impossible to envisage that many more than several score of persons could have crowded together into the built-up, urban core of Obulcula's territory as permanent inhabi-tants, on the reasonable assumption that a portion of the *oppidum* was de-voted to public, open space. A comparison of Obulcula's surface area with some better-known Baetican towns is telling: Urso possesses a surface area of 115.5 hectares, Gades 81, Corduba 56, Astigi 40–50 hectares, and Siarum 10 hectares.[51]

What larger conclusion may be drawn, with all due caution, from the particular rural-urban split in settlement numbers and *oppidum* area at Obulcula? Is it possible to make inferences about the social structure of the population of the *municipium* centered at Obulcula from the survey data? The answer, in the judgment of this author, is affirmative. It is easily within the realm of possibility, on the basis of the foregoing discussion, to suppose that decurionals, *honestae feminae*, and *honesti* outside the *ordo* constituted a significant proportion—perhaps as much as 25 percent, or even more— of Obulcula's population, including slaves and freedmen.

Most of the preceding points would also apply to the *municipium igno-tum* centered at Alameda in Málaga province. Extensive survey there, rep-resenting literally a generation's effort in the identification and cataloging of Chalcolithic through medieval sites in its municipal district, yields a total of sixty-six Roman-era first- through third-order rural sites in an area of approximately 70 square kilometers.[52] Even so, the coverage represents only roughly half of the territory of the unknown *municipium* at Alameda. On the principle, therefore, of the undercount of sites, and on the basis of the limited coverage of an inventory based on sporadic extensive survey, it is reasonable to assume that the *territorium* of the *municipium ignotum* with its center at Alameda would have counted in the order of plus or minus 125 first- through third-order rural sites. The very same observations made above in connection with Obulcula, the size of its *ordo,* and the status and rank of the rural inhabitants/proprietors there may apply also *mutatis mutandis* to the population at Alameda. On the other hand, we are in no position to guess about the possible numerical relationship between those living in the *oppidum* at Alameda and those in its surrounding territory from the fact that the modern town lies atop the Roman one.

Does the situation of Obulcula describe the general urban-rural split in the population of Baetican towns and cities? Absolutely not. On a priori grounds alone, we must suppose that a large number of persons lived in the *oppida* or built-up portions of more substantial towns such as Hispalis, Urso, Gades, Corduba, and Astigi. A fragmentary honorary inscription of A.D. 147 proves that an unknown but significant number of people must have lived in Siarum's *oppidum,* with its surface area of 10 hectares. The relevant portion of the inscription records a cash donation to various components of the municipium's population in the following terms: "– – – – – – / plebeis singulis incolis viris et mulieribus intra muros habitantibus pra[ese]ntibus singulis X (denarios) [– – – – – –] / – – – – – –." The surviving portion of the inscription records a monetary donation of an indeterminate sum—probably 10 *denarii*—to each of the town's plebeians and 10 *denarii* to each of the male and female *incolae* or resident aliens of the town actually living within the walls of the *municipium.* The plebeians of the passage are *originarii* of Siarum and are set off from the *incolae* by an unexpressed conjunction such that the relevant clause should read "– – – – – – / plebeis singulis <et> incolis viris et mulieribus. . . ."[53]

On the other hand, the example of Obulcula is representative of a large number of communities in all portions of the province whose *oppida* housed only a small fraction of their population—or even none at all, as is possibly the case of Iponoba. Estimates of the surface area of this town vary from as low as one hectare to 4, with the figure of around 2.5 hectares representing the best-informed calculation.[54] More important still: the *oppidum* of Iponoba consisted essentially of an open, monumental area. It is hard to imagine any but a tiny handful of persons as living in the *oppidum* or town itself; on the other hand, unsystematic survey of the territory of Iponoba suggests a thickly settled countryside (Morena López 1990). Let us finally, in this connection, consider the question of El Laderón in Córdoba province. Stylow categorizes it as an *oppidum ignotum* and assigns it a *territorium*.[55] The possession of an *ager* or *territorium* in the context of Roman imperial Baetica means municipalization for a center such as El Laderón. Almagro-Gorbea gives the surface area of El Laderón as 0.9 hectares.[56] This means a priori that only a handful of persons can have lived in the *oppidum* of the putative *municipium* with its center at El Laderón.

It may be fruitful, at this point, to reflect more closely on municipal populations—in specific, local *honesti* and, a fortiori, *honestae,* who did not serve on local town councils. There is another dimension—a spatial one, as it were—to the existence of *honesti* outside the *ordo.* A close analysis of the *tituli picti* of the Dressel 20 oil-bearing amphoras suggests that the majority of *fundi* and associated *possessores* and/or tenants supplying the oil shipped to Rome and elsewhere were situated in the lowlands of the Baetis valley—more specifically, in the fluvially linked triangular area bounded by Hispalis to the west, Corduba to the east, and Astigi to the south. This study has examined one such site, namely the villa establishment at Cuesta del Espino in Córdoba province. This area was marked, above all, by relatively numerous *territoria,* each of which contained a relatively high proportion of cultivable land. In other words, the towns along the north bank of the Guadalquivir within this area, as well as the few towns south of the Baetis—but within this producing triangle—were sufficiently well-equipped in productive land proximate to the Baetis and its main tributary, the Singilis, to enable a considerable portion of their free population to acquire the means to enter the ranks of the non-politically active *honesti.* A large number of the persons named on the amphoras are therefore probably *originarii* of Hispalis, Italica, Ilipa Ilia, Axati, Naeva, Oducia, Munigua, Iporca, Canania, Arva, Celti, Carmo, Segovia(?) on the Singilis, Detumo, Obulcula, Segida Augurina, Astigi, Carbula, and Corduba. One *titulus pictus,* in fact, offers explicit indication of the *origo* within this area of a *possessor* devoted to the growing of the olive destined for conversion into oil for export. The *titulus pictus* was recovered in excavations during 1989 of the Monte Testaccio, the large dump of mostly Spanish amphoras southwest of the Aventine hill, undertaken by the Spanish School at Rome. Position delta of the *titulus* refers to the control district Astigi, bears the consular date corresponding to A.D. 161, and names in line 2 "Iuni Optati Arvesis." According to Rodríguez Almeida, "Arvesis" is the *origo* of the *possessor,* and the line may be read as "(oleum) Iuni Optati, Arvensis" or construed as "Iuni Optati Arvense (oleum)."[57] In the first instance, the *titulus* refers to oil of Iunius Optatus, who possesses as *origo* Arva; in the second instance, the *titulus* refers to Iunius Optatus, the producer of oil that emanates from Arva.

In short, there are good grounds for seeing the agriculturally rich and exporting *civitates* of the valley of the Guadalquivir and towns in the western portion of the *conventus Gaditanus* as those which tended to have the largest proportion of *honesti* outside the *ordo* and potential municipal jurors in their populations. And to these areas we can also add the *territorium* of Iliberri (Granada), which probably corresponds to a substantial portion of the extremely fertile and extensive Vega of Granada lying to the west of the ancient *municipium.* It should come as no surprise that Iliberri produces an appreciable complement of senators. That there were such persons in significant numbers in these lowland communities is virtually certain from the identity between many of the *negotiatores* attested in Dressel position beta of the amphoras—persons who enjoyed de facto and legal immunity from local *honores* and *munera*—and the proprietors, producers, or wholesale buyers whose names are attested in the form of initials, usually, in the stamps on the handles of these same containers. The identification of such persons will be a concern of the next chapter.

The older, Phoenician centers along the Atlantic and Mediterranean coasts allegedly reflect a different reality. López Castro makes the forceful argument that the slave-based economy of these cities from the last third of the second century B.C. onward gradually created substantial social and economic cleavages in the populations of Gades, Malaca Abdera, and Sexi.[58] In these cities, the population would have been dominated by a landowning elite also involved in *garum* production in or near the urban centers themselves—an elite that stood, in prestige, power, and income, well above the remnants of the freeborn population devoted to less remunerative, small-scale artisanship in the towns and other centers along the southern littoral of Baetica. But if López Castro and others are right to insist that Gades became a *municipium civium Romanorum* in 49 B.C., then the clear consequence is that a substantial number of Gades' *municipes* were relatively impoverished Roman citizens at the same time that the Roman citizenship was being offered as a plum to local elites elsewhere in the province. There must be something wrong, consequently, with the premise of a substantial, permanent cleavage in Gades' urban population, as envisaged by López Castro. A way out of this dilemma might be to suppose that a substantial number of Gades' *municipes* became prosperous precisely through sea-borne trade as middlemen, and not through the exploitation of rural *fundi*. A possible point in favor of the preceding assertion is the enumeration of 500 persons possessing the equestrian census in Gades in A.D. 14(?), as recorded by Strabo (3.5.3). On the other hand, Chic García makes the attractive suggestion that the mercantile aristocracy of Gades invested in agriculture in that part of the hinterland of Gades called "isla de Cartare." The "isla de Cartare" seems to have constituted a chunk of territory through which ran, in antiquity, a water connection between the Guadalquivir and Guadalete rivers. The "isla" may have been formed from the union of the two streams by the junction of the estuary of Asta and Nabrissa or, alternatively, to the south of Jerez de la Frontera by a natural canal following the Cañadas de la Loba and Amarguillo.[59] That said, the peculiar circumstances of Gades' setting, its urbanism, and a consideration of the scores of simple funerary inscriptions from its necropoleis referring to a host of persons of uncertain status suggest that the *plebs* may have been a larger component of the urban population here than in many other Baetican towns.[60]

The *municipia* resulting from Vespasian's edict and Domitian's municipal law in the upland areas of the *conventus Astigitanus, Gaditanus,* and *Cordubensis* may have had relatively few *honesti* outside the *ordo* in their midst, as surveys are fairly consistent in revealing that the number of rural first- through third-order sites in each of their probable *territoria* is roughly equal to the likely complement of their local *ordines,* namely of fifty to sixty-five decurions maximum per *municipium.* The main problem here is the lack of systematic or well-published excavation in these *oppida,* which makes estimates of an urban-rural split in local populations difficult to conjecture. It is relevant to note, in this connection, that Fear in his study of Baetica alludes to lower-class housing of moderate means at Rute.[61] Is it possible to categorize the structures at Rute differently? The site report to which he refers concerns the remains of fifteen houses built of substantial dressed stones, a meter in length, at the ancient site of Cisimbrium. The houses, discovered in June 1950, produced remains of pavement, walls, terracotta sculpture—including a Bacchus figure—stone mills, numerous gold coins, some silver ones, many bronze coins, stone hatchets, indeterminate bronze objects, amphora remains, *sigillata,* Campanian ware, weights, an iron candelabrum, mosaic remains, stucco remains, and agricultural implements.[62] Are these the houses and possessions of poor people? Likely not. The problem of the urban-rural split in the population of Baetica invites a consideration of another cleavage, namely that between free and dependent laborers. It is appropriate to turn, therefore, to the problem of the labor found on Baetican estates. The main question at this point is: Did rural production in Baetica depend mainly on tenancy or chattel slavery?

※

Foxhall offers compelling grounds for thinking that tenants constituted an important source of agricultural labor not only in Egypt and North Africa, but in Italy and Greece as well, during the late Republican and imperial periods.[63] If tenants were in any way abundant as a source of estate management and labor in Baetica in the early Principate, the sources do not say. Efforts to establish the widespread presence of *coloni* involved in the production and processing of olives and olive oil rest on a few scattered bits of evidence in the form of Dressel 20 amphora stamps. Liou and Tchernia, following Mayet and Manacorda, read the letters COL in the stamps K. V. FIG. GRUM // COL. SIC. ET ASI, AUGGGNNN / COLEARI. FGRU, AUGGGNNN / OLEARI. FGR, and K. V. FIG. GRUM / COL. SIC. ET. ASI from the *figlina Grumese* ("La María," Lora del Río); the stamps . . .FIGCEP. // COLLEOP . . , [A]UGGG NNN. / [C]OLEARI. F. CEPA, and K. V. FIG. CEPA / COLLEOPAR from the *figlina Ceparia* ("El Portillo," Palma del Río); and the stamps AUGGGNNN. / COLEARI. F. BARB and K. V. FIG. BAR / COLSICETASI from the *figlina Barba* ("El Sotillo," Almodóvar del Río) as "col(onus)," and take "Eari(nus)," "Leopar(dianus)," "Sic(ulus)," and "Asi(aticus)" to be tenants who leased the aforementioned amphora workshops from the emperor. Liou and Tchernia reject Remesal's reading "c(onductor) ol(earius)" for COL, noting that the term "conductor" is followed by the genitive of the operation involved or by the name of the domain taken under *conductio,* but only once is followed by an adjective.[64] Lomas and Sáez have suggested the expansion "c(uratores) ol(earii),"[65] a post otherwise unknown, but the reading OLEARI that Sáez and Chic García allege in the stamps represents a misunderstanding:[66] the "C" of the element COLEARI has simply not survived on the stamp from Rome that they cite.[67] They also adduce Callender for stamps from Strasbourg and Cirencester that putatively lack the "C" of

"COLEARI," but that investigator provides no relief. The "C" in the stamp from Strasbourg has simply not survived, which is the reason why Callender brackets the letter, while the stamp cited by the aforementioned scholar from Cirencester, but not illustrated in *Roman Amphorae*, does not lack the "C."[68] The sole unequivocal evidence for *coloni* in Baetica during the Principate comes from a stamp found in Rome that reads SOSUMAE / COLONA K V (K V reversed) / T TC ET IA.[69] Again, the context here refers to an imperial property in Baetica, namely the *Kalendarium Vegetianum*. The *Kalendarium Vegetianum* consisted of the estates and other properties of the senatorial Valerii Vegeti in Baetica, which passed from private ownership, either by testamentary bequest or confiscation, to the *fiscus* in c. A.D. 160. As its name suggests, the *Kalendarium Vegetianum* was concerned with loans on interest from monies generated by the agricultural activity of the Valerii Vegeti. The recipients of the loans would have been either tenants or clients of the family. After the passage of their properties to the *fiscus,* the competence of the procurator in charge of the *Kalendarium Vegetianum* extended beyond accounting for loans on interest to imperial tenants to the collection of rents owed by them and services (*operae*) expected of them.[70] Fairly good grounds exist, in short, for seeing a regime of tenancy in properties belonging to the *fiscus,* and grouped under the designation of the *Kalendarium Vegetianum,* in the period from Marcus through the reign of Septimius Severus.

On more general grounds, it is possible to envisage widespread tenancy in properties belonging to absentee senatorials in Baetica. So argue Sáez and Chic on the basis of the nomina of *possessores* in Dressel inscription delta that may belong to the freedmen, or their descendants, of Baetican senators. They adduce Annius Callistus and Annius Felix as having a connection with the Annii of Baetica, and Dasumius Epaphroditus as possibly a freedman — or his son — of the Corduban senator Dasumius.[71] Aubert is not the first scholar to suggest, moreover, that an estate could be subject at the same time to a regime of agency — through a slave *vilicus*— and tenancy; Sáez and Chic García say or imply virtually the same thing in suggesting that senatorial properties in Baetica could be in part leased to tenants and in part managed directly through slaves.[72] It is the conviction of this author, however, that the large majority of *fundi* in Baetica during the Principate were under the direct management of their owners through the *vilicus* system, and that they were worked by chattel slaves, whether organized through tenancy or through agency — or in some cases, through both. Sillières very definitely emphasizes the ubiquity of chattel slaves on *fundi* larger than 100 *iugera* in Hispania, in general, during the early Empire.[73] And there are solid grounds for thinking that tenancy may not even have been necessary in the case of absentee senatorials or equestrians. The case of Helvia, who was left behind in Baetica to supervise family estates while her husband Seneca the Elder was in Rome, receives mention above; and there is the parallel case of the supervision of Agricola's estates in Narbonensis by his mother after the death of Agricola's father, as Griffin notes.[74] Thus immediate blood relatives may have been directly involved, in numerous cases, in the management of family properties in Baetica.

Moreover, it is unlikely that tenancy constituted the main form of estate management in those *municipia* of Baetica with relatively restricted territories. Communities with constricted *territoria* would almost by necessity have seen all or most of their *decurionales* living on *fundi* and, therefore, in a position to directly manage their affairs, particularly in those *municipia* where so-called urban centers were little more than central places for administrative, religious, or marketing activity. To be sure, Kehoe has underscored as one of the main factors in the promotion of tenancy as a form of estate management the need for "upper-class" Romans to manage geographically scattered properties.[75] He may well be correct to assert that tenancy constituted the principal method of upper-class estate exploitation in most provinces of the Roman Empire. But aside from exceptional cases that occurred relatively late in the history of the province,[76] the sheer lack of widely scattered properties in the possession of most Baetican elites and would-be elites of decurional or sub-decurional rank simply obviated the need for indirect management through tenants. The widespread practice of erecting herms to urban and rural *possessores* and *patres familiarum* also constitutes, it can be argued, powerful indirect evidence that proprietors in Baetica lived on, or were frequently present at, their rural properties, and therefore were in a position to directly manage their affairs. Herms with the portrait busts of the dedicatees belong to a slave-owning milieu,[77] and would seem to have little or no place on those *fundi* managed by — or, for that matter, worked to any significant degree by — tenants. This last point brings us to the question of the labor force found on Baetican estates.

The labor of chattel slaves was in certain contexts supplemented at peak periods of the agricultural year by hired free or unfree labor or *mercenarii*.[78] For example, some nonslave labor along the Mediterranean and Atlantic littorals of Baetica may have come from North Africa. Temporary, migrant laborers from the African continent may have participated in the annual tuna catch and associated *garum* production in the area of the Strait of Gibraltar.[79] The evidence of burials from Baelo points in this direction. Though Baelo's epigraphy has yet to reveal an explicitly designated African, the southeastern necropolis of the town has yielded up nonanthropomorphic Betilos, or funerary sculptures, and tomb types that find exclusively African parallels.[80] More significant is the chronology of these tombs, which date from the reign of Tiberius to the Flavian period: Almagro Gorbea demonstrates that the majority (14, or 66 percent of the tombs) date from the reign of Claudius, or precisely that period when Baelo, benefiting from reconstructed *garum* installations, probably achieved municipal status and would have attracted a considerable population of temporary, migrant workers, many of them from Africa.[81] The well-founded suggestion is that it is precisely this population of temporary laborers that occupied the simpler earthen tombs marked with Betilos, as opposed to Baelo's natives, who would have utilized the freestanding monuments of the necropolis.[82] In other words, while the Betilos may point to the pre-Roman Punic tradition of Baelo, as Remesal suggests, their continued use in the Julio-Claudian and Flavian periods may have been fostered by a continuous stream of temporary migrants from the African shore opposite.

A study of all the epigraphic evidence suggests that slave numbers in the Baetican countryside—particularly those portions south of the Baetis—were large, and that slaves and freedmen constituted a substantial proportion of the total population of the province, perhaps as much as 30 to 40 percent by the mid-first century A.D.[83] An accounting of certain and possible slaves and freedmen in rural contexts will yield good results. The identification of possible slaves and freedmen flows from the firmly established principle that in urbanized contexts of the Roman West during the Principate, persons with a single name in the inscriptions are *grosso modo* slaves, and that furthermore, the possession of a Greek cognomen generally, though not invariably, points either to servile status or to extraction.[84] The emphasis below on slaves and freedmen in the *conventus Cordubensis* and *Astigitanus* derives from the fact that the aforementioned two assize districts alone have been subject to the reediting of *CIL* II at the time of the completion of this study.[85]

There is, however, abundant evidence for slaves and freedmen in rural contexts outside the *conventus Astigitanus* and *Cordubensis*. One of the more compelling pieces of evidence concerns the famous formula Baetica on bronze from Bonanza (Sanlúcar de Barrameda), discovered in 1868.[86] In the document, Dama L. Titi ser(vus), acting on behalf of the creditor L. Titius, accepts through fiduciary *mancipatio* a security from the debtor L. Baianus in the form of real estate and its attached chattel slaves (the "fundus Baianus" in the "pagus Olbensis" and the chattels represented by the slave Midas). The parties to the transaction—even if stock figures—and the reference to the *mancipia* of L. Baianus show clearly the presence of agricultural slaves in this portion of the province at an early, Augustan date. Curchin refers to the document as a land- and slave-sale tout court.[87] The most remarkable assemblage of rural slaves, all probably part of a single *familia rustica,* comes from the Cortijo de los Baños (Beas de Segura, Jaén province) in an area that is not in Baetica at all, but in the upper Guadalquivir valley in a zone of Tarraconensis that is ecologically similar to that of the upper-middle portions of the river valley within the provincial confines of Baetica.

The Cortijo de los Baños produces a villa settlement, possessing a *pars urbana,* and includes a necropolis that yields a remarkable assemblage of funerary stelae, all of which attest slaves.[88] Two of the stones were discovered in the early 1970s and complement other stelae that were discovered in the same place in 1923 but that have almost entirely perished. One stele discovered in the 1920s has a semi-circular focus adorned by two symmetrically disposed *hederae.* It discloses a certain Pacatus, whose age at death is unknown. The epitaph dates to the second or third century A.D. A second stele found in the 1920s, whose inscription was recorded, names Fidentina, who died at age 17, in addition to a certain Nectareus, who died at age 40. The second stele seems to be contemporaneous with the first. Of the two stelae discovered in the early 1970s, one records Saturnina, who died at age 40 and was commemorated by an unnamed daughter; the epitaph also names Aurelia, who died at age 11, and Maritima, who died at age 50. The second, a limestone stele, records Valentina, who died at age 22. The two latter stelae are contemporary with the preceding ones, or perhaps slightly earlier in date, that is, from the second century. González Román suggests that all four stelae disclose members of the *pars rustica* of the villa situated on fertile soil next to the Arroyo del Ojanco. Four more stelae from the villa came to light in the autumn of 1985, and they collectively name or refer to five slaves and ex-slaves from this same rural slave *familia.* The new *serviles* include the freedwoman [A]e(lia?) Locris, who died at age 22; the slave C(h)restus, who died at age 5; the slave Poletice, who died at age 30 and was commemorated by her slave husband and sons; an unknown slave or ex-slave, who died at age 12; and a certain Princeps(?), who died at age 2.[89] Examples could rapidly multiply of other rural slaves and freedmen outside of the *conventus Astigitanus* and *Cordubensis,* but as there is no means of readily comparing their numbers to the total epigraphic context in which they are attested, due to the laggard publication of the new fascicles of the second volume of the *Corpus of Latin Inscriptions,* it is not possible to adduce all the evidence here.

Servi and *liberti* represent a high proportion of all named individuals in rural contexts in the *conventus Cordubensis.* The percentage of certain and possible slaves and freedmen is high in all portions of the *conventus,* both north of the Guadalquivir in the upland areas of the Sierra Morena and south of the river. Some examples will be illustrative of the preceding observation. The new edition of the second volume of the *Corpus of Latin Inscriptions* lists eleven inscriptions from the *ager* of Obulco (*CIL* II^2/7, 125-127a, 128-134). The inscriptions, a combination of votive, honorary, and funerary texts and a fleet diploma, name seventeen individuals. Of these, six are certain or possible slaves and freedmen. Eight persons attested in Obulco's territory are explicitly designated or certain *ingenui.* The territory of Solia in the northern part of the *conventus* offers twenty-two non-Christian inscriptions, including several votives and one inscribed *terminus* (*CIL* II^2/7, 766-773, 775-778, 781-790). These inscriptions name nineteen individuals, of whom seven are certain or possible slaves or freedmen. The same inscriptions name five individuals who are explicitly designated *ingenui.* Baedro and its likely territory in the north-central portion of the *conventus* produce thirty-five inscriptions of all types (*CIL* II^2/7, 815-850). These inscriptions record a total of thirty-nine persons whose names survive wholly or in part. Of these persons, twelve are certain or possible slaves or freedmen; only seven are explicitly designated as freeborn. Freedmen may be overrepresented in the inscriptions,[90] but the same cannot necessarily be said of slaves, who are abundant in the rural epigraphy of the *conventus Cordubensis* south of the Baetis and in the *conventus Astigitanus.* On a priori grounds, though, it may be reasonable to suppose that slaves and freedmen constituted a higher percentage of the rural population, at least in those areas of the eastern portion of the province of Baetica where the Roman institutional presence was oldest in the form of colonial or municipal establishments. Of course, the prime example of a colonial establishment in eastern Baetica is the *colonia immunis* Tucci (Martos, Jaén

province), situated within the *conventus Astigitanus;* and it may be no co-
incidence that from its territory (or, if not from part of its *ager,* then from
part of a place that was obviously strongly influenced by the colony, namely
Torre de la Fuencubierta, located 10 kilometers to the west-northwest of
Martos) there comes possible evidence of a slave *columbarium*—the sole
possible example on record in this portion of the province. The place yields
a funerary cist of white stone on which is inscribed the name of Clodia Appi
l(iberta) Hospita, appearing in an epitaph of possibly first-century A.D.
date.[91] Also from the same spot comes a funerary urn of limestone, which
names Satu(l)a Aviti l(iberta) in an epitaph of first-century A.D. date.[92] Also
from this putative *columbarium* comes another funerary urn, which attests
Tertiola Aviti liberta in an epitaph also of the first century A.D.[93] Camacho
Cruz suggests that this and the preceding urns, homogeneous in appearance and date, come from a *columbarium* of Appius Clodius Avitus constructed for a "family of clients," which we can surely take to refer to his
familia rustica.[94] A possible *columbarium* here would, in turn, suggest the
presence of a relatively large slave household in some unknown *praedium*
of the second century A.D.

It is wrong to minimize the presence of slaves as rural labor in the upper
Guadalquivir valley to the point of denying their presence altogether in
the context of small- and medium-sized *fundi,* as some investigators have
done.[95] The evidence laid out above demonstrates a servile presence even
in remote portions of the campiña of Jaén, although it remains open to anyone to suggest that slave *familiae* here and in more upland areas of the province were modest in size, amounting to, for the sake of hypothesis, no more
than eight to fifteen slaves per *fundus* on average, or even fewer on occasion.
Survey evidence from the campiña of Sevilla may be very much in line with
the aforementioned supposition. Meticulous site investigation, based on a
program of semi-intensive survey, in the municipal territory of Fuentes de
Andalucía and in those of adjoining municipalities reveals necropoleis
that are evidently attached to rural settlements. It is possible to identify two
second-order sites and their inhumation cemeteries. Situated in the municipal district of Carmo, "Tinajuela II" possesses a surface scatter of roughly
7,000 square meters. The site, which probably represents an ex novo
Flavian foundation, yields various common ceramics, amphoras, and finewares; it also produces semi-circular column bricks. Its adjoining necropolis consists of fifteen to twenty scatters of *tegulae,* each of which is approximately 20 square meters. The second-order site "Santa Juliana I," situated

in the municipal territory of Fuentes de Andalucía, possesses a surface scatter of roughly 150 square meters. The site produces a fragment of a granite grain mill, suggesting that the property of which it was a part grew cereals. In immediate proximity to the site and slightly elevated with respect to the main scatter are a further eight to ten scatters of 10 square meters each that clearly represent inhumation tombs. Like the preceding rural establishment, "Santa Juliana I" represents an ex novo Flavian-era settlement.[96] It is certainly possible that some or all of these inhumation tombs belong to the members of the *familia rustica* of these two rural settlements. It is also obviously open to anyone to suppose that a number of the slaves and freedmen revealed in all of the varying rural contexts mentioned above represent domestic servants, particularly in the larger, more complex first-order establishments; but it would be extreme to deny the distinct probability that a certain number of them were chattels who worked in the productive sphere. It would be a safe bet to suppose that it is virtually impossible that the context and particulars of the formula Baetica from Bonanza, described above, were unique in Baetica during the early Principate.

How is it possible, finally, to reconcile the simultaneous existence of relatively large *fundi* with comparatively restricted *familiae* of slaves and freedmen working them? A solution to this quandary might be to posit that the increasing importance of oleiculture in the province by the later first century A.D. involved a less-intensive commitment of labor throughout the year,[97] punctuated only at certain times by the necessities of the harvesting and processing of olives. A modest number of permanent chattel slaves complemented by the labor of family members and supplemented at peak agricultural seasons by free or unfree *mercenarii* in the form of *servi vicarii*, for example, would have been adequate not only to the challenges posed by the extensive type of agriculture represented by the growing and processing of olives, but also to the more intensive requirements of subsistence arable cultivation. The production of oleiculture would have been destined for consumption beyond the *fundus*, while arable cultivation and the growing of legumes was intended primarily, though not exclusively, for the maintenance of the family and dependents within the confines of the estate.

CHAPTER SIX

Wealthy Baetici

It is now time to name some of the beneficiaries of economic activity and growth in Baetica from c. 50 B.C. to c. A.D. 200. The first three sections of this chapter will consider those *viri honesti* and *feminae honestae* whose connections with specific wealth-producing activities may be established or inferred with some degree of confidence. A fourth and final section will be reserved for freedpersons and those likely *honesti* outside the *ordo* for whom specific wealth-making activities cannot be identified, but whose inclusion in this study finds its justification in that such persons illustrate the generalized growth that the province experienced between the rule of Augustus and that of Septimius Severus. Many persons whose specific sources of wealth are identifiable belong to the senatorial, equestrian, and decurional orders. But their numbers are far surpassed by men and women who belong to the middle stratum in Baetican society. The essential truth of the preceding statement is one that only a positivistic enumeration of persons can reveal. Only the meticulous identification of such persons can put flesh and sinew, as it were, onto the skeletal concept of the middle stratum. The discussion begins with senators, and the ordering principle will be alphabetical, according to nomina.

Senators

Caballos underscores the economic base and urbanization of Baetican communities producing senators. He also emphasizes the problem of distin-
guishing between native Spaniards and the descendants of Italians. The
cultural advantages of urban life and desire for imperial service also count
as factors in the entry of provincials into the senate.[1] Of particular interest
must be the sources of wealth of Spanish senators. The concern in this section will be to name those Baetican and non-Baetican senators, along with
known relatives, whose specific sources of wealth in Baetica or elsewhere
are identifiable.

A

P. Aelius P.f. Serg. Hadrianus was born in Rome but possesses *origo* in Italica.[2] More uncertain are efforts to link the amphora stamps PORTPAH,
PORPA, POR.P.A.H., and PORPAHS from the *figlina Virginensia* (Villar
de Brenes) and Cruz Verde with the proprietor P(ublius) A(elius) H(adri-
anus), that is, the emperor.[3] Birley, in his biography of Hadrian, though,
takes it as virtually certain that the stamps can be understood to refer to
"'the warehouse, port(us), of Publius Aelius Hadrianus,'" and therefore as
marks of the proprietorship of the emperor over the oil contained in amphoras produced on his estate, the *fundus Virginiensis*.[4] Hadrian's father,
the *vir praetorius* P. Aelius Serg. Hadrianus Afer, an *originarius* of Italica,
was married to the Gaditana Domitia Paulina.[5] L. Annaeus Seneca, the elder, born in Corduba, possessed an indeterminate number of properties in
Baetica. When he returned to Rome in or before A.D. 5, he left his wife
Helvia behind to administer them.[6] The great-grandfather of M. Aurelius,
Annius Verus, who was made a senator by Nero, was born in Ucubi.[7] On a
priori grounds, we can assume that he owned productive properties in the
vicinity of that town. The son of the preceding and *consul suffectus I* in
A.D. 97 was M. Annius Verus.[8] The father of the emperor, (M.) Annius M.f.
Verus, possibly possessed brick works in the vicinity of Rome.[9] M. Annius
M.f. Libo, *consul ordinarius* in A.D. 128, was the paternal uncle of M. Aure-
lius.[10] Both Caballos and Castillo argue for the Baetican and Corduban
origin of the suffect consul of A.D. 90, L. Antistius L.f.(?) Gal. Rusticus.[11]
Caballos, citing Callender, links Rusticus with the oil amphora stamps
L. AT., L. AT. RU., and L. AT. RUS; but he goes too far in connecting the
consul with L. Antistius Rusticus, a *duovir* of Corduba.[12]

C

The *consul II ordinarius* of A.D. 199 and proconsul of Baetica, P. Cornelius P.f. Gal. Anullinus, was an *originarius* of Iliberri.[13] Sáez and Chic suggest that the producer Anullinus, named in a *titulus pictus* of A.D. 140–145, is the same as our P. Cornelius Anullinus, although chronological considerations alone make the identification unlikely.[14] Of possible Baetican origin is L. Stertinius Quintilianus Acilius Strabo Q. Cornelius Rusticus Apronius Senecio Proculus, who was suffect consul in A.D. 146.[15] Son of the preceding is the *legatus provinciae Asiae* in 161/162 or 162/163, Q. Cornelius L.f. Senecio Proculus, who may be an *originarius*, like his father, of Carteia.[16] Sáez and Chic may well be correct to link Proculus or his father with the olive-oil producer Cornelius Proculus, named in a *titulus pictus* of 153.[17] Of possible Gaditane origin (more specifically, Portus Gaditanus) is the suffect consul of 70 or 71, L. Cornelius L.f. Gal. Pusio.[18] A son, it seems, of the preceding is the suffect consul of A.D. 90, L. Cornelius Pusio Annius Messalla.[19] The latter may be the same person as a ". . . Cornelio Pusioni" mentioned in the so-called *testamentum Dasumii*. If this is the case, it reinforces the Baetican origins of the consul of 90.[20] There is prima facie warrant for seeing either the father or the son, or both, as the proprietors of the fish-sauce amphora-producing installation, active during the first two centuries A.D., at the Cortijo del Tesorillo (Jerez de la Frontera). A funerary inscription there names Martial, the slave of L. Cornelius Pusio.[21] The slave may have served as the foreman of the amphora-producing facility.

F

Caballos follows Chic García in seeing the Dressel 20 amphora stamps attesting initials followed generally by the letters "c.v." (= "c(larissimus) v(ir)") and reading L.F.C.SENTIC., L.F.LUC(?), C.F.P(?), Q.F.S., and C.F.TITIANUS from amphoras produced in the area of Posadas and Ecija as referring to a family of senators of Baetican origin who entered the senate at the end of the second century A.D.[22] Caballos, following Remesal, postulates the existence of a L. Fabius Lucilianus, and takes him to be the son of the *consul II ordinarius* of 204, L. Fabius Cilo Septiminus Catinius Acilianus Lepidus Fulcinianus.[23] Various scholars assign a Spanish origin to L. Fabius M.f. Gal. Cilo Septiminus Catinius Acilianus Lepidus Fulcinianus.[24] Remesal links stamps found at the *figlina Scalensia* (Cerro de los Pesebres) LCF, LFCCVFSCAL and variants, LFFSCA, and LFLUC-

CVFS with Cilo, his son L. Fabius Lucilianus, and his grandson L. Fabius Fortunatus Victorinus.[25] On the other hand, the stamps LFCRESCVFP and LFCRESCCVFP lead Liou and Tchernia to argue that the stamps LFC are better expanded as "L F(   ) Crescens," and that the *clarissimus vir* of the stamps remains unidentified.[26] Jacques will go only so far as to say with certainty that a family represented by the abbreviated *gentilicium* F(   ), and counting in its ranks certain *clarissimi* at the beginning of the third century, owned widely spread properties and associated potteries producing amphoras bearing their abbreviated names. This family's properties were concentrated in the middle Guadalquivir valley between Celti and Posadas, with some properties and associated amphora-producing installations along the Genil (Singilis). Jacques is agnostic on the certain identification of any of the persons represented by the stamps with any known or inferable senatorials of the later second and third centuries A.D., suggesting only that it is highly likely that the family members represented by the abbreviated nomen F(   ) were Fabii and that the most likely identification, without insisting on the point, between the stamps and any known senator is the one that would link stamps reading LFC and variants with the consular and *praefectus urbi* L. Fabius Cilo, mentioned above.[27]

H

Caballos, following Panciera, suggests the Baetican origin of the suffect consul of A.D. 85, P. Herennius Pollio.[28] Publius is the son of another suffect consul (of July 85), M. Annius Herennius Pollio, who was a *dominus* of a *figlina* at Rome.[29] Chic adduces the amphora stamps PMOCV//FIGED, made by the pottery "La Corregidora" and dating to the reigns of Elagabalus and Severus Alexander, suggesting they were produced by the "c(larissimus) v(ir)" P(   ) M(   ) O(   ), though Liou and Tchernia reject the expansion as facile.[30] The vital point remains that the stamp refers to an otherwise unknown *clarissimus* of the first half of the third century, as Jacques notes.[31]

M

Caballos links the stamps L.M.VE. from Mejía and Villar Tesoro near Arva and the "f(undus) Veg(etianus?–etinus?)," revealed in position delta of a painted inscription from the Testaccio, with the *legatus (proconsulis) provinciae Baeticae* of uncertain date L. Marius L.f. Gal. Vegetinus Marcianus Minicianus Myrtilianus.[32] From Siarum is the suffect consul of

A.D. 114, L. Messius Rusticus.[33] The brother, probably, of the preceding is the friend of Hadrian, M. (Messius) Gal. (Rusticus) Aemilius Papus, who was married to a certain Cutia Prisca.[34] A son of the preceding is the *Xvir stlitibus iudicandis* late in Hadrian's reign M. Messius M.f. Gal. Rusticus Aemilius Afer Cutius Romulus Priscianus Arrius Proculus.[35] The brother, probably, of M. Messius Proculus is the *legatus Augusti legionis XX Valeriae Victricis,* among other posts, M. Cutius M.f. Gal. Priscus Messius Rusticus Aemilius Papus Arrius Proculus Iulius Celsus.[36] The probable son of M. Cutius Celsus is the *Quaestor Antonini Pii* M. Messius M.f. Gal. Rusticianus Aemilius Lepidus Iulius Celsus Balbinus Arrius Proculus.[37] The likely brother of the preceding is (M.?) Messius M.f. Gal. Rust[icus Aemilius] Papus A[rrius?] [Proc?]lianus (perhaps [Pris?]cianus or [Aci?]lianus) Iu[lius Af]er.[38] Caballos sees also as a member of the Aemilii Papi M. Messius M.f. Gal. Rusticus Aemilius Verus Aelius Romulus Priscianus Tit(i?)us Proculus, attested in Hispalis.[39] The same investigator suggests interests and properties of the Aemilii Papi in Hispalis, possibly Italica, and on the banks of the ancient *Lacus Ligustinus* (area of Utrera, Montellano, and Los Palacios).[40] Didierjean links the Hacienda de Mejina (Espartinas, Sevilla province) with Messius Rusticus Aemilius Afer (sic), seeing in the modern name the "fundus Messianus" of *CIL* XV 4432.[41] Bonsor, on the other hand, connects *CIL* XV 4432 with the despoblado "Gallos," located 5 kilometers south of Lora and 3 kilometers west of Lora la Vieja. He notes that the place was called Meçina in the thirteenth century, a name that derives putatively from the estate name Messianus, formed, in turn, from the nomen Messius.[42] Remesal, with all due caution, makes the interesting, though indemonstrable, suggestion that M. Cutius Celsus, named in full above, has a connection of some sort with the oil merchant Cutius Celsianus.[43] And Remesal may be right to connect with Caesia Senilla, who had honored with an inscription the aforementioned M. Cutius Celsus (*CIL* II 1283), the oil merchants Q. Caesius Caesianus, Caesius Eumenes, Caesius Macrinus, and Caesius Senecio, who are attested in *tituli picti* of 149 and 150.[44]

L. Mummius Niger Q. Valerius Vegetus Severinus Caucidius Tertullus, a consul possibly in the reign of Pius, was the probable proprietor of the oil-producing *Kalendarium Vegetianum,* which he either established or inherited.[45] Lomas and Sáez connect the stamps reading L.M.VE with L(ucius) M(ummius) Ve(getus), that is, our senator.[46] Caballos suggests the origin in Iliberri of Vegetus, who may be the grandson of the *consul suffectus* of

A.D. 91, namely Valerius Vegetus of Iliberri. L. Mummius Vegetus also possessed properties in Viterbo and possibly Apulia.[47]

Casas del Picón is a site on the left bank of the Genil that yields Dressel 20 amphora stamps that read IIMVSETPR. The stamps and associated amphoras date to c. A.D. 150. Remesal suggests that the stamps reflect either the association of two individuals of the same family "MV(   ) S(   ) et [MV(   )] PR(   ) or P(   ) R(   )" or the "II(duorum) MV(   ) S(   ) ET P(   ) R(   )," that is to say, two persons with the nomen MV(   ) and cognomen S(   ) plus a third individual with the nomen P(   ) and cognomen R(   ).[48] Remesal, in addition, underlines the stamp PMSC, also found at Casa del Picón, which dates anytime from c. A.D. 150 through the third century. Remesal sees a reference here to a certain P(   ) M(   ) S(   ) and the "[(figlina)] C(eparia)." The same scholar sees the abbreviation MV(   ) as a reference to the nomen Mummius, and suggests that the stamps designate either Mummius S(isenna?, -ecundinus?) and a Mummius Pr(   ) or P(   ) R(utilianus?), or two Mummii S(   ) and a third person from a different family. Taking the chronology of the stamps into account, Remesal suggests that the stamp IIMVSETPR refers to the ordinary consul of 133, P. Mummius Sisenna, and the suffect consul of 146, P. Mummius Sisenna Rutilianus, and that the stamp PMSC represents either one of the Sisennas or Mummius Secundinus, whom the author of the *Historia Augusta* (*HA Sev.* 13) includes at the head of a list of prominent persons put to death by Septimius Severus. Remesal postulates that Mummius Secundinus may be a son of Sisenna Rutilianus without insisting on the point, but seems to be more confident that Secundinus' *fundi* and associated *figlinae* were confiscated by Severus and passed directly into the *res privata* after a preliminary incorporation into the *patrimonium Caesaris*. Remesal is not the only commentator to note the family connection of the Mummii with the Valerii Vegeti, as embodied by L. Mummius Niger Q. Valerius Vegetus Severinus Caucidius Tertullus.[49]

Chic García, on the other hand, views the stamps as referring to two P. Mussidii Semproniani, whom he identifies on the basis of a bronze seal from Irni(?), which names a certain P. Mussidius Sempronianus twice.[50] Remesal rejects the identification, noting a dissimilarity in the typology of the stamps found on the handles of Dressel 20 amphoras and the seal as well as a difference with the stamps found in the stoppers of non–Dressel 20 amphora types.[51] Against Remesal's first point is the similarity between the seal from Irni(?) and those bronze seals from Rome that name *diffusores* and *mercatores olearii*. Apropos Remesal's second point: a probable Dressel 20 stopper has appeared in excavations near the forum of Aquileia, and it does not resemble the seal from Irni(?).[52] The nonresemblance of the seals is a moot point, however, given the likelihood that the seal from Irni(?) would have served a purpose other than stamping finished Dressel 20 containers, namely that of marking storage areas, whether in Baetica or in Italy, allotted the Mussidii Semproniani by the *annona*.

P

The ordinary consul of A.D. 184, Cn. Papirius Aelianus, was probably born in Iliberri.[53] We might conjecture, on general principles, that he owned oil-producing lands and/or pasturage in the vicinity of that town. Caballos opts for the origin in Italica of the suffect consul with Hadrian in March–April 119, A. Platorius A.f. Serg. Nepos Aponius Italicus Manilianus C. Licinius Pollio.[54] He is mentioned as *dominus* on brick stamps of 123 and 134.[55] Tutilius Lupercus Pontianus was consul in 135. A second consul bearing this name, the suffect of 183, was L. Tutilius Pontianus Gentianus.[56] Either one or both of the Tutilii seems to have had olive-producing properties in Baetica, to judge from *tituli picti* of 149 and 161.[57] Bennett reasonably suggests olive oil as a likely basis for the wealth of Trajan's ancestors, but goes badly astray in insinuating a connection between the red-slip ware *officinator* Traius Masculus, attested on a pottery fragment from Ilici, and the Traii.[58]

V

From Iliberri, apparently, was the suffect consul of A.D. 91, Q. Valerius Vegetus.[59] From Iliberri also was his son, the suffect consul in A.D. 112, Q. Valerius Q.f. Vegetus.[60] The possibility is a strong one that it was either the father or the son who established the oil-producing properties subsumed under the rubric *Kalendarium Vegetianum*, and not their putative grandson, L. Mummius Niger Q. Valerius Vegetus, mentioned above.

Equestrians

The evidence does point positively to the involvement of numerous senators in Baetican olive-oil or other production, but it is, with two more or less certain exceptions, silent on any similar involvement in agricultural production on the part of those equestrians who are explicitly connected in our sources with civil administration and/or military command.[61] The reason is surely in large part the salaried nature of equestrian posts during the Principate. Out of a total of forty or so equestrians, whether connected with official duties or not, whose Baetican origins are certain,[62] only six can be linked with a greater or lesser degree of probability to identifiable mining or agricultural activities. From a total of approximately ninety known Baetican senators,[63] we identified above roughly thirty whose specific sources of wealth can be identified or conjectured within a reasonable margin of certainty. On the other hand, the number of *equites Romani* who were not involved with military command or civilian equestrian posts but who were engaged with *negotia* must have been considerable. The *locus classicus* for Baetican equestrians most likely involved in trade is Strabo's allusion—reflecting probably a census of his own day—to the 500 persons rated as equestrians at Gades (3.5.3). The *equites Romani* at Carmo who collectively paid for a statue and inscribed pedestal honoring the *quattuorvir* L. Iunius L.f. M.n. L.pron. Gal(eria) Rufus also merit mention here, although their precise sources of wealth cannot be ascertained.[64] And it may well be the case that a number of persons placed in the category of decurionals, below, actually possessed the equestrian census. One reason, therefore, for our inability to identify the specific sources of wealth for equestrians may be their overall lower profile in Spanish epigraphy.

Possessing *origo* in Italica is the praetorian prefect of 118/119, P. Acilius Attianus.[65] Caballos sees him as a remote descendant of Italian emigrants to Italica, and links Attianus with a *fundus Attianus* mentioned on *tituli picti* of the reign of Pius from the Monte Testaccio in Rome.[66] The connection remains unproven. In any case, Caballos assumes, it seems justifiably, that Attianus owned properties in the area of Italica. Guichard's suggestion, furthermore, is attractive in that the M'. Acilii of Singili(a?) Barba, who circulated in an equestrian milieu, derived their wealth from olive cultivation and olive-oil production.[67] Their connection with olive oil would explain, in large part, the *amicitia* of Acilia Plecusa with P. Magnius Rufus Magonianus, a procurator of the *Kalendarium Vegetianum* between 180 and 198, and with Rufus' wife Carvilia Censonilla.[68] Acilia Plecusa's position as a landowner of substantial means approaching or even exceeding the equestrian census is now certain from the discovery of her elaborately constructed *sepulchrum* and marble sarcophagus from the necropolis of the Roman villa "Las Maravillas," situated 6 kilometers west-northwest of Singili(a?) Barba.[69] Caballos unhesitatingly categorizes Acilia Plecusa's husband and *patronus,* Manius Acilius Quir(ina) Fronto, as an equestrian from his position as "praef(ectus) fabrum,"[70] although Atencia Páez is skeptical of the claim.[71]

On the other hand, and apropos of the sources of the wealth of the Acilii, there are no certain grounds whatsoever for seeing the *figlinae* BARBA, BARB, or BAR or the name SINGILIESE in Dressel position delta on an amphora from the Testaccio as proof of the production of amphoras, as Guichard alleges, in the territory of Singili(a?) Barba itself. The aforementioned names bear no necessary relationship with the name of the city.[72] The toponym SINGILIESE may refer to the "pagus Singiliensis" mentioned in the epitaph of P. Acilius P.l. Antiochus from Herrera (Sevilla).[73] Although we know of olive-oil production in its territory, there is not one scintilla of archaeological evidence for the production of oil-bearing amphoras at or near Singili(a?) Barba. Workers installing modern irrigation pipes in the Cortijo de Valsequillo, situated 1.6 kilometers west-southwest of Singili(a?) Barba, accidentally discovered the remains of an *opus signinum*-lined vat and a cylindrical sandstone oil-press counterweight.[74]

L. Iunius L.f. Gal. Moderatus Columella, from Gades, served as *tribunus militum legionis VI Ferratae,* and wrote on agriculture during the mid-first century A.D.[75] Columella records that his uncle was a substantial landowner in the vicinity of Ceret (Jerez de la Frontera) and an expert in viticulture. The most famous rich equestrian from Baetica during the Principate is Sextus Marius. Sextus Marius was the owner(?) of both copper and gold mines, which were confiscated by Tiberius in A.D. 33 after Sextus had been accused of incest with his daughter and hurled from the Tarpeian rock.[76] The extension and scale of Marius' mines must have been vast, stretching in the area of the Sierra Morena from north of Corduba westward to north of Sevilla. T. Mercello Persinus Marius served as aedile and *duovir* at Corduba and was subsequently a *procurator Augusti* (in Baetica presumably) under Augustus.[77] It remains an interesting but unverified hypothesis that his sources of wealth involved both mining and quarrying.[78] C. Rocius Rocianus V[a]leria[nus], from Corduba, attested in a posthumous honorary inscription of the later second century, served as *tribunus militum* of an unknown legion and as *praefectus* of an unknown *cohors equi-*

tata.[79] His name appears in *tituli picti* from the Monte Testaccio and the *Fos-sur-mer* shipwreck, revealing him to be an oil-producing *possessor* in Baetica.[80]

On the other hand, the sources name *negotiatores* and *possessores,* about whom see more below, who are a priori likely to have had, in many cases, sufficient wealth to propel them into the ranks of Roman equestrians. This is another way of saying that these merchants would have possessed the requisites of birth and wealth sufficient to entitle them to the *anulus aureus* and to the other prerogatives and trappings of the equestrian status, but did not enter imperial civilian or military service. Another reason why more explicitly designated equestrians do not appear in the sources is simply that the relevant testimonia, specifically the *tituli picti* on Dressel 20 amphoras, are, for the most part, silent on the explicit status and rank of *mercatores* and *possessores,* save for a handful of instances in which their filiation or libertination is indicated.

Decurions and Honesti Outside the Ordo

·I will signal first those persons of explicitly attested decurional status who may have had some connection with *negotia*. A benefactor and *duovir* of Naeva (Cantillana, Sevilla), L. Aelius Quir. Aelianus, named in an inscription having a Flavian terminus post quem, or one of his relatives, may have been involved in oil production and trade, to judge from homonymous individuals named in positions beta and delta from *tituli* of the Monte Testaccio.[81] Knowledgeable commentators connect the *gens* Egnatia of the wife of the benefactor at Naeva, a certain Egnatia Lupercilla, with the production and commerce of Baetican oil at Arva.[82] The dedicant, L. Aelius Aelianus, of a statue of Venus and its inscribed base, of Antonine date, set up in the *ager* of Corduba between El Higuerón and Villarubia, may well be the same person as the magistrate at Naeva and the oil trader L. Aelius Aelianus.[83] P. Aelius P.f. Fabianus served as a magistrate and priest at Ulia under Tiberius.[84] Curchin, on uncertain grounds, suggests a familial link with the oil merchant C. Aelius Fabianus.[85] The *duovir* at Corduba, L. Antistius Rusticus, may have had some sort of involvement with Baetican olive-oil production and trade.[86] Curchin identifies, on uncertain grounds, as the possible relative of C. Attius Severus, named on a *hospitium* bronze of A.D. 31 from Iptuci (Cabezo de Hortales, Prado del Rey, Cádiz province), the oil merchant P. Attius Severus.[87] L. Cornelius P.f. L.n. Balbus Minor,

IIIIvir at Gades (Cádiz) in 44–43 B.C. and suffect consul in 32, made his greatest impact on the economic development of the future province of Baetica by constructing the city of Portus Gaditanus, which has now been conclusively located at Los Altos de Bolaños, next to the ancient shoreline of the Bahía de Cádiz, 10 kilometers inland from the present littoral.[88] The city, laid out according to Hippodamian principles, is as yet unexcavated. Insufficient grounds exist, unfortunately, to establish a definite link between the *duovir* and *flamen perpetuus* at Barbesula, L. Fabius Gal(eria) Caesianus, and the oil trade.[89] Caesianus was honored with a statue and *epulum* (public banquet) by his heirs Fabia C.fil. Fabiana and Fulvia Sex.fil. Honorata through a testamentary wish. Chic García would like to see a connection between the magistrate at Barbesula and Dressel 20 amphora stamps that read L.F.F. and FF, found along the Genil and Guadalquivir rivers.[90] The same investigator points to amphora stamps from the Monte Testaccio that putatively read PFFABIAN, PFFAB, and FFAB, but the claim is fallacious. Contrary to Chic's claim, the first stamp does not necessarily refer to a Fabianus, but, following Dressel's expansion, not noted by Chic, reads P. F(   ) FABA(TI?).[91] The link, circumstantial at best, between L. Fabius Caesianus and the oil trade remains unsubstantiated. On the other hand, C. Iuventius C.F. Quir. Albinus, an aedile, *duovir,* and patron of Axati (Lora del Río, Sevilla province) during the rule of the Antonines, seems to have had extensive involvement with oil production and commerce.[92] Albinus will reappear in the discussion below.

The number of local magistrates and decurions in Baetica who can be connected with agricultural production and commerce in an explicit fashion is exiguous. But it remains possible to argue that their numbers increase appreciably on a priori grounds on a consideration of the likely places in Baetica where they lived during the Principate. And it is certainly open to anyone to suggest that many of the persons in our sources who can be connected with agricultural production and *negotia* possessed the requisites of birth, moral probity, and wealth sufficient to enable them to have entered the *ordo* if they had so wished but who, for a variety of reasons, declined to do so and who, therefore, enter the category of *honesti* or *possessores* outside the *ordo.*

It may be useful to indicate, if only in summary fashion, all those persons and families not mentioned previously, or only in passing, who fall potentially or certainly into the category of *honesti* outside the *ordo* and local jurors, following, in part, the list established by Melchor Gil of local Spanish elites whose sources of wealth can be established with certainty or guessed at with some degree of confidence.[93] The discussion will turn mainly on olive oil and its distribution as a source of wealth. It is necessary to repeat in this context the point raised above in Chapter Four about traders and exemption from liturgies: traders in the service of the imperial *annona* are automatically nondecurions precisely because they could enjoy exemptions from liturgies, whereas decurions could not. It is worth re-emphasizing that much of the evidence consists of the stamps and *tituli picti* found on amphoras, particularly Dressel 20 oil-bearing ones. The majority of persons named in the following pages are those traders attested in position beta of the *tituli*. They are persons who enjoyed a contractual relationship with the *annona* that conferred immunity from liturgies and preferential access to Rome's supply infrastructure. On the other hand, the interpretation of the stamps found on the handles of Dressel 20 amphoras remains, as noted above, a controversial point. There are those who would see the names as reflecting the proprietors of amphora-producing workshops, accompanied at times by the names of the workshop *officinatores* and/or slaves. Others would insist that the names in the stamps—usually, but not invariably, represented by the abbreviated *tria nomina*—refer to the producers and/or initial owners of the oil. It may be possible to see in certain of the names wholesale buyers of oil, who were frequently oil-producing estate owners themselves. But whatever the truth is, one thing is certain: the persons represented by the stamps profited in some fashion from olive oil. That said, in the absence of evidence to the contrary, some of the persons named in the stamps may represent town councilors or magistrates. Moreover, *honestae feminae* will also figure in the comments below: women appear in Dressel position beta as oil merchants of substantial means, and the ranks of local benefactors in Baetica were filled with females.[94]

Careful examination of the epigraphical evidence reveals the existence of Baetican families with interests in trade extending over two or even three or more generations. It is unnecessary, as a consequence, to believe the statement that "trading fortunes built up in one generation seem to have been invested elsewhere or become submerged by the next."[95] And to characterize the individuals in Dressel position beta as a mere list of names does not seem a fruitful course of action.[96] Furthermore, it is simply not true that Roman traders in Baetica, or at least those connected with the province, as in the case of *mercatores* and/or *navicularii* from Narbonensis, sought to convert gain from commerce into the predictable returns from landowning and agricultural production or money-lending as quickly as possible. Even Trimalchio continued to engage in maritime commerce *after* he had become a landowner of means. But not for long, as D'Arms admits, emphasizing that after retiring from direct involvement in *negotia,* Trimalchio continued to extend loans of a commercial nature through freedmen.[97] Veyne's analysis of Trimalchio as a paradigm for a freedman entrepreneur turned into landowner-usurer still seems to hold the field.[98] It is a pity that this is so. One of the aims of this book is to show the central importance of the names appearing on Dressel 20 and other amphoras in reconstructing the socioeconomy of Baetica during the Principate. Careful analysis of these amphoras reveals persons engaging in *negotia* for years or even decades, whose activity in commerce sometimes extended through generations. And surely the scant evidence for the sons of freedmen entering *ordines decurionum* in Hispania and Baetica, in particular,[99] constitutes additional, if only indirect, grounds for thinking that the freeborn sons and grandsons of freedmen *mercatores olearii* eschewed the *ordo* and *honores* in favor of profitable *otium* or leisure devoted to production and trade. Trimalchio, in short, does not seem to be a suitable model for the activity of *mercatores* associated with the production and distribution of Spanish oil. We now turn to the detailed evidence.

As a preliminary point, it is worth noting that Aubert confesses not to know of instances in which the names on the stamps match the names in Dressel position beta.[100] The following discussion, based in large part on the path-breaking work of Chic García, will include instances of certain or probable identity between the names in the stamps and those in the *tituli picti.* It will also serve to illustrate how broad strata of Baetican society, including *ingenui,* whose census rating could span the spectrum from local *iudices* to those possessing the equestrian census, and not just senatorials, equestrians, or decurionals on one side, or slaves and freedmen on the other, were involved in or profited from oil production and trade. The persons enumerated below will also include merchants whose Baetican origin is likely, on the basis of either nomenclature or other indications.

A

The stamps L.AEL, L.AL, and variants, found in the *figlina* Las Valbuenas and in the Monte Testaccio, dating to c. A.D. 150, may refer to the trader L. Aelius Lupatus known from the Testaccio in a *titulus pictus* of A.D. 154, and operating in conjunction with other Lucii Aelii: Optatus, Caesianus, and Aelianus.[101] A really interesting aspect of these names is that Caesianus and Aelianus are not freedman names — they most likely refer to *ingenui* whose parents or grandparents may have been slaves. The stamp L.AE OP COL, found in Azanaque-Castillejo, next to Arva, may refer to a L. Aelius Optatus, known from *tituli* of the Testaccio and Horti Torlonia, one of which dates to A.D. 154.[102] L. Aelius Optatus may be the son or brother of the Q. Aelius Optatus who seems to have been honored with a statue that Aelia Optata ordered by testament, erected in Celti through the agency of her heirs C. Appius Superstes and C. Annius Montanus.[103] The latter two individuals appear in another inscription from Celti that honors a certain Q. Fulvius Lupus, in fulfillment of a testamentary wish; the inscription dates to the second century A.D.[104] Q. Aelius Optatus seems to be the person in the stamps Q AE.O.POR, from La Catría, Q.AE OPCO, from El Judío, and Q.AE OPTATI and Q AE OPCOL, from Azanaque-Castillejo.[105] It is doubtful that the Aelia Optata who dedicated a statue in Nescania to her son L. Aelius Quirina Mela (*CIL* II 5492) is the same as the aforementioned Optata in Celti, and that there is any link between the M. Ae(lius) Me(la)(?) of the stamps MAEM, MAEAME, and MEM from Azanaque-Castillejo and the person honored in Nescania.[106]

Some of the amphora stamps do disclose more or less complete names. One such example concerns two stamps found in Volubilis that refer to a M.A.E.VALER and MAEVALER. Mayet and Chic García see a reference here to a certain M. Aelius Valerianus, active in some aspect of the production or trade of olive oil and oil containers during the Flavian period.[107] The matter cannot be proved, but it is possible that Valerianus is an *honestus* outside the *ordo*. Another, relatively unabbreviated, name appearing in a Dressel 20 stamp may refer to a further *honestus vir* outside the *ordo*. That stamp appears on an amphora dating to the period 70–105 from the legionary encampment at Nijmegen, and reads Q.AELI.MINICIANI, or Q. Aelius Minicianus.[108] The same person is also named in a stamp from London.[109] In the same category, arguably, are Gn. Aelius Cornelianus, named in stamps emanating from the pottery Embarcadero at Peñaflor, and P. Aelius Fuscianus, named in stamps from the *figlina Edopiana* ("La Corregidora," Posadas).[110]

Otherwise, we are mostly dependent on the initials of the *tria nomina*. Many of these stamps, though, permit us to discern various familial relationships. From a number of sites in Germany and Britain come the stamps

L(   ) A(   ) PAE(   ) and POR(tu) L(   ) A(   )
R(   ), which appear on Dressel 20s of Flavian-Trajanic date produced in La Catria; Remesal suggests that the two individuals indicated by
the initials of their *tria nomina* may be brothers or represent father and
son.[111] Why is it important to raise the possibility that the two persons in
the preceding stamps are father and son? If this is the case, then the son is
most likely the freeborn offspring of either an ex-slave or a freeborn father.
Furthermore, from the fact that so many of the persons indicated in the
stamps and the *mercatores* named in Dressel position beta of the *tituli picti*
are one and the same persons or closely related, it follows that the son—or
father—of the stamps from Germany, and others like them, may conceivably represent *honesti* outside the *ordo*.

A workshop at Azanaque-Castillo produced Dressel 20 amphoras bearing the stamps G(   ) A(   ) F(   ) and C(   )
AP(   ) F(   ); Remesal suggests that the latter represents a descendant of the individual indicated by the first stamp.[112]

Amphora workshops at Malpica produced containers bearing the
stamps L(   ) A(   ) BR(   ) and M(   ) A(   )
C(   ). They show up in German sites and reflect two related individuals, according to Remesal.[113]

It can be ventured, furthermore, that the *diffusores* L. Aelius Aelianus,
L. Aelius Caesianus, and C. Aelius Fabianus, named in *tituli* from the
Monte Testaccio—the first two from a.d. 154 and the third from 160—are,
if not in the ranks of equestrians, then Spanish *honesti* outside the *ordo*.[114]

Bonsor identified pottery kilns at Arva itself, and one of the stamps
found there reads M.AEM.RUS. The stamp refers to a certain M(arcus)
Aem(ilius) Rus(ticus?), and Chic suggests that he was a relative of Aemilia
Rustici f(ilia) Artemisia, who set up at Celti a statue of Venus adorned with
a gold band encrusted with a precious gem.[115] Chic may be right to link
with them Aemilia C.f. Rustica, named in a funerary inscription of the
second half of the first or beginning of the second century from Palma del
Río.[116] Callender dates the stamp between a.d. 80 and 130(?); Martin-
Kilcher dates an example from Augst between 90 and 190;[117] Remesal dates
the mark from the reign of Augustus to the Flavians; while Mayet dates
an example from Volubilis to the beginning of the second century.[118]
M. Aemilius Rusticus appears in a *titulus pictus* from the Monte Testaccio
of possibly the year 149.[119] Again, the notable thing about Rusticus is that

he is, with the greatest likelihood, freeborn. Melchor Gil seems overly optimistic in connecting Artemisia's husband, M. Annius Celtitanus, with L. Annius Annianus and C. Annius Rufinus, attested on Dressel 20 handle stamps from Arva.[120] On the other hand, it is possible that L. Aemilius Rusticus, named on an unparalleled Dressel 20 stamp found at Colchester, is a relative of Marcus Aemilius Rusticus.[121] The Aemilii Rustici would then represent another example of different members of the same family involved in various aspects of the processing, bottling, and commercialization of Baetican oil. A similar arrangement is discernible in the production and commercialization of *sigillata* from Tritium Magallum (modern Tricio, La Rioja province), involving two freeborn relatives belonging to the *gens* Mamilia.[122]

More briefly, the oil trader M. Aemilius Cutianus, attested in *tituli picti* from the Testaccio of A.D. 146–147, may be from Astigi;[123] his cognomen certainly suggests his freeborn status.

The evidence of the Monte Testaccio, a bronze stamp found at Rome, and epigraphy from the Mediterranean littoral of Baetica provide a particularly vivid example of the conjunction of wealth-creating activity and social mobility, involving a family with no obvious connection with the *ordo* or local *honores*, save for a priesthood in the case of a female member. A statue base of white marble from Barbesula (cortijo Los Canos) records a dedication of second-century date to *Iuno Augusta*.[124] The statue base and accompanying inscription, in addition to a statue of the divinity made out of 100 pounds of silver, were set up, under authorization of the *ordo* of Barbesula, by C. Iulius Alfius Theseus, his wife Alfia Domitia Tertullina, and their son Q. Alfius Iulius Severus Optatianus in honor of their daughter and sister Alfia Domitia Severiana, a *flaminica perpetua*. The dedicant, C. Iulius Alfius Theseus, as González points out, is obviously the same individual as the trader of the same name cited in *tituli picti* of 154 from the control district Astigi. The merchant is also implicit in a *titulus* of c. 149 recording the "(Trium) Iul(iorum) Alf(iorum) Firm(i) Na . . . " who acted in association.[125] The same person is named on a bronze stamp discovered in Rome, now in the Louvre, with a diameter of 7.2 centimeters, which is dated by the ordinary consuls of 156, Silvanus and Augurinus.[126] A *titulus pictus* of 145, representing the control district Astigi, names in position beta the oil merchant Q. Alfius Theseus, who traded the product of the *possessor* Iulianus.[127] It is easy to agree with González, as does Chic García,[128] that the merchants of the *tituli* of 145 and 154, as well as the one implied in the *titulus* of c. 149, are one and the same person, and that Q. Alfius Theseus became C. Iulius Alfius Theseus through adoption by a certain C. Iulius, who is represented in Dressel position delta of the *titulus pictus* of 145. Theseus' son, moreover, was certainly a *honestus vir,* if not an *eques Romanus,* and there are no obvious grounds for inferring that he was a member of Barbesula's or another community's *ordo.*

Dressel 20 stamps name C. Annius Rufinus and Publius Annius Rufus (or Rufinus).[129] The first name appears in stamps of A.D. 75–150, produced at Arva. The stamps of C. Annius Rufinus show up in Britain and along the Rhine. The second individual appears on stamps manufactured at La Catria that show up at a variety of British, Gallic, and German sites, as well as at Rome. Remesal dates the stamps bearing the name of Publius Annius Rufus (or Rufinus) to the Flavian-Trajanic eras. The interest of both these persons is that their cognomina suggest their freeborn status.[130] It is possible, therefore, to reckon them among the ranks of Baetican *honesti* who profited in some fashion from the production and bottling of olive oil. Whether they are to be counted as *honesti* outside the *ordo* is impossible to determine. Nor is it possible to establish a family connection between the two.

We met above the fish-sauce trader and likely freeborn Spaniard C. Annius Senecio. Senecio is named on fish-sauce containers recovered from a south Italian shipwreck of the first half of the first century A.D. Whether Senecio was an *honestus* outside the *ordo* is unknown.

C. Antonius Balbus, active in the trade of olive oil during the reign of Antoninus Pius, may have been a freeborn trader of Baetican origin.[131] His surname is not borne by any explicitly designated Spanish slave or freedman.

A benefactor of Astigi, Aponia C(ai) f(ilia) Montana, was a *sacerdos Divarum Augustarum* in c. A.D. 150.[132] She gave circus games *ob honorem* and erected two statues, one of 100 pounds of silver and the other of 150 pounds of the same metal. Her son's name was Caesius Montanus, and it may be reasonable to connect this name with the Caesii who are on record as *mercatores* and/or *navicularii* associated with the production and commerce of olive oil from Astigi and its environs. It is a stretch, on the other hand, to believe that Urchail Atitta f(ilia) [or Atitta(e) f(ilius or filia?)], who undertook the construction of certain arched gates at Ilipa, perhaps during the reign of Augustus, is an ancestor of one Rufinus Atitta, whose name appears on Dressel 20 stamps of possibly the second half of the first century A.D., from *figlinae* and villas located at Las Sesenta, Palo Dulce, El Berro, La Mallena, and La Catria(?), all in the control district of Hispalis.[133]

One *diffusor olearius* who was active in A.D. 149 was Decimus Aticus Atticus Trophimianus.[134] He was freeborn, to judge from his polyonomy and on the assumption—a reasonable one—that he was the son of the *diffusor* Decimus Aticus Trophimus, who, like his putative son, is attested in the Monte Testaccio.[135] The cognomen of the father points to his status as a freedman.

Women—both freeborn and ex-slave—are on record as high-profile *negotiatrices oleariae* during the high imperial period. One such individual is Atilia T.f. Pa[terna?], who was active probably during the late Antonine period.[136] The *negotiatrix* may well be a relative, perhaps a daughter, of the *diffusor* and possible *ingenuus* T. Atilius Atilianus, active in c. A.D. 150 and attested on a bronze seal from Rome.[137]

C

The Caecilii of Astigi are central to this discussion. Caecilia Trophime and her husband Caecilius Silo ordered the dedication, by testamentary disposition, of a statue of *Pietas,* to be made from 100 pounds of silver.[138] Their heirs, D. Caecilius Hospitalis, Caecilia D.f. Materna, and Caecilia Philete, erected the statue in Astigi, probably during the reign of Pius. The relationship between all the named parties remains a controversial point, though Caecilia Materna is freeborn and quite possibly an *honesta femina;* she may well also be the daughter of the olive-oil merchant D. Caecilius Maternus and the sister of D. Caecilius Hospitalis—that same Hospitalis who is likely attested on a statue base at Rome, set up on behalf of the "negotiatores olearii ex Baetica" in honor of the prefect of the *annona* M. Petronius Honoratus. D. Caecilius Hospitalis is also attested in *tituli picti* of A.D. 145, 147, and 154, and operated in association with Maternus.[139] Melchor counts the Caecilii, including the *negotiator olearius ex Baetica* D. Caecilius Hospitalis, as benefactors of Astigi, and as having their wealth rest on the commerce of olive oil.[140] On the basis of nomenclature alone, it is possible to identify D. Caecilius Maternus as freeborn; as such, he would represent another instance of a Baetican *honestus* outside the *ordo.*

It is possible that the stamps Q.C.C. and Q.C.C.F, found at "Las Sesenta" next to the Guadalquivir, correspond to the trader Q. Caesius Caesianus, attested in the Testaccio in *tituli picti* of 149.[141] Caesianus as a likely *ingenuus* would represent a further example of the direct participation of the freeborn in trade, although the possibility always remains that Caesianus' forebears were slaves. Chic García links the stamp QCM with the *diffusor* Q. Caesius Macrinus, attested in the Testaccio under the year 149.[142] Macrinus, similarly, is probably the cognomen of an *ingenuus.*

The cognomina of the *diffusores olearii* C. Calpurnius Legulianus and C. Cantus Sulpicianus are fairly sure pointers to freeborn status. They are attested in the Testaccio and Horti Torlonia in *tituli picti* of c. A.D. 150 and 149, respectively.[143]

Melchor Gil insinuates a family connection between the *diffusor olearius* M. Cassius M.f. Gal(eria tribu) Sempronianus, attested at Tocina, and the *duovir* and benefactor of Italica M. Cassius Caecilianus, although, on Loyzance's admission, there are no epigraphical elements to confirm such a connection.[144] The vital point to emphasize is that Sempronianus was a person of substantial means who, by his service to the *annona,* was ipso facto an *honestus* outside the *ordo.* The stone recording Sempronianus states that he set up and dedicated some sort of structure ("a solo fecit et dedicavit"). There is no agreement on the nature of the structure: one scholar suggests it was a funerary monument; another argues that it was either a statue or a public building of religious or civil function; a third investigator simply categorizes it as a public edifice.[145] The important point is that Sempronianus, although possessing *origo* in Olisipo, had intimate ties—perhaps as a landowner—with Canania, in the possible territory of which the stone naming him was found. There are many like Sempronianus discernible in our sources from the far Roman West.

Chic García implies a link between the stamp MCLSI, found at the "Hoyo de San Sebastián," and its variants, dating to 140–180 in the Testaccio, and the oil trader M. Claudius Senecio, named in *tituli picti* of 149 and 154.[146] The same investigator suggests that the stamps MMCSAE, MMCSM, MMCSV, MMCSVR, and MMCSANTOF refer to a father-son association of the MM. Claudii Seneciones, who appear in the Testaccio in mid-second-century A.D. *tituli picti.*[147] Remesal, similarly, suggests that the marks MM(   ) C(   ) S(   ) ANTO(   ), MM(   ) C(   ) S(   ) VR(   ), and M(   ) C(   ) S(   ), which were found on Dressel 20s from German sites and were produced in or near Arva, may refer to a father and son or, alternatively, two brothers.[148] It is strange that no scholar seems to have noted that commercial enterprises in the Principate were frequently the preserve of families who invariably bequeathed the same cognomen from generation to generation, an oddity that leaves open the distinct possibility that the name had a value equivalent to a company trademark today. More to the point: in a Spanish context, the cognomen Senecio designates an *ingenuus.*

Q. Cornelius Quadratus is another likely candidate to be a freeborn *diffusor olearius;* he was active during the Antonine period.[149] Rodríguez Almeida makes the interesting but unconfirmed suggestion that Quadratus is to be identified as the brother of the imperial tutor Fronto. Our diffusor's status was probably not so lofty, but, even so, he may be counted among the ranks of local Baetican *honesti* outside the *ordo.*

At the end of the Antonine period, Cornelia Q(uinti) f(ilia) Placida, another high-profile freeborn *negotiatrix* involved with the sale and commerce of Baetican olive oil, was active. Placida is attested in *tituli* of A.D. 191 from the Monte Testaccio and nearby Horti Torlonia.[150]

Aulus Cosconius Avitus was an olive-oil merchant, active at some point during the first century A.D. He is attested in a *titulus pictus* from an amphora fragment recovered in the Baths of Diocletian.[151] He is almost certainly freeborn: of 212 instances of the cognomen Avitus recorded by Kajanto, only four belong to explicitly designated slaves or freedmen.[152]

From German sites come the stamps on Dressel 20s reading L(   ) C(   ) ANT(   ) P(ortu), L(   ) C(   ) HE(   ), and L(   ) C(   ) M(   ). The first and third stamps date to the mid-second century, while the second mark is of third-century date. Remesal suggests that the first and third stamps may refer to brothers or to a father and son; the second stamp might refer to a descendant of those named in the first and third stamps. The three stamps appearing on Dressel 20s manufactured at La Catria could thus represent three generations of persons devoted to the production and trade of olive oil.[153]

Representing Dressel 20 production at Malpica are the stamps M(   ) C(   ) L(   ) S(   ) R(   ) and S(   ) C(   ) L(   ) C(   ), found at German sites, which reflect related persons involved in the production and/or commerce of olive oil, according to Remesal.[154]

D

It would be unfair to omit from this accounting Marcus Decius Rufinus. He, too, deserves his place in a study devoted to wealth and social mobility in Rome's richest and most important province. Rufinus is named in a *titulus pictus* from the Monte Testaccio, which dates to approximately c. A.D. 150.[155] He may be confidently identified as freeborn: his cognomen is not borne by any Spanish slave or freedman. Of 490 examples of the name catalogued in Kajanto's repertorium, only nine are borne by non-Spanish slaves or freedmen.[156]

E

The *mercator* Q. Ennius Proculus Cornelianus is named in position beta of *tituli picti* from the Testaccio, dating to the period 153–161.[157] He is certainly freeborn. Another Ennius and likely *ingenuus,* C. Ennius Ennianus, is known from a *titulus* from the Horti Torlonia.[158] The members of this family are also indicated in amphora stamps of Flavian to mid-second-century date.[159] In addition, an inscription found at Seville and now lost names the *sevir Augustalis* Q(uintus) Ennius [En]niorum Albaniani et Enniani [lib(ertus)] Herma.[160] Without being able to establish the precise relationships, it is reasonable to suppose that Hermes was a freedman member of the family of the Ennii, and that his patrons Quintus Ennius Albanianus and Quintus Ennius Ennianus were somehow involved with oil production and commerce.

F

An opistographic marble plaque found in the territory of Oducia (Mesa de Lora or Lora la Vieja?) names a certain Lucius Flavius Flavianus.[161] Hübner in *CIL* dates the inscription attesting Flavianus, who died at age 48, to the Antonine period. The editors of the re-edited *Corpus Inscriptionum Latinarum,* following Remesal's lead, suggest that Flavianus was possibly a relative of the Quintus Flavius Flavianus who is named on Dressel 20 amphora stamps of second-century date. Quintus Flavius Flavianus is named in stamps emanating from the amphora-producing site La Catria, which lay in the territory of Oducia. The stamps may be expanded Q(uinti) F(lavii) F(laviani) and p(ortus) Q(uinti) Fl(avii) Fl(aviani).[162] Two points about the Flavianus of the epitaph from Mesa de Lora are important: first, he was probably, as his nomenclature suggests, freeborn, and second, the absence of any indication of magistracies or service as a decurion possibly means that he was, on the reasonable assumption of freeborn status, an *honestus* outside the local town council. The fact that Lucius Flavius Flavianus was interred in the very heart of the region of Baetica richest in olive orchards and oil production can be taken as a priori grounds for thinking that the *CIL* editors are right to connect him, if only indirectly, with the production and distribution of olive oil.

A pottery in the vicinity of Celti produced amphoras bearing the mark Q.F.C., which is datable to the mid-second century from the fact that it appears on amphoras from the Monte Testaccio bearing *tituli picti* of 149. Chic García links the stamp with the *patronus* and *pontifex* of neighboring Arva, Q. Fulvius Q. Fulvi Attiani f(ilius) Q. Fulvi Rustici n(epos) Gal(eria tribu) Carisianus, who was honored by the "centuriae Ores, Manens, Halos, Erques, Beres, Arvabores, Isines, and Isurgut."[163] Carisianus may also be the same as the Fulvius Charisianus who is named as a *mercator* in a *titulus pictus* from the Testaccio of 179–180, and who operated in association with Fulvius Rogatus; this on the assumption that the *titulus* that reads FULVIORUM II CHARI/SIANORUM ET ROGATI names one person bearing the name Q. Fulvius Charisianus.[164] Remesal, on the other hand, sees two individuals named Q. Fulvius Charisianus in the *titulus* and suggests that the Carisianus named in *CIL* II 1064 may be either one of the homonyms of the *titulus pictus* or one of their ancestors. In the same discussion, Remesal links those stamps from Arva naming a certain Q(   ) F(   ) R(   ) with the Fulvius Rogatus of the *titulus*.[165] The possibility does remain open, however, that the person indicated by the stamp Q.F.R. RIV is the same as the grandfather Quintus Fulvius Rusticus named in the honorary inscription from Arva that also names the priest Q. Fulvius Carisianus.[166] Chic García also links the mark Q.F.C. with the stamp Q.F.LUPI, found in Alexandria; the latter stamp refers, in all probability, to the wealthy Celtitanus Q. Fulvius Lupus, mentioned above.[167] On any interpretation, we probably ought to count the C(h)arisiani of the stamps, *tituli picti,* and inscription from Arva as further examples of those who were socially prominent outside the *ordo* in Baetican communities. And the likely oil trader Q. Fulvius Q. Fulvi Attiani f(ilius) Q. Fulvi Rustici n(epos) Gal(eria tribu) Carisianus was, without any doubt, a landowner of substantial means at or near Arva. It is likely that behind the native names of the "centuriae" that honored him are associations or communities of rural proprietors—probably of the territory of Arva.[168] Carisianus' relationship with them was undoubtedly complex, but it will have derived in the first instance, it is reasonable to suppose, from the fact that he acquired or channeled their olive and/or olive-oil production as a *diffusor olearius.* Another probable member of this family is the Q. Ful(vius)

Nig(er or -inus?), attested on stamps produced at Arva and found in Rome and Autun.[169]

G

Titus Gesatius Frontinus was active as an oil merchant at the beginning of the second century A.D.[170] He may be part of the *societas* of the Gesatii, named in a painted inscription on a Dressel 20 of approximately the mid-second century A.D.[171] Frontinus was evidently freeborn, to judge by his cognomen, which is not borne by any explicitly attested slave or freedman in Kajanto's catalogue.[172] It is certainly not possible to point to any Baetican slave or ex-slave with the cognomen.

I

C. Iulius Senex, active as an oil merchant c. A.D. 180 and named in a *titulus pictus* from the Testaccio, may count as an *honestus* outside the *ordo,* as Latin epigraphy discloses no freedman bearing his cognomen.[173] In the same category may also belong C. Iulius Valerianus, active as an oil merchant between 147 and 161 and named in the Testaccio.[174] In a spot decreed by the *ordo* of Astigi, M. Iulius Hermes Frontinianus and his son M. Iulius Hermesianus erected a pedestal with dedicatory inscription to their father and grandfather M. Iulius Hermesianus, a *diffusor olearius* or, alternatively, a "diffusor olei ad annonam urbis," as an unpublished inscription from Sevilla terms him.[175] Rodríguez Almeida points out that the son and grandson also profited from the supply of olive oil to Rome. *Tituli picti* from the Testaccio of Severan and post-Severan contexts suggest that the senior M. Iulius Hermesianus was active in the Antonine period, that M. Iulius Hermes Frontinianus was active at some period extending from the reign of Commodus into that of Septimius Severus, and that the grandson M. Iulius Hermesianus was active in the late Severan period.[176] The nomenclature of Frontinianus points to his freeborn status, and we can virtually assume freeborn status in the case of the grandson. The MM. Iulii from Astigi provide explicit proof of the activity of at least one family in the distribution of Baetican olive oil across three generations.

Iunia D(ecimi) f(ilia) Rustica was *sacerdos perpetua et prima* at Cartima.[177] It is an inspired suggestion that identifies her as the daughter of the olive-oil trader D. Iunius R . . . , attested in amphoras recovered from the Monte Testaccio and Mâcon dating to c. A.D. 120–125.[178] Rustica was a perpetual priestess, as was the daughter, Alfia Domitia Severiana, of the *diffu-*

sor olearius C. Iulius Alfius Theseus, mentioned above, in neighboring Barbesula.

C. Iunius Priscianus deserves a place in the roster of potentially freeborn *negotiatores olearii* from Baetica. A *titulus pictus* from the Monte Testaccio shows his activity in A.D. 146.[179] The -ianus ending of his cognomen leaves open his possible free birth.

The *Saint-Gervais 3* wreck and other sites yield the stamps Q.I.AL, C.I.A, CIALB, CIVENALBEP, Q.I.C.SEG, Q.I.M., Q.I.MF, and QIMFN impressed on amphoras produced at Casilla de Malpica, 9 kilometers from Palma del Río, on the Singilis.[180] It is likely that the marks refer to C. Iuventius C.f. Quir. Albinus, an aedile, *duovir,* and patron of Axati (*CIL* II 1054), mentioned previously, and his family/*familia* members. Albinus or a relative owned the amphora workshop at Malpica that seems to have reached a peak of activity in the mid-second century A.D., and that may have produced for other clients or lessees, such as a certain Calpurnius, whose name appears on stamps found at Malpica, Rome, and throughout western Europe.[181] Remesal dates the stamp Q(   ) I(   ) C(   ) SEG(   ) to the Flavian-Trajanic period; the mark C(   ) I(   ) ALB(   ) to the first half of the second century A.D.; and the stamps Q(   ) I(   ) AL(   ) and Q(   ) I(   ) M(   ) to c. A.D. 150, and sees in the marks evidence of three generations of the same family, of which the *duovir* at Axati formed a part, involved in the commerce of olive oil.[182] Remesal, in line with his conviction that the stamps refer to the producers and/or initial owners of the product, suggests that the Iuventii were landowners in the area of Malpica. On whatever interpretation of the stamps we take, Albinus and relatives seem to have profited from the production, sale, and trade of oil, in addition to the manufacture of amphoras.

Remesal suggests that the persons represented by the stamps S(   ) I(   ) RVF(   ) and S(   ) I(   ) SEN(   ) are members of the same family.[183] The likely cognomen, Rufus or Rufinus, of the person indicated by the first stamp points to freeborn status.

L

M. Licinius Maternus, named in position beta of a *titulus* from the Testaccio of c. 150, is another likely candidate as a freeborn Spaniard of Baetican origin outside the *ordo.*[184] No explicitly designated Spanish slave or freedman bears his cognomen.

M

The *tituli picti* in Dressel position beta reveal something unique in Latin epigraphy. The painted inscriptions disclose the existence and activity of two prominent businesswomen and sisters in the Roman Empire. They are the *ingenuae* Maria Q.f. Fesia[na?] and Maria Q.f. Postumina. We might imagine that the two were legally independent—either through the death of their father or through emancipation—and so were able to own property, and were free to transact business, subject only to the formal approval of a tutor.[185] The sisters were active in roughly the mid-second century A.D.[186]

Another likely freeborn *diffusor* is Lucius Memmius Hispanus, who was active in roughly the mid-second century.[187] The trader bears a cognomen that is never borne by Spanish slaves or freedmen. Of the forty-eight examples of the cognomen collected by Kajanto, only one belongs to a *servilis*—a slave recorded at Rome.[188] Hispanus is one of a number of Lucii Memmii active in the oil trade c. A.D. 150. Another possible freeborn member of this family with apparently both servile and freeborn members is L. Memmius Memmianus.[189] Lucius Mevius Rufus was active during the interval c. 15 to 5 B.C. in the commerce of fish sauce.[190] With caution, it may be possible to identify him as freeborn; although a Baetican freedman in Corduba bears the cognomen Rufus during the early Principate, the numbers, nevertheless, favor Mevius' free birth: of the 1,433 instances of the name in Kajanto's study, only twenty-four are borne by explicitly designated slaves or freedmen.[191] It remains possible that the fish-sauce amphora producer L. Mevius Faustus, attested on a Dressel 8 container found at the pottery "Villanueva" in the Bay of Cádiz,[192] as well as the oil merchant P. Mevius Faustus, named on an oil amphora from the Castra Praetoria in Rome, are descendants of Rufus.[193] Both of the latter two *negotiatores* seem to have been active in the Julio-Claudian period. Also attested in the Castra Praetoria is the Baetican fish-sauce trader C. Minicius Rusticus, whose cognomen is prima facie evidence for his freeborn status.[194]

N

Dressel found a fragmentary amphora on the Testaccio, deposited in approximately the mid-second century A.D., that names the *diffusor olearius* Lucius Nigidius Senecio.[195] Nigidius' cognomen is sufficient warrant for suggesting that he is yet another example of an *ingenuus* active in trade on behalf of the food supply of the city of Rome, and, as such, another *honestus* outside the *ordo* in the Antonine period.

O

The example of the *mercator olearius* M. Ovius Avillianus demonstrates that oil traders, on occasion, distributed the products of their own estate(s). Avillianus is named in Dressel position beta of *CIL* XV 3981 from the Testaccio, while position delta, dated A.D. 149, of the same container names the producer Avillia[nus], clearly the same person.[196] The cognomen of the trader, Avillianus, suggests his freeborn status. In this case, M. Ovius Avillianus would count as another specimen of an *honestus* outside the *ordo* in Baetica. There exist at least two further, more or less certain cases of oil merchants distributing oil from their own *fundi:* the traders T. Cassius Apolaustus, a likely freedman, attested in the Testaccio, and the merchant T. Testius Titullus, named in the *Port-Vendres II* wreck.[197] There are likely more instances of known *diffusores* who commercialized the oil of their own estate(s), but whose activity in this regard is obscured by the comparative rarity of Dressel 20 amphoras that preserve all the elements of the *tituli picti* on the same container. In any event, the examples of Avillianus, Apolaustus, and Titullus show that landowning or tenancy on the one hand, and commercial activities on the other, could be complementary and simultaneous activities.

P

The claim that was made above concerning Marcus Licinius Maternus might also be fairly made of T. Pompeius Maternus and T. Pompeius Paternus, attested on the Testaccio in *tituli* of c. 150.[198] The latter persons would be in the category of *honesti viri* outside the *ordo* both from their names, which are characteristic of *ingenui,* and from the fact that they had the means to act as merchants in the service of the *annona,* and therefore enjoyed immunity from both onerous local *munera* and, as a practical matter, officeholding and service as decurions for the duration of their involvement in the supply of Rome and the army.

The cognomen of the oil trader L. Postumius Pollio, attested in the Horti Torlonia in a *titulus* of possibly mid-second-century A.D. date, may point to his free birth; of 114 imperial-era instances of the name, only four are borne by certain slaves or freedmen.[199]

S

The -ianus ending of their cognomina leaves open the strong possibility that we are dealing with freeborn olive-oil merchants in the persons of M. Sempronius Livianus and C. Sempronius Sempro<nianus?>. The former is attested on a Dressel 20 fragment of unknown date from the Horti Torlonia in Rome; the second is named on a similar container, corresponding to period V (A.D. 120 to 140), from the Roman auxiliary encampment and associated settlement at Vindolanda in Britannia.[200] The same observation might be made also of L.(?) Severus Severianus, another probable freeborn oil trader, active during the Principate.[201]

In Chapter Three, we encountered the likely freeborn Spanish fish-sauce merchant L. Sempronius Fuscus. Fuscus seems to have been active during the Julio-Claudian period and supplied, among other places, the civilian community at Augst in Upper Germany.

It is worth emphasizing that only rarely is it possible to establish a connection between the names represented by the stamps and those persons of subequestrian status found in funerary or honorary inscriptions. Chic García is almost certainly right to connect the stamps L.S.A.R. with a certain L. Sergius Aelius Rusticus Quir(ina tribu). Rusticus is attested in a funerary inscription found near Cazalla de la Sierra (Sevilla province), which, on formulaic grounds, is datable to the period c. 120–190.[202] Callender dates examples of the stamp L.S.A.R, found at Rome, Heddernheim, and Vienne, to "probably the first half of the second century."[203] The critical point about Rusticus is that his epitaph is silent on any decurional status or *honores*—a peculiarity that alone leaves open his status as an *honestus* outside the *ordo decurionum*. There must exist scores of individuals of similar status and situation lurking in the handle stamps of Dressel 20s whose identities are hidden by the fact that they are usually referred to with their *tria nomina* reduced to bare initials or otherwise heavily abbreviated.

Remesal identifies the stamps LSPBOEQ, M.S.P., and II SER on amphoras produced in the vicinity of Arva as referring to the Servilii Polliones and envisages four generations of this family active in the production of olive oil.[204] They are L. Servilius L.f. Pollio, a *IIIIvir bis;* his son(?) and *conductor vectigalium* (tax collector) at Munigua in the reign of Titus, namely Servilius Pollio; a son of the preceding who is reflected in the stamp

II SER; a Lucius Servilius Pollio named in the stamp LSPBOEQ and active between 145 and 161; and finally, an M. Servilius Pollio of the stamp M.S.P., active in the period 160 to 180. Remesal, furthermore, suggests that the *figlinae* Guadajoz, Adelfa, Juan Barba, and Villar Tesoro, active c. A.D. 150, were under the control of the Servilii Polliones. P. Izquierdo suggests that the two stamps QSP, found on Dressel 20s from the *Cala Culip IV* shipwreck of c. A.D. 70–80, refer to a Quintus Servilius(?) Pollio(?), who is related to this family.[205]

V

C. Valerius Paternus was involved with commerce in olive oil in the years A.D. 149 and 154. He operated in association with his brother(?) C. Valerius Valerianus in the latter year. A delta inscription from a Dressel 20 amphora discloses the oil producer Vale . . . (?), and it may well be the case that the putative brothers distributed, on occasion, their own oil.[206] Paternus was, without any doubt, a freeborn Spaniard, on the basis of his cognomen, which is never borne by Baetican slaves or freedmen. Other probable freeborn Valerii, perhaps unrelated, involved in Baetican oil and its commerce are Valerius Ru[fus] and M. Valerius Valgo;[207] both may have been active in the mid-second century.[208] A certain Vinisius Vinisianus, active in A.D. 154 with Baetican oil, may also have been freeborn, to judge from his cognomen.[209]

Other *diffusores olearii* whose nomina cannot be reconstructed completely but who have, on surviving onomastic grounds, a fair warrant to being considered freeborn include [   ]onius Aper, [   ]lius Asper, [   ]us Marcellus, [   ] Montanus, and [   ]eius Senecio.[210] The free birth of the son, at least, of the *Vibianorum patris et iunioris* is virtually certain; they are attested in the Testaccio in *tituli* of the late 170s A.D.[211] The fish-sauce trader L. Verrius Aper, attested on an amphora of Julio-Claudian date from the Castra Praetoria in Rome, may also be freeborn.[212]

Not all *diffusores olearii* were of Baetican origin. M. Cassius Sempronianus, discussed above, was an *originarius* of Olisipo, but had a residence in Baetica. The best known, probably, of the olive-oil merchants in the Principate in the Roman West was C. Sentius Regulianus, attested at Rome.[213] Regulianus is an explicitly designated *eques Romanus,* and he seems to be from Gallia Lugdunensis.[214] Sextus Fadius Secundus Musa was from Gallia Narbonensis, and more specifically Narbo Martius (modern Narbonne), where he held all the local magistracies.[215] He seems to be the same person as the oil merchant Sextus Fadius Secundus, attested in *tituli picti* from the Testaccio of A.D. 146, 149, 154, and 161.[216] Coelia Cn.f. Mascellina, possibly of Narbonensian origin, was involved with the trade in Baetican olive oil in roughly the mid-second century A.D.[217] A remarkable aspect of the career of this freeborn daughter of Cn. Coelius Masculus is that she carried on the business not of her father but of her mother, who was a "negotiatrix olearia ex provincia Baetica item vini Arelate."[218] The merchant and possible *navicularius* Quintus Urittius Revocatus, named on oil-bearing amphoras from the *Port-Vendres II* shipwreck of Claudian date, was probably from Gaul.[219]

At this point, and still in connection with olive oil, it may be appropriate to mention, if only summarily, those persons who, on a priori grounds, can be counted among the ranks of *honesti viri* and *honestae feminae* of senatorial to decurional rank or below, but whose precise rank and census cannot be determined in the absence of further information. Several have already been mentioned above, such as those emperors whose Baetican *fundi* provided olive oil, the senatorial Tutilii Pontiani and the equestrian oil-producer Rocius Rocianus. These individuals, both male and female, show up in the genitive on inscription delta of Dressel 20 oil-bearing amphoras and constitute, on the most likely interpretation of the meaning of the names found in this component of the *tituli picti,* those known *possessores* and *coloni* whose properties produced oil. Some of them were undoubtedly freedmen and freedwomen, but many, if not most, were freeborn.[220] It becomes even more difficult, therefore, to accept Remesal's insistence that these names in Dressel position delta represent *publicani* connected with the collection of *portoria* levied on the export of Baetican oil, from the fact that over thirty women are attested among the total of 270 names on record. These women are obviously, in many instances, *honestae feminae;* and furthermore, it is reasonable to suppose that many of the males representing oil producers would have been in the category of *honesti* outside the *ordo.* Liou and Tchernia, for example, make the plausible suggestion that the producer Aelia Marciana, named on amphoras commercialized by the "Antonii Melissus et Peregrinus" discovered in the *Saint-Gervais 3* wreck, is perhaps a relative of Aelius Marcianus, who was proconsul of Baetica under Antoninus Pius.[221]

Freedmen and the Miscellaneous Wealthy

Freedmen on record with specific, wealth-creating activities and occupations are the subject of several studies published in the late 1980s that discuss, in detail, the juridical, social, and economic aspects of ex-slaves in the Iberian peninsula, including Baetica.[222] It is not necessary to rehearse here, for example, every single epigraphic or literary attestation of *liberti* involved in the various *artes liberales* or artisanal professions.

Many of the Dressel 20 handle stamps refer to freedmen who are ubiquitous as oil traders and as amphora manufacturers. The beta inscriptions of the Dressel 20 *tituli* also name numerous freedmen *diffusores,* such as D(ecimus) Aticus D(ecimi) l(ibertus) Onesimus, active during the reign of Antoninus Pius.[223] In spring 1990, Caballos and Eck found five amphora stamps at the "Molino de la Peña de la Sal," which corresponds to the port of Arva (El Castillejo).[224] The most interesting mark reads MEGN and supports Callender's suggestion that the mark MEE known previously, and also found at the site, is related to the *sevir* M. Egnatius Venustus named in an inscription from Arva (*CIL* II 1066). Venustus received the *ornamenta decurionalia* (insignia and title of a decurion) and a statue from Arva at the beginning of the second century A.D. Venustus, the individuals indicated by the stamps, and a certain L. Egnatius who was an *Augustalis* at Orippo, and who appears in a fragmentary dedication to Mercury of Claudian date,[225] are probably all related, and point to the involvement of this *familia* in oil production and trade. The *sevir Augustalis* at Suel L. Iunius Puteolanus was probably involved with the production and/or commerce of Baetican fish sauce.[226] Puteolanus erected a dedication to Neptune Augustus and gave an *epulum* for some or all of the inhabitants of that coastal Baetican town. The fish-sauce trader P. Clodius Athenio, who resided in Rome or Ostia during the first half of the second century A.D., was mentioned in Chapter Four. His cognomen suggests his status as a freedman.[227] Of possible Baetican origins are the fish-sauce traders and obvious freedmen Marcus Valerius Euplus, Marcus Memmius Agathemerus, and Caius Clodius Alexander; they are named on amphoras carrying fish sauce from Lixus in Mauretania Tingitana and Sexi in Baetica discovered in the *Pecio Gandolfo (Almería)* shipwreck of c. A.D. 50–100.[228]

Deserving of brief mention, additionally, are those *honesti viri* who were certainly or possibly outside the *ordo,* and *honestae feminae* whose sources of wealth are not known. Their ranks include all explicitly attested freeborn *incolae* and probably a large majority of foreigners of nonservile status. On general grounds, it remains possible to see their more or less permanent geographical movement as having economic motives, as they sought to better their situation or that of their dependents.[229] Geographical mobility, in short, may be seen as a consequence of economic activity, however ill defined, and thus freeborn *alieni* deserve mention in this study. The following freeborn and freed persons — not necessarily all migrants — are attested in both rural and urban contexts.

Mackie already identified *incolae*, or resident aliens, as those persons of social distinction who remained outside local town councils. We might extend this category to include all those *alieni* in Baetica who are not explicitly designated *incolae*, but who seem to have enjoyed more than an ephemeral relationship with a community other than that of their birth. The numbers of such individuals could multiply rapidly. For the sake of example, let us focus brief attention on "M(arcus) Iunius Quir(ina tribu) [Hi]spanus, Segoviensis," who ordered a dedication, by testament, to *Vesta Augusta.* The *ordo* of Naeva decreed a spot for the dedication to be erected. Although the stone was found in Sevilla, it is likely that it was brought there from Cantillana, the site of the *municipium Naevense.* Hispanus, a Roman citizen and *originarius* of Baetican Segovia, is named on a pedestal of white marble, measuring 125 by 49.5 by 48 centimeters. The inscription naming Hispanus dates to the first half of the second century A.D.[230] Although he is not an explicitly designated *incola* of Naeva, some kind of protracted relationship with that town is implied by Hispanus' dedication. In any event, Hispanus counts probably as an *honestus* who remained outside of any *ordo decurionum.*

Mackie also indicated as certain *honesti* outside the *ordo* local priests. She singled out a Marcus Fabius Probus, a *flamen* and "pontifex perpetuus Div[- - -] Aug(ust-)" in Aurgi.[231] Probus' priesthoods date probably to the second half of the second century A.D. The application of the criterion of the tenure of priesthoods and the absence of any attestation of magistracies or rank as decurion will result, indeed, in the identification of other likely *honesti* outside local, Baetican *ordines* besides Probus. There is, for example, Gaius Mummius G(ai) f(ilius) Quir(ina tribu) Hispanus, a *pontifex* at Singili(a?) Barba honored by the "cives et incolae" of that Flavian *municipium* at some point during the first half of the second century A.D.[232] The point is not to accumulate a long list of examples, but simply to underline the frequency with which probable and possible persons of social repute who are not on record as having held magistracies or served as decurions appear in Baetican epigraphy of the early Principate. But local and provincial priestesses in Baetica invariably count, also, as *honestae feminae*. The phenomenon of Baetican priestesses is the subject of a recent and exhaustive inventory and analysis.[233]

Other possible *honesti* outside the *ordo* merit inclusion in this survey. They include the Fabii Fabiani. Canto sees the various Fabii Fabiani attested in Baetica as representing a single family with various branches; sadly, there are no solid grounds for establishing such a connection save for the possible accident of homonymy. A total of seventeen inscriptions, clustering in the penibético between the Baetis and the Mediterranean, name eight Fabii Fabiani and five Fabiae Fabianae. The males employ the praenomina Caius, Lucius, or Quintus. Canto's point, nevertheless, is well taken that these persons seem to show a uniformly high economic attainment, and it is noteworthy that only one can be linked in a certain way with local magisterial or priestly offices.[234] A certain L. Fabius L.f. Gal. Fabianus is named in three inscriptions from the unknown *oppidum* located in the Cortijo del Tajo (Teba del Condado, Málaga province). In one of the inscriptions, he is named as the heir of a certain Q. Fabius L.f. Gal. Fabullus, probably also a nondecurional, who made testamentary provisions for the erection of a statue of *Victoria Augusta*.[235] The same Fabianus is named in the two other inscriptions from the Cortijo del Tajo as commemorating his freeborn wife Cordia L.f. Sergiana and his freeborn mother Nummia M.f. Rustica.[236] One C. Fabius C.f. Quir. Fabianus is the dedicant of a statue and statue base in Singili(a?) Barba to *Libertas Augusta* (*ILS* 3780). This latter Fabianus is probably the same as the "Gaius Fabius G.f. Quir. Fabianus Singiliensis" attested in a fragmentary funerary plaque, datable to the second half of the second century A.D., from Singili(a?) Barba.[237] An inscription of late Flavian or early second-century A.D. date from Cartima names the *sacerdos perpetua* Iunia D.f. Rustica, who made a variety of benefactions to that town. The inscription records her husband as a certain C. Fabius Fabianus.[238] Again, it is important to emphasize that there is no warrant, save for homonymy, to think that the Fabii Fabiani enumerated so far in Singili(a?) Barba, Cartima, or the *oppidum ignotum* at the Cortijo del Tajo near Teba are related. A funerary(?) inscription from Setenil near Acinippo names two more Fabii Fabiani, this time C. Fabius Fabianus father and son.[239] An honorary inscription from Barbesula names L. Fabius Gal. Caesianus, a *duovir* honored by his heirs, Fabia C.fil. Fabiana (his niece?)

and Fulvia Sex.fil. Honorata.[240] The same Fabia C.f. Fabiana may be named in another inscription, possibly from Barbesula, if not from Carteia, which records a dedication of a statue adorned with jewels to *Diana Augusta*.[241] An inscription of uncertain reading seems to record a certain Fabia [C.f.?] Fabiana in Iptuci (Prado del Rey), who was honored by a statue, the erection of which was entrusted to her brother Fabius Montanus.[242] A funerary inscription from Fuente Alhama (Luque) records a certain Fabia Q.f. Fabiana.[243] An honorary inscription from Ulia of A.D. 222–235 to Severus Alexander seems to have been dedicated by a polyonomous individual whose full name is uncertain but seems to include the elements Q. Fabius Fabianus [-c. 2-]ratus. . . .[244] Another funerary inscription, this time from Curiga, names a certain Fabia L.[f.] Fabiana, who died at age 40.[245] The honorary inscription from Aratispi, discussed below, that was set up to M. Fulvius Senecio names as one of his *amici* one C. Fabius Fabianus. A funerary inscription, possibly of the second half of the second century A.D., this time from Hispalis, names a certain "Q. Fabius Q.f. Quirina Fabianus Ilurconensis idem Patriciensis," who died at the age of 43.[246] The dual *origo* of the penultimate Fabianus may be connected to his role as a *negotiator*.[247]

The best interpretation of the social position of the various Fabii Fabiani and Fabiae Fabianae would be to suggest that they are all members of that broad class of Baetici who belong to the socioeconomic spectrum of persons including sub-decurional jurors, *honestae feminae,* and *honesti viri* remaining outside local *ordines.* The number of certain and possible Baetican *honesti* outside the *ordo*—the persons named here are selected representatives of a larger sample—exceeds that of all known decurions and local magistrates in Baetica. Of course, the danger of too crude a positivistic approach to the evidence of the inscriptions is not something to be lightly brushed aside. Perhaps some of the persons named in this section, including certain Fabii Fabiani, were, after all, members of local *ordines* who, for some reason or other, are not designated as officeholders or decurions. It is a notorious fact that explicitly designated decurions in Baetican epigraphy are comparatively rare. Nevertheless, it must surely be the case that a substantial proportion of persons, aside from the obvious cases of local priests, *alieni, incolae,* soldiers, or *negotiatores olearii,* who do not indicate offices held or service as decurion were, indeed, individuals who remained outside local *ordines decurionum.*

Two inscriptions from Aratispi may well point to more *honesti* outside the *ordo.* Aratispi received municipal status under Vespasian. Aratispi is not yet rich in published epigraphy, but those inscriptions, on various supports, that have been published do illustrate certain aspects of Aratispi's life as a *municipium*. Four inscriptions are embedded in the tower of the church that is immediately to the south of the hilltop portion of the *oppidum*. One is a pedestal, apparently of limestone, which measures 95 by 57 by 48 centimeters and is set in the corner of the tower.[248] The letters are inscribed in *scriptura libraria* of the first half of the second century. The inscription consists of a dedication to a certain "M. Fulvius [S]enecio Aratispitanus." He is described as an "optumus [sic] et praestantissimus civis" and is celebrated "ob merita" by certain *amici*. It is clear that Senecio, an obvious *ingenuus*, if not *honestus*, is being commemorated because of some unspecified benefaction(s). Just as significant is the fact that Senecio's *amici* are named in the inscription. They are, in the order of their appearance in the text: Publius Licinius Aemilianus, Publius Licinius R[   ], Lucius Licinius Vibianus, L. Licinius Licinianus, L. Fabius Silvinus, C. Fabius Fabianus, L. Fabius Optatus, M. Iunius Montanus, M. Iunius Martialis, M. Iunius Maternus, M. Flavius Maxuminus, L. Flavius Severus, C. Calpurnius Celer, C. Calpurnius Perpetuus, C. Aemilius Anthus, Annius Dionysius, and L. Aurelius Capratinus. All of the *amici* are arguably freeborn, with the possible exceptions of the last three named. It is not obvious that the *amici* are members of Aratispi's *ordo,* although that conclusion cannot be ruled out. Otherwise, it is also possible that the named "friends" are not members of the council, but, all the same, are of a status sufficient to merit their inclusion in the roster of certain "friends" of a civic benefactor. It may be worth hazarding, without being able to achieve certainty on the matter, that Senecio and his friends belong to the wider group of the municipal "juror class" of Aratispi and other Baetican communities.

A second inscription from Aratispi provides additional testimony for one of Senecio's *amici,* and may point to another person in the *municipium* outside the *ordo.* That person is "L. Licinius Licinianus Aratispitanus," who is named on a funerary pedestal embedded in the southeast corner of the church tower above the aforementioned pedestal.[249] The second altar naming Licinianus measures 76 by 53.5 by 45 centimeters. The text is also inscribed in *scriptura libraria* and is contemporary with the aforementioned inscription. A crucial point here is that the pedestal naming Licinianus is not the commemoration of a poorer member of the *municipes Aratispitanorum.* Another salient point is that the text in the pedestal does not name any offices or charges associable with the deceased. The absence of any such mention is surely, and I would insist on this point, indicative of the distinct possibility that Lucius Licinius Licinianus was never a decurion of Aratispi or an officeholder in that *municipium*.

Finally, the intersection of *honesti,* whether in the *ordo* or not, and production is brought out intimately in the form of pottery or brick stamps, that is, through those items of *instrumentum domesticum* with which Baetici indicated their ownership or manufacture of things, usually transport or storage containers and their contents, but sometimes also bricks. There is, for instance, the stamp, made of lead and measuring 6.5 by 2.9 by 1.6 centimeters, from an unknown place within Baetica, probably the valley of the Baetis, recording FABIAE L(uci) F(ilia) VIETAE.[250] It is impossible to know precisely the function of her stamp. But Vieta has the ring of a *femina honesta* who profited in some way from the production and distribution of pottery and the products it contained. A stamp found in the vicinity of Mesa de Lora (ancient Oducia) reads G(ai) LVCI F(ilii) SEMP(ronii) A(N)NVL(i). It is of bronze and measures 3.2 by 6.7 by 0.5 centimeters.[251] Gaius Sempronius An(n)ulus is not attested on any Dressel 20 amphora stamp. Perhaps An(n)ulus sealed *dolia* with this stamp. We do not know. Nor do we know whether he was a local decurion or magistrate of Oducia. Perhaps, even, he was an *honestus* outside the *ordo.* He does, nevertheless, stand on record as a freeborn Baetican who profited in some fashion from the product(s) of the province.[252] A somewhat more enigmatic seal is that found outside of Montilla (*oppidum ignotum*) in Córdoba province. The bronze seal measures 2.5 by 5 by 0.5 centimeters, and reads C(ai?) G(ai?) F(ilii?) MAR(   ). It dates to the first or second century A.D.[253] The *CIL* II² editor reports seeing in 1996, at a spot north of Montilla, a brick, broken on all sides, with the letters C Q F P, impressed by a rectangular stamp of dimensions similar to those of the aforementioned bronze stamp from Montilla. The element "Q F" of the stamp impression probably is the filiation of this unknown individual. Another bronze seal, this one measuring 2.7 by 5.5 centimeters and found on the Cerro de las Caleras, 6 kilometers east of Montilla, reads C(ai) VALERI POLLIONIS; the stamp dates to the first or second century A.D. and seems to refer to an *ingenuus.*[254] On any reading, the stamps and stamp impressions from the territory of the unknown *oppidum* at Montilla seem to refer to *ingenui* who stamped bricks produced in pottery installations that they either owned or leased.

The meticulous exposition of *honesti* outside the *ordo* and *feminae honestae* above invites us to reconsider the usefulness of Harris' tripartite (re)organization of Roman society, an outline of which was summarized in the introduction. How is it possible to integrate into his scheme wealthy *negotiatores olearii ex Baetica?* These are individuals who in many demonstrable instances were substantial landowners and who had, undoubtedly, numerous dependents at their disposal, both servile and free. At the same time, they were, by virtue of their service to the *annona* of the city of Rome, unencumbered by political activity at both the local and the imperial level. They therefore do not fit into any of the three categories of 1) slaves, *mercenarii*, or other dependents, 2) those with a modicum of land or a shop eking out a living by their own labor, or 3) those who were politically active and had a large number of slaves or other dependents to provide their wealth. It should be apparent, before all else, that *negotiatores* or *mercatores olearii ex Baetica* were themselves directly involved in wealth-creating activity. These merchants are only the more immediately recognizable examples of persons of substantial wealth in Baetica who had the means and desire to remain outside local *ordines decurionum*, or whose civic activity was restricted to the holding of a local priesthood, service as a municipal juror, or euergetistic activity.

CHAPTER SEVEN

✳

The Nature of Economic Growth
in Roman Imperial Baetica:
A Theoretical Perspective

All nonslaves in the province will have seen a general growth in their per capita income and accumulated wealth during the period c. 25 B.C. to A.D. 170.[1] There is no decisive evidence for a substantial growth in the population of the province between the Julio-Claudian and late Antonine eras. It is in the Julio-Claudian and, particularly, Flavian periods that we see a remarkable proliferation of productive rural settlements. Thus agricultural production that can increase either at the intensive margin (that is, through greater inputs of capital and labor, in part through an expanding population that results in net diminished productivity per capita), or at the extensive margin (that is, by bringing more land into use) would a priori have increased at the extensive margin.[2] But abundant evidence for the presence of slaves, as well as productive investment in farmsteads and their associated equipment and infrastructure, such as dams, cisterns, and irrigation canals, means that the inputs of capital and labor also saw substantial, if perhaps irregular, increases in Baetica during the Principate. Per capita income, consequently, would have increased in Baetica in the period from c. 25 B.C. TO A.D. 170, on any reckoning. Jongman's explanation for inhibited growth in productivity—as opposed to total production—and thus per capita income during the Principate is a brilliant tour de force that has no relevance, it is evident, for Baetica. Jongman, following Lipsey et al., writes of "changes in factor supplies (labor, capital and land)" versus "increasing factor productivity (output per unit of factor input)" as elements of growth.[3] Jongman argues that as factor productivity through technological innovation is mainly a feature of modern economic growth, and as land was at a premium and the population high in Campania, "per capita" incomes were, on average, low and did not grow during the Principate. It can be argued that for a substantial length of time in Baetica, all three factor supplies making up the production function were increasing, whereas Jongman, arguing from the case of peninsular Italy, would emphasize that at most two can supply further marginal doses, insisting that in the "real world the supply of at least one of the factors is usually more or less fixed."[4] Further, the contribution of slaves to increasing accumulated wealth or capital and income is ignored by Jongman. Jongman takes as a premise the existence of a mass of tenants living at or just above subsistence who represent the great majority of the inhabitants of Pompeii's territory and its rural workforce.[5] I will return to the question of subsistence. But Jongman's thesis is universalizing: the *coloni* of Pompeii represent, by implication, the rural free of the Empire as a whole. But do they really? Did Pompeii's diversified cereal agriculture and viticulture depend fundamentally on the labor of *coloni*? The unfortunate fact of the matter is that we do not really know the status of that Campanian town's agricultural workforce.

In essence, Jongman adopts as alternative conceptual models to explain Pompeii's economy Jan de Vries' peasant versus specialization models. De Vries originated these models to explain the transformation of Dutch agriculture during the sixteenth and seventeenth centuries. In both models, the trigger is population pressure and/or growth. The two models, following Jongman's summary, are worth outlining briefly. In the end, Jongman describes Pompeii's (rural) economy in terms of the peasant model. In the peasant model, peasants see a reduction in the size of their holdings. Their labor productivity declines, as a static amount of land must feed a high or increasing population. The peasants may need, moreover, to supplement their income with day labor. The price of food rises. Peasants have no marketable surplus of food. Peasants' purchase of non-food items decreases. The result is an increase in social inequality as powerful interests retain or expand landholdings. Rents go up. Many peasants are forced to lease back land. In this model, as summarized by Jongman, urban crafts production is limited to satisfying elite demand for consumer goods.[6] It is striking how

similar all this sounds to the traditional historiography on the agrarian crisis of second-century Italy and the Gracchan response.

In de Vries' specialization model of peasant response to high prevailing
population density and/or population growth, first and foremost, peasants'
land is not split up. Peasants spend more of their time producing a marketable surplus. They are thus able to purchase nonagricultural goods and
"become participants in a proper market economy."[7] As in the peasant
model, labor productivity declines, but the decline is mitigated by the production of marketable crop(s) with less steeply declining marginal labor
productivity, such as the products of viticulture or market gardening. One
beneficial aspect of the specialization response is that the crops that are
most suitable for local conditions can be grown. Another benefit is that
the specialized urban production of consumer goods may result in better
and/or cheaper products. The key element in this model seems to be that
an increased demand for urban goods can siphon off population (growth)
from the land to the cities. Peasants, in the end, become more resistant to
urban elite predators. Moreover, "possibilities for investment and enrichment do exist" in urban manufacturing.[8]

Baetican conditions more closely approximate de Vries' specialization
response, though it is not possible to adduce as the trigger a high prevailing
population density and/or growth in the province. Jongman follows Beloch
in postulating a population density of 180 persons per square kilometer in
Campania.[9] Beloch, it is worth noting by way of comparison, estimated a
density of 20 humans per square kilometer in Baetica.[10] Another crucial difference between the postulates of the de Vries specialization model and
conditions in the province merits underscoring: it is unnecessary, and indeed it is inconsonant with the evidence, to posit in Baetica an urban-rural
dichotomy in terms of the production of nonagricultural goods. The trigger
in the case of Baetica will have been, therefore, external demand for Baetica's agricultural products. Garnsey thinks that "the existence or growth of
demand for an agricultural surplus" was an important element in stimu-
lating productivity and production during the late Empire.[11] Demand for
Baetica's agricultural production seems to have grown in the early Principate. The growing, processing, and sale of agricultural staples, in the main,
such as wine, fish sauce, and olive oil, met a demand that was elastic. The
direct purchase of these staples from producers, in large part by private
negotiatores acting on behalf of the state, would have constituted a primary,

if not the most important, mechanism by which cash entered and circulated within Baetica.

What was the scale of the demand? The short answer is: unknown. In the case of olive oil, though, whatever number of amphoras we fix as the average deposited yearly in the Monte Testaccio, we can, at a minimum, double as the number produced and filled in Baetica in one year. On one recent estimate, 7,000,000 liters of Baetican oil were shipped to Rome per year.[12] To oil-consuming bellies and lamps in Rome and environs, there were added those of Mauretania Tingitana, the legions and civilian centers in the Rhine and Danubian provinces, and the legions and civilians in Britain, Gaul, Dalmatia, Alexandria, and other regions and localities of the Empire, including Lusitania and Tarraconensis.[13] It is clear that much of this Baetican oil would have appeared in the aforementioned places and regions from the redistribution of oil forming part of, or shipped alongside, consignments of oil destined for the *annona*. Rome would have acted as a major point in the transshipment of oil to eastern Mediterranean destinations. It is probably the case that over time, high-density, high-value cargoes from Baetica in the form of metals subsidized the transport of lower-value staples, at least during the early Principate. In this context, it may be worth adding that Chic García suggests that *IG* II² 1100, set up in Athens, refers to an empire-wide disposition of Hadrian regulating the mandatory sale of a certain proportion, in this case a third, of oil production by *possessores* to the Roman state.[14] Also worth noting here is the discovery at Castulo in 1956 of a marble altar, measuring 91.5 by 59 by 32.5 centimeters, of possibly Hadrianic date, that reads "rescriptum sacrum de re olearia."[15] The altar may have formed part of a larger epigraphic monument promulgating a western version of the oil law from Athens. The absence of any other direct evidence for such an empire-wide Hadrianic regulation with significant implications for the production and distribution of oil from Baetica is unfortunate. In light of the absence of evidence, it is a leap of faith to suppose that the procuratorship of the *Kalendarium Vegetianum* goes back to the reign of Antoninus Pius, and to connect that office with the mandatory sale to the state of a percentage of Baetican oil production.[16] All the same, the term *solamina,* which appears in the honorary inscription in Hispalis to the *adiutor praefecti annonae,* Sextus Iulius Possessor, may have the alternative meaning of "indemnifications" or "compensatory payments."[17] It is a tantalizing possibility that J. M. Carrié is right to read the word in the inscription in this way, namely, as a prosaic synonym for the word "solacium,

-a," and it is tempting to see as part of Possessor's duties the compensation, by the Roman state, to Baetican oil producers for the compulsory sale to the *annona* of a (third) part of their crop/produce.[18] But let us suppose that Carrié were right: that would not exclude the possibility that the indemnifications were directed to the ad hoc purchase of oil for civilian or military purposes, that is to say, were not, pace Chic, part of a permanent yearly purchase by the state of a part of the production of olive-oil producers.

It is high time to discuss in detail the question of subsistence. What does a subsistence income mean for Jongman in terms of sesterces? Let us first be clear about what Jongman actually says. He writes, "I have deliberately provided a minimum estimate for elite wealth, excluded the emperor's wealth, and assumed that everyone who did not belong to these orders lived at the level of bare subsistence. That is, of course, unrealistic." But "bare subsistence" is what Jongman assumes to have been the case, anyway, for the income of the mass of the population. For elsewhere he writes: "As incomes for the vast majority of the population were at or near subsistence. . .," and "The vast majority of the Italian population was probably engaged in generating elite income and producing the goods and services for elite consumption — apart from providing their own subsistence, of course." It is precisely this part of Jongman's argument that has not been picked up, so far as I know, for scholarly debate. We can, on Jongman's own reckoning, attach a number to subsistence. That number, of course, refers to the wheat-equivalent annual subsistence ration expressed in sesterces and comes out to a figure of 115 sesterces.[19] That number, although neither Jongman nor any other critic states the matter flatly, is what he means by a subsistence income. Jongman's figure is the same as that derived by dividing Hopkins' minimum estimated annual subsistence wheat ration of 250 kilograms by Rostovtzeff's average price of wheat in the Principate of three sesterces per *modius* (equivalent to 6.55 kilograms).[20] Hopkins' implicit figure rises from 114.5 sesterces per capita subsistence wheat equivalent to 143.1 sesterces if seed — taken to constitute a quarter of the yearly crop — is included. But Raymond Goldsmith, in an article published in 1984 that Jongman does not cite, estimated an average per capita income in the Roman Empire of the first century A.D. of 380 sesterces plus or minus 15 percent, for a range of 320 to 440 sesterces.[21] It is reassuring to note in this context that F. Jacques and J. Scheid, also unaware of Goldsmith's work, suggested an average annual subsistence level of 400 to 500 sesterces for adults in the Roman Empire during the first two centuries A.D.[22] Moreover, T. Pekáry, writing in the mid-1970s, seems to set the subsistence outlay for a family of indeterminate size in the earlier imperial period in an urban context at 3-400 sesterces, although, in that scholar's dire conception, the family would have produced its own clothing and eaten a meatless diet.[23] Of the sum of 380 sesterces, Goldsmith postulated an expenditure of 130 sesterces per annum for wheat and on all other bread grains, mainly barley. And Goldsmith estimated—in the most sober terms—that the average recipient of monetary or imputed income gained close to an average of 1,000 sesterces per annum. This latter figure is, curiously, the same as the yearly earnings of about 250 *denarii* or 1,000 sesterces of the sandal-maker Micyllus in Lucian's *The Cock,* written in about A.D. 170.[24] This latter figure derives from a calculation of Mac-Mullen, an estimation that rests on his perfectly acceptable, though tacit, assumption that the fictional cobbler will have plied his craft throughout the year. All this means that throughout the Roman world, the average tenant, small-scale farmer, and urban or rural skilled or semi-skilled artisan or worker gained a yearly average income that was roughly nine times bare subsistence.

We also need to take into account a step-up to average income not reckoned by Goldsmith. At issue is the notional value of periodic distributions of money or food to the inhabitants of *municipia* and *coloniae* in the Roman world in the form of *sportulae* and *epula.* Mrozek may be optimistic in suggesting that each inhabitant of a community in Italy during the middle Principate gained the equivalent of 120 *denarii* or 480 sesterces per annum as a result of systematic participation at cash handouts.[25] Be that as it may, and taking into account the possibility that public banquets in Baetica were more frequent than cash handouts,[26] we might, on a conservative basis, estimate that in Rome's wealthiest province, an annual step-up to per capita average income would be in the order of 50 percent of the average step-up postulated for Italy, that is to say, 60 *denarii,* or roughly 240 sesterces per year. Consequently, our minima for earned income and average per capita income would increase by a factor of 60 percent across the board, and our subsequent reckonings in the following discussion ought to take this annual supplement to earned income into consideration.

Let us play the numbers game a little more and combine it with the documentary sources for the Roman social order in Baetica in a novel way.

Most students of the Roman world and economy assume—quite rightly it seems—that the mass of the Roman population was more or less directly engaged in agriculture. That assessment would be as true for Baetica as it would be for Italy or elsewhere. The standard rate of return, whether imputed or in coin, on agricultural investment is taken to be 6 percent per annum.[27] Now let us turn briefly to the testimony of the Flavian municipal law of the later first century A.D. as embodied in the so-called Lex Irnitana. Chapter 86 of the Lex Irnitana stipulates that local jurors at Irni, aside from decurions and *conscripti,* are to be chosen from that body of candidates who, assuming certain qualifications of birth, age, and moral probity have been met, either possess themselves or, if they are in the *potestas* of another, have a father, paternal grandfather, paternal great-grandfather, or adoptive father who possesses a minimum census of 5,000 sesterces.[28]

The census refers to accumulated property and not to income. An average 6 percent return on a capital of 5,000 sesterces results in a yearly profit and/or income of precisely 300 sesterces. The figure of 300 sesterces is not far below that figure of 380 sesterces, imputed or in coin, posited by Goldsmith as representing the average yearly income of every man, woman, and child in the Roman Empire. Interestingly, Frier's analysis of "subsistence" annuities recorded mostly by the Antonine jurist Cervidius Scaevola shows that testators left to freedmen or foster children sums that cluster in the range of 376 to 600 sesterces, that is, sums that are precisely within or slightly above the range posited by Goldsmith as representing average per capita income in the Empire.[29] Lamberti, furthermore, makes the attractive suggestion that the census minimum for jurors in Malaca would be double that in Irni, that is, 10,000 sesterces.[30] On this accounting, then, the yearly minimum return on capital of a local juror in that coastal Flavian *municipium* would be roughly 600 sesterces, or precisely in the upper range of subsistence annuities posited by Frier. It is of vital interest to note, furthermore, that, as Frier points out, Scaevola's cases are generally of provincial origin, including one on record from Gades. Frier's definition of "subsistence" is more realistic — and more generous in its scope — than Jongman's: it includes food, clothing, and shelter, namely rent.[31]

Now for a bit more of the documentary evidence, again from the Lex Irnitana. How does the Lex, and therefore the Roman authorities, conceive of or designate those Irnitani who are called to serve as local jurors? These persons are those *municipes* who, on unimpeachable, simple arithmetic, would command a minimum yearly agricultural income — whether imputed, such as produce in kind, or in coin — in the order of 300 sesterces or slightly more. The Lex Irnitana uses the term *idoneus,* one redolent of moral approbation and reflective of elite values, to describe those individuals who are called to local jury duty. The Lex is explicit on this point: the *duoviri* are to appoint, in addition to decurions, those "ex reliquis municipibus" who, in addition to the qualifications spelled out above, are persons "quos maxime idoneos arbitrabitur." To be sure, there were *municipes* who were more equal than others, but the terminology of the Lex makes it crystal clear that the quality of being an *idoneus,* once other requirements are met, begins with a *res* or property qualification of 5,000 sesterces and above.[32] In the jurists and literary sources, *honestus vir* equals *vir locuples,* and the adjective *idoneus,* in two definite instances and possibly a third, is synonymous with *honestus.*[33] Several investigators seem to misunderstand the Lex Irnitana on this fundamental point when they imply that those chosen for jury duty "ex reliquis municipibus" are those who, in every respect, are eligible to serve as decurions.[34] Curchin is more helpful on this matter, observing the existence of men at Irni with property worth a minimum of 5,000 sesterces "who did not qualify as decurions" and suggesting that the property qualification for entry into the *ordo* was higher.[35] The Lex formally offers an exemption clause for those prospective jurors with a census minimum that would, all other qualifications being met, disqualify them for service as decurions. The Lex is explicit on this point and worth quoting in full:[36]

(he [the duovir] is to choose) from the other municipes [all those suitable] . . . ; provided that he does not choose anyone who will be prevented by illness from being able to attend to judging matters in that year, or who will be over 65, or who will be aedile or quaestor, or who will be absent on public business or on the common business of the municipes of that municipium, or who will without wrongful intent not be in that area and therefore not be able in that year to attend to judging matters, or who will be in such a position that he cannot be chosen as or be one of the decuriones or conscripti, unless he cannot be chosen as or be (one of the decuriones or conscripti) because his own property, or his father's or his paternal grandfather's or his paternal great-grandfather's or his father's, in whose power he is, is such that he cannot be chosen as or be one of the decuriones or conscripti.

The provision for those who are vaguely described as not being in the position of eligibility for service as a decurion or one of the *conscripti* refers,

as Lebek notes, to individuals belonging to one of the ignominious professions or to those judicially condemned.[37] Otherwise, prospective and chosen jurors are equated with decurions and *conscripti* in all respects, save for
their census. And nondecurional jurors at Irni did not necessarily possess
the *civitas romana*, but were, like other *municipes* at that and other communities affected by the Flavian municipal law, assimilated to Roman citizens with respect to the application and scope of the Roman civil law.[38]

The preceding points are worth pondering, to put the matter blandly. Roman legislation and the custom it buttresses and reflects conceive as *idonei*
all those freeborn *municipes* at Irni who possess an average income of
roughly three times minimum nutritional subsistence, an income that is
essentially on a par with the estimated average per capita income of the
Roman Empire. And just as pertinent is the observation that the 5,000-
sesterces minimum census at Irni required for local jury service separated
those persons incapable of an autonomous and responsible civic career
from those, by contrast, who were capable of full participation in municipal
life.[39] To be sure, the yearly *minimum* income of 300 sesterces postulated —
on reasonable grounds — for Baetican jurors at Irni is somewhat lower than
Goldsmith's estimated average yearly income and the lower figure(s) of attested "subsistence" annuities. The lower minimum of *honesti* at Irni surely
reflects the likelihood of lower prices and cost of living in those areas of
the province away from the larger urban centers, such as Malaca, Gades,
Hispalis, and Corduba. In other words, the census minimum at Irni was a
sum that probably obtained at other smaller centers of the province, situated inland and away from the main arteries of communication, riverine or
terrestrial. D'Ors, it may be worth recalling in this connection, suggests that
the sum of 5,000 sesterces is a downward adjustment from a higher figure
in the model of the Lex Irnitana.[40] Goldsmith, to be sure, claims lower costs
of living in the provinces than in Italy.[41] And Harl demonstrates how prices
for staples in Italy outside Rome could be a fraction of those which obtained in the *urbs*, while those outside Italy, such as in Africa, could have
been half of those in Italy itself.[42] Harl reckons that in the period from
c. A.D. 75 to 125, each member of a family of four in Italy would have ex-
pended an average of 2 to 2.5 *asses* per diem for cereals, oil, and wine, a sum
that is equivalent to 182.5 to 228 sesterces per year per person. Given the
undoubtedly lower prices in most areas of Baetica in the same period, a

minimum per capita income of roughly 300 sesterces would have provided a comfortable existence. And the minimum figure for *idonei* at Irni was just that: sub-decurional *honesti* at Irni outside the *ordo* would have represented a group whose census ranged from 5,000 to 20,000–25,000 sesterces, yielding incomes—whether notional or in coin—of roughly 300 to 1,200–1,500 sesterces. *Honesti* with patrimonies inadequate for service as decurions or local magistrates would have represented, therefore, an element in the population that, on a priori grounds, was sizable. It is not possible to overemphasize this last point.

Some larger conclusions are in order. The foregoing discussion suggests that many, if not most, of the persons named in the epigraphy of Baetica who, on onomastic or other grounds, can be identified as freeborn have a fair claim, therefore, to being *honesti*. The costs of setting up a commemorative inscription were certainly no bar to the self-representation of those *honesti* who barely met or exceeded the census minimum stipulated by the Flavian municipal law for service as a local juror. The preceding seems a safe supposition from the testimony—unique in the Iberian peninsula, so far as I know—of a costed funerary inscription from Casa de Don Pedro in the *territorium* of Mirobriga.[43] The inscription was engraved on a plaque of yellowish limestone, measuring 60 by 42 by (?) centimeters, fringed by molding. The plaque, built into the wall of the finca "El Carneril," names "Cosconia L(ucii) f(ilia) Materna Mirobrigen[si]s," who died at age 60. Her epitaph states that Materna ordered the plaque (and accompanying epitaph) to be made at a cost of 8 sesterces ("tes[t]amento fier(i) iussit ex (sestertiis) VIII"). The cost of Materna's funerary plaque is a small fraction even of the wheat-based, bare-subsistence minimum posited by Hopkins and Jongman. It hardly needs stating in this context that the freeborn *plebs* at Irni and at places similar to it in size and location—such as Mirobriga— were those males and females possessing a yearly earned income of fewer than roughly 300 sesterces. They, too, are undoubtedly represented in the funerary inscriptions. Hence the cautious approach to the identification of *honesti* in this study. But it is hard to believe that they can have constituted the majority of inhabitants in Baetican communities if Goldsmith's figures for the average yearly income of every man, woman, and child in the early Roman Empire are even approximately correct. As a working hypothesis, and using maximal estimates, it is possible to suggest the breakdown of the population of Baetica in both urban and rural contexts, during the period c. A.D. 70–190, according to status and wealth, along the following lines:

slaves and freedmen: 40%

freeborn *plebs:* 35%

honesti: 25%

Honesti, it is important to remember, include those *idonei,* as defined above, both within and outside the *ordo.* What happens if we import the anachronistic notion of the middle stratum into the reckoning? With the "middle stratum," I refer to those Romans in Baetica—freeborn and ex-slave—with property worth 5,000 to 200,000 sesterces. These are persons who would have had a yearly income, whether imputed or in coin, of approximately 300 to 12,000 sesterces per annum. If we divide the population of the province from Augustus to Commodus into three groups, according to their census, corresponding to those worth less than 5,000 sesterces, those worth 5,000 to 200,000 sesterces, and a third group worth over 200,000 sesterces, then I think it is plausible to hypothesize that those whose census ranged between 5,000 and 200,000 sesterces would have constituted a group whose numbers approached 50 percent of the total population of the province. Just how large in absolute numbers this intermediate or "middle" stratum was in this period is impossible to say, but, to reiterate, it is not a stretch to suppose that it represented a substantial minority of the population, falling not too far short of the total numbers of freeborn plebeians and slaves.[44] Again, it is important to emphasize that in no way is the claim put forward in this study that there existed a discrete, readily definable "middle class" in the early Roman Principate. But as an analytical or heuristic proposition, the consideration of income and income distribution enables one to recognize the palpable material gains that the Roman peace represented for a sizable proportion of the population of southern Spain between Augustus' reign and the Severan dynasty. Speaking of the Roman Empire as a whole, one knowledgeable commentator has even gone so far as to suggest that the "disparity in income between the average Roman and one of those incredible senators was far less than between the average American today and the corresponding percentage of the super-rich in our own society."[45]

So far, we have been dealing with the known statutory lower threshold defining Baetican *honesti.* There is good, independent evidence that shows that wealth and, by implication, incomes were increasing during the earlier second century A.D. It consists of those imperial letters and rescripts aimed at preventing the fraudulent claim to immunity from civic *munera* on the basis of service in the supply of the *annona* of the city of Rome. A letter of Hadrian and rescript of Marcus Aurelius and Lucius Verus stipulate that those *negotiatores* and *navicularii* enjoying immunity had to invest at least half of their property in the supply of the city. The letter of Hadrian, cited by Callistratus, demonstrates that there were *negotiatores,* presumably those aiding the *annona,* claiming or enjoying immunity whose investment had fallen to a level representing less than half of their total wealth. It was not the initial investment that had to remain stable, but the proportion of one's total wealth that had to be always more than half of a person's fortune.[46] The language of the letter shows clearly that individuals' fortunes were increasing: "Negotiatio pro incremento facultatium exercenda est. Alioquin si quis maiore pecuniae suae parte negotiationem exercebit, rursus locuples factus in eadem quantitate negotiationis perseveraverit, tenebitur muneribus . . ." (Call.1 cogn.*Dig.* 50.6.6.8: "Business must be carried on according to an increase in one's resources. Moreover, if anyone carries on a business with more than half of one's wealth but, having become wealthy, sticks, on the contrary, to the same amount of commerce, that person will be bound to perform obligations . . ."). The letter goes on to make a comparison with those *locupletes* whose investment had fallen to a level below that mandated for award of immunity. Sirks identifies these *locupletes* fundamentally as rich landowners, acting as "navicularii qui annonae urbis serviunt," who will have stayed at home and put a *magister navis* in charge of their ships. The rescript of the Divi Fratres, similarly, refers to both *negotiatores* and *navicularii* enjoying or claiming immunity. We are a long way here from the world of Trimalchio. The Hadrianic letter contains clear references to personal wealth increasing through commerce ("pro incremento facultatium") and the entry of persons into the ranks of the *locupletes* ("rursus locuples factus"). The increase in individual means and wealth does not belong to the realm of the unforeseen or happenstance but seems to cohere with the program of the *princeps* himself, for it is Hadrian who is proclaimed in coins and in a surviving inscription as *locupletator,* or "enricher," of the world.[47]

The implication of the letter—and rescript—is that any increase in personal fortunes became known to the authorities—in the first instance the local town council, and subsequently the provincial governor. The primary mechanism by which the details of one's *res* became known was probably the annual or semi-annual census declaration, an outline of which is preserved in Ulpian's *forma censualis.*[48] As a working hypothesis, it may also be reasonable to assume that the information of the Dressel 20 amphora *tituli* was contained in more or less permanent records at each urban center of the fiscal districts named on the amphoras, and that this information could, if necessary, be used to check the accuracy or veracity of the information of the census declarations. The Hadrianic letter and rescript of Marcus Aurelius and Lucius Verus are precisely relevant in a discussion of wealthy Baetici from the fact that many *negotiatores* and, presumably, some *navicularii* aiding the *annona* of the city of Rome were of Baetican origin or domicile. As yet, there is no inscriptionally designated Baetican *navicularius*.[49]

There can be no doubt that it is the existence of per capita income growth, coupled with a substantial element of *honesti* and *honestae* in Baetica in the high Principate—both within and outside local *ordines*—that explains, in large measure, the vitality of civic institutions and the importance and self-esteem of Baetican *municipes* of all social and economic strata from the late first century B.C. to the Severan period.[50] This last point raises an issue of inestimable importance for the proper understanding of the construction of Roman society in the Roman West during the early Principate. All of the evidence presented and analyzed in this study shows the possibility of rising incomes across all levels and strata of Baetican society from the reign of Augustus to the Severans. It should be obvious by now that persons belonging to the *plebs* were not locked immutably into that category. The distinction *honesti-plebs,* about which so much is made in this book, was not one based on rigid castes. There was no caste system in the early Roman Empire in the West. In the fluid, dynamic, and growing economy of Baetica during the early Principate, a person's fortune, and hence classification, could and did change. A person classifiable as a plebeian in the course of one local census could, in subsequent assessments of personal property, enter the ranks of the municipal *honesti.* In sum, Baetica during the Principate does not seem to reflect the underdevelopment model of the Roman economy that prevails in contemporary scholarship.

Growth in Baetican per capita incomes probably moderated and possibly stagnated during the fourth quarter of the second century A.D. The likely reasons for this state of affairs are multiple. For one thing, the province experienced a shock in the form of several invasions/incursions of so-called Mauri from North Africa in the 170s. We know that the orderly life of the province was disrupted as a result; Singili(a?) Barba was besieged, and it is telling that the ceramics evidence suggests a severe downturn in the operations of the mines in the Río Tinto in c. 175. Perdiguero suggests that the urban oilery at Aratispi, discussed above, was incinerated by the Mauri.[51] The excavators of the villa at Sierra de Yeguas, not far to the northwest of Singili(a?) Barba, associate signs of collapsed and incinerated structures there, datable to the second century, along with a hoard of first- and possibly second-century sesterces, with the invasion of the Mauri in 177.[52]

Scholars, furthermore, seem to be unanimous in positing an increasing concentration of property in the province from roughly the mid-second century A.D. onward. The evidence for this phenomenon is partly epigraphical and partly archaeological, chiefly the results of archaeological survey. Mayet connects the increasing appearance in the Dressel 20 amphora stamps of the names of *figlinae* accompanied by the indication FIG, FIGUL, FIGLIN, FIGLINA, or simply F from c. A.D. 150 on as a certain indication of the concentration of the ownership of the amphora workshops and, at the same time, of rural properties. A prime example of this putative concentration of properties and associated amphora installations concerns the *figlinae Barba, Ceparia,* and *Grumensis,* which, sometime after c. A.D. 150, allegedly passed into the ownership of the Aurelii Heraclae, father and son. The *figlinae* and associated *fundi* were confiscated by Septimius Severus at the end of the second century, subsequently passed under the control of the *Kalendarium Vegetianum,* and may, finally, have fallen again into private hands at some point between 214 and 226. The likely presence of the same tenant in all three *figlinae* would constitute proof, if I understood Mayet correctly on this point, that the same *dominus* owned *figlinae* and *fundi.* And the mere fact that the *figlinae,* each apparently located in a different *conventus,* were confiscated must mean that they had, or were attached to, associated estates.[53]

Remesal, though, has indicated serious problems in Mayet's understanding of the chronology of the various sections and layers of the Monte Testaccio and material recovered from it, and can demonstrate, convincingly in my opinion, and following Dressel, that the stamps attesting the Aurelii Heraclae, father and son, are of third-century date. On Remesal's reconstruction of the vicissitudes of the *figlinae Barba, Ceparia,* and *Grumensis,* the *figlinae* and associated *fundi* were in the possession of the senator Mummius Secundinus, the son or nephew of Mummius Sisenna Rutilianus. Secundinus was executed by Septimius Severus in 197/198, and his properties were confiscated by the emperor. The properties were immediately absorbed into the *patrimonium Caesaris,* but subsequently passed into the *res privata.* Upon the death of either Septimius or Caracalla, the properties were sold, ceded, or leased to the Aurelii Heraclae. The chronology, therefore, for Mayet's arguments for adducing the *figlinae Barba, Ceparia,* and *Grumensis* as evidence for the concentration of property seem to lack a firm base. Her overall contention that the aforementioned *figlinae* point to the concentration of property may, all the same, have a certain validity if Remesal is right to argue that the consular Mummii consisted of two branches: one that included L. Mummius Niger Q. Valerius Vegetus, with properties at Iliberri and environs, and a second branch that included Mummius Sisenna, Rutilianus, and Secundinus, whose properties were in the central Guadalquivir valley, specifically in the area of Arva, Axati, and Celti.[54] It is worth mentioning, incidentally, that it is during the reign of Severus Alexander that the beta *tituli* disclose the activity—at first limited—after a long hiatus, of private *mercatores olearii.* The *mercatores* had been replaced by agents of the *ratio privata* in the procurement of Baetican oil during the 190s A.D.[55] The private merchants drop out of the epigraphical record with the cessation of amphora-dumping at the Testaccio in the 260s.

There is also a series of stamps attesting the *figlinae Medianae, Salsenses, Statianenses,* and "ST SIP," all of which are situated within the *territorium* of Arva, and all linked to an individual indicated by the initials Q. F(   ) R(   ). Mayet sees these stamps, which she dates to the end of the second and third centuries, as indicative of the concentration of amphora-producing installations in the hands of a certain Q. F(   ) R(   ), and is agnostic on the identification of the person lurking behind the initials of the stamps with either Quintus Fulvius Rusticus or Quintus Fulvius Rogatus, discussed in Chapter Six.[56] The certain identity of the owner remains elusive. Jacques emphasizes those stamps on Dressel 20s produced by the family represented by the abbreviated nomen F(   ) in numerous *figlinae* along the middle Baetis and Singilis, principally, as evidence of property concentration at the end of the second and third centuries A.D. The family counted *clarissimi* in its ranks, and, without being able to establish a certain link between any of the abbreviated names in the stamps and any known senators of the Severan period, Jacques suggests that the most likely context for the amassing by this family of geographically diverse properties was the confiscation by Severus of lands belonging to Clodius Albinus' supporters in Baetica.[57]

CHAPTER EIGHT

Conclusions

The imperial peace generated a substantial middle social and economic stratum in Baetica between c. 30 B.C. and A.D. 200. The fundamental basis of this stratum's wealth was metals and, increasingly, exportable agricultural production. Baetica's geography, its resources, its climate, its riverine system, and the elastic demands of the Roman state, army, and *plebs* for its products combined to generate wealthy Baetici.

The Augustan peace generated complex and widespread changes in the nature of the Baetican rural landscape. At the administrative level, the inhabitants of Baetica were bound up in Roman schemes of land division, tax assessment, and tax collection. The physical face of the province was perhaps not profoundly altered by these arrangements in the Augustan and Julio-Claudian periods. Comparatively few areas of the province were subjected to *limitatio,* that is, the physical division of parcels of land, according to Roman schemes of land division into *centuriae* and their sub-units. The towns of the province do show increasing monumentalization, along Roman lines, in the reign of Augustus and under his immediate successors. This is a theme touched on repeatedly elsewhere by competent investigators. Certain areas of the province, generally in the lower Guadalquivir valley, do suggest ex novo, Roman-style rural foundations, but their geography seems, in substantial measure, dictated by their placement within or on the periphery of communities that either received colonial deductions or achieved municipal status under Augustus or in the triumviral era. But the nature of habitation in rural areas of the province does change in at least one significant way during the early Principate, continuing a process that is discernible in the late Republican period as well. At issue here is the denucleation of certain native sites, as their inhabitants increasingly chose to live in isolated rural settlements close at hand to productive, particularly arable, land. This is certainly a trend that is observable in that portion of the province most easily subject to analysis, namely those areas of Baetica situated between the Baetis and the Atlantic and Mediterranean littorals. The aforementioned are the areas that have seen the brunt of systematic extensive and intensive rural survey during the last generation.

Why did Baetici want to be closer to productive land from the triumviral period onward? Perhaps it would be better to rephrase that question. Why would they not? Here, too, the contemporary voice of Chairman Deng Xiao Ping, although reflecting different circumstances, might speak to the attitude of Baetican Romans toward gain in the lapidary phrase: "It is glorious to become wealthy." The inhabitants of the province of Hispania Ulterior Baetica, as a whole, were confronted with a multiplicity of benefits under Augustus and his successors. Their main possessions and gifts were the land; the incomparable natural infrastructure of the Singilis, the Baetis, and the *Lacus Ligustinus;* peace — aside from the inevitable and sporadic incidents of rural thievery — on land and sea; and the need of Augustus and his successors for constant and predictable supplies of metals and comestibles for the *plebs* of Rome and the army. Industrious undoubtedly, and inheritors in part, surely, of the commercial drive and genius of the Phoenicians, the Baetici met the opportunities afforded them by nature and by Rome. The supply of the city of Rome, the *plebs,* and the army represented a combination of the Republican legacy of rented public land and the initiative and participation of private traders and interests. The world of private initiative is vividly displayed in the so-called Murecine tablets of Julio-Claudian date.[1] Mention of the archive of C. Sulpicius Cinnamus and C. Sulpicius Faustus is relevant here because it dates to a few years before the first signs of active and official intervention in favor of the trade and importation to Rome of foodstuffs in the form of Claudius' incentives to *negotiatores* supplying the *urbs* with grain. The scale and nature of such imperial benefits widens and intensifies in the following century. That is a familiar theme. But it clearly means that the picture of purely free commerce or market-driven initiative in Roman trade in the West is an illusion.

Alongside the aforementioned developments are the collapse of the Julio-Claudian dynasty and the arrival of an energetic ruling family whose acts vis-à-vis Hispania represent a watershed in its history, with especially great consequences for Baetica. The bestowal of the Latin right to scores of Baetican communities and their assumption of Roman-style charters and the *ius civile* brought manifold pressures on local elites to both assimilate and conform to Roman ways. The financial costs associated with these changes were high. Nonetheless, the Roman authorities showed obvious sensitivity to local conditions and the capacities of local elites and proto-elites by adjusting the census minima for service as municipal jurors and, in all probability, those fortunes necessary for service as a decurion or officeholder. The result was that numerous provincials were counted as *honesti* whose wealth was really modest, at least on the conventional assumptions of what constitutes the wealthy in the Roman Empire. Price levels in most areas and towns of Baetica were probably modest in comparison with those of Rome, Pompeii, or Italy, as a whole. It must be said that our picture of the social and economic standing of municipal elites, both in Italy and elsewhere, has for too long been dominated by the stray statements of our literary sources, such as Pliny's accidental revelation of the 100,000-sesterces census minimum for service as a decurion in his hometown of Comum (*Ep.* 1.19).

The archaeological and epigraphical record shows that Baetici in all parts of the province adapted to the new conditions of the Flavian epoch, no doubt after some initial stumbles. The uniform upsurge in municipal benefactions during the Flavian era in all four *conventus* of the province is an indication of this adjustment. So are the numerous instances of town building and rebuilding throughout the province. But the most dramatic index of the change brought about in Baetica by Vespasian and his sons is the remarkable rural construction of greenfield settlements, and reconstruction, along Roman lines, of pre-existing habitats. In nearly all instances in which really precise and informative rural survey and site excavation allow us to discern diachronic changes in the settlement pattern, the boom in the number and quality of rural settlements throughout Baetica during the Flavian era is readily apparent. The causes of this settlement boom are complex and sometimes interlocking. Increasing tax demands by the Roman state are certainly a factor. So is the constant or growing demand for Baetican staples and commodities, which is part of the explanation for more intensive agriculture in many areas of the province. Remesal and his students may be right to see Vespasian's concessions to Spain and Baetica as part of a larger plan for the Spanish provinces as a logistical anchor for the increasingly organized and static *limes* (fortified frontier) in Germany and along the upper Danube.[2]

But the preceding is not the full story. The Flavian "reconstruction" of Spain and Baetica, in particular, produced far-reaching social changes that themselves were in large part a consequence of the altered political and administrative landscape. In Chapter Four we canvassed some of the costs associated with the acquisition of Roman citizenship and the spread of Roman-style town constitutions. A central element in Roman aristocratic values was the high premium placed on agriculture as the bedrock foundation of wealth. Roman ideology placed a concomitant value on the possession of rural *fundi* equipped for sojourns of variable duration by the owner. The realities of urbanism in most parts of Baetica, away from a handful of the larger centers, meant that local elites embraced Roman values to the extent of living more or less permanently on their rural properties—a reflection not only of economic requirements but also of their full acceptance of and assimilation into the Roman order. The first- through third-order Roman rural *aedificia* dotting the Baetican countryside in increasing numbers from the early Flavian epoch onward represent a mixture of social aspirations and economic exigency. The labor on rural estates rested on a combination of free and unfree persons. In most areas of the province, rural chattel slaves existed, but their numbers in each *fundus* were probably modest. Extensive agriculture in the form of oleiculture dictated that the needs of owners or tenants could be met by a relatively modest number of slaves, complemented and supplemented, particularly at peak seasons, by the labor of family members and of *mercenarii*.

All of the evidence shows with limpid clarity that external demand and internal push produced, by A.D. 100, a Baetican social order in which the wealthy—even the moderately wealthy—did not inevitably join local town councils or hold office. *Honesti* or local worthies outside the local *ordo* existed in varying proportions in the towns of Baetica. It is obvious that the larger and wealthier communities of Baetica had in their populations a higher proportion of *honesti* than did the smaller towns with smaller territories. The stamps and *tituli picti* of Dressel 20 oil-bearing amphoras afford a window into *honesti* outside the *ordo:* both they and the independent epigraphical evidence reveal families whose interests in trade extended over several generations. It was a peculiarly Roman genius both to foment their existence and to exploit them in the interests of their communities and the Roman state. For the small-fry *honesti,* it was in the form of local jury duty that they served their fellow Romans. For the bigger fish, it was in the form of local benefactions or oceanic traverses and the building and outfitting of ships to feed and supply the imperial *plebs,* the emperor, and his army. Some *locupletes,* nevertheless, got through the net. Repeated imperial letters and constitutions from late in Hadrian's reign on show that a tension existed between the authorities and the understanding that local *honesti* outside the *ordo* had of their own prerogatives and responsibilities. Abuses of the system clearly existed. Not the least interesting aspect of second-century imperial efforts to curb abuses of immunity-seeking *navicularii* and *negotiatores* is the light they shed on the reality of growing fortunes and incomes in the Hadrianic and Antonine eras.

Widespread wealth-creation in Baetica and rising per capita income ended in the fourth quarter of the second century A.D. The causes were various, and external to the Iberian peninsula. The successive incursions of the Mauri incapacitated much of the productive infrastructure of the province during the 170s. The civil wars and confiscations of the properties and facilities of Baetican elites during the 190s had negative repercussions. The cessation of the activity of private oil traders and their replacement by agents of the state in that same decade also stymied elite and proto-elite growth in the province. Anyone tempted to look for the reasons for a decline in wealth creation and per capita income increase either in some inherent defect in the structure or nature of the Roman economy itself or in demographic factors is working on the basis of faulty assumptions.

✖

Notes

Introduction

1. Whittaker 1985 and 1993; Parkins 1997; Harris 1993; Jongman 1988; Pleket 1990 and 1993.

2. Molina Vidal 1997.

3. Morley 1996.

4. Garnsey and Saller 1987, 43 and 51; Hopkins 1980, 104; Jongman 1988, passim; Frier 1991, 245–246; Alcock 1993, 221.

5. So Frier 1991, 245–246.

6. Purcell 1990, passim.

7. Ibid., 115.

8. This is the line of Corbier 1991, esp. 234.

9. So Garnsey and Saller 1987, 116, on the basis of Purcell 1983.

10. Purcell (1983, 165) reckons approximately 1,000 living *apparitores* in the early Principate.

11. Engels 1990, 40–41, citing Aristotle *Politics* 1267a–1268b.

12. Thompson 1982, 401 and passim. He has in his crosshairs Deman 1975.

13. Harl 1996, passim, esp. 3–4 and 250–269.

14. Cf. de Ligt 1990, 52, based mainly on the evidence from the Roman East, for the slightly peculiar-sounding formulation "middling stratum" to describe "reasonably well-off peasants," who, in his view, constituted always a "small" minority of the farming population in the Empire. I am more optimistic on the size of this minority.

15. The *ducenarii* (200,000-sesterces men) are a virtually forgotten category of freeborn Italians and provincials, possessing a census of 200,000 to 400,000 sesterces, who sat on two of the five panels of jurors serving at Rome. Demougin 1988, 449–453, 457.

16. See, on this point, Christ 1980, 216.

17. So, e.g., Garnsey and Saller 1987, 115–116.

18. For the expression "middle layer," see D'Arms 2000, discussed below at Chapter Seven, note 42.

19. Harris 1988, passim, esp. 604–605, inspired—like Engels—by Aristotle (*Politics* 4.11.1295bl–3).

20. See Chapter Six, note 222, for some bibliography.

21. Duncan-Jones 1963, 171. Tovar 1974 lists 246 named places and jurisdictions in Baetica. Despite the fact that a number of the toponyms in his catalogue represent road stations that may not have possessed municipal status, or *pagi*, from the continual appearance of previously unknown *municipia*, such as the *res publica Aiungitanorum* in the *conventus Astigitanus*, an estimate of 225–275 named communities in Baetica seems reasonable. For Aiungi, see Stylow and López Melero 1995.

22. Le Roux 1991b, 106.

23. Garnsey 1970, 235, 252, and esp. 256–258, citing, e.g., Ulpian's reference to the "ordo et possessores" of communities, in general (*Dig.* 50.9.1).

24. For the evolution of the jury panels during the early Principate, see Demougin 1988, 443–498. For the evidence of the Lex Irnitana, see below, Chapter Seven.

25. Le Roux 1987, 278 n. 54; idem 1991b, 105–106, taking as analogy the relationship between *ducenarii*, i.e., those with a census minimum of 200,000 sesterces serving on the jury panels at Rome, and Roman senators.

26. Alföldy 1984, 110.

27. T. Kruse, reviewing Haley 1991 in *JRA* 8 (1995): 477, adduces Alföldy 1976 and 1984.

28. Le Roux 1991b, 106.

29. Mackie 1983a, 57 and 69 n. 12, noting as *honesti* outside the *ordo* resident aliens (*incolae*), individuals in military service, a *flamen* and *pontifex* at Aurgi (*CIL* II 3362), and a bridge-builder at Oretum (*CIL* II 3221 = 6339): these and no more!

30. *CIL* II 1047 (Iporca), *CIL* II 1276 (Siarum), *CIL* II^2/5, 985 (Los Castellares), and *CIL* II^2/5, 389 (Ipsca).

31. Garnsey 1970, 235.

32. Jacques and Scheid 1990, 302, contrasting "les 'honnêtes gens' et les humbles."

33. Woolf 1998, 163–164.

34. Ibid., 242.

35. See Chapter Six for Baetican traders or those having a trading connection with the province.

36. This study has been influenced by D'Arms 1981.

37. Whittaker 1985, 57–58. Cf. Finley 1973, passim, esp. 35–61.

38. Harris 1993, 22, though he concedes that curial merchants in Gaul were "fairly common."

39. Remesal (1990 and 1997b) is a forceful proponent of this view, followed by Berni Millet (1998).

40. Wickham 1988, 191–192.

41. So Carreras Monfort (1999), on the basis of techniques derived from Geographic Information Systems (GIS). His work shows, on the other hand, the market principles of least cost and maximum profits at work, e.g., in the distribution of Gallic wine in the West.

42. Whittaker 1985.

43. Against Whittaker, see also Jacques (1990, 892–893), who notes the profusion of Dr. 20s throughout the Roman West—and not just in Rome—produced by the putative senatorial family represented by the abbreviated *gentilicium* F(   ) in the amphora stamps. In this study, the expression "*possessores* and/or tenants" will be common from the fact that in Roman classical law, tenants did not have *possessio:* see Köhn 1983, 191–193, and Kehoe 1997, 184 n. 3.

44. On this point, see Mattingly 1988, 52–53.

45. Harris 1993, 16–17.

46. Sirks 1991, passim, esp. 1–107.

47. Paterson 1998. The work of Mattingly and Remesal goes unmentioned in Paterson's article.

48. Temin 2001.

49. Remesal 1998, 198.

50. Liou and Tchernia 1994, 134. Contra, Remesal (1983, 105), who characterizes these *mercatores* as "nur Spediteure."

51. Blázquez 1978; Sánchez León 1978.

52. Baetici are the inhabitants of the province of Baetica: for this term, see Pliny *Ep.* 1.7.2, 3.4.6, 3.9, and 6.29.8; and cf. *TLL* II, 1679.4–12, for further testimonia.

Chapter One

1. *MRR* 2:215.

2. *MRR* 2:261.

3. Brunt (1971, 602) suggests 49 for Gades' receipt of municipal status. Similarly, Wiegels 1985, 34. See Richardson 1996, 119, for Gades' acquisition of municipal status either in 49 or within the following six years.

4. For an overview of the events of 49–45 and their prelude, see Richardson 1996, 104–116; Wilson 1966, 34–38; Roldán Hervás 1978; González Román 1978; and Tsirkin 1981.

5. *MRR* 2:236 and 275–276; see also Lacort Navarro et al. 1986, 69–78 (= *CIL* II²/5, 521), for an inscription of 49 from La Rambla that gives Longinus' filiation "C(ai) f(ilius)." La Rambla is possibly the location of Sabetum: *CIL* II²/5, p. 142; Curchin (1990, 164 no. 271), errs in assigning the inscription to Ulia.

6. *MRR* 2:308.

7. Urso: Wiegels 1985, 64–65, with bibliography. Hispalis: ibid., 36–38, with bibliography.

8. Hasta: Caesarian according to Wiegels 1985, 35; Thouvenot 1940, 190; Vittinghoff 1952, 74; and Galsterer 1971, 66 no. 26. Brunt (1971, 591) is agnostic on its Caesarian ascription. Itucci: Wiegels 1985, 45–46, for its location; and Galsterer 1971, 67 no. 41; Thouvenot 1940, 190; and Vittinghoff 1952, 74, for its Caesarian

promotion. Galsterer-Kröll 1972, 121–123 and 127 table I; and García y Bellido 1959, 500, for Itucci's promotion before 27 B.C. Ucubi: Abascal Palazón and Espinosa 1989, 61–62.

9. Role and function of the colonies: Fear 1996, 63–104; Cortijo Cerezo 1990–1991.

10. Fear 1996, 31–62, emphasizing the general instability of the future province. Gabba 1954, 297–305; Richardson 1996, 81–82 and 117; and Marín Díaz (1988), 171–85, for a substantial Roman and Italian presence by c. 50 B.C., and, similarly, Roldán Hervás 1978, 109–130.

11. Fear 1996, 51–54.

12. Brunt 1971, 231.

13. Cf. *OLD* p. 2038 for the meaning of the epithet: "(of troops) locally levied," on the basis of Caes. *B Civ.* 2.20.4; *B Alex.* 53.4; *BHisp.* 7.4 and 10.3; and Tac. *Ann.* 1.31, a meaning that says nothing about whether the troops were natives or Roman-Italians (pace Fear [1996, 51], who adduces Lewis and Short's "of, or belonging to the household slaves" or "native, indigenous" [s.v. "vernaculus"]).

14. Downs 2000, 204–206 and passim. Cf. the suggestion by Bennett (1997, 3) of the possibility of miscegenation in the ancestry of Trajan. One might disagree, however, with Downs' conclusion that the "greater part" of the population of southern Spain in the last two centuries B.C. was of mixed ethnic ancestry, and although she may be right to state that "up to the period of Caesarian colonization . . . there were few Romans" (p. 208), the widespread presence of Italians in Ulterior goes unmentioned in her study.

15. Corell 1999, 63–67, no. 12.

16. Ibid., 67: "La inscripció deu ser contemporània de la craecíó de la colonia." See Brunt 1971, 592 no. 24, following Grant 1946, for the date of the colony.

17. See Marín Díaz 1988, passim, esp. 60–76 and 171–172.

18. See the admirable discussion by Hernández Fernández (1998).

19. Plut. *Crass.* 4.2; *Sert.* 9.1–5.

20. *BHisp.* 3.3–9; Cic. *Att.* 12.2.1; *Fam.* 6.18.2; cf. Val. Max. 9.4 ext. 3.

21. Hernández Fernández 1998, 175–176.

22. Gil Farrés 1966, 157 nos. 430–434 and fig. 35, on whom see Marín Díaz 1988, 61 no. 5, 67 no. 28, and 77–78, citing *RE* I-1 col. 543 on the name Aemilius, and R. S. Conway, *The Italic Dialects* (Cambridge, 1897; reprint ed. Darmstadt, 1967), ss. 32, 155, 257, 307, and note xxxviii (vidi), for the name Iunius in Campania and Latium, at Praeneste and Tusculum, and among the Volsci and Peucetii.

23. On this point, see Marín Díaz 1986–1987, 59–60, and 1988, 61 no. 5, 67 no. 28, and 77–78. "Roman" *gentilicia* include names such as, e.g., Acilius, Aemilius, Fabius, and Iulius, while "Italic" names include, e.g., Aefolanus, Iunius, Lucienus, Messius, and Trinius.

24. For this practice, see Knapp 1978b and Dyson 1980–1981.

25. So Chaves Tristán 1998, 157–158, on the basis of González Román and Marín Díaz 1994 (vidi).

26. Lacort Navarro et al. 1986, 69–78 no. 1; Stylow 1995, 220, for the suggestion that Alpis is probably the descendant of Italians arriving in the Iberian peninsula before the Social War.

27. Knapp (1978a, 152–158, esp. 158, drawing on Brunt 1971) urges us to question the reality of "any 'flusso emigratorio'" from Italy into Spain during the later Republic, particularly during the second century B.C. The phrase "flusso emigratorio" comes from Gabba 1954, 302.

28. See now Chaves Tristán 1999.

29. On the *conventus,* see Schulten 1892. Fear (1996, 41) posits the existence of a *conventus civium Romanorum* at Gades, composed of both native Gaditani and Italian immigrants.

30. Hispalis: Caes. *B Civ.* 2.20.5. Corduba: Caes. *B Civ.* 2.19.2; *B Alex.* 57.5.

31. See Fear 1996, 50, citing Varro *Rust.* 3.16.10ff., for the desire of the Veianii brothers from Falerii to return to Italy and their bees after serving in the governor's army in Spain.

32. Ventura Villanueva 1993, 56 and passim.

33. For *adfines,* or shareholders, of medium- and small-sized *societates* in southern Spain, see Chaves Tristán 1994, 116.

34. See *MRR* 2:327, 343–344, 365, 373, 381, and 385, for C. Asinius Pollio's proconsulship(?) in 44–43, Sextus Pompeius' departure in 44, and Octavian's rule over Spain from 42 on through legates.

35. Le Roux 1982, 56, on the evidence of the *Acta triumphalia.*

36. González 1989, arguing specifically for a *legatio* of 15/14 B.C. to the change of era. See *MRR* 2:312 for activity in 45.

37. Carteia: *CIL* II 4967, 1a; *CIL* II p. 1004; *IRCádiz* no. 96c (a). Ilipa Ilia: *CIL* II 4967,1b and c. Hasta: *IRCádiz* no. 33a and b. Italica: de Monsalud 1907, 251. Siarum: González 1989, 520–521.

38. On these *oppida,* see now Moret 1996.

39. Cf. Alcock 1989, 16, and at 25, quoting Osborne (1987, 69–70): "As a rule, it 'seems extremely likely that, the more numerous the traces of human activity in the landscape, the more intensively that land was exploited.'"

40. On this point, see Downs 1996, 199.

41. López Castro 1995, 112–143, esp. 138–139, and 160–196.

42. Molina Vidal 1997.

43. Wickham 1988, 189.

44. Molina Vidal 1997, 226.

45. *BHisp.* 26, whose defection is noted by Richardson (1996, 121).

46. Fear 1996, 89–90, after d'Ors 1953, 201ff. The editors of *Roman Statutes* no. 25 take the conventional line that the clause limited the daily production of tiles (pp. 438–439).

47. For army supply as a stimulus to increasing production in general in Hispania during the first century B.C., see Fabião 1989, 78, 80, and 121–128.

48. Fernández Caro 1985 and 1992. For a bar graph showing changes in the

settlement pattern in Fuentes de Andalucía from the Iberian period through the fifth century A.D., see Haley 1996a, 290, fig. 1.

49. For the classification of rural sites into first- through third-order sites, see Carrillo Díaz-Pines and Hidalgo 1991, 44–47, and Carrillo Díaz-Pines 1991a, 228–230.

50. Lacort Navarro 1985, 364–373.

51. Varro *Rust.* 1.57.2.

52. Ramos Muñoz and González Rodríguez 1990, 74 and 75 n. 3.

53. Fabião 1989, 73–74. For the encampment's date, see Fabião and Molina Vidal at note 56 below. For the type A amphora, a predecessor of the Dressel 20, see Chapter Four's section "Olive Oil." Fabião follows the classification scheme of Peacock and Williams 1986, 134–135.

54. Sáez 1987, 217; González Román, in Rodríguez Neila et al. 1999, 146; Beltrán Lloris 1990, 238 and 249, fig. 111; and Fabião 1989, 105–108 and 115, who emphasizes their limited numbers in Portugal relative to Italian wine containers. See Peacock and Williams 1986, 82–83, with bibliography, for the class 1 amphora.

55. Acinippo: Guadán 1969, 183 and pl. 18, nos. 166–168; and Gil Farrés 1966, 280, 290, 308, 340–341 nos. 1150–1163 for *asses* of 47–44 B.C. Orippo: Gil Farrés 1966, 300, 368 nos. 1493–1494 (*dupondius* of 55 B.C.) and 1495–1496 (*as* of 55 B.C.). Osset: Gil Farrés 1966, 304, 368 no. 1497 (*as* of 48 B.C.?) and 1498 (*semis* of 48 B.C.?); ibid., 324, 368 no. 1499 (*as* of 47–44 B.C.), 1500–1501 (*quadrans* of 47–44 B.C.); ibid., 326, 368–369 nos. 1502–1504 (*asses* of 38 B.C. and later). Baesippo: Gil Farrés 1966, 312, 342 no. 1175 (*semis* of 47–44 B.C.). Ulia: Gil Farrés 1966, 138, 141 fig. 37, 153 no. 374 (*asses* of c. 120–90 B.C.). Arva: Gil Farrés 1966, 158 no. 441 (*asses* of c. 120–90 B.C.). Turri Regina: Gil Farrés 1996, 374 nos. 1566–1567 (*asses* of 47–44 B.C.).

56. See Fabião 1989, 48–50 (date), and 61–64, 79, and 125 (amphoras). See also Molina Vidal 1997, 144, for the date of the encampment.

57. So Roldán Gómez 1999, 209, citing García Vargas 1996.

58. García Vargas (1996, 54–58) says nothing about wine and strongly implies, instead, that the containers were made in connection with fish sauce.

59. See, in general, Curtis 1991; Ponsich and Tarradell 1965.

60. See Lagóstena Barrios 1996a, passim.

61. Cobos Rodríguez et al. 1995–1996.

62. On this matter, see Domergue 1990, 235–236, 253–277, esp. 274–277. Domergue suggests that the majority of lead-silver mines were leased out by the state, whereas most copper and gold mines were in private hands.

63. Ventura 1993, 54, for this *societas.*

64. Plin. *HN* 34.165.

65. Apud Diodorus 5.36.1–3, on which see Domergue 1990, 234–235, 247, 276, 321, and 382.

66. He is T. Iuventius, named on an ingot of late Republican or Augustan date; see Domergue 1990, 256 no. 1020 and 322; Mangas and Orejas, in Rodríguez

Neila et al. 1999, 250. It is possible that he worked in association with a certain M. L[   ].

67. On this route and its economic importance in pre-Augustan times, see Melchor Gil 1999b.

68. Fernández Rodríguez and García Bueno 1993; García Bueno and Fernández Rodríguez 1995.

69. Leiva Briones and Madruga Flores 1992, 248.

70. Carrillo Díaz-Pines 1995, 69–70 no. 3.

71. Carrilero Millán and Nieto González 1994, 62.

72. *CIL* II 1199. The inscription dates c. A.D. 150 to c. 250.

73. Serrano Peña and Rísquez Cuenca 1989.

Chapter Two

1. Alföldy 1969, 131–132.

2. Ibid., 133.

3. Ibid., 133–134; Stylow 1989–1990, 199–201 and pl. 21, 2.

4. Syme (1969, 126), puts the separation of Asturia and Callaecia from Ulterior and their assignment to Citerior in 16–13 B.C. Alföldy (1969, 224 n. 9), associates the aforementioned provincial reorganization with the division of Ulterior into Lusitania and Baetica. For the provincial division in 27 B.C., see Albertini 1923, 25–32.

5. Alföldy 1969, 224 n. 9.

6. See, e.g., Le Roux 1982, 74–75, by default, since he erroneously ascribes to Syme the idea of the bipartition of Ulterior as contemporaneous with the assignment of Asturia and Callaecia to Citerior, though Syme speaks of the latter reform only.

7. Mackie 1983b, passim, esp. 353–357.

8. Alföldy 1969, 224 n. 9. Albertini 1923, 34–35, plumps for a date of 7–2 B.C. for the change.

9. *CIL* II 4701; 4702(?); 4703; 4704 = Sillières 1990, 107 no. 46 (Inscription I); 4705–4708; 4709 = 4710; 4711.

10. Dio 55.10a.2; Tac. *Ann.* 4.44.3. Wells 1972, 70, dates Ahenobarbus' expedition to 2 B.C.

11. Map: Nicolet 1991, 99–100 and 114. Mackie (1983a, 16 n. 23) thinks the boundary change may "in fact" belong to 2 B.C.

12. So Mattern 1999, 39: Agrippa "seriously miscalculated the size of the province of Baetica."

13. González 1988a and Castillo 1994.

14. *CIL* VI 1396 = *ILS* 8343, and ibid. for an Augustan date.

15. Alföldy 1992, 74.

16. Proculus: Alföldy 1969, 166–167 and 267. Victorinus: ibid., 38–42 and 170.

17. Alföldy 1995.

18. Fear 1996, 116–127, arguing mainly against Henderson 1942.

19. González (1984, 87–100), following Saumagne 1965, argues that *municipia civium Romanorum* did not exist outside Italy. For a summary of the debate, see Mentxaka 1993, 39–41.

20. See, e.g., Wiegels 1985, 11, apropos the tribe of Acinippo.

21. For arguments that put the creation of the *quadragesima Galliarum* during Augustus' reign, specifically between 20 and 10 B.C., see France 1993, esp. 925–926.

22. Site descriptions in Amores Carredano 1982.

23. Durán and Padilla 1990, 123; Sáez 1998.

24. Beltrán Fortes and Baena del Alcázar 1994.

25. On this phenomenon, involving a *contributio* (administrative fusion) of older and newer communities, see Pérez Macías et al. 1997, 204 and passim.

26. For a description of the structures and their dimensions, see Sáez 1987, 101–103.

27. Lacort Navarro 1982, 171–186.

28. Lacort Navarro and Melchor Gil 1993, 182–188. The *metae* range in diameter from 0.57 to 1.08 meters and in height from 0.15 to 0.67 meters. The *catillus*, from the Cerro de los Pesebres, has a diameter of 0.60 meters and a height of 0.39 meters. The *metae* show up at the *municipium* (Segida Augurina) situated at La Saetilla, in addition to the *oppida* at San Sebastián and Remolino.

29. See Parker 1992, 118 no. 235, citing Hesnard 1980, pl. VI, 1.

30. Parker 1992, 394 no. 1059.

31. See ibid., 414–415 no. 1118 and 221 no. 529, respectively.

32. Mattingly 1996, 219.

33. Sealey 1985, 37, 42, 46, 139, and 160.

34. Martin-Kilcher 1994, 388 and 389 fig. 165.

35. Sáez 1987, 22–26, and see 3–71 for a general overview of viticulture in the province, relying mainly on the literary sources.

36. Bernal Casasola and Lorenzo Martínez 1998a.

37. For the terminal date, see Bernal and Lorenzo 1998b.

38. Bernal 1998a, 179–185.

39. Carranque: Beltrán Fortes and Loza Azuaga 1997, 109–110. Haza Honda: Sotomayor 1997, 14–15; Beltrán Fortes and Loza Azuaga 1997, 112–115. Fontanar: Lagóstena Barrios 1996a, 122–123 no. 38. Jarana or Villanueva: Ponsich 1988, 70; Jiménez Cisneros 1971, 138–142; Beltrán Lloris 1990, 223; Peacock 1974, 236; Lagóstena Barrios 1996a, 70–71 no. 17. Puente Melchor: García Vargas and Lavado Florido 1995. Las Canteras: Ponsich 1988, 71; Lazarich et al. 1989, 99; Lagóstena Barrios 1996a, 93–96 no. 25. El Gallinero: Lagóstena Barrios 1996a, 82–83 no. 20. El Almendral: Lagóstena Barrios 1996a, 103–104 no. 30; idem 1996b, 150 no. 11. Los Tercios: Lagóstena Barrios 1996a, 50–52 no. 9. Orippo: Bendala Galán and Pellicer Catalán 1977.

40. Yardley (1994, 270) translates the relevant passage as follows: "From Spain, in fact, come large quantities not only of wheat, but also of wine, honey and oil."

Van Nostrand (1937, 175) and Richardson (1996, 165–166) misunderstand Justin's Latin, suggesting that he concedes that Spain did not produce very much grain. Justin is elliptical but clear: "Hinc enim non frumenti tantum magna copia est, verum et vini, mellis oleique."

41. Rickman and Remesal could be correct on this point: Rickman 1980, 81; Remesal 1997b, 12, 21, and esp. 64. Contra, Pavis d'Escurac 1976, 166 and 188.

42. For C. Turranius Gracilis and his activity, see Pavis d'Escurac 1976, 317–319.

43. Chic García 1985b, 277–278.

44. For the explosion of epigraphic activity in Baetica during the reign of Augustus, see Stylow 1995, esp. 220–221 and 227–228. For an impressionistic survey of changes in Hispania in general during Augustus' reign, see MacMullen 2000, 50–84.

45. See now Amores and Keay 1999.

46. Keay 1996.

47. See Durán and Padilla 1990 for the settlement pattern at Astigi. Connection of urban habitation and oleiculture: Sáez 1987, 219–220. For the labor requirements of oleiculture, cf. Spurr 1986, 134–140.

Chapter Three

1. Richardson 1996, and Fear 1996, on whom see Haley 1997.

2. González 1988a; *AE* 1984.508 (tabula Siarensis); Eck, Caballos, and Fernández 1996.

3. On Baelo, see Wiegels 1985, 20–21.

4. For Roman settlement in the area of Antequera in general, see Atencia 1987b.

5. There is, e.g., the villa "El Campillo" in the municipal district of Castellar (Jaén province) with a foundation date in the first half of the first century A.D.: Hornos Mata et al. 1985.

6. Survey at Fuentes de Andalucía: see Fernández Caro 1985 and 1992.

7. Gorges 1979, 121 fig. 19 and 125–127.

8. Moret 1990 and 1995.

9. Contra, Downs (1996, 183–198 and appendix A), who postulates the Iberian origin of most of these structures. It is not clear how Downs (p. 330 s.v. La Guardia de Jaén) can date the "recinto-torre" on the Cerro de la Horca as far back as the full Iberian period, when Ruiz et al. (1987, 351) date the structure to c. A.D. 60–80. And she dates the "recinto-torre" at El Higuerón (Córdoba province) to c. 400 B.C. (pp. 192–194), whereas Carrillo Díaz-Pines (1991b, 107) can show that its central, quadrangular structure dates to the first half of the first century A.D. On this quadrangular structure, measuring 20 by 17 meters, and El Higuerón in general, see Fortea and Bernier 1970, 61–114 and fig. 2. There is no data in Carrillo 1998 that demonstrates the pre-Roman origin of any of these *turres* in Baetica.

10. Garcia-Bellido 1994–1995, on the evidence of 102 stamped ingots from the *Comacchio (Ferrara)* shipwreck, for which see Berti (1990, 171–192), who suggests (p. 75) the objects' Spanish origin.

11. Aguilar Sáenz and Guichard 1995, 208–210 and fig. 66.

12. Ortiz Romero 1995, passim, esp. 188–191.

13. Oria Segura et al. 1990, 62 no. 23.

14. Serrano Ramos et al. 1985. "El Tesorillo" is located 4.5 kilometers east of Teba. It is a quadrangular structure, measuring 16.45 by 14.25 meters, inhabited from c. A.D. 30 to the beginning of the second century.

15. Montellano: Oria Segura et al. 1990. The campiña of Sevilla: Ruiz Delgado 1985. Survey of changes to Baetican towns: Keay 1998, 68–74, with bibliography.

16. Fernández Jurado et al. 1992, esp. 305 and 309. Keay (1998, 76) was wrong, I think, to set Onuba's nucleation in the Flavian period.

17. Chic García 1996, 248, on the basis of Pascual Guasch's (1980) analysis of the western Mediterranean shipwreck evidence, and Blanco and Luzón 1966, 76, fig. 1.

18. At the Grau Vell de Sagunt (Valencia), all the first-century issues are Flavian (Aranegui Gascó 1980); of 435 coins of Republican through late imperial date recovered at the Portus Ilicitanus, not one is Neronian (Abascal 1989); and at Barcino, of 260 coins studied, Neronian issues are unknown (Campo and Granados 1978).

19. This is ground covered already, in part, by Haley 1996a; see also the map of the *conventus* in ibid., 287.

20. See Morena López 1992, 258–262.

21. Romero Pérez and Melero García 1999. Finewares from the site include Gallic *sigillata.*

22. Romero Pérez 1993b, passim, esp. 501. The site yields *tessellae*, indicating mosaic remains, in addition to marble fragments.

23. Raya de Cardenas et al. 1987. The site yields no Italian *sigillata*, Campanian B, or imitation Campanian forms, but it does disclose south Gallic ware, Gallic *marmorata*, thin-walled ceramics of Tiberian-Claudian date, as well as Spanish *sigillata.*

24. Gener Basallote et al. 1992, passim, esp. 101–124, for a catalogue of the pottery. The site, situated at an altitude of 485 meters, is immediately to the northwest of Loja. Carbonized olive pits here point to oleiculture (p. 128).

25. So Cortijo 1990–1991.

26. Curchin 1990, 138 no. 8 (Anticaria), 139 nos. 21–22 (Aurgi), 144 nos. 73–76 (Cisimbrium), 148 no. 111 (Igabrum), 149 no. 117 (Ilipula Laus), 149 no. 118 (Iliturgicola), 149 nos. 119–122 (Ilurco), 150 nos. 126–127 (Ipolcobulcula), 150 nos. 128–130 (Ipsca), 160 nos. 228–229 (Osqua), 160 no. 234 (Ostippo), 161 nos. 235–236 (Sabora), 162 nos. 249–251 (Singili[a?] Barba), and 165 nos. 281–282 (Ulisi). Of these inscriptions, only Curchin 160 no. 234 = *CIL* II 5048 certainly dates to the pre-Flavian epoch; the dedicant, a *Xvir Maximus* of Ostippo, honored the younger

Drusus in an inscription of c. A.D. 15–20. To Curchin's list of magistrates, add now *CIL* II²/5, 786 and 789, naming two *duoviri* at Singili(a?) Barba.

27. See Dardaine 1993, 68–72 (summary table listing all known Baetican costed donations).

28. *CIL* II²/5, 394 (= II 1569), on which see Mackie 1990, 184.

29. See Guichard 1993, 72–73.

30. See, e.g., *CIL* II 2960 from Pompaelo (Pamplona), dated A.D. 185, attesting *hospitium* between that community and a certain P. Sempronius Taurinus.

31. Romero Moragas and Campos Carrasco 1986.

32. For the location of Orippo, see Sillières 1990, 313.

33. Romo Salas and Vargas Jiménez 1993, 672–676 and 681–682.

34. Ibid., 676–679, esp. 679.

35. Gorges 1979, 241–244, for the sites.

36. On the villa and its phases, see Bernal Casasola and Lorenzo Martínez 1996.

37. Hacienda de Manguarra y San José: Gorges 1979, 304; Serrano Ramos and Luque Moraño 1979. For Las Torres, see Gorges 1979, 306.

38. For some studies on pre-Roman and early Roman Baeturia, see the bibliography at Keay 1998, 59 n. 25, to which add the general discussion by Canto in *ERBC* 15–46 and 175–202.

39. Mellaria: Vaquerizo et al. 1994b. Mirobriga: Pastor Muñoz et al. 1992. Regina: Alvarez Martínez and Rubio Muñoz 1988. Sisapo: Zarzalejos et al. 1994.

40. Rodríguez Díaz 1995. The abandoned centers include La Alcazaba de Badajoz, Sierra de la Martela (Segura de León), Los Castillejos-2 (Fuente de Cantos), El Castrejón de Capote (Higuera la Real), Ermita de Belén (Zafra), and La Tabla de las Cañas (Capilla).

41. *CIL* II²/5, 994 = *ILS* 5971. The findspot of the stone, El Moralejo, is roughly 3.5 kilometers west-southwest of Estepa.

42. See Pavis d'Escurac 1976, 184; Mackie 1983a, 187 and 197 n. 30.

43. *CIL* II²/5, 495.

44. Carrillo Díaz-Pines 1995.

45. So ibid., 82.

46. Morena López and Serrano Carrillo 1991, 123 no. 14, 136.

47. Romero Pérez 1987.

48. Romero Pérez and Melero García 1999, 13. For other sites devoted to olive growing and processing in the vicinity of Antequera, see Corrales Aguilar 1997–1998, 91–94, and Romero Pérez 1997–1998, 128–129.

49. Carrilero et al. 1995. A *pars urbana* is deducible from the surface discovery of painted red stucco and mosaic *tessellae*.

50. Chic García 1985a, 4–30, for a sites survey.

51. Ibid., 12–14 and 18–20, respectively.

52. Ibid., 31–52, for a sites survey.

53. Ibid., 32–36, 39–40, and 43–44, respectively, for the installations.

54. Ibid., 53–110, for a survey of the sites, and 92–94 for Villar Tesoro.

55. With 20% of recorded farmsteads beginning in the Claudian period or in the first years of the Neronian, against the less than 5% of the survey total in Durán and Padilla 1990 attributable to the Flavian period.

56. Zevi (1966, 244), who seems to have been misunderstood on this point by Chic García (1991, 104).

57. Sealey 1985, 84.

58. Dr. 2–4s at Loma de Ceres: Gener Basallote et al. 1993, 980–981. For the Colchester containers, see Sealey 1985, 37, 42, 46, 139, and 160, dated by stratigraphic context from A.D. 43 to 60/61.

59. Colls et al. 1977, 43–47, esp. 47.

60. *CIL* XV 4700, and Zevi 1966, 234–235.

61. So Beltrán Lloris 1990, 238–239; Sciallano and Sibella 1994, 52 s.v. "Amphore Dressel 28" (suggesting a date range for the amphora's production from the end of the first century B.C. to the middle of the second century A.D.); and García Vargas 2000, passim, esp. 242–243.

62. Bernal Casasola and Lorenzo Martínez 1998a, 33.

63. On the circumstances of its discovery and details of its phases and production, see García Vargas 2000, passim, esp. 242–243.

64. Liou 1998, 96 PN 36 with fig. 8, and 98 and 102 for the date.

65. *CIL* II^2/7, 349, on which see Rodríguez Neila 1994a.

66. So Chic García 1997. For the objects, see Casariego et al. 1987, 23–24 nos. 9–10 (catalogue) and 136–137.

67. Van Nostrand 1937, 181.

68. Gorges 1979, 306.

69. Ponsich 1988, 65; Gorges 1979, 307; Rodríguez Oliva 1997.

70. Atencia and Sola 1978, passim, esp. 83.

71. See Ponsich 1988, 183.

72. Baena del Alcázar 1997, 99.

73. For a preliminary report on the site and associated structures, see Villaseca Díaz and Hiraldo Aguilera 1991, as well as Villaseca 1997.

74. For the Rinconcillo stamps, see Beltrán Lloris 1990, 223. For the Baelo stamps, see Domergue 1973, 56 no. 2098, 112 and 114.

75. For the mark, see Domergue 1973, 112 and 114–115.

76. CAES(ius): *CIL* XV 3496. ANT(onius): Beltrán Lloris 1977, 102 n. 54 (Alcalá del Río); *CIL* XII 5683, 112a (Vienne) and 112b (Geneva). The stamps at Vienne and Geneva simply read "C. FVF. A." For the reading "C. FVF. AVITI," with all the letters of the nomen and cognomen ligatured, on the material from Alcalá del Río— (two Haltern 70 containers), see Mayet, "Appendix," in Colls et al. 1977, 141–143; and Beltrán Lloris 1990, 234.

77. Martin-Kilcher 1994, 401–402 ST 189, and ibid. for a date of 10 B.C.– A.D. 10.

78. Liou 1998, 98 PN 39 and fig. 11.

79. Oil: *CIL* XV 3646; Liou 1998, 98 PN 39 and fig. 11. Colls et al. (1986, 64)

connect the QQ. Caecilii with a homonymous metal trader, for whom see note 100 below.

80. Stamps from Olivar de los Valencianos: Pérez López et al. 1999, 702 nos. 37–38.

81. See *CIL* XV 3639–3641; Liou and Marichal 1978, 112–113 no. 1; Liou 1998, 96–98 PN 37–38 and figs. 9–10, from the Castra Praetoria, Fos-sur-mer, and Port-la-Nautique (Aude), respectively.

82. Etienne and Mayet 1998, 214, for Domesticus. For Cornelia, see *CIL* IV 5618b–d.

83. An explicit case is "Clarus, Ossono(bensis)," from modern Faro in Portugal, named on Pompeian VII (= Spanish) amphoras, for which see *CIL* IV 5611–5616. For Spanish amphoras and associated products in Pompeii in general, see Manacorda 1977b.

84. Parker 1992, 90–91.

85. Cf. Curchin 1991, 133: "Merchants tended to be of low status, usually freedmen and foreigners."

86. Martin-Kilcher 1994, 406 P32.

87. Loza Azuaga and Beltrán Fortes 1988; Beltrán Fortes and Loza Azuaga 1997, 112–115.

88. Baldomero et al. 1997; Mora Serrano and Corrales Aguilar 1997, 34.

89. García Vargas and Sibón Olano 1992.

90. Lagóstena Barrios (1996a, 82–83 no. 20) dates the cessation of activity here to c. A.D. 50, or somewhat later. The installation produced Dressel 7, 8, and 10 containers.

91. Toscanos: Ponsich 1988, with bibliography. El Rinconcillo: Fernández Cacho 1995. Buena Vista: Lagóstena Barrios 1996a, 59–60 no. 13, and 1996b, 149 no. 6.

92. Cf. Pliny *HN* 8.191 for reddish to golden yellow wool from Baetica ("velleris . . . rutili).

93. *CIL* II²/7, 334, and ibid. for Stylow's suggestion that Domergue's alternative reading (1990, 270), "soc(ietatis) aerar(iarum fodinarum)"—where "Cordubensium" is implied—may be the right one.

94. "S(ocietas) C(astulonensis?)": Domergue 1990, 261–263, 268–269. "Soc(ietas) Vesc(   )": ibid., 257 no. 1043, 259–260 and 270.

95. González 1998, 110–111 no. 5, for a description of the object, date, and circumstances of its discovery.

96. Domergue 1990, 236.

97. Domergue 1994, 75. Names of producers on ingots from the *Sud-Perduto 2* (Bouches de Bonifacio, Corsica) wreck of c. A.D. 1–15 include C. Vacalicus, C. Asi[   ], M. H[   ], L. Valerius Severus, M. Valerius Ablo, G. Au[   ], and Ant(   ) or An[   ]. Named "wholesale" merchants include Q. Kamaecus and C. Cacius Philargyrus. The merchants who took over the ingots include L. Agrius, P. Turpilius Germanus, and M. Accius Ant(   ). For the wreck, see Bernard and Domergue 1991.

98. Domergue 1998, 207, on the basis of the *Cabrera 4* and other wrecks.

99. Ibid., adducing the example of Ap. Iunius Zethus. *Sud-Lavezzi B* wreck: Liou and Domergue 1990.

100. Chic García 1992, 2–3; Melchor Gil 1993–1994, 343–344. Other producers from the *Cabrera 5* wreck are P. Caecilius Popillus, Iulius Vernio, Tanniber or T. Annius Ber(   ), P. Postumius Rufus, Q. Haterius Gallus, Ca[   ], M. Valerius Ablo, L. Fla(   ), C. Pom(   ), and [   ]us L.f. Rufus. The ingots suggest the activity of the "grossiste" Q. Pompeius (or -onius) Satullus, intermediary between the aforementioned producers and the merchants L. Fannius (Demetrius?) and Q. Caecilius. For the evidence, see Colls et al. 1986, 43–58 and 75–80.

101. Veny 1979; Veny and Cerdá 1972.

102. Domergue 1972, 619–621.

103. *HAE* 2177.

104. I wish to thank Thomas G. Schattner of the German Archaeological Institute in Madrid for this information.

105. Syme 1977, 377.

Chapter Four

1. For an exhaustive discussion of the motive(s), date, and nature of the *ius Latii,* see Mentxaka (1993, 39–63), who plumps for 73/74 (p. 47). Fear (1996, 144–146), following Bosworth 1973, advocates the earlier date.

2. Massa: Plin. *Ep.* 3.4.4, 6.29.8, and 7.33, on which Sherwin-White 1966, 101–102, 214, 389, and 444–447. Gallus(?): Plin. *Ep.* 1.7, on which Sherwin-White 1966, 101–102 and 186, who presumes that an extortion case is at issue here, with Talbert (1984, 509 no. 28) (date). Classicus: Plin. *Ep.* 3.4, 3.9, and 6.29.8, on which Sherwin-White 1966, 18–19, 56–60, 161, 214–215, 230–238, and 389.

3. Birley 1997, 149–150, noting Dio 69.10.1.

4. But cf. Alföldy (1985, 100), who, following an oral suggestion of H. Halfmann, is agnostic on the question of the emperor's presence in Mauretania.

5. Alföldy 1985, esp. 101–105. For the siege at Singili(a?) Barba, see *CIL* II²/5, 783 = *ILS* 1354a, an honorary inscription to G. Vallius Maximianus from the "ordo Singil(iensium) Barb(ensium) ob municipium diutina obsidione et bello Maurorum liberatum."

6. On the disruption, see, in general, Jones 1980, 161–163.

7. Mayet 1970, 174.

8. *HA Sev.* 12.1–3; cf. Richardson 1996, 238–239.

9. Discussions, incorporating the earlier bibliography, include Abascal Palazón and Espinosa 1989, Cortijo Cerezo 1990–1991, Curchin 1990, Mackie 1983a, and Rodríguez Neila 1994b.

10. Atalayuelas: Castro 1988. Palma del Río: Carrillo Díaz-Pines and Hidalgo 1991. Southeast Córdoba province: Carrillo Díaz-Pines 1991a. Fuentes de Andalucía: Fernández Caro 1985 and 1992. Aguas Blancas and Fardes rivers: Buendía

Moreno and Villada Paredes 1987. For a bar graph showing changes in the settlement pattern in Atalayuelas, Palma del Río, southeast Córdoba province, and Fuentes de Andalucía, see Haley 1996a, 290 fig. 1.

11. Camacho Cruz and Lara Fuillerat 1996, 84.

12. Loza Azuaga 1982–1983. For the inclusion of this area within the territory of Singili(a?) Barba, see the map of the *conventus Astigitanus* in *CIL* II^2/5.

13. Recio Ruiz and Ruiz Somavilla 1989–1990.

14. Tellería Sebastián and Medianero Soto 1995–1996. The forms of Spanish *sigillata* include Dragendorff 24/25, 15/17, 27, and 37. On the site, see also Medianero Soto and Tellería Sebastián 1988.

15. Soto Iborra et al. 1994, 341 and 344 fig. 7.

16. Cf. Balil et al. 1986, passim, esp. 254–255, for the key point that Spanish *sigillata* production, although in its incipient phase during Nero's reign, only really begins to be fully developed and widespread in its typology and quantity in the Flavian and Trajanic periods.

17. Muñíz Jaén et al. 2000, 255–261.

18. See Boto González and Riñones Carranza 1989–1990.

19. Moreno Almenara 1997, 53–55.

20. Iponoba: Muñoz 1987. Iliberri: Rodríguez Oliva 1993, 201. Iliturgicola: Vaquerizo Gil et al. 1991, 124; 1992, 183–184; and 1994a, 69–115, for construction activity, including a possible porticoed public space, in the Flavian era. Atalayuelas: Castro and Choclán 1988, 130–131; Castro et al. 1987, 207–215. Sabora: *CIL* II^2/5, 871 = *ILS* 6092 = *FIRA*² I, no. 74, on which see Atencia 1987a and McElderry 1918, 80. Ipolcobulcula possibly a foundation ex novo: Carrillo 1991a, 235–236. For Olaurum, see Keay 1998, 77, on the basis of Juárez Martín 1989.

21. Edmondson 1990, 167.

22. Perdiguero López 1995, 66–72.

23. Ruiz Nieto and Secilla Redondo 1990.

24. *Municipium (Flavium)*: *CIL* II^2/5, p. 162, and ibid. for Monturque's possible indentification as Spalis.

25. Keay 1998, 78.

26. Ibid., 77.

27. Remesal (1987), who dates the complex on the basis of a head of Bacchus in low relief on white marble, found in the apsidal room.

28. Castro et al. 1993, 456.

29. Fernández Caro 1992, 54–59 and 72–73.

30. Murillo Redondo et al. 1989, 163; Fortea and Bernier 1970, 33–34 no. 6; Bernier et al. 1981, 38–39 no. 23 and fig. 13.

31. Pace Downs (1996, 304 no. 21), who dates its occupation down to the fourth century A.D. Neither Bernier et al. (1981) nor Fortea and Bernier (1970) report the presence of *sigillata* at the site, as Downs alleges.

32. For the site's location and description, see Morena López 1994 and Bernier et al. 1981, 28–29 no. 8 and fig. 8, with pl. I–III.

33. Castro López 1986, 72. The place does disclose one inscription, a funerary tablet from the north necropolis, reading "Vale[---]/viva[s? ---?]," for which see *CIL* II^2/5, 377.

34. Alcock 1993, 48–49.

35. Frederiksen 1976, in extenso, esp. 343–346; Mackie 1983a, 24.

36. For which see Curchin 1985, 329–330 nos. 1–2.

37. *CIL* II^2/7, 864 = *HEp* 5 (1995), 39 no. 113, and ibid. for the suggestion that the name of the *vicus* goes unmentioned because the votive altar was set up within its confines.

38. Castro et al. 1993, 452.

39. As allege Choclán Sabina and Castro López (1986–1987, 149), in the cases of Atalayuelas and Torrebenzalá.

40. *CIL* II^2/5, p. 18, for the identification of Torrebenzalá as Batora on archaeological and epigraphic grounds, including the discovery at the site of a dedication to M. Aurelius of A.D. 166 (*CIL* II^2/5, 59) and an inscription mentioning the "ordo Bator(ensi)s" (*CIL* II^2/5, 60).

41. *CIL* II^2/5, 51 and p. 8. Line 2 of the fragmentary inscription might contain, on Recio's reconstruction, a reference to an unknown *municipium*.

42. Pace González Román (in Rodríguez Neila et al. 1999, 168–170).

43. On the Cerro Boyero, located roughly one kilometer southeast of Valenzuela in Córdoba province, see Bernier et al. 1981, 83–84 no. 115 and fig. 71, with pl. XLVII–XLIX; and Downs (1996, 305 no. 23), who notes the presence of cisterns, drainage canals, silos, and a nearby necropolis.

44. Keay 1998, 62. It was a mistake (Haley 1991, 88) to characterize, following Ponsich (1974, 240 no. 72), the Roman remains at the cortijo de Alcaudete southsouthwest of Carmo as an "agricultural village."

45. For agglomerations at El Centenillo (Jaén province), see Domergue 1971; 1987, 272; 1990, 359–360, and ibid. for other examples in the Sierra Morena.

46. *CIL* II^2/5, 30, on which see Haley 1996b, 21–22, who follows Hübner's dating of *CIL* II 3361 to Trajan's reign.

47. Keay 1988, 68.

48. Didierjean 1978, 20–21 and Table 1.

49. Blázquez 1980.

50. Haley 1996b.

51. So Castro López 1999, 181–182. Pace also Castro López and Gutiérrez Soler (2001, 156–157).

52. Roca Roumens 1976, 100.

53. Orfila Pons 1993. For late Baetican *sigillata* at El Ruedo in southeastern Córdoba province, see Muñíz Jaén et al. 2000, 252.

54. Early date: so Hornos et al. 1986, 207, and Choclán and Castro 1990, 216. Sarcophagus: Recio 1973, 357–360 and fig. 4. Weight (*uncia*): Romero de Torres 1915, 568–569. For parallels of Constantinian date or later, see de Palol 1949, 134 no. 6 (from La Alcazaba, Málaga province), 136 no. 1 (Braga, Portugal), and 138 no. 6 (from Smyrna).

55. Garnsey and Saller 1987, 76.

56. Cf. Alcock (1993, 53), who underscores the ability of intensive surveys in Achaia to pick up the remains of tiny rural habitations that can be connected with small-scale or modest proprietors.

57. On which see Cabello et al. 1992

58. To judge from Cabello et al. (ibid., 537 fig. 1).

59. Le Gall 1991, passim, esp. 316.

60. *CIL* II 1197 = *CILA* 2, no. 97, and ibid. for the inscription's interpretation and date.

61. On his career, see Remesal 1991 and Le Roux 1986, 252–258, who takes "solamina" to refer to emergency consignments of oil to the province of origin (255); I follow *OLD*, p. 1781, in seeing here a probable reference to supplies of grain sent to alleviate a shortage. Cf. Pavis d'Escurac (1976, 128 and 191), who notes that the term "solamina" is deliberately set off from "oleum" in the formula "adiutor Ulpii Saturnini praef(ecti) annonae ad oleum Afrum et Hispanum recensendum item solamina transferenda item vecturas naviculariis exsolvendas" and therefore ought to refer to cereals. But for a different possible sense of the word, see Chapter Seven.

62. *CIL* II²/5, 457.

63. Melchor Gil (1993–1994, 339, and idem 1994, 111), who misattributes the stone to Ipsca; the monument was found "un cuarto de legua de Espejo," according to the *CIL* description.

64. *CIL* II²/5, 753, and ibid. for the date.

65. *CIL* II²/5, 1330.

66. On grain cultivation in Baetica, see also Sáez 1987, 75–145.

67. Silos at El Ruedo: Muñíz Jaén et al. 2000, 261–262. The silos range from 1.25 meters to 1.60 meters in diameter and from 50 meters to 1.12 centimeters in depth.

68. For navigation on the Baetis, see Chic 1978.

69. Rodríguez Almeida 1993, 98 and 100.

70. Chic 1978, 11–19.

71. *VA* 5.6, cited by Blázquez 1988, 207.

72. For this interpretation of the word, see Remesal 1977–1978, 116–117.

73. Baldomero et al. 1997, passim, esp. 152–155.

74. Almayate Bajo: see below, note 114, for references. Calle Carretería: Rambla and Mayorga 1997, 68.

75. Cara and Rodríguez 1995, 90–93.

76. For a summary and description of types A and B, see Berni Millet 1998, 26–33, with figs. 4 and 5.

77. See the discussion in ibid., 20; Mayet 1986, 286; Chic 1994, 77–78.

78. This is the line of Mayet 1986, 299; Liou and Gassend 1990, 198–200; and Liou and Tchernia 1994, 138. Contra, Remesal (1986, 20–21; 1997b, 10 and 19; and 1998, 190), who suggests that the names in the stamps refer to the owners—either the producers or the wholesale buyers—of the oil.

79. Rodríguez Almeida 1993, 98–99.

80. See Fülle 1997, esp. 123–127, for a comparison of Dressel 20 amphora manufacture with *sigillata* production at Arezzo. Remesal (1980, 135) already adduced, on theoretical grounds, the leasing of kilns.

81. Remesal 1980, 136–140, for details, followed by Keay 1988, 99. Chic (1985a, 102–106) is agnostic on the question.

82. On the *tituli picti*, see, in general, Chic 1988, passim, and Berni Millet 1998, 21–22. Peña 1998, 165–170, is inaccurate in detail.

83. And not the weight of the full vessel, as Aubert states erroneously (1994, 266). On the meaning of the number in Dressel position gamma, see Rodríguez Almeida 1980a, 58 n. 4, and Chic 1988, 3.

84. So Liou and Gassend 1990, 177 and 183.

85. On this important point, see Remesal 1998, 188.

86. Chic 1988, 168–172, for the evidence. Dressel's sondages revealed a particularly large number of amphoras with consular dating of the reign of Pius. W. V. Harris, in *The Inscribed Economy* (Ann Arbor, 1993), p. 187, states erroneously that the "delta graffiti . . . begin to appear on Baetican amphorae in the year 140. . . ." He is confusing the delta *titulus* per se with the consular dating element.

87. Chic 1988, 73, for the appearance of the mark only after the reign of Hadrian. Funari (1996, 14–15 no. 2) claims to read the control mark "R" in an unpublished and difficult-to-read *titulus* from Vindolanda, dated by context to the period A.D. 104 to c. 120.

88. See Rodríguez Almeida 1984, 235–236, for discussion.

89. The evidence is collected by Le Roux (1986, 267–271 [appendix 2]).

90. Scaev.1 reg. *Dig.* 50.4.5.

91. So Panciera 1980, 243, and Liou and Gassend 1990, 205–208, esp. 206. For other views, see Loyzance 1986; Tchernia 1980, 158–159, following De Ruggiero (*DE* II, 2, 1782–1783 s.v. "Diffusor") and Rougé (1978, 58); Le Roux 1986; Rodríguez Almeida 1987–1988, 299–304; and Chic 1986, 248.

92. Sirks 1991, 28–34, 37, and 100, for these contracts of the *locatio-conductio* type.

93. Taglietti 1994, 190–191.

94. Sirks 1991, 47–49 and 61.

95. Herz 1988, 114, on the basis of the distinction in *Dig.* 50.6.6.3 between "Negotiatores, qui annonam urbis adiuvant, item navicularii qui annonae urbis serviunt." The different verbs may simply be the result of rhetorical *variatio.* Cf. Garnsey (1983, 124–125), who suggests that trading was subsumed under shipping as a practical matter in the minds of Roman officialdom.

96. Herz 1988, 133; Sirks 1991, 39, 44 n. 28, and 60.

97. Garnsey (1974, 236–237) notes that "decurions as such never benefitted from such grants."

98. Call. 1 cogn. *Dig.* 50.6.6.8 (epist. Hadr.) and *Dig.* 50.6.6 (rescr.).

99. So Keay 1998, 10, on the basis of Domergue (1998), for whom the delta notation was an auto-declaration of oil producers, *navicularii,* and merchants to ad-

vertise the product, aid the shippers in assessing the rate of portage of goods, and allow the state to determine the *portorium*, or customs duty.

100. Though direct evidence from Baetica is lacking, *CIL* II 3664 from Ebusus (Ibiza, Baleares province) in Tarraconensis may provide analogous evidence: there, an unknown individual through testamentary gift established a fund of 90,000 sesterces from which the tribute was to be paid; for the Flavian or post-Flavian date of the inscription, see Castelló 1988, 88–90 no. 26, and Mackie 1983a, 160 n. 11.

101. See, e.g., Krier 1981, 31–35 nos. 7–8, for a decurion of Trier and "nauta Araricus" installed at Lyon in the early second century A.D.

102. As does Berni Millet (1998, 21), citing *CIL* II 1180 and Remesal 1991. For a similar line, see Pleket 1990, 67 n. 12.

103. Sirks 1991, 60.

104. Saller 1994, 189 and passim.

105. For the coins, see Marín Díaz and Mellizo Fernández 1991.

106. Marín Díaz et al. 1989.

107. Bernal Casasola and Navas Rodríguez 1996; Bernal Casasola 1998b.

108. See García Vargas and Lavado Florido 1995, 218–219.

109. Richardson 1996, 163.

110. Liou and Marichal 1978, 131–135 no. 27 and fig. 12.

111. Curtis 1991, 63 n. 86.

112. Chic 1996, 260.

113. On the Huerta del Rincón pottery and its phases, see Baldomero et al. 1997, and Mora Serrano and Corrales Aguilar 1997, 34.

114. Manganeto (Almayate Bajo): Arteaga 1985; Baena del Alcázar 1997, 98 no. 1. El Secretario: Baena del Alcázar 1997, 99; Villaseca Díaz and Hiraldo Aguilera 1991; and Villaseca 1997.

115. Rodríguez Temiño 1990.

116. *CIL* VI 9677 = *ILS* 7278.

117. *CIL* II 1971. Cf. *CIL* II 1970, which names Proculus as *patronus* of Malaca, among his other charges. On Proculus, see Devijver 1976–1993, 825–826 V 29.

118. As does Curchin (1991, 144).

119. *IG* XIV 2540 = *CIL* II p. 251, on which Van Nostrand 1937, 200, and Curchin 1991, 144.

120. So Chic 1996, 265, insinuating also their possible role in the exportation to the eastern Mediterranean of Baetican olive oil.

121. Gozalbes Cravioto and Muñoz Hidalgo 1986.

122. Ortiz Juárez et al. 1981, 248–249.

123. Chic 1985a, 27.

124. See Chic 1984.

125. Jashemski 1992.

126. Chic 1985a, 32–36.

127. Bonsor 1931, 21, and cf. Chic 1985a, 53.

128. Romo Salas 1993.

129. Chic 1985a, 79.

130. Ibid., 89.

131. Ibid., 99. Other sites producing various combinations of amphoras and other items include El Judío, Motores de Malpica, and La Liñana (all in the district of Palma del Río); Juan Barba (Alcolea del Río); Cruz Verde (Alcalá del Río); and Arva; for which see Chic 1985a, 47, 47–49, 49, 94, 106, and Bonsor 1931, 31, respectively.

132. Lara Fuillerat and Camacho Cruz 1995; Lara Fuillerat 1997, 91, on the production at Tejar de Genilla.

133. Camacho Cruz and Lara Fuillerat 1996.

134. Lara Fuillerat 1997, 88, for a preliminary description and analysis.

135. Romero and Medianero 1992.

136. Nieto and Lobón 1990.

137. Cf. the conjunction of villa and ovens firing common ceramics at El Ruedo (Almedinilla) in southeastern Córdoba province, on which see Muñíz Jaén et al. 2000. The ceramics would have supplied the needs of the villa complex, as well as adjoining settlements (p. 255).

138. Romero Moragas 1985.

139. Beltrán Lloris 1990, 193.

140. Serrano Ramos and Rodríguez Oliva 1974.

141. Mora Serrano 1993, 184, 186 nos. 1–3, and 196 no. 1.

142. Serrano Ramos 1995, 227; Beltrán Lloris 1990, 193.

143. Serrano Ramos 1995, 227; Baena del Alcázar 1997, 100; Recio et al. 1989.

144. Baena del Alcázar 1997, 98–99, with bibliography.

145. Rodríguez Neila 1999, 45, citing Setälä 1977.

146. See Serrano Ramos et al. 1984.

147. Serrano Ramos et al. 1992.

148. Serrano Ramos 1991.

149. Atencia Páez and Serrano Ramos 1997, 186–197, and passim.

150. Melchor Gil 1999, 262–263.

151. For production at Cartuja, see Sotomayor 1964–1965, and Serrano Ramos 1979.

152. Atencia Páez and Serrano Ramos 1997, 183.

153. For a full inventory of stamps, typology, and chronology of production at Andújar, see Sotomayor et al. 1999. See also Mayet 1984, 1 : 35–57, for *sigillata* production at Andújar.

154. Price 1987.

155. Curchin 1993, 82.

156. Fuentes 1998, on the basis of glass wasters at the site.

157. *CILA* 2, p. 196 no. 230, where the name is expanded as AUG(ius). Contrary to the indication of *CILA* 2, *CIL* II 6251, 2 ad loc., does not expand the name as "AUC(tus)."

158. Haley 1988. To the piece of ceramic analyzed in the article, add now the base of an undecorated plate of form Dragendorff 15/17 signed "Mamilius" and

found in the baths at Segobriga (Cerro de Cabeza del Griego, Saelices, Cuenca province): see Sánchez-Lafuente Pérez 1990, 202 no. 127 and 212.

159. *CIL* II²/5, 385, dating to the second half of the first or the second century.

160. Segura Arista 1988, 112–130, and 1993.

161. Loza Azuaga and Beltrán Fortes 1990.

162. Canto 1978, 305–310, on the basis of *CIL* II²/5, 847 (= *CIL* II 2011). Melchor Gil (1994, 125) follows Canto in seeing the *servi stationarii* at Nescania as involved in a *statio marmoraria* exploited by the Fabii. Cisneros Cunchillos (1988, 99–100) is skeptical on the ownership of the quarries in Málaga province and on a connection between the *servi stationarii* at Nescania and marble-working.

163. So Mackie 1983a, 156 and 199 n. 37.

164. Canto 1977–1978, 175–178; Grünhagen 1978, 299–300; Cisneros Cunchillos 1988, 26–27, 76–77, and 105–108.

165. *CIL* II 1131 and 1132, on which Canto 1977–1978, 177–178. Contra, Cisneros Cunchillos (1988, 48–51), who does posit the imperial control of the *statio,* but disavows a connection between its ownership and that of the quarries at Almadén.

166. Mayer and Rodà 1998, 218, and passim for other aspects of Baetican quarries not mentioned here.

167. On the mines at Vipasca and their administration, see Domergue 1983.

168. For two imperial procurators, active under Nerva, of the Río Tinto mines, see *CIL* II 956 and *HEp* 3 (1993), 89–90 no. 198.

169. Long and Domergue 1995, passim, esp. 830–834.

170. *AE* 1914.23, and Domergue 1990, 257 no. 3001, for the ingot; Domergue 1990, 266, for its date, and 236, 268 n. 34, and 287, for the suggestion that the mines of the Caenici were private property.

171. Escacena and Padilla 1992, 17 no. 1.

172. Ibid., 20–21 no. 6.

173. So Sánchez-Corriendo Jaén 1997, 154, following Oria Segura et al. 1990, 122.

174. Sánchez-Corriendo Jaén 1997, 253–254.

175. *CIL* II²/5, 660 (= II 5510).

176. Sánchez-Corriendo Jaén 1997, 253–254, citing Gómez-Pantoja 1994.

177. Ponsich 1974, 71–114 and fig. 17, 126–210 and fig. 42; and idem 1991, 199–221 and fig. 64, respectively.

178. Sánchez-Corriendo Jaén 1997, 161, on the basis of Ponsich 1974, 79–80 nos. 41–43.

179. Ponsich 1991, 30–32 and fig. 10; and idem 1998, 176–177 with fig. 2.

180. *Coll.* 11.7.1–2, and *Dig.* 47.14.1 pref, on which Garnsey 1970, 157.

Chapter Five

1. Stylow 1986, 301–303, following Galsterer 1971, 44–50. For an alternative date of the grant, see Fear 1996, 144–146, following Bosworth 1973.

2. Effect of *ius Latii:* Mackie 1983a, 26, 41, 60, 73 n. 26, and appendix II (201–

210); Galsterer 1971, 37–50, esp. 49; Curchin 1990, 87; Abascal Palazón and Espinosa 1989, 44; Millar 1977, 404–405; Stylow 1986, 298. Heightened importance of local councils: see Le Roux 1991a, 570; and Galsterer 1988, 86–87.

3. Carrillo Díaz-Pines 1990, esp. 83–84. On "El Ruedo," see also Vaquerizo Gil and Carrillo Díaz-Pines 1995.

4. On the building phases of the structure, see Jiménez and Martín-Bueno 1992, 71–78, and 66–67 for the discovery of a *sestertius* of Philip, dated A.D. 248, below the mortar bedding of one of the mosaics, providing a secure post quem.

5. Choclán 1988.

6. Morena López and Serrano Carrillo (1991) catalogue a total of thirty-three rural sites with cisterns, constructed of *opus caementicium*.

7. Loza 1982–1983.

8. Pradales Ciprés (1993, 150, 153 map 2, and 155 map 6) notes the presence of Spanish *sigillata* from the upper Ebro valley in certain upland centers of the *conventus Astigitanus*.

9. Greene 1986, 47.

10. Cf. the credit and fiduciary arrangements—constituting monetization—of the Appianus estate in the Fayum district, for which see Rathbone 1991, 318–330, and 398 for the apparently high level of coinage in general circulation in the third century A.D. Egyptian countryside: see also Howgego 1992, 20–22, for the widespread and normal use of exchange by means of coinage in rural areas of the Roman Empire; Howgego emphasizes, however, the persistence of barter. On the complementarity and coexistence of barter transactions and cash payments in rural areas of the Roman Empire, see also de Ligt 1990, 33–43, esp. 38–39.

11. Perdigones Moreno et al. 1986, 58–59, on the basis of an excavation at the calle General Ricardos no. 5 and 7.

12. For a sample of Baetican urban and rural sites yielding early imperial coinage through surface recovery and excavation, see Haley 1996a, appendix. To this list, add the coins from the villa at Alhaurín el Grande, for which see Andérica Frías 1983.

13. So Guichard 1990, 46 and 57, on the basis of Suet. *Vesp.* 16.1: "non enim contentus omissa sub Galba vectigalia revocasse, nova et gravia addidisse, auxisse tributa provinciis, nonnullis et duplicasse" ("For not content to have restored the indirect taxes cancelled under Galba, he added new and burdensome ones, increased the tribute imposed on the provinces, and even doubled that of many [sc. provinces]"). Suetonius is here referring surely to all the provinces with the phrase "auxisse tributa provinciis."

14. Out-of-pocket expenditures: Curchin 1990, 25, 27, 61–62, and 106–111. Indirect taxes: Guichard 1990, 48–49 and 56. Pliny (*Pan.* 37.1–4) alludes to Spanish "cives novi ex Latio," i.e., those who gained Roman citizenship through office holding or immediate kin of former magistrates, when he signals their obligation to pay the 5% inheritance tax as direct heirs under the Flavians, an obligation that was dispensed with in the case of those *veteres cives* whose citizenship predated the Flavians: so Guichard 1990, 45–46 and 57.

15. Vespasian as the founder of the provincial cult: Etienne 1958, 130, and Fishwick 1987, 1.2, 219–239, esp. 238–239. But see now Pailler 1989, who dates the inception of the imperial cult in Narbonensis and Baetica to Domitian, and specifically to A.D. 86.

16. Use of marble: Stylow 1991, 26, noting the self-advertisement of the elites according to the best Roman models; and see also Segura 1993, 116–117, for the utilization of marble from Igabrum in the *conventus Astigitanus* and at Corduba. Local benefactions: Mackie 1990, esp. 184 and 189; Curchin 1983, esp. 237–244 tables I–VI.

17. Melchor 1994, 170–171, who counts a total of sixty-two examples of benefactions aimed at public building(s), of which twelve date securely to the Flavian era and fifteen to the second century A.D.

18. See Melchor 1994, 54–55, 179, 190–191, and 200–201. For probable non-decurionals as euergetists, see, e.g., *CIL* II^2/5, 854 (statue to *Victoria Augusta* set up at the *oppidum ignotum* at the Cortijo del Tajo through the testamentary order of Q. Fabius L.f. Gal[eria] Fabullus), and *CIL* II 1166 (statue to *Vesta Augusta* set up in Naeva[?], also by testamentary disposition, by the Segoviensis M. Iunius Quir[ina] Hispanus). In Singili(a?) Barba, C. Fabius C.f. Quir(ina) Fabianus set up, while alive, a statue and base of *Libertas Augusta* (*CIL* II^2/5, 771 = *ILS* 3780). For further discussion of these three persons with testimonia, see Chapter Six.

19. Montenegro 1975, 47–48. On the relative shortage of public funds and the concomitant importance of individuals for subsidizing public works, see Mackie 1983a, 103 and 119, and cf. Galsterer 1971, 84, who highlights the role of magistrates at Flavian *municipia* in privately financing building projects.

20. Petition and its grounds: see Chapter Four, note 20, for references.

21. See d'Ors 1961, 209–211, on the basis of *AE* 1962.288 (dated September 7, A.D. 79).

22. So Guichard 1990, 65, on the basis of Pliny *Pan.* 29.4–5.

23. For Baetican elite involvement with nonagricultural investments, including public contracts, see the full discussion in Rodríguez Neila 1999, 41–48.

24. Sempronianus: *AE* 1984.526 (Tocina, Sevilla province). Hermesianus: *CIL* II^2/5, 1180. Mussidius: see *CIL* II, 6259, 11, which names P. Musidi Semproniani twice in the genitive on a circular seal 8.4 centimeters in diameter, on display in the Seville archaeological museum. For the seal, see also Chic 1994, 107; Fernández Gómez 1991, 309; and *Bronces* p. 335 no. 329. The piece is apparently from Irni, as *CIL* II describes its discovery in the possession of an antiquities dealer at nearby Algámitas. Mussidius seems to be named in Dr. 20 stamps from "Casa del Picón," a pottery on the left bank of the Genil, recording II MU.S.E.P.R., II MU.S.ET.P.R., and PMSC, sc. a *societas* consisting of P. Mussidii Semproniani (father and son?) and a third individual bearing the initials P.R. See Chic 1994, 107, for the identification of the Semproniani of the seal and those of the stamps. Contra, Remesal 1996, 200 n. 19.

25. On the oilery, see Perdiguero 1995–1996. Cf. the urban oilery at Corduba on the bank of the Baetis of c. A.D. 50 and later: Morena López 1997. Cf. also the

two urban oileries at Munigua of possible Flavian date, for which see Hanel 1989, 206–222, esp. 221.

26. See Márquez Moreno 1989.

27. Márquez Moreno (ibid., 40–43) catalogues a total of thirty-four fragments of *sigillata* out of a larger, unspecified number; of the thirty-four pieces, four are fragments of Italian *sigillata*, and only one corresponds to the base and part of the wall of an unspecified form of Gallic *sigillata*.

28. Ibid., 41 with 52 pl. XIV. The funnel has a diameter of 29 centimeters with a spout just under 9 centimeters wide, and is made from the same clay as the amphora fragments and *dolia* found at the site. It is apparent that Dressel 20 *figlinae* provided their clients with more essentials than merely transport containers necessary for successful olive cultivation and oil production.

29. Remesal Rodríguez et al. 1997.

30. See Romero Corral 1995.

31. The coordinates of the site are 1° 26′ 32″ longitude and 38° 34′ 4″ latitude. On the site and its features, see Romero Corral 1995.

32. Ibid., 300–301.

33. Date of municipalization: *CIL* II^2/7, p. 186.

34. Márquez Trigueros 1996.

35. Curchin 1993, 82; Rodríguez Neila 1999, 26 n. 3.

36. *CIL* II^2/5, 1282. On the site, roughly 12 kilometers east-southeast of Ecija, see Durán and Padilla 1990, 83 no. 52.

37. Portillo et al. 1985, 192–193 no. 10.

38. See Serrano Carrillo and Morena López 1984, 115–116 no. 138.

39. Portillo et al. 1985, 200–201 no. 21.

40. Ibid., 201 no. 22.

41. See Caballero Mesa 1973, 206–212, and Serrano Ramos et al. 1983, for the site and its stratigraphy

42. Portillo et al. 1985, 201–202 no. 23.

43. *AE* 1971.177, and Romero Pérez and Melero García 1999, 13.

44. Arteaga et al. 1990.

45. Keay (1998, 71) notes this "gradual decline for reasons which are not fully understood."

46. See Hornos et al. 1986; Choclán and Castro 1990; Castro et al. 1993, for all relevant details of the site.

47. For the structure and its contents, see Cazabán 1914; Romero de Torres 1915.

48. I had already written these words when I saw the preface in S. Keay, ed., *The Archaeology of Early Roman Baetica* (1998): "In the more remote parts of the *conventus Astigitanus* . . . some 'towns' were little more than monumental centers with little room for a significant urban population" (p. 8).

49. Remesal et al. 1997b, 155.

50. Almagro-Gorbea 1987, 25, based on the plan in Blanco and Corzo 1976,

fig. 9, estimates Obulcula's surface area at 3.3 hectares. Blanco and Corzo (ibid., 157) do suggest that the Roman town extended beyond its Iberian fortifications, especially to the north, but even so, the area of Obulcula's *oppidum* remains small.

51. See Keay 1998, 84 (appendices IA and IB) for a tabulation of the surface area of Baetican *oppida,* including Obulcula.

52. Recio Ruiz 1993.

53. *CIL* II 1282 + suppl. p. 842 = *CILA* 2, 3, no. 930 (fragment c), and ibid. for the mistranslation of the passage "A cada uno de los incolas de la plebe, hombre o mújer. . . ."

54. Keay (1998, appendix IB) gives Iponoba's surface area as one hectare, but Almagro-Gorbea (1987, 25), following Fortea and Bernier 1970, 38, notes its surface area as 4 hectares; at 25 n. 20, however, Almagro-Gorbea reports the excavator A. M. Muñoz's oral suggestion that the actual area is roughly 2.5 hectares.

55. *CIL* II^2/5, pp. 93–94 and map.

56. Almagro-Gorbea 1987, 26, on the basis of the plan of the site in Fortea and Bernier 1970, 50.

57. Rodríguez Almeida 1994b, 96 no. 140.

58. López Castro 1995.

59. Chic 1983, 117.

60. Inscriptions: see López de la Orden and Ruiz Castellano 1995, and *IRCádiz* 78–254 nos. 120–500.

61. Fear 1996, 210.

62. Santos Jener 1950.

63. Foxhall 1990.

64. Liou and Tchernia 1994, 147–148, citing *C. Th.* 1.11.2: "conductores dominicos," against Remesal 1980, 150; and cf. Remesal 1996, 203, for the same expansion or, alternatively, "c(onductio) ol(earia)."

65. Lomas and Sáez 1981, 68–73.

66. Sáez and Chic 1983, 209 n. 112.

67. Rome: *CIL* XV 2565 (in which the initial "A" of "AUGGG" is also missing).

68. Callender 1965, 267 no. 1808(c). For the stamp from Cirencester, see Callender's site report in Richardson 1962, 175 and pl. XXII(d).

69. *CIL* XV 3189 (two examples from the Testaccio and one from the Horti Torlonia).

70. For a lucid description of the *Kalendarium Vegetianum,* see Ojeda Torres 1999, 161–164, drawing on the work of Manacorda (1977a) and Lomas and Sáez (1981).

71. Sáez and Chic 1983, 201. So, similarly, Liou and Tchernia 1994, 151, on Epaphroditus. For Callistus, Felix, and Epaphroditus, see Chic 1988, 91–92 and 96, respectively.

72. Aubert 1994, 133–138; Sáez and Chic García 1983, 201.

73. Sillières in Leveau, Sillières, and Vallat 1993, 246–247.

74. Griffin 1972, 6 n. 66, on the basis of Tac. *Agr.* 7.2.

75. Kehoe 1997, 5, 144–146.

76. One possible exception would be M. Iunius Terentianus Servilius Sabinus, a *duovir, flamen,* and *pontifex* at Corduba and patron of Acinippo (*CIL* II 1347 and p. 701). He may have owned *fundi* at both towns and therefore have benefited from tenancy.

77. Stylow 1988, 127; Portillo et al. 1985, esp. 212–213.

78. Pace Villanueva Acuña (1993, 946), who, while acknowledging the existence of chattel slavery in rural contexts in the more Romanized portions of the Iberian peninsula during the Principate, denies that even in such contexts slaves would have constituted the predominant labor force.

79. Ponsich 1975, 676–677.

80. Remesal 1979, 43–44.

81. Almagro Gorbea 1982, 425–426. See Remesal 1979, 10, for Baelo's *garum* facilities and ability to attract temporary African migrants, after an oral suggestion of Ponsich. For the date of Baelo's municipalization, see Wiegels 1985, 21.

82. Remesal 1979, 46.

83. Beloch (1886, 447–448) estimated a total population of 1.5 million in Augustus' reign, and envisaged some growth in the province during the imperial period (448).

84. Single name: Kajanto 1968, 6–9; Shaw 1984, 470; Knapp 1992, 340. Greek cognomen: Solin 1971, 135 and 158; Taylor 1961, 125–127.

85. For slaves and freedmen in the *conventus Cordubensis* and *Astigitanus,* cf. also the useful but incomplete lists of Camacho Cruz 1997a and 1997b.

86. *CIL* II 5042 = 5406 = d'Ors 1953, 431–446 no. 39, for text, bibliography, and commentary.

87. Curchin 1985, 339 no. 4.

88. González Román 1990.

89. Pastor and Stylow 1996, 284–285 no. 1 (end of the second or beginning of the third century A.D.), 285 no. 2 (second half of the second century A.D. or somewhat later), 285–286 no. 3 (c. 200–250), and 287–288 no. 4 (second century A.D.).

90. On this point, in general, see MacMullen 1987, 360 with n. 5, 368 nn. 50 and 53, and 375–376.

91. *CIL* II^2/5, 211 = Camacho Cruz 1997a, 262 no. 177.

92. *CIL* II^2/5, 212, and ibid. for the date.

93. *CIL* II^2/5, 213, and ibid. for the date.

94. Camacho Cruz 1997a, 262 no. 177.

95. As do Choclán Sabina and Castro López (1990, 207–209), emphasizing the ability of the immediate members of a peasant family to generate the labor sufficient to work more modest *fundi.* But Castro (1988, 321) underscores the presence of slaves in rural properties in the region of Atalayuelas in the campiña of Jaén.

96. "Tinajuela II": Fernández Caro 1992, 131–132 no. 69. "Santa Juliana I": ibid., 133 no. 70.

97. For oleiculture as less labor-intensive than viticulture or arable cultivation (involving both cereals and legumes), see Spurr 1986, 134–140.

Chapter Six

1. Caballos Rufino 1990, passim, esp. 13–14.

2. Ibid., 40–44 no. 7 with bibliography, and *PIR²* A 184.

3. So Caballos (1990, 42), following Chic 1985a, 106 with references. Caballos insinuates a connection of the emperor with the "fundus Aelianus" attested on a Dr. 20 amphora from the *figlina* La Catria.

4. Birley 1997, 24 and 317 n. 7, following Caballos 1990, 42.

5. Caballos 1990, 44–45 no. 8, and *PIR²* A 185.

6. Sen. *Helv.* 14.3 ("tu patrimonia nostra sic administrasti ut tamquam in tuis laborares"), on which see Griffin (1972, 6), who suggests interests in vineyards or olive groves rather than an "export business or mines." How does she know?

7. Caballos 1990, 64–65 no. 30; *HA Marcus* 1.2; and *PIR²* A 694.

8. *PIR²* A 695, and Caballos 1990, 65–67 no. 31, with bibliography, who suggests his birth in Ucubi but migration to Gades, where his children were born, citing Syme 1958, 791ff. But Syme (792) simply notes another Annius, L. Cornelius Pusio Annius Messalla, in Gades, for whom no necessary relation with the family of the future emperor is implied or suggested.

9. Caballos 1990, 67–68 no. 32; Setälä 1977, 55 n. 1; and *PIR²* A 696.

10. Caballos 1990, 59–60 no. 25; Castillo 1982, 491 no. 16. Etienne (1965, 66 no. 17) cites *PIR²* A 667 to the effect that Libo came from Gades, a notion reproduced by Caballos. *PIR²* A 667 says no such thing. More secure is the identification of Libo as a *dominus* in brick stamps from Rome, on which see Setälä 1977, 54–55.

11. Caballos 1990, 69–72 no. 34; Castillo 1982, 493 no. 25. See also *PIR²* A 765.

12. Caballos 1990, 71, on the basis of Callender 1965, 148 no. 803. But Callender simply notes the homonymously named *duovir* in Corduba (*CIL* II²/7, 349) without making a link with the consular. Caballos also notes the "fundus ANTISTIA(NUM)" (sic), for which see Chic 1988, 79; cf. Chic 1985a, 65, for the stamps Q. ANT. R from La Catria from the second half of the first century A.D. Contrary to the claim of Stylow (*CIL* II²/7, 349 ad loc.), Syme (1983, 371) does not suggest that the *duovir* is the father of the suffect consul of 90; Syme only writes (360) that the suffect's *patria* is Corduba, "which exhibits a homonymous magistrate."

13. *CIL* II²/5, 623 = *ILS* 1139 and *PIR²* C 1322.

14. Sáez and Chic 1983, 195, on the basis of *CIL* XV 4282; cf. Caballos Rufino 1990, 100, and Liou and Tchernia 1994, 150–151, for the possible connection. For the *titulus pictus,* see also Chic 1988, 92, and ibid. for the date.

15. Caballos 1990, 106–108 no. 53; Castillo 1982, 513–514 no. 89; and *PIR²* C 1423.

16. So Caballos 1990, 113–114 no. 57. On Senecio, see also *PIR²* C 1451.

17. Sáez and Chic 1983, 195, on the basis of *CIL* XV 4274.

18. Caballos 1990, 108–110 no. 54, after González, *IRCádiz* nos. 535 and 450. See also *PIR²* C 1425.

19. Caballos 1990, 110–112 no. 55.

20. See ibid., 111.

21. *IRCádiz* no. 535. For the Cortijo del Tesorillo, see Lagóstena Barrios 1996a, 64–66 no. 15 and 159.

22. Caballos 1990, 127–128 nos. 63A–F; Chic 1985a, 20–23, 38, and 40.

23. Caballos 1990, 128–129 no. 64, on the basis of *CIL* III 4120 (*ager Poetoviensis*), which seems to presuppose that Cilo had at least one son and grandson, and Remesal 1989.

24. On Cilo, see Caballos 1990, 132–135 no. 66. From Iluro, according to Instinsky (1944) and Alföldy (1968, 142, 156, and 159); Alföldy does not suggest origin in Singili(a?) Barba, pace Caballos (1990, 133–134). See also *PIR*² F 27.

25. Fortunatus: Caballos 1990, 137 no. 68. See Remesal 1989 for the stamps and connections.

26. Liou and Tchernia 1994, 142.

27. Jacques 1990.

28. *AE* 1975.21, and Caballos 1990, 153–154 no. 81, after Panciera 1973, 96.

29. Caballos 1990, 154–155 no. 82; and Setälä 1977, 127–128. See also *PIR*² 119.

30. Chic 1985a, 24, followed by Caballos 1990, 199 no. 106; but see now Liou and Tchernia 1994, 143.

31. Jacques 1990, 883 n. 63.

32. Caballos 1990, 209–210 no. 115. See Chic 1985a, 88 and 93, for the stamp. Painted inscription: Rodríguez Almeida (1980a, 87 no. 35 and fig. 15), who expands "f(undo, -iglina) veg(etiano, -ana)" in line 3. Bonneville (1982, 5–32) sees "Myrtilianus" as an *origo* designation.

33. *CIL* VI 1240, 31552 = *ILS* 5931; and Caballos 1990, 215 no. 121.

34. *CIL* XIV 3516; and Caballos 1990, 217–218 no. 123. Friend of Hadrian: *HA Hadr.* 4.2.

35. *CIL* XIV 3526; and Caballos 1990, 216 no. 122.

36. *CIL* II 1282, 1283, 1371; and Caballos 1990, 220–225 no. 125.

37. *AE* 1983.517; and Caballos 1990, 213–215 no. 120.

38. *I.Eph.* 697b = Eck 1980, 40–45; and Caballos 1990, 218–220 no. 124.

39. *CIL* II 1175; and Caballos 1990, 229–230 no. 129A.

40. Caballos 1990, 223.

41. Didierjean 1978, 22, citing (24 n. 1) Beltrán Lloris 1970, 281.

42. Bonsor 1931, 27. *CIL* XV 4373 (A.D. 179) refers to a "fundus Messianus" and to the fiscal control district Hispalis. See also Ponsich 1974, 40 no. 57, for the Hacienda de Mejina, following Pabón 1953, 131 (vidi), in the municipality Espartinas as deriving from Messina, i.e., from Messius.

43. Remesal 1983, 104, where the references to *CIL* II 1172 and 1173 instead of 1282 and 1283 must be the result of a typographical error. Cutius Celsianus: *CIL* XV 3849.

44. Remesal 1983, 104. Caesianus: *CIL* XV 3797–3799. Eumenes: *CIL* XV 3800–3801. Macrinus: *CIL* XV 3797–3799. Senecio: *CIL* XV 3802.

45. Castillo 1982, 510 no. 78; Caballos 1990, 231–235 no. 129B; *PIR*² M 707.

46. Lomas and Sáez 1981, citing G. Chic, "Bases y desarrollo del comercio aceitero de la Bética," Ph.D. thesis (Sevilla, 1977), 497, and Callender 1965, 162

no. 898. Caballos (1990, 234) notes this expansion without comment, but cf. 208–210 no. 115 for the identification of the stamp with L. Marius L.f. Gal. Vegetinus!

47. Viterbo: *CIL* XI 3003 = *ILS* 5771; Aecae in Apulia: *CIL* IX 948. It is unclear on what warrant Caballos (1990, 229–230 no. 129A) posits an antecedent of L. Mummius Niger Q. Valerius Vegetus (named in the Aecae inscription) by the name of Mummius Niger Valerius Vegetus (named in the Viterbo text). It may well be the case that the same person is named in the inscriptions from Viterbo and Aecae, with the only difference being that the inscription from Viterbo omits his praenomina.

48. Remesal 1996.

49. Cf. Caballos 1990, 232, for the family connection.

50. Chic 1994, 107–108. For the seal, see above, Chapter Five, note 24.

51. Remesal 1996, 200 n. 19.

52. See Gomezel 1994 for a description of the object and circumstances of its find.

53. *CIL* VI 2099; and Caballos 1990, 247 no. 136.

54. *CIL* V 877 = *ILS* 1052; and Caballos 1990, 249–252 no. 138.

55. *CIL* XV 1363–1366.

56. Consul of 135: *CIL* VI 31125; and Groag, "Tutilius," *RE* VII 1614 no. 2. Consul of 183: *CIL* VI 2099; and Groag, "Tutilius," *RE* VII 1615 no. 5.

57. *CIL* XV 4174 (149): PONTIANI; *CIL* XV 3826 (161): TUTILI PONTIANI. On the two consuls, see Sáez and Chic (1983, 194–195), who note that the Tutilii must also have had Lusitanian property, to judge from *CIL* II 550.

58. Bennett 1997, 3, categorizing erroneously Traius Masculus as the proprietor of an amphora manufactury. For Masculus, see *CIL* II 6257, 199; Bennett (224 n. 12) mistakenly cites *CIL* I 6257 no. 199, instead of *CIL* II 6257, 199.

59. *CIL* II^2/5, 627; Castillo 1982, 515 no. 95; and Caballos 1990, 301–303 no. 165.

60. *CIL* II^2/5, 624; Castillo 1982, 515–516 no. 96; and Caballos 1990, 303–305 no. 166.

61. For Baetican equestrians involved in civilian and military posts and commands, see Caballos Rufino 1998.

62. For the figure of thirty-nine equestrians with certain Baetican origins, see Caballos 1998, 126–128, to which add Sextus Marius. For the latter's possible equestrian status, see Knapp 1983, 43, citing Wiegels 1972, no. 299.

63. This number derives from Caballos Rufino 1999, 138.

64. *CIL* II 1380, on which see Eck (1997, 69–70), who sees more than two *equites* involved here.

65. For his *origo* in Italica, see Castillo 1982, 488 no. 3; *PIR*² A 45.

66. Caballos 1990, 31 and 35. Contra, Fear (1996, 273), who suggests native origins.

67. Guichard 1991.

68. Magonianus: *CIL* II^2/5, 780 = *ILS* 1405. Censonilla: *CIL* II^2/5, 781.

69. See Romero Pérez 1993a and 1993–1994, and *CIL* II^2/5, 830, for the tomb

and the inscription discovered within it that reads "D(is) M(anibus) s(acrum) / Acilia Plae / cusa Sing(iliensis) / [Ba]rbensis / [ann(orum) -2-3- h(ic)] s(ita) e(st) / - - -." Clustered around the tomb, which measures 10.5 by 8.64 meters, are seven inhumation tombs of the third century or later.

70. Caballos 1998, 128 no. 36 and 134.

71. *CIL* II²/5, 784 ad loc.

72. *CIL* XV 2559 (BARBA), 2560 and 2563a (BARB), 2561a and b and 2563b (BAR). Guichard's mark BA (1991, 304) is a misreading of *CIL* XV 2563c, which reads "F. BA • R." SINGILIESE: *CIL* XV 4456. Chic (1985a, 6–7) suggests a connection between the name C.IVL.BAR on an amphora stamp from El Sotillo, in the control district Corduba, and the *figlina Barba*.

73. So Chic 1988, 86, on the basis of Collantes de Terán et al. 1951, 207.

74. Atencia Páez 1988, 49–50.

75. *CIL* IX 235 = *ILS* 2923; Devijver 1976–1993, 499 I 147.

76. Tac. *Ann.* 6.19; Dio 58.22.2–3. Pliny (*HN* 34.4) refers to "(aes) Marianum . . . quod et Cordubense dicitur." See Domergue 1990, 235, for his ownership of the mines; contra, Mangas and Orejas (in Rodríguez Neila et al. 1999, 272), for his leasing of the mines.

77. *CIL* II²/7, 342 (aedile and *duovir*), and *HEp* 2 (1990), 108 no. 345 (*procurator*).

78. For his possible sources of wealth, see Ventura Villanueva 1999, 71–72, and Carrillo et al. 1999, 49–50, with testimonia, alleging familial relationships with various Persii and Marii, attested at Corduba and Epora and supposedly involved with mining, and adducing the mark M.P. on cornices from the theater at Corduba, for which see Ventura Villanueva 1999, 68–69 no. 12 with fig. 17, which they expand as "M(ercellonis) or M(arii) P(ersini)." The arguments seem circumstantial, at best.

79. *CIL* II²/7, 286.

80. *CIL* XV 3870–3871; Liou and Marichal 1978, 128 no. 16.

81. *CIL* II 1191 = Curchin 1990, 156 no. 186. A certain L. Aelius Aelianus is named in Dressel beta in *tituli picti* of 154 (*CIL* XV 3693, and see also 3694). Aelius Aelianus in the genitive is named in Dressel delta of *CIL* XV 4049, encountered in Dressel's sounding M of the Testaccio (A.D. 140–145). For the possibility that the person named in Cantillana and in the Monte Testaccio are the same, see Chic 1988, 89. Melchor Gil (1993–1994, 341) is hasty to state categorically that the *duovir* of Naeva and the producer/trader of oil are one and the same person.

82. Rodríguez Neila and Melchor Gil 2001, 206.

83. *CIL* II²/7, 725.

84. *CIL* II²/5, 495 = Curchin 1990, 164 no. 274.

85. C. Aelius Fabianus: *CIL* XV 3692, dated A.D. 160. For the connection, see Curchin 1990, 164 no. 274, and see also Rodríguez Neila and Melchor Gil 2001, 206. Chic (1988, 5) is skeptical, rightly I think, of a link between the two.

86. Rusticus: *CIL* II²/7, 349. For stamps that may refer to the *duovir* or a relative, see above, note 12.

87. C. Attius Severus: *AE* 1955.21 = Curchin 1990, 150 no. 132. P. Attius Severus: *CIL* XV 3642–3645.

88. Balbus: *PIR²* B 1331 = Curchin 1990, 146–147 no. 96, and ibid. for other references and discussion. Portus Gaditanus: see Rambaud 1996 and 1997.

89. *CIL* II 1941.

90. Chic 1996, 247–248, with testimonia.

91. *CIL* XV 2849 ad loc.

92. *CIL* II 1054 = Curchin 1990, 139 no. 23, who misreads Albinus' title as "IIvir munificentissimus." He was a "civis munificentissimus": *CIL* II index p. 772.

93. Melchor Gil 1993–1994.

94. On these oil *negotiatrices* and proprietors/tenants of olive-producing estates, see Gallego Franco 1991, 100–103. Kampen (1981, 114), from the nonepigraphical evidence, notes Roman female involvement in large-scale business ventures in the early Roman Empire.

95. Duncan-Jones 1990, 46.

96. Whittaker 1985, 55.

97. So D'Arms 1981, 100–102, on the basis of Petron. *Sat.* 76.2–8.

98. Veyne 1961, 231–240. Cf. Kehoe 1997, 73: "Once having made his fortune, Trimalchio began investing his wealth in land, limiting his involvement in commerce to lending money through freedmen," citing Veyne and D'Arms.

99. On this point, see Serrano Delgado 1988, 220–221.

100. Aubert 1994, 263.

101. Chic 1994, 86–87. Lupatus: *CIL* XV 3693–3694.

102. Chic 1994, 87. Optatus: *CIL* XV 3693–3694 and 3795; Chic 1988, 5; and ibid. for Optatus' appearance in *societas* with the DD. Caecilii. Funari (1996, 10–11) reads the beta text of an unpublished Dr. 20 inscription from Vindolanda, dated by context to the period A.D. 100–120, as <L>AELIOPTAELI<AN>LUP, and sees a reference to the traders L. Aelius Optatus, L. Aelius Aelianus, and L. Aelius Lupatus.

103. *CIL* II 2329. On the family and its interests, see Thevenot 1952.

104. Chic 1985a, 77, and 1975, 357–358.

105. Chic 1985a, 67–68, 75, 77.

106. Ibid., 78, for the possible identification.

107. Mayet 1978, 373 nos. 53 and 54, with pl. VII nos. 53–54; Chic 1992, 10–11.

108. Stuart 1977, 90 no. 3 and pl. 25 no. 422.

109. Funari 1996, 22 no. 26.

110. Chic 1992, 17, for discussion and references.

111. Remesal 1997b, 38 and 87–88 nos. 17, 17a–d, 18, and 18a for the stamps L(   ) A(   ) PAE(   ) and variants; Remesal 1997b, 38 and 88 no. 20, on the basis of Callender 1965, 211 no. 1370(9), for the stamp POR(tu) L(   ) A(   ) R(   ). For the latter stamp in London and Colchester, see Funari 1996, 20 nos. 18, 18a–c.

112. Remesal 1997b, 39, and 85 no. 5 and 93–94 no. 43, for the stamps.

113. Ibid., 43, and 85 nos. 3–4, for the stamps. Remesal dates the stamp L(   ) A(   ) BR(   ) to the Flavian-Trajanic periods.

114. Aelianus: see note 81 above. Caesianus: *CIL* XV 3693–3694. Fabianus: *CIL* XV 3692.

115. Chic 1985a, 82–83. Statue of Venus: *CIL* II 2326. The full name of the benefactor, responding to the testamentary wishes of her husband M. Annius Celtitanus, is Aemilia Rustici f. Artemisia: see *CIL* II 2326 ad loc. and *CIL* II suppl. index p. 1054. Melchor Gil (1993–1994, 340) mistakenly turns her into two persons: Aemilia Artemisia and Aemilia Rustica.

116. For Aemilia Rustica, see *CIL* II^2/5, 1319 = Stylow 1988, 121–123 no. 3.

117. Callender 1965, 173–174 no. 1003; Martin-Kilcher 1987, 96 no. 10a and 262–263 no. 1318.

118. Remesal 1986, 123 no. 30, but at 61 fig. 14a and 249 no. 30 he dates the stamp, I assume inadvertently, to the second half of the second century; Mayet 1978, 372–373 no. 50.

119. Rodríguez Almeida 1979, 885 no. 20.

120. Melchor Gil 1993–1994, 340.

121. Funari 1996, 22 no. 27, for the stamp reading L.AEMILI/RUST, and ibid. for a date of A.D. 60–61/200.

122. See Haley 1988.

123. Rodríguez Almeida 1979, 911–912 nos. 16–17; Chic (1988, 6) notes a second-century inscription from Astigi attesting the MM. Aemilii Faustus, Clara, and Op[tatus], as well as other unknown persons, and the Aemilius Optatus on a Dr. 20 amphora stamp from La Catria, a *figlina* in the control district of Astigi.

124. *IRCádiz* 55–57 no. 80.

125. González 1983, 190–191. *Tituli picti* of 154: *CIL* XV 3883 and 3884. *Titulus* of 149: *CIL* XV 3889.

126. *CIL* XV, 2, 2, 8272.

127. Rodríguez Almeida 1972, 152–156 no. 6 and fig. 13.

128. Chic 1988, 7 and 27, following González 1983, 190–191.

129. Rufinus: Funari 1996, 23 no. 32, and ibid. for the date; Remesal 1986, 124 no. 33, and 1997b, 91 no. 37; Callender 1965, 90 no. 241; Ponsich 1974, 164 and fig. 65; and Chic 1985a, 76 and 81. Rufus (or Rufinus): Funari 1996, 23–24 no. 33; Remesal 1986, 124–125 nos. 34 (and ibid. for the date), 34a, and 34b, reading RVF (i or -ini); Remesal 1997b, 91 nos. 39 (and ibid. for the date), 39a, and 39b; Callender 1965, 200 no. 1280 and fig. 12, 27–28; and Chic 1985a, 69.

130. The name Rufinus points to freeborn status: of 490 examples in Kajanto 1965, 229, only nine are used by explicitly designated slaves or freedmen. So, similarly, the cognomen Rufus: of 1,433 instances of the name noted by Kajanto, only twenty-four are borne by explicitly designated slaves or freedmen.

131. *CIL* XV 3699; Chic 1988, 8.

132. *CIL* II^2/5, 1162 and *HEp* 3 (1993), 137 no. 344 = Chic 1987–1988, 365–367. Melchor Gil (1993–1994, 340 n. 19) connects her with the producer Caesius in the

zone of Astigi named in *CIL* XV 3901 and with the merchant Q. Caesius Caesianus, at note 44 above.

133. As suggested by Melchor Gil 1993–1994, 341. For Urchail Atitta, see *CIL* II 1087, dated too early (to the first half of the first century B.C.) by Melchor Gil. Chic (1985a, 61) is more guarded on a possible connection between the benefactor of Ilipa and the individual of the amphora stamps. For the stamps, see Chic 1985a, 56, 58–59, 61, and 72 (mark ATITAC of uncertain reading). For a tentative date of the second half of the first century B.C., with non-Spanish examples, see Callender 1965, 236 no. 1547.

134. *CIL* XV 3731–3734; Chic 1988, 10.

135. Rodríguez Almeida 1972, 159–162 no. 10, and ibid. for the suggestion that he was the father of D. Aticus Atticus Trophimianus.

136. *CIL* XV 3742; Chic 1988, 11, attested in the Horti Torlonia.

137. *CIL* XV 2, 2, 8097. The cognomen ending in -ianus points to his free birth.

138. *CIL* II²/5, 1165.

139. So Tchernia 1980, 155–156, followed by Remesal 1983, 104. For D. Caecilius Hospitalis, see *CIL* XV 3762–3764, 3769–3771, 3773–3781; Rodríguez Almeida 1972, 164–166 no. 12 and fig. 19; *CIL* VI 1625b = *ILS* 1340; and *CIL* II²/5, 1165.

140. Melchor Gil 1993–1994, 339.

141. Chic 1994, 90, following Callender 1965, 221–222 no. 1428 and 226 no. 1460. *Tituli picti: CIL* XV 3797–3799.

142. Chic 1994, 90, on the basis of *CIL* XV 3797–3799.

143. Legulianus: Rodríguez Almeida 1979, 926 no. 36; *CIL* XV 3803. Sulpicianus: Rodríguez Almeida 1979, 927 no. 37.

144. Melchor Gil 1993–1994, 341. Sempronianus: *AE* 1984.526. Caecilianus: *AE* 1982.520, for whom see Loyzance 1986, 278.

145. González 1983, 186, for its identification as a funerary monument; Le Roux (1986, 267 no. 2) suggests the inscription refers to a statue or a public edifice, either religious or civil in nature; Loyzance (1986, 274) conjures up a public edifice.

146. Chic 1994, 90–91.

147. Ibid., 92.

148. Remesal 1997b, 43.

149. Rodríguez Almeida 1994a, 120–123 nos. 9–10. Of 165 instances of the cognomen Quadratus in Kajanto 1965, 232, fourteen are borne by explicitly designated slaves or freedmen.

150. *CIL* XV 3845–3847.

151. *CIL* XV 3653; Chic 1988, 22–23, and ibid. for the date.

152. Kajanto 1965, 304.

153. Remesal 1997b, 38, and 99 no. 63, 101 no. 68, and 102–103 no. 73 for the stamps.

154. Remesal 1997b, 43, which reads M(   ) C(   ) L(   ) S(   ) B(   ), probably through a misprint, and 102 no. 71 and 101–102 no. 70 for the stamps.

155. *CIL* XV 3850–3851; Chic 1988, 23.

156. Kajanto 1965, 229.

157. Rodríguez Almeida 1994a, 123 nos. 11, 12, and 13(?).

158. *CIL* XV 3852.

159. See Remesal 1997b, 108–109 nos. 97–98.

160. *CIL* II 1195.

161. *CIL* II²/5, 1342 (= II 1058 + p. 837).

162. Remesal 1977–1978, 105 nos. 29–30 and 113, for the provenance of the stamps, date, and expansion of "p" in one of the stamps as "p(ortus)" from the findspot, "el puerto," of *CIL* II 1058. Remesal suggests a possible link between the individual in the stamps from La Catria and the Q.FL.FLAVIANI of a stamp found in Amiens listed as Callender 1965, 225 no. 1453.

163. Chic 1985a, 53, for the stamp and apparent connection with Carisianus, named in *CIL* II 1064. *Tituli picti: CIL* XV 3813 and 4267. Melchor Gil (1993–1994, 342) designates the Fulvii as decurionals, on the basis of Carisianus' pontificate—though he may simply have held a local priesthood of Arva, without ever having been either a magistrate or a decurion.

164. So Chic 1988, 25, on the basis of *CIL* XV 3876, in which he sees one Charisianus as named; but he leaves open the possibility that two persons of the same name are mentioned in the *titulus.*

165. Remesal 1983, 99, citing the stamps Q. F(   ) R(   ) SALS, Q. F(   ) R(   ) MED, and Q. F(   ) R(   ) RIV, which he dates to the beginning of the third century.

166. Chic 1985a, 83.

167. Ibid., 53–54. For the stamp, see Will 1983, 405–406 no. 35. Q. Fulvius Lupus in Celti: *CIL* II 2330.

168. On this point, Sáez 1978, passim, esp. 259.

169. Callender 1965, 225 no. 1456, and Chic 1985a, 84, for the stamps and his affiliation with the family of C(h)arisianus. If "Niger" is his cognomen—"Nigrinus" is also possible—then he is most likely freeborn: of 253 examples of the cognomen in Kajanto 1965, 228, only twenty belong to explicitly designated slaves or freedmen. Of eighty-nine nonsenatorial men in imperial inscriptions bearing the cognomen Nigrinus, none is an explicitly designated slave, and only one can be positively identified as a freedman: Kajanto 1965, 228.

170. Liou and Marichal 1978, 113–116 nos. 2 and 3; Chic 1988, 26, and ibid. for the date.

171. *CIL* XV 3878; Chic 1988, 26; Rodríguez Almeida 1984, 227.

172. Kajanto (1965, 236) collects fifty-two examples of the name.

173. *CIL* XV 3899; Chic 1988, 29, noting its position (K) in the Testaccio, while citing Rodríguez Almeida (1984, 228), who suggests c. 230. Of thirteen instances of the name in Kajanto 1965, 301, not one belongs to an explicitly designated slave or freedman.

174. *CIL* XV 3903–3905; Chic 1988, 30.

175. The inscription was discovered in the base of the tower (the Giralda) of the cathedral of Sevilla; see Chic 1999, 42 and 55 n. 122.

176. Rodríguez Almeida 1990, 369–378.

177. *CIL* II 1956.

178. Chic 1996, 261, on the basis of *CIL* XV 3914 and Liou (1987), 134 no. 3, from Mâcon (Saône-et-Loire).

179. *CIL* XV 3911; Chic 1988, 30.

180. *Saint-Gervais 3:* see Liou and Gassend 1990. For Casilla de Malpica, see Chic 1985a, 44–46.

181. Calpurnius: Chic 1985a, 45–46; and Callender 1965, 89, for the diffusion of the stamps naming Calpurnius.

182. Remesal 1997b, 43–44.

183. Ibid., 38, referring to 127 no. 173—which reads SEX(   ) I(   ) RUFI—and 127 no. 174.

184. *CIL* XV 3929; Chic 1988, 32–33.

185. On women's capacity to undertake *negotia*, see Gardner 1986, 233–237, and 9, 14–15 for emancipation.

186. Fesia[na?]: Rodríguez Almeida 1979, 942–944 no. 63, and ibid. for the suggestion that the two Mariae Q.f. are sisters (Chic 1988, 34). Postumina: *CIL* XV 3960 and perhaps 3961; Chic 1988, 34.

187. *CIL* XV 3963; Chic 1988, 35.

188. Kajanto 1965, 199. See *CIL* VI 37541 for the slave Hispanus.

189. Rodríguez Almeida 1972, 186 no. 25; Chic 1988, 35.

190. Desbat et al. 1987, 164 no. 6 with fig. 11, from Saint-Romain-en-Gal, and ibid. for the date.

191. Rufus in Corduba: *CIL* II²/7, 415a. The name Rufus is at Kajanto 1965, 229.

192. Pérez López et al. 1999, 698 no. 6.

193. *CIL* XV 3663, on whose possible relationship with L. Mevius Rufus, and that of L. Mevius Faustus, see Chic 1991, 107, and Pérez López et al. 1999, 698 n. 27.

194. *CIL* XV 4738.

195. *CIL* XV 3971; Chic 1988, 36.

196. For Avillianus, see *CIL* XV 3977–3979 and 3981–3982; Rodríguez Almeida 1984, 229; Chic 1988, 37.

197. Apolaustus: *CIL* XV 3972–3973; Rodríguez Almeida 1972, 188 no. 27 and fig. 31; idem 1981, 116–118 no. 1; Chic 1988, 18. Titullus: Colls and Lequément 1980, 186; Chic 1988, 41.

198. Licinius Maternus: *CIL* XV 3929; Chic 1988, 32–33. Pompeius Maternus: Rodríguez Almeida 1972, 193–195 no. 31 with fig. 34; idem 1979, 950 no. 76, and 952 no. 76A; Chic 1988, 38. Paternus: Rodríguez Almeida 1979, 952 no. 78; Chic 1988, 38. Paternus' status is that of an *ingenuus* from his cognomen, which is never borne by Spanish slaves or freedmen. Of 283 instances of the cognomen in Kajanto 1965, 304, not one is borne by an explicitly designated slave or freedman.

199. *CIL* XV 3991; Chic 1988, 39. Cognomen: see Kajanto 1965, 164. This trader may be the same as a certain Pollio attested in *tituli picti* of c. A.D. 150: see *CIL* XV 3881, and possibly Rodríguez Almeida 1979, 948–949 no. 73.

200. Livianus: *CIL* XV 4000; Chic 1988, 40. Sempro<nianus?>: Funari 1996, 13–14, and ibid. for the date.

201. Rodríguez Almeida 1972, 205–207 no. 39; Chic 1988, 40.

202. *CIL* II 1048; and Chic 1992, 15–16, for the identification and suggestion that Rusticus died on his estate.

203. Callender 1965, 164–165 no. 925(d).

204. Remesal 1980, 142–144, and ibid. for relevant testimony.

205. Izquierdo 1989, 68 no. 7.

206. *CIL* XV 4023–4027; Chic 1988, 42–43, and ibid. for the suggestion that the brothers(?) distributed their own oil. For the producer Vale . . . (?), see *CIL* XV 4026. For C. Valerius Valerianus, see *CIL* XV 4025–4027; Rodríguez Almeida 1994a, 128 nos. 17–18. Valerianus, whose name suggests his free birth as well, also operated in isolation in 161.

207. Ru[fus]: Rodríguez Almeida 1979, 956 no. 85, and ibid. for a post-Severan date; Chic 1988, 43. Valgo: Rodríguez Almeida 1972, 209 no. 41; Chic 1988, 43.

208. Rodríguez Almeida (1984, 231) also suggests Rufus' activity c. A.D. 150. Chic García (1988, 43) suggests a date for Valgo of A.D. 140 to 147 from the position of his *titulus* in the Testaccio.

209. *CIL* XV 4052–4055; Chic 1988, 45.

210. Aper: Rodríguez Almeida 1979, 959 no. 88. Asper: Colls and Lequément 1980, 183. Marcellus: *CIL* XV 4077. Montanus: *CIL* XV 3689 (A.D. 91 from the Viminalis in Rome); he may be the same as a certain [   ] Montanus attested in the Castra Praetoria, for whom see *CIL* XV 3670–3672. Senecio: Rodríguez Almeida 1972, 215–217 no. 46; and *CIL* XV 4090(?).

211. *CIL* XV 4044–4045; Chic 1988, 51, who notes the father-son association of the Vibiani.

212. *CIL* XV 4767. His cognomen is not borne by one explicitly designated slave or freedman in Hispania.

213. *CIL* VI 29722; see Chic 1988, 40.

214. On his origins, see Le Roux 1986, 269 no. 8, and Wierschowski 1995, 61 n. 108, 178, 181, and esp. 185 n. 162.

215. *CIL* XII 4393.

216. *CIL* XV 3863–3870 and 3872–3873; Chic 1988, 25.

217. *CIL* XV 2, 2, 8166 = *IG* XIV 2412, 24; see Taglietti 1994, 172–174.

218. *AE* 1973.71; Panciera 1980, 244–245.

219. Colls et al. 1977, 62 nos. 12–14 with figs. 24–25; Colls and Lequément 1980, 183; Chic 1988, 46. For his Gallic origin, see Berni Millet 1998, 73 n. 93.

220. The evidence is collected by Chic (1988, 88–112), with the exception of "Iunius Optatus, Arvesis," for whom see Rodríguez Almeida 1994b, 96 no. 140.

221. Liou and Tchernia 1994, 151.

222. See Schulze-Oben 1989, esp. 87–116; Serrano Delgado 1988; and Gimeno Pascual 1988.

223. *CIL* XV 3740; Chic 1988, 11.

224. Caballos and Eck 1992.

225. *HEp* 5 (1995), 202 no. 696.

226. On Puteolanus and his putative activity, see Haley 1990a, followed by Etienne and Mayet 1998, 215.

227. So Curchin 1991, 144.

228. Liou 2000.

229. On migration within, and into, Hispania, see Haley 1991.

230. *CIL* II 1166 + suppl. p. 841 = *ILS* 3318 = *CILA* 2, no. 4, and ibid. for the circumstances of the pedestal's recovery, description, and date.

231. *CIL* II 3362 = *CIL* II^2/5, 29, and ibid. for the date.

232. *CIL* II^2/5, 788, and ibid. for the date. Cf., similarly, Rodríguez Neila 1999, 88, adducing likely nondecurional and nonmagisterial local and provincial priests at Arva, Acinippo, Cartima, Tucci, Castro del Río (*municipium ignotum*), Anticaria, Astigi, and Hispalis, in addition to Hispanus at Singili(a?) Barba.

233. Delgado 1998, 52–53, 72–87, and passim.

234. For the exception, a *duovir* attested in a fragmentary inscription, apparently from the cortijo de Moguerejo, 5 kilometers southwest of El Coronil, see Canto 1978, 293–294 = *AE* 1979.351.

235. *CIL* II^2/5, 854, and ibid. for a possible date of c. A.D. 150.

236. *CIL* II^2/5, 856 and 859, respectively.

237. So Serrano Ramos et al. 1991–1992, 199–200 and pl. XI = *CIL* II^2/5, 804, and ibid. for the date.

238. *CIL* II 1956, l. 9.

239. *CIL* II 1356.

240. *CIL* II 1941.

241. Presedo Velo 1974 = *AE* 1974.384. On the statue base, see also Beltrán Fortes and Ventura Villanueva 1992–1993, 373–374, who suggest its origin in Algeciras, which they identify as Iulia Traducta (380 n. 5).

242. *CIL* II 1923 = *IRCádiz* no. 501.

243. *CIL* II^2/5, 270.

244. *CIL* II^2/5, 493.

245. *CIL* II 1045.

246. *CIL* II 1200 = *CILA* 2, 70–71 no. 59 with fig. 24, and ibid. for the date.

247. Haley 1991, 104–105.

248. *CIL* II^2/5, 733 = Perdiguero López 1995, 23–25, with a description of the stone.

249. *CIL* II^2/5, 734.

250. Fernández Gómez 1991, 313 and fig. 4, with pl. II-2.

251. *CILA* 2, no. 219 and fig. 117.

252. Note also a bronze seal (*CILA* 2, no. 232 and fig. 122), measuring 2.2 by

6 centimeters, from Arva, naming the probable *ingenuus* Gaius Licinius Propinquus, which stamped pottery products — amphoras? Of thirty-one instances of the male name and four female cases, not one is borne by a slave or freedman in Kajanto 1965, 303.

253. *CIL* II²/5, 540 (= II 6259, 5).

254. *CIL* II²/5, 566 (= 4975, 65). Of 144 instances of the name Pollio in Kajanto 1965, 164, only four are borne by slaves or freedmen.

Chapter Seven

1. Cf. Goldsmith 1987, 35: "But again real income per head may well have increased very slowly up to the early second century A.D. but to have lost any gain by the beginning of its fourth quarter [sic]."

2. For the distinction "intensive-extensive" agriculture, see Spurr 1986, 1, and Kehoe 1988, 12–13.

3. Jongman 1988, 26–27, following R. G. Lipsey, P. O. Steiner, and D. D. Purvis, *Economics,* 7th ed. (New York, 1984), ch. 38 (vidi).

4. Jongman 1988, 76.

5. Ibid., 134, 143, 146, 192, and 194–195.

6. Ibid., 92–93, following de Vries 1974, 4–7 (vidi).

7. Jongman 1988, 93.

8. Ibid., 94, following de Vries 1974, 7–10 (vidi).

9. Jongman 1988, 108, following Beloch 1890, 457.

10. Beloch 1886, 447. Cf. Pleket 1993, 329, on Baetica, "for which there does not seem to be much evidence for demographic growth."

11. Garnsey 1996, 150.

12. Remesal 1998, 197.

13. Baetican oil in Lusitania: Fabião 1993–1994. Northeastern coast of Tarraconensis and Ebro River valley: Berni Millet 1998. Pannonia: Gabler and Kelemen 1984. Britain: Funari 1996; Carreras and Funari 1998. Northeast France: Baudoux 1996, 85–106 and 114–138. Dalmatia: Cambi 1983. Alexandria: Will 1983.

14. Chic García 1979.

15. *AE* 1958.9 = *CILA* 6, no. 90 and pl. XVII no. 61.

16. As does Ojeda Torres (1999, 164).

17. Cf. C. Lewis and C. Short, *A Latin Dictionary* (Oxford, 1879; reprint ed. 1989), 1718.

18. See J. M. Carrié's review of Pavis d'Escurac 1976 in *REA* 82 (1980): 360–362, at 361, followed by Chic 1996, 250–251.

19. Jongman 1988, 194, 195, 192 (quotations); 22 n. 4 and 195 n. 2 (subsistence income).

20. Hopkins 1980, 118–120, citing M. I. Rostovtzeff, *RE* s.v. "frumentum," 149 (119 n. 54).

21. Goldsmith 1984, 273 and table 1.

22. Jacques and Scheid 1990, 309.

23. Pekáry 1976, 111.

24. See MacMullen 1974, 187 n. 18, citing Lucian *The Cock* 22. We can ignore MacMullen's *obiter dictum* that the 250 *denarii* represents the "subsistence level."

25. Mrozek 1987, 104.

26. On this point, see Melchor 1994, 122.

27. For 6% as a typical rate of return on land in Italy, see Duncan-Jones 1982, 33 n. 3 and 133. Kehoe (1997, 78) mentions a "conventional annual return on capital of 6 percent," but does not specify whether it is capital invested in agriculture, out on loan, or invested in some sort of trading venture.

28. Tab. Irn. IX B (ch. 86) 49–52–IX C (ch. 86) 1–2, on which see González 1986, 231.

29. Frier 1993.

30. Lamberti 1993, 170 n. 95.

31. *Dig.* 32.41.6; Frier 1993, 225.

32. Tab. Irn. IX B (ch. 86) 49; IX C (ch. 86) 2; and IX C (ch. 86) 1–2.

33. So Garnsey 1970, 232, on the basis of *Dig.* 47.2.52.21 (*honestus* synonymous with *locuples*), 47.2.67.4, 47.9.9, and possibly 48.10.18 (*idoneus* synonymous with *honestus*).

34. This is the line of Abascal Palazón and Espinosa 1989, 145, and Lamberti 1993, 171, who erroneously assume that 5,000 sesterces is the census minimum for decurions at Irni.

35. Curchin 1990, 25.

36. Tab. Irn. IX B (ch. 86) 49–52–IX C 1–16 (trans. M. Crawford). González (1986, 231) writes: "[Lines] 12–16 . . . make it clear that the property qualification for a decurio was more than 5,000 HS at Irni."

37. Lebek 1993, 175–176.

38. On this point, see Le Roux 1991b.

39. So Jacques and Scheid 1990, 311.

40. D'Ors 1986, 174.

41. Goldsmith 1987, 262–263 n. 2.

42. Harl 1996, 273–275 and 279.

43. *HEp* 5 (1995), 23 no. 67, where the expansion "(sextertiis)" in line 6 must be the result of a misprint.

44. It does not seem helpful to confine the notion and reality of a "middle layer" in the social and economic fabric of towns in the Roman West to the restricted group of *Augustales,* as does D'Arms (2000, 129, and ibid. for the expression "middle layer").

45. MacMullen 1997, 90, referring to the findings of Goldsmith (1984 and 1987).

46. On the passage from Callistratus and on the rescript of Marcus and Lucius Verus (*Dig.* 50.6.6.6), see Sirks 1991, 50–52.

47. Coins: *BMC* III p. 415 nos. 1193–1194 (A.D. 119–120 or 121), on which see Birley 1997, 99. Inscription: *CIL* XIV 2799 of A.D. 128 or later from Gabii, calling Hadrian and Sabina "locupletatores municipii." The idea of the emperor as an enricher of the Roman world and its inhabitants seems to go back to Trajan's reign;

cf. *CIL* VI 958 = *CIL* VI.8.2, 40500 and 40501 of A.D. 108 from Rome, calling Trajan the "propagator orbis terrarum" and "locupletator civium."

48. *Dig.* 50.15.4 pref.

49. Cf. the suggestion of Keay (1988, 102) that *navicularii* shipping Baetican oil came predominantly from Narbonensian families such as the Fadii, Valerii, Segolatii, and Olitii.

50. On the evolution and spirit of the civic experience in Hispania in general, and Baetica in particular, from Caesar to the beginning of the Severan dynasty, see the perceptive discussion in Le Roux 1995, 79–109.

51. Perdiguero 1995–1996, 142.

52. Tellería Sebastián and Medianero Soto 1995–1996, 175.

53. Mayet 1986, 300–301 and 302–303.

54. Remesal 1996, 209–211, and passim.

55. Rodríguez Almeida 1980b, 282–283; Chic 1988, 67–71; Berni Millet 1998, 49–50.

56. Mayet 1986, 301–302, who refers to the "figlina Stip(. . .)" (sic). See Callender 1965, 225 no. 1454, for the reading "Q.F.R ST SIP" of this mark, found in Rome, Langres, Tottweil, and Arva.

57. Jacques 1990.

Chapter Eight

1. Camodeca 1992.

2. Remesal 1997b, 49; Remesal et al. 1997, 155.

❋

Bibliography

Abascal Palazón, J. M. 1986. *La cerámica pintada romana de tradición indígena en la península ibérica.* Madrid.

———. 1989. *La circulación monetaria del Portus Ilicitanus.* Valencia.

Abascal Palazón, J. M., and U. Espinosa. 1989. *La ciudad hispano-romana: Privilegio y poder.* Logroño.

Aguilar Sáenz, A., and P. Guichard. 1995. *La ciudad antigua de Lacimurga y su entorno rural.* Badajoz.

Alarcão, J. de. 1988. *Roman Portugal.* 2 vols. Warminster.

Albertini, E. 1923. *Les divisions administratives de l'Espagne romaine.* Paris.

Alcock, S. E. 1989. "Roman Imperialism in the Greek Landscape." *JRA* 2:5–34.

———. 1993. *Graecia Capta: The Landscapes of Roman Greece.* Cambridge.

Alföldy, G. 1968. "Septimius Severus und der Senat." *BJ* 168:112–160.

———. 1969. *Fasti Hispanienses.* Wiesbaden.

———. 1976. "Die römische Gesellschaft—Struktur und Eigenart." *Gymnasium* 83:1–25.

———. 1984. *Römische Sozialgeschichte.* 3d ed. Wiesbaden.

———. 1985. "Bellum Mauricum." *Chiron* 15:91–109.

———. 1992. "A proposito dei monumenti delle province romane nel Forum Augustum." In *Studi sull'epigrafia augustea e tiberiana di Roma* (*Vetera* 8), 67–75. Rome.

———. 1995. "Der Status der Provinz Baetica um die Mitte des 3. Jahrhunderts." In R. Frei-Stolba and M. A. Speidel, eds., *Römische Inschriften-Neufunde, Neulesungen und Neuinterpretationen. Festschrift für Hans Lieb*, 29–42. Basel.

Almagro Gorbea, M. 1982. "Nota sobre la seriación de las urnas de la necrópolis SE. de Belo." *MCV* 18:419–426.

———. 1987. "El área superficial de las poblaciones ibéricas." In *Los asentamientos ibéricos ante la romanización, Coloquio: 27–28 Febrero 1986*, 21–34. Madrid.

Alvarez Martínez, J. M., and A. Rubio Muñoz. 1988. "Excavaciones en el yacimiento romano de Regina Turdulorum." *Extremadura Arqueológica* 1:221–230.

Amaro, C. 1990. "Olaria romana da Garrocheira, Benavente." In A. Alarcão and F. Mayet, eds., *Les Amphores Lusitaniennes: Typologie, Production, Commerce*, 87–95. Paris.

Amores, F., and S. J. Keay. 1999. "Las sigillatas de imitación tipo Peñaflor o una serie de hispánicas precoces." In M. Roca Roumens and M. I. Fernández García, eds., *Terra Sigillata Hispánica: Centros de fabricación y producciones altoimperiales*, 235–252. Jaén and Málaga.

Amores Carredano, F. 1982. *Carta arqueológica de los Alcores (Sevilla)*. Seville.

Andérica Frías, J. R. 1983. "Hallazgos numismáticos en la villa romana de 'La Fuente del Sol' (Alhaurín el Grande, Málaga)." *Numisma* 180–185:55–67.

Andreau, J. 1974. *Les affaires de Monsieur Jucundus*. Rome.

Aranegui Gascó, C. 1980. "La circulación monetaria en el Grau Vell de Sagunt (Valencia)." *Numisma* 165–167:59–86.

Arteaga, O. 1985. "Los hornos romanos del Manganeto, Almayate Bajo (Málaga). Informe preliminar." *NAH* 23:175–193.

Arteaga, O., and M. Blech. 1985. "Untersuchungen auf dem Cerro de Maquiz: Vorbericht der Kampagne Mai 1984." *MDAI(M)* 26:177–184.

Arteaga, O., et al. 1990. "El abandono de un sector urbano de Obulco en época flavia." In *AAA 1990. II* [publ. 1992], 310–317. Seville.

Atencia Páez, R. 1987a. "Sobre los restos arqueológicos del 'Cortijo de la Colada' (Cañete la Real, Málaga) y la localización de 'Sabora.'" *Baetica* 10:139–159.

———. 1987b. "El poblamiento antiguo en la depresión de Antequera." In *Actas del II Congreso Andaluz de Estudios Clasicos*, 205–229. Málaga.

———. 1988. *La ciudad romana de Singilia Barba (Antequera-Málaga)*. Málaga.

Atencia Páez, R., and E. Serrano Ramos. 1997. "El taller antikariense de terra sigillata hispánica." In *Figlinae Malacitanae* 1997, 177–215.

Atencia Páez, R., and A. Sola. 1978. "Arqueología romana Malagueña." *Jábega* 23:73–84.

Aubert, J. J. 1994. *Business Managers in Ancient Rome: A Social and Economic Study of Institores, 200 B.C.–A.D. 250*. Leiden.

Baena del Alcázar, L. 1997. "Arquitectura y tipología de los hornos romanos malacitanos." In *Figlinae Malacitanae* 1997, 95–106.

Baldomero, A., et al. 1997. "El alfar romano de la Huerta del Rincón: Síntesis tipológica y momentos de producción." In *Figlinae Malacitanae* 1997, 147–176.

Balil, A., et al. 1986. "Terra sigillata hispánica: A propósito de un libro reciente." *BSEAA* 52:248–262.

Baudoux, J. 1996. *Les amphores du nord-est de la Gaule*. Paris.

Beloch, K. J. 1886. *Die Bevölkerung der griechisch-römischen Welt*. Leipzig.

———. 1890. *Campanien: Geschichte und Topographie des antiken Neapel und seiner Umgebung*. 2d rev. ed. Breslau.

Beltrán Fortes, J., and L. Baena del Alcázar. 1994. "La arquitectura funeraria romana del alto Guadalquivir (Jaén). Informe final." In *AAA 1994. II* [publ. 1999], 125–131. Seville.

Beltrán Fortés, J., and M. L. Loza Azuaga. 1997. "Producción anfórica y paisaje costero en el ámbito de la Malaca romana durante el alto imperio." In *Figlinae Malacitanae* 1997, 107–146.

Beltrán Fortes, J., and A. Ventura Villanueva. 1992–1993. "Basis marmorea cum signo argenteo." *Tabona: Revista de Prehistoria y de Arqueología* [Universidad de La Laguna] 8, 2:373–389.

Beltrán Lloris, M. 1970. *Las ánforas romanas en España.* Zaragoza.

———. 1977. "Problemas de la morfología y del concepto histórico geográfico que recubre la noción tipo: Aportaciones a la tipología de las ánforas béticas." In *Méthodes classiques et méthodes formelles dans l'étude typologique des amphores, Actes du Colloque de Rome, 27–29 Mai 1974*, 97–131. Rome.

———. 1990. *Guía de la cerámica romana.* Zaragoza.

Bendala Galán, M., and M. Pellicer Catalán. 1977. "Nuevos hallazgos en el solar de la antigua Orippo (Dos Hermanas, Sevilla)." *Habis* 8:321–330.

Benítez Mota, R., et al. 1992. "Intervención arqueológica de urgencia en la Loma del Puerco, Chiclana de la Frontera (Cádiz)." In *AAA 1992. III* [publ. 1995], 90–96. Cádiz.

Bennett, J. 1997. *Trajan, Optimus Princeps: A Life and Times.* Bloomington and Indianapolis.

Bernal Casasola, D. 1995. "Tecnología de manufactura de lucernas en época romana: Dos elementos de fabricación a molde en la P. ibérica." In M. Vendrell-Saz et al., eds., *Studies on Ancient Ceramics: Proceedings of the European Meeting on Ancient Ceramics*, 147–150. Barcelona.

———. 1997. "Novedades de epigrafía anfórica en la Bética: Talleres costeros granadinos del bajo imperio." *Boletín de la Asociación Española de Amigos de Arqueología* 37:99–110.

———. 1998a. "Las ánforas de producción local: Tipología, caracterización y epigrafía." In D. Bernal, ed., *Excavaciones arqueológicas en el alfar romano de la Venta del Carmen, Los Barrios (CADIZ)*, 143–198. Madrid.

———, ed. 1998b. *Los Matagallares (Salobreña, Granada): Un centro romano de producción alfarera en el siglo III d.C.* Salobreña.

Bernal Casasola, D., and L. Lorenzo Martínez. 1996. "Los Altos del Ringo Rango (Los Barrios, Cádiz): Un complejo residencial e industrial de época romana (ss. I-V d.C.) en la bahía de Algeciras." *CPAM* 23:191–211.

———. 1998a. "Producciones cerámicas de época romana: Los alfares de la Venta del Carmen." *Revista de Arqueología* 203:24–33.

———. 1998b. "Las cerámicas importadas y la cronología del complejo alfarero." In D. Bernal, ed., *Excavaciones arqueológicas en al alfar romano de la Venta del Carmen, Los Barrios (CADIZ)*, 63–80. Madrid.

Bernal Casasola, D., and J. Navas Rodríguez. 1996. "Los Matagallares: Un centro alfarero romano en Salobreña." *Revista de Arqueología* 182:42–51.

Bernard, H., and C. Domergue. 1991. "Les lingots de plomb de l'épave romaine Sud Perduto 2 (Bouches de Bonifacio, Corse)." *Bulletin de la Société des sciences historiques et naturelles de la Corse* 111:41–95.

Berni Millet, P. 1998. *Las Ánforas de aceite de la Bética y su presencia en la Cataluña romana.* Barcelona.

Bernier Luque, J., et al. 1981. *Nuevos yacimientos arqueológicos en Córdoba y Jaén.* Córdoba.

Berti, F., ed. 1990. *Fortuna Maris: La nave romana di Comacchio.* Bologna.

Birley, A. R. 1997. *Hadrian: The Restless Emperor.* London.

Blanco, A., and R. Corzo. 1976. "El urbanismo romano de la Bética." *Symposium de Ciudades Augusteas,* 137–162. Zaragoza.

Blanco Freijeiro, A., and J. M. Luzón Nogué. 1966. "Mineros antiguos españoles." *AEA* 39:73–88.

Blázquez Martínez, J. M. 1978. *Economía de la Hispania Romana.* Bilbao.

———. 1980. "¿Gran latifundio o pequeña propiedad en la Bética (Hispania) en época imperial?" *Miscellanea di studi classici in onore di Eugenio Manni,* vol. 1, 245–255. Rome.

———. 1988. "Hispania en época julio-claudia." In J. González and J. Arce, eds., *Estudios sobre la Tabula Siarensis,* 201–232. Madrid.

Bonneville, J. N. 1982. "Remarques sur l'indication de l'origo par la tribu et le toponyme après des tria nomina sans filiation." *MCV* 18, 1:5–32.

Bonsor, G. 1931. *The Archaeological Expedition along the Guadalquivir, 1889–1901.* New York.

Bosworth, A. 1973. "Vespasian and the Provinces: Some Problems of the Early 70s A.D." *Athenaeum* 51:49–78.

Boto González, M. J., and A. Riñones Carranza. 1989–1990. "Villa romana de Auta Riogordo (Málaga)." *Mainake* 11–12:111–124.

Broughton, T.R.S. 1952. *The Magistrates of the Roman Republic.* Vol. 2. New York.

Brunt, P. A. 1971. *Italian Manpower, 225 B.C.–A.D. 14.* Oxford.

Buendía Moreno, A. F., and F. E. Villada Paredes. 1987. "Prospección arqueológica de superficie realizada en las cuencas de los ríos Fardes y Aguas Blancas (Granada)." In *AAA 1987.* II [publ. 1990], 118–129. Seville.

Caballero Mesa, F. 1973. "Neolíticos-Iberos [sic] y Romanos en la cuenca media del Guadalhorce: Introducción al estudio de cuatro nuevos yacimientos arqueológicos." *Gibralfaro* 25:195–215.

Caballos Rufino, A. 1990. *Los senadores hispanorromanos y la romanización de Hispania (siglos I al III p. C.), I: Prosopographia.* Ecija.

Caballos Rufino, A. 1993. "Un nuevo municipio flavio en el conventus Astigitanus." *Chiron* 23:157–169.

———. 1998. "Cities as a Basis of Supraprovincial Promotion: The *equites* of Baetica." In S. Keay, ed., *The Archaeology of Early Roman Baetica,* 123–146. Portsmouth, R.I.

———. 1999. "Preliminares sobre los caballeros romanos originarios de las provincias hispanas: Siglos I-III d.C." In J. F. Rodríguez Neila and F. J. Navarro Santana, eds., *Elites y promoción social en la Hispania romana,* 103–144. Pamplona.

Caballos Rufino, A., and E. Eck. 1992. "Nuevos documentos en torno a los Egnatii de la Bética." *FlorIlib* 3:57–69.

Cabello, N. J., et al. 1992. "Excavación de emergencia en el yacimiento romano del Cortijo de la Cancha, en Ronda (Málaga)." In *AAA 1992. III* [publ. 1995], 536–539. Cádiz.

Callender, M. H. 1965. *Roman Amphorae with Index of Stamps.* London.

Camacho Cruz, C. 1997a. *Esclavitud y Manumisión en la Bética Romana: Conventus Cordubensis y Astigitanus.* Córdoba.

———. 1997b. "Esclavitud en los Conventus Cordubensis y Astigitanus: Testimonios epigráficos." *MHA* 18:109–167.

Camacho Cruz, C., and J. M. Lara Fuillerat. 1996. "'La Alcantarilla' (Carcabuey, Córdoba), una nueva instalación alfarera en las Subbéticas: Aproximación a su medio físico y su estructura económica." *Antiquitas* [Museo de Priego] 7:69–92.

Cambi, N. 1983. "Le anfore Dressel 20 nella Jugoslavia." In *Producción y comercio del aceite en la antigüedad: II Congreso Internacional,* 363–389. Madrid.

Camodeca, G. 1992. *L'archivio puteolano dei Sulpicii.* Vol. 1. Naples.

Campano Lorenzo, A. 1992. "Excavación arqueológica en el horno de ánforas de 'El Olivar de los Valencianos,' Puerto Real, Cádiz: Comentarios sobre la estructura." In *AAA 1992. III* [publ. 1995], 130–138. Cádiz.

Campo, M., and J. Granados. 1978. "Aproximación a la circulación monetaria de Barcino." *Numisma* 150–155:221–240.

Canto, A. M. 1977. "Inscripciones inéditas andaluzas. II." *Habis* 8:407–428.

———. 1977–1978. "Avances sobre la explotación del marmol en la España romana." *AEA* 50–51:165–188.

———. 1978. "Una familia bética: Los Fabii Fabiani." *Habis* 9:293–310.

———. 1997. *Epigrafía Romana de la Beturia Céltica.* Madrid.

Cara Barrionuevo, L., and J. M. Rodríguez López. 1995. "Estructura económica y comercio marítimo en el extremo oriental de la Bética: Cerámica sigilada y recipientes anfóricos del puerto romano de Guardias Viejas, El Ejido, Almería." *XXI Congreso Nacional de Arqueología, Teruel 1991,* vol. 1, 85–98. Zaragoza.

Carreras Monfort, C. 1999. "The Nature of the [sic] Roman Trade: An Archaeological Perspective." *MBAH* 18, 2:87–114.

Carreras Monfort, C., and P.P.A. Funari. 1998. *Britannia y el Mediterráneo: Estudios sobre el abastecimiento de aceite bético y africano en "Britannia."* Barcelona.

Carrilero Millán, M., and B. Nieto González. 1994. "La Depresión natural de Ronda en la Bética romana: Paisaje agrario y estructure social en el alto imperio." In C. González Román, ed., *La Sociedad de la Bética: Contribuciones para su estudio,* 51–73. Granada.

Carrilero Millán, M., et al. 1995. "La villa romana de Las Viñas (Cuevas del Becerro, Málaga) y el poblamiento rural romano en la depresión de Ronda." *FlorIlib* 6:89–108.

Carrillo Díaz-Pines, J. R. 1990. "Técnicas constructivas en la villa Romana de el Ruedo (Almedinilla, Córdoba)." *AAC* 1:81–107.

———. 1991a. "El poblamiento romano en la subbética Cordobesa." *AAC* 2: 225–252.

———. 1991b. "Panorama actual de la arqueología romana en la campiña de Córdoba (Tipología y jerarquización de los asentamientos)." In J. Aranda Doncel, ed., *II encuentros de historia local: La campiña*, vol. 1: 101–115. Córdoba.

———. 1995. "Testimonios sobre la producción de aceite en época romana en la Subbética Cordobesa." *Antiquitas* [Museo de Priego] 6:53–91.

———. 1998. "Turres Baeticae: Una reflexión arqueológica." *AAC* 10:33–86.

Carrillo Díaz-Pines, J. R., and R. Hidalgo Prieto. 1991. "Aproximación al estudio del poblamiento romano en la comarca de Palma del Río (Córdoba): La implantación territorial." *Ariadna* 8:37–68.

Carrillo Díaz-Pines, J. R., et al. 1999. "Córdoba: De los orígines a la Antigüedad Tardía." In *Córdoba en la Historia: La construcción de la urbe, Actas del Congreso, Córdoba 20–23 de mayo, 1997*, 37–74. Córdoba.

Casariego, A., et al. 1987. *Catálogo de plomos monetiformes de la Hispania Antigua*. Madrid.

Castelló, J. J. 1988. *Epigrafía romana de Ebusus*. Ibiza.

Castillo, C. 1982. "Los senadores béticos: Relaciones familiares y sociales." In S. Panciera, ed., *Epigrafia e ordine senatorio II (Tituli 5)*, 465–519. Rome.

———. 1984. "Los senadores de la Bética: Onomástica y parentesco." *Gerión* 2: 239–50.

———. 1994. "El nuevo juramento a Augusto encontrado en la Bética." In Y. Le Bohec, ed., *L'Afrique, la Gaule, la Religion à l'époque romaine: Mélanges à la mémoire de Marcel Le Glay*, 681–686. Bruxelles.

Castro López, M. 1986. "Consideraciones preliminares para la reconstrucción de la etapa romana en el Alto Guadalquivir: Una perspectiva arqueológica." In A. Ruiz Rodríguez, M. Molinos Molinos, and F. Hornos Mata, eds., *Arqueología en Jaén (Reflexiones desde un proyecto arqueológico no inocente)*, 69–74. Jaén.

———. 1988. "El poblamiento romano de las campiñas occidentales del alto Guadalquivir: El Imperio." In *Actas del Ier Congreso peninsular de Historia Antigua*, vol. 2, 315–324. Santiago de Compostela.

———. 1999. "Reconstruyendo un paisaje agrario: La Campiña de Jaén en los siglos I–II." In V. Salvatierra, and C. Rísquez, eds., *De las Sociedades Agrícolas a la Hispania Romana: Jornadas Históricas del Alto Guadalquivir. Quesada (1992–1995)*, 175–195. Jaén.

Castro López, M., and C. Choclán. 1988. "El poblamiento rural de la campiña de Jaén en época imperial." *Dédalo* 26:119–137.

Castro López, M., and L. Gutiérrez Soler. 2001. "Conquest and Romanization of the Upper Guadalquivir Valley." In S. Keay and N. Terrenato, eds., *Italy and the West: Comparative Issues in Romanization*, 145–160. Exeter.

Castro López, M., F. Hornos Mata, and C. Choclán. 1993. "Cabeza Baja de Encina Hermosa (Castillo de Locubín-Jaén): Una reflexión sobre el desarrollo del territorio ciudadano en la Campiña." In J. F. Rodríguez Neila, ed., *Actas del I Coloquio de Historia Antigua de Andalucía. Córdoba 1988*, vol. 2, 451–467. Córdoba.

Castro López, M., J. López Rozas, N. Zafra de la Torre, J. Crespo García, and C. Chóclan. 1987. "Prospección con sondeo estratigráfico en el yacimiento de Atalayuelas, Fuerte del Rey (Jaén)." In *AAA 1987. II* [publ. 1990], 207–215. Seville.

Cazabán, A. 1914. "Casa comercial, romana, en la Sierra de Castillo de Locubín." *Don Lope de Sosa* 13:142–144.

Chaves Tristán, F. 1994. "Indigenismo y romanización desde la óptica de las amonedaciones hispanas de la Ulterior." *Habis* 25:107–120.

———. 1998. "The Iberian and Early Roman Coinage of Hispania Ulterior Baetica." In S. Keay, ed., *The Archaeology of Early Roman Baetica*, 147–170. Portsmouth, R.I.

———. 1999. "El papel de los 'itálicos' en la amonedación hispana." *Gerión* 17: 295–315.

Chic García, G. 1975. "Inscripciones de Peñaflor." *Habis* 6:357–363.

———. 1978. "Consideraciones sobre la navegabilidad del Guadalquivir en época romana." *Gades* 1:7–20.

———. 1979. "El intervencionismo estatal en los campos de la producción y la distribución durante la época de los antoninos." *MHA* 3:125–137.

———. 1979–1980. "Lacca." *Habis* 10–11:255–276.

———. 1983. "Portus Gaditanus." *Gades* 11:105–120.

———. 1984. "Lebrillos y macetas en los antiguos alfares romanos del Guadalquivir y del Genil." *Habis* 15:275–280.

———. 1985a. *Epigrafía anfórica de la Bética.* Vol. 1. Seville.

———. 1985b. "Aspectos económicos de la política de Augusto en la Bética." *Habis* 16:277–299.

———. 1986. "El comercio del aceite de la Astigi romana." *Habis* 17:243–264.

———. 1987–1988. "Datos para el estudio del culto imperial en la Colonia Augusta Firma Astigi." *Habis* 18–19:365–381.

———. 1988. *Epigrafía anfórica de la Bética.* Vol. 2. Seville.

———. 1991. "Economía y Política en la Epoca de Tiberio: Su Reflejo en la Bética." *Laverna* 2:76–128.

———. 1992. "Los Aelii en la producción y difusion del aceite bético." *MBAH* 11: 1–22.

———. 1994. "Economía y sociedad en la Bética altoimperial: El testimonio de la epigrafía anfórica. Algunas notas." In C. González Román, ed., *La Sociedad de la Bética*, 75–122. Granada.

———. 1996. "Producción y comercio en la zona costera de Málaga en el mundo romano en época altoimperial." In F. Wulff Alonso and G. Andreotti, eds., *Historia Antigua de Málaga*, 245–266. Málaga.

———. 1997. "La miel y las bestias." *Habis* 28:153–166.

———. 1999. "Comercio, fisco y ciudad en la provincia romana de la Bética." In J. González, ed., *Ciudades Privilegiadas en el Occidente Romano,* 33-59. Seville.

Chic García, G., et al. 1980. "Horno cerámico romano del Rancho Perea (San Isidro del Guadalete)." *Boletín del Museo de Cádiz* 1:43-49.

Choclán Sabina, C. 1988. "Excavación de urgencia en el Cerro del Espino (Torredelcampo-Jaén) 1988." In *AAA 1988. III* [publ. 1990], 157-163. Seville.

Choclán Sabina, C., and M. Castro López. 1986-1987. "Ciudad y territorio en la Campiña de Jaén: La distribución de los 'asentamientos mayores' durante época Flavia." *SHHA* 4-5, no. 1:145-160.

———. 1990. "La Campiña del Alto Guadalquivir en los siglos I-II d.C. Asentamientos, estructura agraria y mercado." *Arqueología Espacial 12: Seminario sobre arqueología espacial, Lisboa-Teruel 1988,* 205-221. Teruel.

Christ, K. 1980. "Grundfragen der römischen Sozialstruktur." In E. Eck, H. Galsterer, and H. Wolff, eds., *Studien zur antiken Sozialgeschichte: Festschrift Friedrich Vittinghoff,* 197-228. Köln.

Cisneros Cunchillos, M. 1988. *Mármoles hispanos: Su empleo en la España romana.* Zaragoza.

Cobos Rodríguez, L., et al. 1995-1996. "Intervención arqueológica en el solar del antiguo Teatro Andalucía de Cádiz: La factoría de salazones y la representación gráfica del faro de Gades." *Boletín del Museo de Cádiz* 7 [publ. 1997]:115-132.

Collantes de Terán, F., et al. 1951. *Catálogo arqueológico y artístico de la provincia de Sevilla III.* Seville.

Colls, D., C. Domergue, and V. Guerrero Ayuso. 1986. "Les lingots de plomb de l'épave Cabrera 5 (Ile de Cabrera, Baléares)." *Archaeonautica* 6:31-80.

Colls, D., R. Étienne, R. Lequément, B. Liou, and F. Mayet. 1977. "L'épave Port-Vendres II et le commerce de la Bétique à l'époque de Claude." *Archaeonautica* 1:1-145.

Colls, D., and R. Lequément. 1980. "L'épave *Port-Vendres II:* Nouveaux documents épigraphiques." In *Producción y comercio del aceite en la antigüedad: I Congreso Internacional,* 177-186. Madrid.

Corbier, M. 1991. "City, Territory and Taxation." In J. Rich and A. Wallace-Hadrill, eds., *City and Country in the Ancient World,* 211-239. London and New York.

Cordeiro Raposo, J. M. 1990. "Porto dos Cacos: Uma oficina de produção de ânforas romanas no vale do Tejo." In A. Alarcão and F. Mayet, eds., *Les Amphores Lusitaniennes,* 117-151. Paris.

Corell, J. 1999. *Inscripcions Romanes d'Ilici, Lucentum, Allon, Dianium i els seus respectius territoris.* València.

Corrales Aguilar, P. 1997-1998. "Actividades económicas en la comarca de Antequera (Málaga) en época romana." *Mainake* 19-20:89-105.

Cortijo Cerezo, M. L. 1990-1991. "La política territorial julio-claudia y flavia en la Bética." *MHA* 11-12:249-293.

Crawford, M. H., et al., eds. 1996. *Roman Statutes.* London.

Cuomo di Caprio, N. 1971–1972. "Proposta di classificazione delle fornaci per ceramica e laterici nell'area italiana, dalla preistoria a tutta l'epoca romana." *Sibrium* 11:371–464.

Curchin, L. A. 1983. "Personal Wealth in Roman Spain." *Historia* 32:227–244.

———. 1985. "*Vici* and *pagi* in Roman Spain." *REA* 87:327–343.

———. 1990. *The Local Magistrates of Roman Spain.* Toronto.

———. 1991. *Roman Spain: Conquest and Assimilation.* London.

———. 1993. "Local Elites in Baetica in the Time of Trajan." In J. González, ed., *IMP. CAES. NERVA TRAIANVS AVG.,* 77–86. Seville.

Curtis, R. I. 1988. "Spanish Trade in Salted Fish Products in the First and Second Centuries A.D." *International Journal of Nautical Archeology* 17:205–210.

———. 1991. *Garum and salsamenta: Production and Commerce in Materia Medica.* Leiden.

Dardaine, S. 1993. "Liberalités chiffrées et richesse des notables municipaux en Bétique." In J. F. Rodríguez Neila, ed., *Actas del Iᵉʳ coloquio de historia antigua de Andalucía, Córdoba 1988,* 57–72. Córdoba.

D'Arms, J. H. 1981. *Commerce and Social Standing in Ancient Rome.* Cambridge, Mass.

———. 2000. "Memory, Money, and Status at Misenum: Three New Inscriptions from the Collegium of the Augustales." *JRS* 90:126–144.

Delgado Delgado, J. A. 1998. *Elites y organización de la religión en las provincias romanas de la Bética y las Mauritanias: Sacerdotes y sacerdocios.* British Archaeological Reports, International Series 724. Oxford.

Deman, A. 1975. "Matériaux et réflexions pour servir à une étude du développement et du sous-développement dans les provinces de l'empire romain." *ANRW* II.3, 3–97. Berlin and New York.

Demougin, S. 1988. *L'ordre équestre sous les Julio-Claudiens.* Rome.

Desbat, A., et al. 1987. "Inscriptions peintes sur amphores: Lyon et Saint-Romain-en-Gal." *Archaeonautica* 7:141–166.

Devijver, H. 1976–1993. *Prosopographia Militarium Equestrium quae fuerunt ab Augusto ad Gallienum.* 5 vols. Leuven.

Didierjean, F. 1978. "Le paysage rural antique au nord-ouest de Seville (Campo et Aljarafe)." *MCV* 14:7–33.

Domergue, C. 1971. "El Cerro del Plomo, mina 'El Centenillo' (Jaén)." *NAH* 16:265–380.

———. 1972. "Rapports entre la zone minière de la sierra Morena et la plaine agricole du Guadalquivir à l'époque romaine." *MCV* 8:614–622.

———. 1973. *Belo I. La stratigraphie.* Paris.

———. 1983. *La mine antique d'Aljustrel (Portugal) et les tables de bronze de Vipasca.* Paris.

———. 1987. *Catalogue des mines et des fonderies antiques de la péninsule ibérique.* Paris.

———. 1990. *Les mines de la péninsule ibérique dans l'antiquité romaine.* Rome.

———. 1994. "Production et commerce des métaux dans le monde romain: L'exemple des métaux hispaniques d'après l'épigraphie des lingots." In *Epigrafia della produzione e della distribuzione, Actes de la VIIe Rencontre franco-italienne sur l'épigraphie du monde romain*, 61–91. Rome.

———. 1998. "A View of Baetica's External Commerce in the First Century A.D. Based on Its Trade in Metals." In S. Keay, ed., *The Archaeology of Early Roman Baetica*, 201–215. Portsmouth, R.I.

Downs, M. E. 1996. "'Romanization' in Southern Spain: A Regional Study of Iberian and Roman Settlement in the Guadalquivir Valley." Dissertation, Indiana University.

———. 2000. "Refiguring Colonial Categories on the Roman Frontier in Southern Spain." In E. Fentress, ed., *Romanization and the City: Creation, Transformations, and Failures*, 197–210. Portsmouth, R.I.

Dressel, H. 1878. "Ricerche sul Monte Testaccio." *Annali dell'Instituto di Correspondenza Archeologica*, 118–192.

Duarte, A.L.C. 1990. "Quinta do Ronxinol: A Produção de ânforas no vale do Tejo." In A. Alarcão and F. Mayet, eds., *Les Amphores Lusitaniennes*, 97–115. Paris.

Duncan-Jones, R. P. 1963. "Wealth and Munificence in Roman Africa." *PBSR* 31: 159–177.

———. 1982. *The Economy of the Roman Empire: Quantitative Studies*. 2d ed. Cambridge.

———. 1990. *Structure and Scale in the Roman Economy*. Cambridge.

Durán, V., and A. Padilla. 1990. *Evolución del poblamiento antiguo en el término municipal de Ecija*. Ecija.

Dyson, S. L. 1980–1981. "The Distribution of Roman Republican Family Names in the Iberian Peninsula." *AncSoc* 11–12:257–299.

Eck, W. 1980. "Epigraphische Untersuchungen zu Konsuln und Senatoren des 1.-3. Jh.n.Chr." *ZPE* 37:31–68.

———. 1997. "Italica, die bätischen Städte und ihr Beitrag zur römischen Reichsaristokratie." In A. Caballos and P. León, eds., *Italica MMCC: Actas de las Jornadas del 2.200 Aniversario de la Fundación de Itálica (Sevilla, 8–11 noviembre 1994)*, 65–86. Seville.

Eck, W., A. Caballos, and F. Fernández. 1996. *Das senatus consultum de Cn. Pisone patre*. Munich.

Edmondson, J. 1990. "Romanization and Urban Development in Lusitania." In T. Blagg and M. Millett, eds., *The Early Roman Empire in the West*, 151–178. Oxford.

Engels, D. W. 1990. *Roman Corinth: An Alternative Model for the Classical City*. Chicago.

Escacena Carrasco, J. L., and A. Padilla Monge. 1992. *El poblamiento romano en las márgenes del antiguo estuario del Guadalquivir*. Ecija.

Etienne, R. 1958. *Le culte impérial dans la Péninsule Ibérique*. Paris.

———. 1965. "Les sénateurs espagnols sous Trajan et Hadrien." In *Les empereurs romains d'Espagne*, 55–82. Paris.

Etienne, R., and F. Mayet. 1998. "Le garum à Pompéi: Production et commerce." *REA* 100:199–215.

Fabião, C. 1989. *Sobre as ânforas do acampamento romano da Lomba do Canho (Arganil).* Cadernos da UNIARQ 1. Lisboa.

———. 1993–1994. "O azeite da Baetica na Lusitania." *Conimbriga* 32–33: 219–246.

Fear, A. T. 1996. *Rome and Baetica: Urbanization in Southern Spain, c. 50 B.C.–A.D. 150.* Oxford.

Fernández Cacho, S. 1995. "Las industrias derivadas de la pesca en la provincia romana de la Bética: La alfarería de 'El Rinconcillo' (Algeciras, Cádiz)." *Spal. Revista de prehistoria y arqueología* 4:173–214.

Fernández Caro, J. J. 1985. "Avance sobre la carta arqueológica de la comarca de Fuentes de Andalucía (Sevilla), 1985." In *AAA 1985. II* [publ. 1987], 109–113. Seville.

———. 1992. *Carta Arqueológica del Término de Fuentes de Andalucía (Sevilla).* Ecija.

Fernández Castro, M. C. 1983. "Fábricas de aceite en el campo hispano-romano." In *Producción y comercio del aceite en la antigüedad: II Congreso Internacional,* 569–599. Madrid.

Fernández Gómez, F. 1991. "Conjunto de matrices de sellos romanos procedentes de Sevilla." In *Alimenta: Estudios en homenaje al Dr. Michel Ponsich,* 309–314. Madrid.

Fernández Jurado, J., et al. 1992. "Nuevas evidencias de Onuba." *CPAM* 19: 289–317.

Fernández Rodríguez, M., and C. García Bueno. 1993. "La minería romana de época republicana en Sierra Morena: El poblado de Valderrepisa (Fuencaliente, Ciudad Real)." *MCV* 29, 1:25–41.

Figlinae Malacitanae: La producción de cerámica romana en los territorios malacitanos. 1997. A series of papers published by the Área de Arqueología de la Universidad de Málaga. Málaga.

Fishwick, D. 1987. *The Imperial Cult in the Latin West.* Leiden.

Fortea, J., and J. Bernier. 1970. *Recintos y fortificaciones ibéricas en la Bética.* Salamanca.

Foxhall, L. 1990. "The Dependent Tenant: Land Leasing and Labor in Italy and Greece." *JRS* 80:97–114.

France, J. 1993. "Administration et fiscalité douanières sous le règne d'Auguste: La date de la création de la Quadragesima Galliarum." *MEFRA* 105:895–927.

Frederiksen, M. 1976. "Changes in the Patterns of Settlement." In P. Zanker, ed., *Hellenismus in Mittelitalien,* 341–355. Göttingen.

Frier, B. W. 1991. "Pompeii's Economy and Society." Review of Jongman 1988. *JRA* 4:243–247.

———. 1993. "Subsistence Annuities and Per Capita Income in the Early Roman Empire." *CP* 88:222–230.

Fuentes, A. 1998. "El vidrio: Estudio de los restos de fabricación de un taller de ungüentarios." In D. Bernal Casasola, ed., *Excavaciones arqueológicas en el alfar romano de la Venta del Carmen, Los Barrios (CADIZ)*, 255–276. Madrid.

Fülle, G. 1997. "The Internal Organization of the Arretine Terra Sigillata Industry: Problems of Evidence and Interpretation." *JRS* 87:111–155.

Funari, P.P.A. 1996. *Dressel 20 Inscriptions from Britain and the Consumption of Spanish Olive Oil*. British Archaeological Reports, British Series 250. Oxford.

Gabba, E. 1954. "Le origini della Guerra Sociale e la vita politica romana dopo l'89 a.C." *Athenaeum* 32:293–345.

Gabler, D., and M. H. Kelemen. 1984. "Olio betico in Pannonia: Anfore ispaniche nella Valle danubiana." *AEA* 57:121–142.

Gallego Franco, M. del Henar. 1991. *Femina dignissima: Mujer y sociedad en Hispania antigua*. Valladolid.

Galsterer, H. 1971. *Untersuchungen zum römischen Städtewesen auf der Iberischen Halbinsel*. Berlin.

———. 1986. "Roman Law in the Provinces: Some Problems of Transmission." In M. H. Crawford, ed., *L'Impero romano e le strutture economiche e sociali delle province*, 13–27. Como.

———. 1988. "Municipium Flavium Irnitanum: A Latin Town in Spain." *JRS* 78:78–90.

Galsterer-Kröll, B. 1972. "Untersuchungen zu den Beinamen von Städten des Imperium Romanum." *ES* 9:44–145.

Garcia-Bellido, M. P. 1994–1995. "Las Torres-recinto y la explotación militar del plomo en Extremadura: Los lingotes del pecio de Comacchio." *Anas* 7–8:187–218.

García Bueno, C., and M. Fernández Rodríguez. 1995. "Minería y metalurgia en Sierra Morena: El poblado romano republicano de Valderrepisa." *Revista de Arqueología* 170:24–31.

García Vargas, E. 1996. "La producción anfórica en la Bahía de Cádiz durante la república como índice de romanización." *Habis* 27:49–62.

———. 2000. "Ánforas romanas producidas en Hispalis: Primeras evidencias arqueológicas." *Habis* 31:235–260.

García Vargas, E., and Mª L. Lavado Florido. 1995. "Ánforas alto, medio y bajo-imperiales producidas en el alfar de Puente Melchor (= Villanueva, Paso a Nivel: Puerto Real, Cádiz)." *Spal. Revista de prehistoria y arqueología* 4:173–214.

García Vargas, E., and J. F. Sibón Olano. 1992. "Intervención arqueológica de emergencia: 'El Gallinero' (Puerto Real, Cádiz)." In *AAA 1992. III* [publ. 1995], 124–129. Cádiz.

García y Bellido, A. 1959. "Las colonias romanas de Hispania." *Anuario de Historia del Derecho Español* 29:447–509.

Gardner, J. F. 1986. *Women in Roman Law and Society*. Bloomington and Indianapolis.

Garnsey, P. 1970. *Social Status and Legal Privilege in the Roman Empire*. Oxford.

———. 1974. "Aspects of the Decline of the Urban Aristocracy in the Empire." *ANRW* II.1, 229–252. Berlin and New York.

———. 1983. "Grain for Rome." In P. Garnsey, K. Hopkins, and C. R. Whittaker, eds., *Trade in the Ancient Economy*, 118–130. London.

———. 1996. "Prolegomenon to a Study of the Land in the Later Roman Empire." In J.H.M. Strubbe, R. A. Tybout, and H. S. Versnel, eds., *Energeia: Studies on Ancient History and Epigraphy Presented to H. W. Pleket*, 135–153. Amsterdam.

Garnsey, P., and R. Saller. 1987. *The Roman Empire: Economy, Society and Culture*. Berkeley.

Gener Basallote, J. M., J. M. Hita Ruiz, N. Marín Díaz, M. A. Pérez Cruz, M. Puentedura Béjar, A. Ventura Villanueva, and F. Villada Paredes. 1992. *Loja durante el dominio romano*. Granada.

Gener Basallote, J. M., P. F. Marfil Ruiz, and M. Puentedura Béjar. 1993. "Loma de Ceres, un centro de producción anfórico." In *II Congreso Peninsular de História Antiga*, 971–993. Coimbra.

Gil Farrés, O. 1966. *La moneda hispánica en la edad antigua*. Madrid.

Gimeno Pascual, H. 1988. *Artesanos y técnicos en la epigrafía de Hispania*. Bellaterra.

Goldsmith, R. W. 1984. "An Estimate of the Size and Structure of the National Product of the Early Roman Empire." *Review of Income and Wealth* 30: 263–288.

———. 1987. *Premodern Financial Systems: A Historical Comparative Study*. Cambridge.

Gómez-Pantoja, J. 1994. "Occultus Callis." *MCV* 30, 1: 61–73.

Gomezel, C. 1994. "Un tappo di anfora Dressel 20 ad Aquileia?" In *Epigrafia della produzione e della distribuzione, Actes de la VIIe Rencontre franco-italienne sur l'épigraphie du monde romain*, 543–545. Rome.

González Fernández, J. 1982. *Inscripciones romanas de la provincia de Cádiz*. Cádiz.

———. 1983. "Nueva inscripción de un difusor olearius en la Bética." In *Producción y comercio del aceite en la antigüedad: II Congreso Internacional*, 183–191. Madrid.

———. 1984. "Tabula Siarensis, Fortunales Siarenses et Municipia Civium Romanorum." *ZPE* 55: 55–100.

———. 1986. "The Lex Irnitana: A New Copy of the Flavian Municipal Law." *JRS* 76: 147–243.

———. 1988a. "The First Oath Pro Salute Augusti Found in Baetica." *ZPE* 72: 113–127.

———. 1988b. "Epigrafía del yacimiento de La Cañada." In J. González and J. Arce, eds., *Estudios sobre la Tabula Siarensis*, 91–126. Madrid.

———. 1989. "M. Petrucidius M.f. legatus pro pr." *Athenaeum* 67: 517–523.

———. 1991. *Corpus de Inscripciones latinas de Andalucía*. Vol. 2, *Sevilla*, book 1: *La Vega (Hispalis)*. Seville.

———. 1996. *Corpus de Inscripciones latinas de Andalucía.* Vol. 2, *Sevilla,* book 3: *La Campiña.* Seville.

———. 1998. "Varia Epigraphica II." *Habis* 29:105–115.

González Román, C. 1978. "Guerra civil y conflictos sociales en la P.H.U. en el 48–44 a.C." In *Actas del I Congreso de Historia de Andalucía: Andalucía antigua,* 131–142. Córdoba.

———. 1990. "Inscripciones romanas inéditas de la provincia de Jaén, III." *FlorIlib* 1:147–159.

González Román, C., and A. Marín Díaz. 1994. "Prosopografía de la Hispania Meridional en época republicana." In C. González Román, ed., *La Sociedad de la Bética,* 241–318. Granada.

González Román, C., and J. Mangas Manjarrés. 1991. *Corpus de Inscripciones Latinas de Andalucía.* Vol. 3, *Jaén,* book 1. Seville.

Gorges, J. G. 1979. *Les villas hispano-romaines.* Paris.

Gozalbes Cravioto, C., and F. Muñoz Hidalgo. 1986. "Fuente de Piedra: La via romana de la sal." *Jábega* 53:20–23.

Granino Cecere, M. G. 1994. "D. Caecilius Abascantus, diffusor olearius ex provincia Baetica (CIL VI 1885)." In *Epigrafia della produzione e della distribuzione, Actes de la VIIᵉ Rencontre franco-italienne sur l'épigraphie du monde romain,* 705–719. Rome.

Grant, M. 1946. *From Imperium to Auctoritas.* Cambridge.

Greene, K. 1986. *The Archaeology of the Roman Economy.* Berkeley.

Griffin, M. 1972. "The Elder Seneca and Spain." *JRS* 62:1–19.

Grünhagen, W. 1978. "Farbiger Marmor aus Munigua." *MDAI(M)* 19:290–306.

Guadán, A. M. de. 1969. *Numismática ibérica e ibero-romana.* Madrid.

Guichard, P. 1990. "Politique flavienne et fiscalité en Hispania." *MCV* 26.1:45–73.

———. 1991. "Sur les procurateurs du Kalendarium Vegetianum et quelques notables municipaux." In *Alimenta: Estudios en homenaje al Dr. Michel Ponsich,* 297–308. Madrid.

———. 1993. "Les effets des mesures flaviennes sur la hiérarchie existant entre les cités de la Péninsule ibérique." In *Ciudad y comunidad cívica en Hispania: Siglos II y III d.C.,* Collection de la Casa de Velázquez 40, 67–84. Madrid.

Haley, E. W. 1988. "Roman Elite Involvement in Commerce: The Case of the Spanish TT. MAMILII." *AEA* 61:141–156.

———. 1990a. "The Fish Sauce Trader L. Iunius Puteolanus." *ZPE* 80:72–78.

———. 1990b. "The Lamp Manufacturer Gaius Iunius Draco." *MBAH* 9, 2:1–13.

———. 1991. *Migration and Economy in Roman Imperial Spain.* Barcelona.

———. 1996a. "Rural Settlement in the Conventus Astigitanus (Baetica) under the Flavians." *Phoenix* 50:283–303.

———. 1996b. "The Land as Map: Problems of Roman Land Division in Baetica." *CB* 72:19–28.

———. 1997. "Town and Country: The Acculturation of S Spain." *JRA* 10: 495–503.

Hanel, N. 1989. "Römische Öl- und Weinproduktion auf der Iberischen Halbinsel am Beispiel von Munigua und Milreu." *MDAI(M)* 30:204-238.

Harl, K. W. 1996. *Coinage in the Roman Economy, 300 B.C. to A.D. 700.* Baltimore and London.

Harris, W. V. 1988. "On the Applicability of the Concept of Class in Roman History." In T. Yuge and M. Doi, eds., *Forms of Control and Subordination in Antiquity,* 598-610. Leiden.

———. 1993. "Between Archaic and Modern: Some Current Problems in the History of the Roman Economy." In idem, ed., *The Inscribed Economy: Production and Distribution in the Roman Empire in the Light of "instrumentum domesticum,"* 11-29. Ann Arbor.

Helly, B., et al. 1986. "Un dépôt d'amphores Dressel 20 à inscriptions peintes découvert à Sainte-Colombe (Rhône)." *Archaeonautica* 6:121-145.

Henderson, M. I. 1942. "Julius Caesar and Latium in Spain." *JRS* 32:1-13.

Hernández Fernández, J. S. 1998. "Los Vibii Pac(c)iaeci de la Bética: Una familia de hispanienses mal conocida." *Faventia* 20:163-176.

Herz, P. 1988. *Studien zur römischen Wirtschaftsgesetzgebung: die Lebensmittelversorgung.* Wiesbaden.

Hesnard, A. 1980. "Un dépôt augustéen d'amphores à La Longarina, Ostie." In J. H. D'Arms and E. C. Kopff, eds., *The Seaborne Commerce of Ancient Rome: Studies in Archaeology and History,* 141-156. Rome.

Hopkins, K. 1980. "Taxes and Trade in the Roman Empire (200 B.C.-A.D. 400)." *JRS* 70:101-125.

Hornos Mata, F., M. Castro López, M. Angel Lagunas, and S. Montilla. 1986. "Actuación arqueológica de urgencia en Cabeza Baja de Encina Hermosa (Castillo de Locubín-Jaén)." In *AAA 1986. III* [publ. 1987], 203-209. Seville.

Hornos Mata, F., C. Choclán Sabina, and J. T. Cruz Garrido. 1985. "Excavación de urgencia en la villa de el Campillo (Castellar, Jaén)." In *AAA 1985. III* [publ. 1987], 217-221. Seville.

Howgego, C. 1992. "The Supply and Use of Money in the Roman World, 200 B.C. to A.D. 300." *JRS* 82:1-31.

Instinsky, H. U. 1944. "Die Herkunft des L. Fabius Cilo." *Philologus* 96:293-294.

Izquierdo, P. 1989. "Àmfores." In J. Nieto Prieto et al., *Excavacions arqueològiques subaquàtiques a Cala Culip I,* 59-83. Girona.

Jabaloy, M. E. 1998. "La villa romana del Cortijo del Canal (Albolote, Granada)." In M. Mayer et al., eds., *De les estructures indígenes a l'organització provincial romana de la Hispània citeriòr: Homenatge a Josep Estrada i Garriga,* 265-273. Barcelona.

Jacques, F. 1990. "Un exemple de concentration foncière en Bétique d'après le témoignage des timbres amphoriques d'une famille clarissime." *MEFRA* 102:865-899.

Jacques, F., and J. Scheid. 1990. *Rome et l'intégration de l'empire (44 av. J.-C.-260 ap. J.-C.).* Paris.

Jashemski, W. F. 1992. "Vasa Fictilia: Ollae Perforatae." In R. M. Wilhelm and H. Jones, eds., *The Two Worlds of the Poet: New Perspectives on Vergil,* 371–391. Detroit.

Jiménez, J. L., and M. Martín-Bueno. 1992. *La casa del Mitra (Cabra, Córdoba).* Cabra.

Jiménez Avila, F. J. 1989–1990. "Notas sobre la minería romano-republicana bajo-extremeña: Las explotaciones de plomo de la Sierra de Hornachos (Badajoz)." *Anas* 2–3 : 123–134.

Jiménez Cisneros, M. J. 1971. *Historia de Cádiz en la Antigüedad.* Cádiz.

Jiménez Pérez, C., et al. 1992. "Excavaciones de urgencia en el solar de la calle San Nicolás N° 7: Una nueva factoría de Salazones en Algeciras (Cádiz)." In *AAA 1992. III* [publ. 1995], 65–69. Cádiz.

Jones, G.D.B. 1980. "The Roman Mines at Riotinto." *JRS* 70 : 146–165.

Jongman, W. 1988. *The Economy and Society of Pompeii.* Amsterdam.

Juárez Martín, J. M. 1989. "Informe de la excavación de urgencia en el Cerro del Hachillo (Lora de Estepa): Junio, Julio y Agosto de 1989." In *AAA 1989. III* [publ. 1991], 480–487. Seville.

Kajanto, I. 1963. *Onomastic Studies in the Early Christian Inscriptions of Rome and Carthage.* Helsinki and Helsingfors.

———. 1965. *The Latin Cognomina.* Helsinki and Helsingfors.

Kampen, N. 1981. *Image and Status: Roman Working Women in Ostia.* Berlin.

Keay, S. J. 1988. *Roman Spain.* London.

———. 1996. "Ideology and the Location of Roman Towns in Baetica." *CB* 72 : 51–57.

———. 1998. "The Development of Towns in Early Roman Baetica." In idem, ed., *The Archaeology of Early Roman Baetica,* 55–86. Portsmouth, R.I.

Kehoe, D. 1988. *The Economics of Agriculture on Roman Imperial Estates in North Africa.* Göttingen.

———. 1997. *Investment, Profit, and Tenancy: The Jurists and the Roman Agrarian Economy.* Ann Arbor.

Knapp, R. C. 1978a. *Aspects of the Roman Experience in Iberia, 206–100 B.C.* Valladolid.

———. 1978b. "The Origins of Provincial Prosopography in the West." *Anc-Soc* 9 : 187–222.

———. 1983. *Roman Córdoba.* Berkeley.

———. 1992. *Latin Inscriptions from Central Spain.* Berkeley.

Köhn, J. 1983. "Die Kolonen in den Rechtsbestimmungen." In K.-P. Johne et al., *Die Kolonen in Italien und den westlichen Provinzen des Römischen Reiches,* 167–257. Berlin.

Krier, J. 1981. *Die Treverer außerhalb ihrer Civitas.* Trier.

Lacort Navarro, P. J. 1982. "Sobre las construcciones romanas de Carchena (Término municipal de Castro del Río, Córduba)." *Habis* 13 : 171–186.

———. 1985. "Cereales en Hispania Ulterior: Silos de época ibero—romana en la campiña de Córdoba." *Habis* 16 : 363–386.

Lacort Navarro, P. J., and E. Melchor Gil. 1993. "Nuevos vestigios de época romana en el entorno de Palma del Río (Córdoba)." *Ariadna* 12:169-188.

Lacort Navarro, P. J., et al. 1986. "Nuevas inscripciones latinas de Córdoba y su provincia." *Faventia* 8:69-109.

Lagóstena Barrios, L. 1993. "Una tésera de plomo hallada en el yacimiento romano de 'Puente Melchor,' Puerto Real (Cádiz)." *Habis* 24:307-309.

———. 1996a. *Alfarería Romana en la Bahía de Cádiz*. Cádiz.

———. 1996b. "Explotación del salazón en la Bahía de Cádiz en la Antigüedad: Aportación al conocimiento de su evolución a través de la producción de las ánforas Mañá C." *FlorIlib* 7:141-169.

Lamberti F. 1993. *"Tabulae Irnitanae": Municipalità e "ius Romanorum."* Naples.

Lara Fuillerat, J. M. 1997. "Testimonios sobre los centros de producción cerámica de época romana y Antigüedad Tardía en la provincia de Córdoba." *Antiquitas* [Museo de Priego] 8:83-96.

Lara Fuillerat, J. M., and C. Camacho Cruz. 1995. "Hornos romanos en los términos municipales de Priego de Córdoba y Fuente Tójar." *Antiquitas* [Museo de Priego] 6:33-52.

Lazarich González, M., et al. 1989. "Informe preliminar de la primera campaña del proyecto de prospección arqueológica sistemática de la campiña sur gaditana: Termino de Puerto Real." In *AAA 1989. II* [publ. 1991], 98-100. Seville.

Leal Linares, P. 1995. *Obulco*. Ecija.

Lebek, W. D. 1993. "La Lex Lati di Domiziano (Lex Irnitana): Le strutture giuridiche dei capitoli 84 e 86." *ZPE* 97:159-178.

Le Gall, J. 1991. "Quelques moyens de gagner sa vie à FLAVIA IRNITANA au temps de l'empereur Domitien." In *Alimenta: Estudios en homenaje al Dr. Michel Ponsich*, 315-321. Madrid.

Leiva Briones, F., and J. V. Madruga Flores. 1992. "La villa romana de 'Las Viñas'; en Zamoranos." *BRAC* 122:247-253.

Le Roux, P. 1982. *L'armée romaine et l'organisation des provinces ibériques d'Auguste à l'invasion de 409*. Paris.

———. 1986. "L'huile de Bétique et le Prince sur un itinéraire annonaire." *REA* 88:247-271.

———. 1987. "Cité et culture municipale en Bétique sous Trajan." *Ktema* 12: 271-284.

———. 1991a. "Municipium Latinum et municipium Italiae: À propos de la lex Irnitana." In *Epigrafia: Actes du Colloque international d'épigraphie latine en mémoire de Attilio Degrassi*, 565-582. Rome.

———. 1991b. "Le Juge et le citoyen dans le municipe d'Irni." *CCG* 2:99-124.

———. 1995. *Romains D'Espagne: Cités et politique dans les provinces II⁶ siècle av. J.-C.-III⁶ siècle ap. J.-C.* Paris.

Leveau, P., P. Sillières, and J.-P. Vallat. 1993. *Campagnes de la Méditerranée Romaine*. Paris.

Ligt, L. de. 1990. "Demand, Supply, Distribution: The Roman Peasantry between

Town and Countryside: Rural Monetization and Peasant Demand." *MBAH* 9: 24–56.

Liou, B. 1980. "Les amphores à huile de l'épave Saint-Gervais 3 à Fos-sur-Mer: Premières observations sur les inscriptions peintes." In *Producción y comercio del aceite en la antigüedad: I Congreso Internacional,* 161–175. Madrid.

———. 1987. "Inscriptions peintes sur amphores: Fos (suite), Marseille, Toulon, Port-la-Nautique, Arles, Saint-Blaise, Saint-Martin-de-Crau, Mâcon, Calvi." *Archaeonautica* 7: 55–139.

———. 1998. "Inscriptions peintes sur amphores de Narbonne (Port-la-Nautique, Aude), III." *RAN* 31: 91–102.

———. 2000. "Les inscriptions peintes des amphores du Pecio Gandolfo (Almería)." *MEFRA* 112: 7–25.

Liou, B., and C. Domergue. 1990. "Le commerce de la Bétique au Ier siècle de nôtre ère: L'épave Sud-Lavezzi 2 (Bonifacio, Corse du Sud)." *Archaeonautica* 10: 56–94.

Liou, B., and J. M. Gassend. 1990. "L'épave Saint-Gervais 3 à Fos-sur-Mer (milieu du IIe siècle ap. J.-C.): Inscriptions peintes sur amphores de Bétique: Vestiges de la coque." *Archaeonautica* 10: 157–264.

Liou, B., and R. Marichal. 1978. "Les inscriptions peintes sur amphores de l'anse Saint-Gervais à Fos-sur-mer." *Archaeonautica* 2: 109–182.

Liou, B., and A. Tchernia. 1994. "L'interprétation des inscriptions sur les amphores Dressel 20." In *Epigrafia della produzione e della distribuzione, Actes de la VIIe Rencontre franco-italienne sur l'épigraphie du monde romain,* 133–156. Rome.

Lomas, F. J., and P. Sáez. 1981. "El Kalendarium Vegetianum, la Annona y el comercio del aceite." *MCV* 17: 55–84.

Long, L., and C. Domergue. 1995. "Le 'véritable plomb de L. Flavius Verucla' et autres lingots: L'épave 1 des Saintes-Maries-de-la-Mer." *MEFRA* 107: 801–867.

López Castro, J. L. 1995. *Hispania Poena: Los Fenicios en la Hispania Romana.* Barcelona.

López de la Orden, M. D. 1979–1980. "Hornos cerámicos romanos en el 'Olivar de los Valencianos' (Puerto Real, Cádiz)." *Boletín del Museo de Cádiz* 2 [publ. 1981]: 59–62.

López de la Orden, M. D., and A. Ruiz Castellano. 1995. *Nuevas inscripciones latinas del Museo de Cádiz.* Cádiz.

Loyzance, M.-F. 1986. "A propos de Marcus Cassius Sempronianus Olisiponensis, diffusor olearius." *REA* 88: 273–283.

Loza Azuaga, M. L. 1982–1983. "Nuevos yacimientos romanos en la depresión de Antequera (Málaga)." *Mainake* 4–5: 191–200.

Loza Azuaga, M. L., and J. Beltrán Fortes. 1988. "Estudio arqueológico del yacimiento romano de Haza Honda (Málaga)." In E. Ripoll Perelló, ed., *Actas del Congreso Internacional "El Estrecho de Gibraltar": Ceuta, 1987,* vol. 1, 999–1001. Madrid.

————. 1990. *La explotación del Mármol blanco de la Sierra de Mijas en época romana.* Bellaterra.

Mackie, N. 1983a. *Local Administration in Roman Spain, A.D. 14–212.* Oxford.

————. 1983b. "Augustan Colonies in Mauretania." *Historia* 32:332–358.

————. 1990. "Urban Munificence and the Growth of Urban Consciousness in Roman Spain." In T. Blagg and M. Millett, eds., *The Early Roman Empire in the West,* 179–192. Oxford.

MacMullen, R. 1974. *Roman Social Relations, 50 B.C. to A.D. 284.* New Haven and London.

————. 1987. "Late Roman Slavery." *Historia* 36:359–382.

————. 1997. "The Roman Empire." In C. G. Thomas, ed., *Ancient History: Recent Work and New Directions,* 79–102. Claremont, Calif.

————. 2000. *Romanization in the Time of Augustus.* New Haven and London.

Manacorda, D. 1977a. "Il kalendarium Vegetianum e le anfore della Betica." *MEFRA* 89:313–332.

————. 1977b. "Anfore spagnole a Pompei." In *L'instrumentum domesticum di Ercolano e Pompei nella prima età imperiale, Quaderni di cultura materiale* 1, 121–133. Rome.

Marín Díaz, M. A. 1986–1987. "La emigración itálica a Hispania en el siglo II a.C." *SHHA* 4–5:53–63.

————. 1988. *Emigración, colonización y municipalización en la Hispania republicana.* Granada.

Marín Díaz, N., and J. A. Mellizo Fernández. 1991. "Hallazgos numismáticos en la 'Villa Romana' de Loma de Ceres, Molvízar (Granada)." In *VII Congreso Nacional de Numismática: Memoria,* 281–288. Madrid.

Marín Díaz, N., et al. 1989. "Informe de la excavación arqueológica de emergencia en Loma de Ceres, 1987–88: Molvízar-Granada." In *AAA 1989. III* [publ. 1991], 220–227. Seville.

Márquez Moreno, C. 1989. "Excavación de un yacimiento romano en Cuesta del Espino. Posadas (Córdoba)." *Ariadna* 7:7–61.

Márquez Trigueros, E. 1996. "Agricultura romana en Sierra Morena." *BRAC* 131:211–223.

Martin-Kilcher, S. 1987. *Die römischen Amphoren aus Augst und Kaiseraugst. 1: Die südspanischen Ölamphoren (Gruppe 1).* Augst.

————. 1994. *Die römischen Amphoren aus Augst und Kaiseraugst. 2: Die Amphoren für Wein, Fischsauce, Südfrüchte (Gruppen 2–24).* Augst.

Mattern, S. P. 1999. *Rome and the Enemy: Imperial Strategy in the Principate.* Berkeley and London.

Mattingly, D. J. 1988. "Oil for Export? A Comparison of Libyan, Spanish and Tunisian Olive Oil Production in the Roman Empire." *JRA* 1:33–56.

————. 1996. "First Fruit? The Olive in the Roman World." In G. Shipley and J. Salmon, eds., *Human Landscapes in Classical Antiquity: Environment and Culture,* 213–253. London and New York.

Mattingly, H. 1936. *Coins of the Roman Empire in the British Museum*. Vol. 3, *Nerva to Hadrian*. London.

Mayer, M., and I. Rodà. 1998. "The Use of Marble and Decorative Stone in Roman Baetica." In S. Keay, ed., *The Archaeology of Early Roman Baetica*, 217–234. Portsmouth, R.I.

Mayet, F. 1970. "Parois fines et céramique sigillée de Riotinto (Huelva)." *Habis* 1: 139–176.

———. 1978. "Marques d'amphores de Maurétanie Tingitaine (Banasa, Thamusida, Volubilis)." *MEFRA* 90:357–406.

———. 1984. *Les céramiques sigillées hispaniques*. 2 vols. Paris.

———. 1986. "Les figlinae dans les marques d'amphores Dressel 20 de Bétique." *REA* 88:285–305.

McElderry, R. 1918. "Vespasian's Reconstruction of Spain." *JRS* 8:53–102.

Medianero Soto, F. J., and M. Romero Pérez. 1990. "Intervención arqueológica de urgencia en la Casería de la Mancha, Antequera (Málaga)." In *AAA 1990. III* [publ. 1992], 389–393. Seville.

Medianero Soto, F. J., and J. C. Tellería Sebastián. 1988. "Algunas consideraciones en torno al yacimiento 'Cerro Sánchez' (Sierra de Yeguas, Málaga)." In *AAA 1988. III* [publ. 1990], 245–250. Seville.

Melchor Gil, E. 1993–1994. "Las élites municipales de Hispania en el alto imperio: Un intento de aproximación a sus fuentes de riqueza." *FlorIlib* 4–5:335–349.

———. 1994. *El mecenazgo cívico en la Bética: La contribución de los evergetas al desarrollo de la vida municipal*. Córdoba.

———. 1995. *Vías romanas de la provincia de Córdoba*. Córdoba.

———. 1999a. "Contactos comerciales en el Alto Guadalquivir, el valle medio del Betis y la zona costera malagueña durante el Alto Imperio." *Habis* 30:253–269.

———. 1999b. "La red viaria romana y la comercialización de los metales de Sierra Morena." In R.M.S. Centeno et al., eds., *Rutas, ciudades y moneda en Hispania*, 311–322. Madrid.

Melchor Gil, E., et al. 1997. "El camino de Corduba a Ategua: Nuevos hallazgos de infraestructura romana viaria en la provincia de Córdoba." *AAC* 8:161–180.

Mentxaka, R. 1993. *El senado municipal en la Bética Hispana a la luz de la lex irnitana*. Vitoria.

Millar, F. 1977. *The Emperor in the Roman World*. Ithaca, N.Y.

Molina Vidal, J. 1997. *La dinámica comercial romana entre Italia e Hispania Citerior*. Alicante.

Monsalud, Marqués de. 1907. "Epigrafía romana, griega y visigótica de Extremadura y Andalucía." *BRAH* 50:248–252.

Montenegro, A. 1975. "Problemas y nuevas perspectivas en el estudio de la Hispania de Vespasiano." *HAnt* 5:7–88.

Montilla Pérez, S. 1987. "Prospección arqueológica superficial en el término municipal de Alcaudete (Jaén): Análisis y conclusiones en torno a un muestreo probabilístico planteado entre las cuencas fluviales de los ríos Víboras y S. Juan." In *AAA 1987. II* [publ. 1990], 132–138. Seville.

Mora Serrano, B. 1993. "Hallazgos monetarios en los territorios malacitanos."
Baetica 15:183–197.

Mora Serrano, B., and P. Corrales Aguilar, P. 1997. "Establecimientos salsarios y producciones anfóricas en los territorios malacitanos." In *Figlinae Malacitanae* 1997, 27–59.

Morena López, J. A. 1990. "Prospección arqueológica superficial de urgencia en los terrenos afectados por el trazado de la variante de Baena (Córdoba)." In *AAA 1990. II* [publ. 1992], 78–82. Seville.

———. 1992. "Avance de resultados de la intervención arqueológica de urgencia en la variante de Montilla." In *AAA 1992. III* [publ. 1995], 252–262. Cádiz.

———. 1994. "El poblado y la necrópolis del Cerro de los Molinillos (Baena, Córdoba)." *BRAC* 126:159–191.

———. 1997. "Apuntes sobre urbanismo y economía en el sector meridional de la Córdoba romana: Excavación arqueológica de urgencia en calle Caño Quebrado, esquina a Ronda de Isasa." *BRAC* 132:85–122.

Morena López, J. A., and J. Serrano Carrillo. 1991. "Obras hidráulicas romanas en la campiña oriental de Córdoba (Baena-Cañete)." In J. Aranda Doncel, ed., *II encuentros de historia local: La campiña, Córdoba*, vol. 1, 117–149. Córdoba.

Moreno Almenara, M. 1997. *La villa altoimperial de Cercadilla (Córdoba): Análisis arqueológico*. Seville.

Moret, P. 1990. "Fortins, 'tours d'Hannibal' et fermes fortifiées dans le monde ibérique." *MCV* 26, 1:5–43.

———. 1995. "Les maisons fortes de la Bétique et de la Lusitanie romaines." *REA* 97:527–564.

———. 1996. *Les fortifications ibériques de la fin de l'âge du bronze à la conquête romaine*. Madrid.

Morley, N. 1996. *Metropolis and Hinterland: The City of Rome and the Italian Economy, 200 B.C.–A.D. 200*. Cambridge.

Mrozek, S. 1987. *Les distributions d'argent et de nourriture dans les villes italiennes du Haut-Empire romain*. Bruxelles.

Muñíz Jaén, I., et al. 2000. "Sobre alfares, silos y almazaras en la villa romana de El Ruedo (Almedinilla, Córdoba)." *Antiquitas* 11–12:233–266.

Muñoz, M. 1987. "Un ejemplo de continuidad del tipo de vivienda ibérica en el municipio de Iponoba: El Cerro del Minguillar (Baena, Córdoba)." In *Los asentamientos ibéricos ante la romanización*, 63–68. Madrid.

Murillo Redondo, J. F., et al. 1989. "Aproximación al estudio del poblamiento protohistórico en el sureste de Córdoba: Unidades políticas, control del territorio y fronteras." In *Arqueología Espacial 13. Fronteras*, 151–172. Teruel.

Nicolet, C. 1991. *Space, Geography, and Politics in the Early Roman Empire*. Ann Arbor.

Nieto, B., and R. Lobón. 1990. "Cubrición de los hornos romanos de Cuevas de Becerro." In *AAA 1990. III* [publ. 1992], 413–416. Seville.

Ojeda Torres, J. M. 1999. "Luces y sombras del estado burocrático: La administración de las provincias hispanas durante el Alto Imperio: El caso de la Bética."

In J. F. Rodríguez Neila and F. J. Navarro Santana, eds., *Elites y promoción social en la Hispania romana,* 145–166. Pamplona.

Orfila Pons, M. 1993. "Terra Sigillata hispánica tardía meridional." *AEA* 66: 125–148.

Orfila Pons, M., et al. 1996. "Estudio preliminar de los elementos constructivos hidráulicos de época romana del río Cubillas (tramo Deifontes-Albolote, Granada)." *AAC* 7:83–114.

Oria Segura, M., et al. 1990. *El poblamiento antiguo en la sierra sur de Sevilla: Zona de Montellano.* Seville.

Ors, A. d'. 1953. *Epigrafía jurídica de la España romana.* Madrid.

———. 1961. "Miscelánea epigráfica: Los bronces de Mulva." *Emerita* 29:203–218.

———. 1986. *La ley Flavia municipal.* Text and commentary. Rome.

Ortiz Juárez, D., et al. 1981. *Catálogo Artístico y Monumental de la Provincia de Córdoba.* Vol. 1, *Adamuz-Bujalance.* Córdoba.

Ortiz Romero, P. 1995. "De recintos, torres y fortines: Usos (y abusos)." *Extremadura Arqueológica* 5, 177–193. Cáceres.

Osborne, R. 1987. *Classical Landscape with Figures.* London.

Pabón, J. M. 1953. "Sobre los nombres de la 'villa' romana en Andalucía." In *Estudios dedicados a Menéndez Pidal,* vol. 4, 87–165. Madrid.

Pailler, J.-M. 1989. "Domitien, la 'loi des Narbonnais' et le culte impérial dans les provinces sénatoriales d'Occident." *RAN* 22:171–189.

Palol, P. de. 1949. "Ponderales y exagia romanobizantinos en España." *Ampurias* 11:127–150.

Panciera, S. 1973. "Osservazioni sui consoli dell'85 d.C." *Rivista Storica dell'Antichità* 3:95–101.

———. 1980. "Olearii." In J. H. D'Arms and E. C. Kopff, eds., *The Seaborne Commerce of Ancient Rome,* 235–250. Rome.

Parker, A. J. 1992. *Ancient Shipwrecks of the Mediterranean and the Roman Provinces.* Oxford.

Parkins, H. M., ed. 1997. *Roman Urbanism: Beyond the Consumer City.* London and New York.

Pascual Guasch, R. 1980. "La evolución de las exportaciones béticas durante el Imperio." In *Producción y Comercio del aceite en la antigüedad: I Congreso Internacional,* 233–242. Madrid.

Pastor, M., and A. U. Stylow. 1996. "Miscelánea epigráfica de la provincia de Jaén II/III." *AAC* 7:283–292.

Pastor Muñoz, M., et al. 1992. *Mirobriga: Excavaciones arqueológicas en el 'Cerro del Cabezo' (Capilla, Badajoz): Campañas 1987–1988.* Mérida.

Paterson, J. 1998. "Trade and Traders in the Roman World: Scale, Structure, and Organisation." In H. Parkins and C. Smith, eds., *Trade, Traders and the Ancient City,* 149–167. London and New York.

Pavis d'Escurac, H. 1976. *La préfecture de l'annone: Service administratif impérial d'Auguste à Constantin.* Rome.

Peacock, D.P.S. 1974. "Amphorae and the Baetican Fish Industry." *AntJ* 54: 232–243.

Peacock, D.P.S., and D. F. Williams. 1986. *Amphorae and the Roman Economy: An Introductory Guide.* London and New York.

Pekáry, T. 1976. *Die Wirtschaft der griechisch-römischen Antike.* Wiesbaden.

Peña, J. T. 1998. "The Mobilization of State Olive Oil in Roman Africa: The Evidence of Late Fourth-Century Ostraca from Carthage." In J. T. Peña et al., *Carthage Papers,* 117–238. Portsmouth, R.I.

Perdigones Moreno, L., et al. 1986. "Excavación en el solar de la calle General Ricardos N° 5–7." In *AAA 1986. III* [publ. 1987], 55–60. Seville.

Perdiguero López, M. 1995. *Aratispi (Cauche el Viejo, Antequera): Investigaciones Arqueológicas.* Málaga.

———. 1995–1996. "La fase romana en Aratispi: (Cauche el Viejo, Antequera): El molino de Aceite." *Mainake* 17–18:125–169.

Pérez López, I., et al. 1999. "Contribución al catálogo de sellos y grafitos anfóricos de la bética: Las producciones de Puerto Real." *XXIV Congreso Nacional de Arqueología. Cartagena 1997,* 695–706. Murcia.

Pérez Macías, J. A., et al. 1997. "Arucci y Turobriga: El proceso de romanización de los llanos de Aroche." *CPAM* 24:189–208.

Pleket, H. W. 1990. "Wirtschaft." In F. Vittinghoff, ed., *Europäische Wirtschafts- und Sozialgeschichte in der römischen Kaiserzeit,* 25–160. Stuttgart.

———. 1993. "Agriculture in the Roman Empire in Comparative Perspective." In H. Sancisi-Weerdenburg, et al., eds., *De agricultura: In memoriam Pieter Willem de Neeve,* 317–342. Amsterdam.

Ponsich, M. 1974. *Implantation rurale antique sur le Bas-Guadalquivir.* Vol. 1. Madrid.

———. 1975. "Perennité des relations dans le circuit du Détroit de Gibraltar." *ANRW* II.3, 655–684. Berlin and New York.

———. 1979. *Implantation rurale antique sur le Bas-Guadalquivir.* Vol. 2. Madrid.

———. 1987. *Implantation rurale antique sur le Bas-Guadalquivir.* Vol. 3. Madrid.

———. 1988. *Aceite de oliva y salazones de pescado: Factores geo-económicos de Bética y Tingitana.* Madrid.

———. 1991. *Implantation rurale antique sur le Bas-Guadalquivir.* Vol. 4. Madrid.

———. 1998. "The Rural Economy of Western Baetica." In S. Keay, ed., *The Archaeology of Early Roman Baetica,* 171–182. Portsmouth, R.I.

Ponsich, M., and M. Tarradell. 1965. *Garum et industrie antiques de salaison dans la Méditerranée occidentale.* Paris.

Portillo, R., et al. 1985. "Porträthermen mit Inschrift im römischen Hispanien." *MDAI(M)* 26:185–217.

Pradales Ciprés, D. 1994. "Orígenes y distribución de la *terra sigillata* en Andalucía: Nuevos datos para el comercio cerámico en la antigüedad." In J. F. Rodríguez Neila, ed., *Actas del I Coloquio de Historia Antigua de Andalucía. Córdoba 1988,* 143–169. Córdoba.

Presedo Velo, F. 1974. "Hallazgo romano en Algeciras." *Habis* 5:189–203.

Price, J. 1987. "Glass Vessel Production in Southern Iberia in the First and Second Centuries A.D.: A Survey of the Archaeological Evidence." *Journal of Glass Studies* 29:30-39.

Puerta, C., and A. U. Stylow. 1985. "Inscripciones romanas del sureste de la provincia de Córdoba." *Gerión* 3:317-346.

Purcell, N. 1983. "The Apparitores: A Study of Social Mobility." *PBSR* 51: 125-173.

———. 1990. Review of W. Jongman, *Economy and Society of Pompeii. Classical Review* 40:111-116.

Rambaud, F. 1996. "Portus Gaditanus: Hipótesis de un nuevo emplazamiento." *Revista de Arqueología* 187:24-35.

———. 1997. "Portus Gaditanus." *MDAI(M)* 38:75-88.

Rambla Torralvo, J., and J. Mayorga Mayorga. 1997. "Hornos de época altoimperial en calle Carretería, Málaga." In *Figlinae Malacitanae* 1997, 61-78.

Ramos Muñoz, J., and R. González Rodríguez. 1990. "Prospección arqueológica superficial en el término municipal de Jerez de la Frontera, Cádiz. Campaña 1990." In *AAA 1990. II* [publ. 1992], 64-75. Seville.

Rathbone, D. 1991. *Economic Rationalism and Rural Society in Third-Century A.D. Egypt.* Cambridge.

Raya de Cardenas, M., and I. Toro Moyano. 1987. "Villa romana del Cortijo Lapuente (Albolote, Granada)." In *AAA 1987. III* [publ. 1990], 233-238. Seville.

Raya de Cardenas, M., et al. 1987. "Excavaciones de urgencia relativas a la villa romana del Cortijo del Canal." In *AAA 1987. III* [publ. 1990], 225-232. Seville.

Recio, A. 1973. "Fragmentos de Sarcófagos Romano-Cristianos en Andalucía." *Antonianum* 48:343-360.

Recio, A., et al. 1989. "Un horno de fabricación cerámica en Vélez-Málaga." *Jábega* 63:21-24.

Recio Ruiz, A. 1993. "Prospecciones arqueológicas en Alameda (Málaga)." In *AAA 1993. III* [publ. 1997], 457-462. Seville.

Recio Ruiz, A., and I. Ruiz Somavilla. 1989-1990. "Prospecciones arqueológicas en el t.m. de Sierra de Yeguas (Málaga)." *Mainake* 11-12:93-110.

Recio Veganzones, A. 1976. "Inscripciones romanas de la Bética: Estepa, Osuna, Martos y Porcuna." *Boletín del Instituto de Estudios Giennenses* 90:71-104.

Remesal Rodríguez, J. 1977-1978. "La economía oleícola bética: nuevas formas de análisis." *AEA* 50-51:87-142.

———. 1979. *La necrópolis sureste de Baelo.* Excavaciones Arqueológicas en España, 104. Madrid.

———. 1980. "Reflejos económicos y sociales en la producción de ánforas olearias béticas (Dressel 20)." In *Producción y comercio del aceite en la antigüedad: I Congreso Internacional,* 131-152. Madrid.

———. 1983. "Ölproduktion und Ölhandel in der Baetica: Ein Beispiel für die Verbindung archäologischer und historischer Forschung." *MBAH* 2, 2:91-111.

———. 1986. *La annona militaris y la exportación de aceite bético a Germania.* Madrid.

———. 1987. "Informe preliminar sobre la primera campaña de excavaciones en Arva (Alcolea del Río, Sevilla)." In *AAA 1987. II* [publ. 1990], 346-353. Seville.

———. 1989. "Tres nuevos centros productores de ánforas Dressel 20 y 23: Los sellos de Lucius Fabius Cilo." *Ariadna* 6:119-153.

———. 1990. "El sistema annonario como base de la evolución económica del Imperio romano." In T. Hackens and M. Miró, eds., *Le commerce maritime romain en Méditerranée occidentale: Colloque international tenu à Barcelone du 16 au 18 mai 1988,* 355-367. Strasbourg.

———. 1991. "Sextus Iulius Possessor en la Bética." In *Alimenta: Estudios en homenaje al Dr. Michel Ponsich,* 281-295. Madrid.

———. 1996. "Mummius Secundinus: El Kalendarium Vegetianum y las confiscaciones de Severo en la Bética (HA Severus 12-13)." *Gerión* 14:195-221.

———. 1997a. "Evergetismo en la Bética, nuevo documento de un municipio ignoto (=¿Oducia?)." *Gerión* 15:283-295.

———. 1997b. *Heeresversorgung und die wirtschaftlichen Beziehungen zwischen der Baetica und Germanien.* Stuttgart.

———. 1998. "Baetican Olive Oil and the Roman Economy." In S. Keay, ed., *The Archaeology of Early Roman Baetica,* 183-199. Portsmouth, R.I.

Remesal Rodríguez, J., et al. 1997. "Arva: Prospecciones en un centro productor de ánforas Dressel 20 (Alcolea del Río, Sevilla)." *Pyrenae* 28:151-178.

Riccobono, S., et al. 1940-1943. *Fontes Iuris Romani Anteiustiniani.* 3 vols. Florence.

Rickman, G. 1980. *The Corn Supply of Ancient Rome.* Oxford.

Richardson, J. S. 1996. *The Romans in Spain.* Oxford.

Richardson, K. M. 1962. "Excavations in Parsonage Field, Watermoor Road, Cirencester, 1959." *AntJ* 42:160-182.

Roca Roumens, M. 1976. *Sigillata hispánica producida en Andújar.* Jaén.

Rodríguez Almeida, E. 1972. "Novedades de epigrafía anforaria del monte Testaccio." In *Recherches sur les amphores romaines,* 107-241. Rome.

———. 1979. "Monte Testaccio: I mercatores dell'olio della Betica." *MEFRA* 91: 873-975.

———. 1980a. "El monte Testaccio, hoy: Nuevos testimonios epigráficos." In *Producción y comercio del aceite en la antigüedad: I Congreso Internacional,* 57-102. Madrid.

———. 1980b. "Vicissitudini nella gestione del commercio dell'olio betico da Vespasiano a Severo Alessandro." In J. H. D'Arms and E. C. Kopff, eds., *The Seaborne Commerce of Ancient Rome,* 277-290. Rome.

———. 1981. "Varia de Monte Testaceo." *Cuadernos de Trabajos de la Escuela Española de Historia y Arqueología en Roma* 15:105-164.

———. 1983. "Altri mercatores dell'olio betico." *Dialoghi di Archeologia* 1:79-86.

———. 1984. *Il Monte Testaccio: Ambiente, storia, materiali.* Rome.

———. 1987-1988. "Diffusores, negotiatores, mercatores olearii." *BCAR* 92:299-306.

———. 1990. "Revisitando el Testaccio." In T. Hackens and M. Miró, eds., *Le com-*

merce maritime romain en Méditerranée occidentale: Colloque international tenu à Barcelone du 16 au 18 mai 1988, 369-390. Strasbourg.

———. 1993. "Graffiti e produzione anforaria della Betica." In W. V. Harris, ed., *The Inscribed Economy*, 95-106. Ann Arbor.

———. 1994a. "Scavi sul Monte Testaccio: Novità dai Tituli Picti." In *Epigrafia della produzione e della distribuzione, Actes de la VIIᵉ Rencontre franco-italienne sur l'épigraphie du monde romain*, 111-131. Rome.

———. 1994b. "Los *tituli picti*." In J. M. Blázquez, ed., *Excavaciones arqueológicas en el Monte Testaccio (Roma): Memoria Campaña 1989*, 36-129. Madrid.

Rodríguez Almeida, E., and S. Schupbach. 1982-1983. "Nota su un nuovo mercator olearius del commercio betico." *BCAR* 88:99-103.

Rodríguez Díaz, A. 1995. "El 'problema de la Beturia' en el marco del poblamiento protohistórico del Guadiana Medio." *Extremadura Arqueológica* 5:157-175.

Rodríguez Neila, J. F. 1973. *Los Balbos de Cádiz*. Seville.

———. 1994a. "El epígrafe CIL, II. 2242—Corduba—y las 'locationes' de propiedades públicas municipales." In C. González Román, ed., *La Sociedad de la Bética*, 425-460. Granada.

———. 1994b. "Organización territorial romana y administración municipal en la Bética." In *Actas del II Congreso de Historia de Andalucía: Córdoba, 1991: Historia Antigua*, vol. 3, 201-248. Córdoba.

———. 1999. "Elites municipales y ejercicio del poder en la Bética romana." In J. F. Rodríguez Neila and F. J. Navarro Santana, eds., *Elites y promoción social en la Hispania romana*, 25-102. Pamplona.

Rodríguez Neila, J. F., C. González Román, J. Mangas, and A. Orejas. 1999. *El trabajo en la Hispania romana*. Madrid.

Rodríguez Neila, J. F., and E. Melchor Gil. 2001. "Evergetismo y cursus honorum de los magistrados municipales en las provincias de Bética y Lusitania." In C. Castillo, F. J. Navarro, and R. Martínez, eds., *De Augusto a Trajano: Un siglo en la historia de Hispania*, 139-238. Pamplona.

Rodríguez Oliva, P. 1993. "Transformaciones urbanas en las ciudades de la Baetica durante el alto imperio." In *La ciudad en el mundo romano: Pre-Actas: XIV Congreso Internacional de Arqueología Clásica*, 187-204. Tarragona.

———. 1997. "Los hornos romanos de Torrox." In *Figlinae Malacitanae 1997*, 271-303.

Rodríguez Temiño, I. 1990. "Hallazgos de dos ánforas con 'tituli picti' en Écija (Sevilla)." *AEA* 63:292-295.

Roldán Gómez, L. 1999. "La presencia del vino en el entorno de Jerez en época romana: Elementos arqueológicos e iconográficos." In S. Celestino Pérez, ed., *El vino en la Antigüedad Romana*, 201-224. Madrid.

Roldán Hervás, J. M. 1978. "La crisis republicana en la Hispania Ulterior." In *Actas del I Congreso de Historia de Andalucía: Andalucía antigua*, 109-130. Córdoba.

Romero Corral, R. M. 1995. "La presa romana de Torretejada (Belalcázar, Córdoba)." *AAC* 6:295-309.

Romero de Torres, E. 1915. "Antigüedades romanas e ibéricas de Castillo de Locubín y Fuensanta de Martos, en la provincia de Jaén." *BRAH* 66:564–575.

Romero Moragas, C. 1985. "Un horno de cerámica común romana en Marchena (Sevilla)." In *AAA 1985. III* [publ. 1987], 285–287. Seville.

Romero Moragas, C., and J. M. Campos Carrasco. 1986. "La villa romana del Cortijo de Miraflores: Sevilla." In *AAA 1986. III* [publ. 1987], 321–328. Seville.

Romero Pérez, M. 1987. "El Callumbar: Una villa Romana dedicada a la producción del aceite." In *AAA 1987, III* [publ. 1990], 500–508. Seville.

———. 1993a. "Arqueología de urgencia en la comarca de Antequera: Nuevos descubrimientos." *Revista de Arqueología* 151:56.

———. 1993b. "Sondeo arqueológico de urgencia en la villa romana del Batán: Antequera, Málaga." In *AAA 1993. III*, 498–502. Seville.

———. 1993–1994. "La necrópolis romana de las Maravillas: Bobadilla: Málaga." *Mainake* 15–16:195–222.

———. 1997–1998. "Algunas reflexiones sobre la producción de aceite en las villae de la comarca de Antequera." *Mainake* 19–20:115–141.

Romero, M., and J. Medianero. 1992. "Informe preliminar de excavación de urgencia: Casería 'La Mancha.' Antequera (Málaga)." In *AAA 1992. III* [publ. 1995], 501–503. Cádiz.

Romero Pérez, M., and F. Melero García. 1999. "Resultado de la primera intervención en la villa romana de la Estación. Antequera (Málaga)." *Jábega* 80:3–14.

Romo Salas, A. S. 1993. "El conjunto alfarero romano de Azanaque (Lora del Río, Sevilla): Intervención de 1993." In *AAA 1993. III* [publ. 1997], 766–777. Seville.

Romo Salas, A. S., and J. M. Vargas Jiménez. 1993. "Prospección arqueológica y diagnosis en la finca de Doña Ana (Dos Hermanas, Sevilla)." In *AAA 1993. III* [publ. 1997], 670–682. Seville.

Rougé, J. 1978. "Aspects économiques du Lyon antique." In *Les martyrs de Lyon (177)*, Colloques Internationaux du Centre National de la Recherche Scientifique no. 575, 47–63. Paris.

Ruggiero, E. de, ed. 1895–. *Dizionario Epigrafico di Antichità Romane*. Rome.

Ruiz, A., et al. 1987. "La excavación arqueológica de urgencia en el cerro de la Horca, La Guardia, Jaén." In *AAA 1987. III* [publ. 1990], 344–353. Seville.

Ruiz Delgado, M. M. 1985. *Carta arqueológica de la campiña sevillana Zona Sureste*. Vol. 1. Seville.

Ruiz Nieto, E., and R. Secilla Redondo. 1990. "Intervención arqueológica de emergencia en los Paseillos (Monturque, Córdoba)." In *AAA 1990. III* [publ. 1992], 54–59. Seville.

Sáez Fernández, P. 1978. "Las centurias de la Bética." *Habis* 9:255–271.

———. 1987. *Agricultura romana de la Bética*. Vol. 1. Seville.

———. 1994. "Notas sobre pervivencias del elemento indígena en la Bética romana: Cuestiones a debate." In C. González Román, ed., *La Sociedad de la Bética*, 461–493. Granada.

———. 1998. "Transformaciones agrarias de la República al Imperio en la zona meridional hispana." In J. Mangas, ed., *Italia e Hispania en la crisis de la república romana,* 99-106. Madrid.

Sáez Fernández, P., and G. Chic García. 1983. "La epigrafía de las ánforas olearias béticas como posible fuente para el estudio del colonato en la Bética." In *Producción y comercio del aceite en la antigüedad: II Congreso Internacional,* 193-210. Madrid.

Saller, R. P. 1994. *Patriarchy, Property and Death in the Roman Family.* Cambridge.

Sánchez León, M. L. 1978. *Economía de la Hispania meridional durante la dinastía de los Antoninos.* Salamanca.

Sánchez-Corriendo Jaén, J. 1997. "La ganadería en la Hispania antigua." Diss., Univ. Complutense de Madrid.

Sánchez-Lafuente Pérez, J. 1990. "Terra sigillata de Segóbriga y ciudades del entorno: Valéria, Complutum y Ercavica." Diss., Univ. Complutense de Madrid.

Santos Jener, S. 1950. "Rute (Córdoba): 'Zambra. Las Viñuelas.'" *NAH* 1:229.

Saumagne, C. 1965. *Le droit latin et les cités romaines sous l'empire.* Paris.

Schulten, A. 1892. *De conventibus civium Romanorum.* Berlin.

Schulze-Oben, H. 1989. *Freigelassene in den Städten des römischen Hispanien.* Bonn.

Sciallano, M., and P. Sibella. 1994. *Amphores: Comment les identifier?* 2d ed. Aix-en-Provence.

Sealey, P. R. 1985. *Amphoras from the 1970 Excavations at Colchester Sheepen.* British Archaeological Reports, British Series 142. Oxford.

Segura Arista, M. L. 1988. *La ciudad ibero-romana de Igabrum (Cabra, Córdoba).* Córdoba.

———. 1993. "Explotación romana de las canteras de 'Mármol rojo de Cabra': Fuente económica del municipio de Igabrum." In J. F. Rodríguez Neila, ed., *Actas del I Coloquio de Historia Antigua de Andalucía: Córdoba, 1988,* 111-124. Córdoba.

Serrano Carrillo, J., and J. A. Morena López. 1984. *Arqueología inédita de Córdoba y Jaén.* Córdoba.

Serrano Delgado, J. M. 1988. *Status y promoción social de los libertos en Hispania Romana.* Seville.

Serrano Peña, J. L., and C. Rísquez Cuenca. 1989. "Informe de la obra de emergencia: Prospección con sondeo y limpieza en el yacimiento arqueológico Horno del Castillo Guarromán (Jaén)." In *AAA 1989. III* [publ. 1991], 255-265. Seville.

Serrano Ramos, E. 1979. "Sigillata hispánica de los hornos de la Cartuja (Granada)." *BSEAA* 45:31-80.

———. 1991. *Terra sigillata hispánica de los alfares de Singilia Barba.* Málaga.

———. 1993. "Notas sobre el yacimiento arqueológico de la Loma de Benagalbón." *Baetica* 15:199-205.

———. 1995. "Produciones de cerámicas comunes locales de la Bética." In X.

Aquilué and M. Roca, eds., *Ceràmica comuna romana d'època Alto-Imperial a la Península Ibèrica: Estat de la qüestió*, 227–249. Empúries.

Serrano Ramos, E., R. Atencia Páez, and A. de Luque Moraño. 1983. "Informe preliminar sobre la estratigrafía del yacimiento Iberromano del Cerro de los Castillones, Campillos (Málaga)." *XVI Congreso Arqueológico Nacional*, 813–828. Zaragoza.

———. 1985. "Memoria de las excavaciones del yacimiento arqueológico en 'El Tesorillo' (Teba, Málaga)." *NAH* 26:117–162.

Serrano Ramos, E., R. Atencia Páez, and P. Rodríguez Oliva. 1984. "Un nuevo taller de sigillata en la Baetica: Alameda (Málaga)." *Baetica* 7:171–184.

———. 1991–1992. "Novedades epigráficas de Singilia Barba. *Mainake* 13–14: 171–203.

Serrano Ramos, E., A. Gómez Valero, and J. C. Castaños Ales. 1992. "Un nuevo taller de sigillata en la Baetica: Teba (Málaga)." *Baetica* 14:181–202.

Serrano Ramos, E., and A. de Luque Moraño. 1979. "Una villa romana en Cártama (Málaga)." *Mainake* 1:147–164.

Serrano Ramos, E., and P. Rodríguez Oliva. 1974. "Cerro Alcaide: Un alfar romano en Casabermeja." *Jábega* 6:56–62.

Setälä, P. 1977. *Private Domini in Roman Brick Stamps of the Empire: A Historical and Prosopographical Study of Landowners in the District of Rome*. Helsinki.

Shaw, B. D. 1984. "Latin Funerary Epigraphy and Family Life in the Later Roman Empire." *Historia* 33:457–497.

Sherwin-White, A. N. 1966. *The Letters of Pliny: A Historical and Social Commentary*. Oxford.

Sillières, P. 1990. *Les voies de communication de l'Hispanie méridionale*. Paris.

Sirks, B. 1991. *Food for Rome: The Legal Structure of the Transportation and Processing of Supplies for the Imperial Distributions in Rome and Constantinople*. Amsterdam.

Smit Nolen, J. U. 1988. "A villa romana do Alto do Cidreira (Cascais)-os materiais." *Conimbriga* 27:61–140.

Solin, H. 1971. *Beiträge zur Kenntnis der griechischen Personnenamen in Rom I*. Helsinki.

———. 1982. *Die griechischen Personennamen in Rom: Ein Namenbuch*. 3 vols. Berlin.

Soto Iborra, A., et al. 1994. "Memoria definitiva de la prospección arqueológica de urgencia efectuada sobre el trazado del tramo Ardales-Campillos de la C-341 (Málaga)." In *AAA 1994. III* [publ. 1999], 336–346. Seville.

Sotomayor, M. 1964–1965. "Excavaciones en la Huerta de la Facultad de Teología de Granada." *NAH* 8–9 [publ. 1966]: 193–202.

———. 1972. "Andújar centro de producción y exportación de sigillata a Mauritania." *NAH* 1:263–289. Madrid.

———. 1997. "Algunas observaciones sobre hornos y excavaciones de alfares romanos." In *Figlinae Malacitanae* 1997, 9–26.

Sotomayor, M., et al. 1979. "Los alfares romanos de Andújar: Campañas de 1974, 1975 y 1977." *NAH* 6:441-497.

Sotomayor Muro, M., et al. 1999. "Centro de producción de Los Villares, Andújar (Jaén)." In M. Roca Roumens and M. I. Fernández García, eds., *Terra Sigillata Hispánica*, 19-60. Jaén and Málaga.

Spurr, M. S. 1986. *Arable Cultivation in Roman Italy, c. 200 B.C.-c. A.D. 100.* London.

Stuart, P. 1977. *Gewoon aardewerk uit de Romeinse legerplaats en de bijbehorende grafvelden te Nijmegen.* Beschrijving van de verzamelingen in het Rijksmuseum G. M. Kam te Nijmegen 6.

Stylow, A. U. 1983. "Inscripciones latinas del sur de la provincia de Córdoba." *Gerión* 1:267-303.

———. 1985. "Ordenación territorial romana en el valle de los Pedroches ('Conventus Cordubensis')." *XVII Congreso Nacional de Arqueología*, 657-666. Zaragoza.

———. 1986. "Apuntes sobre epigrafía de época flavia en Hispania." *Gerión* 4: 285-311.

———. 1988. "Epigrafía romana y paleocristiana de Palma del Río. Córdoba." *Ariadna* 5:115-150.

———. 1989-1990. "Más Hermas." *Anas* 2-3:195-206.

———. 1991. "El Municipium Flavium V(———) de Azuaga (Badajoz) y la municipalización de la Baeturia Turdulorum." *SHHA* 9:11-27.

———. 1995. "Los inicios de la epigrafía latina en la Bética: El ejemplo de la epigrafía funeraria." In F. Beltrán Lloris, ed., *Roma y el Nacimiento de la Cultura Epigráfica en Occidente*, 219-238. Zaragoza.

Stylow, A. U., and R. López Melero. 1995. "Epigraphische Miszellen aus der Provinz Jaén. 1. Eine Grabbuße zugunsten der Res publica Aiungitanorum." *Chiron* 25:357-386.

Stylow, A. U., et al. 1995. *Corpus Inscriptionum Latinarum: Editio altera.* Vol. 2, part 7: *Conventus Cordubensis.* Berlin.

———. 1998. *Corpus Inscriptionum Latinarum: Editio altera.* Vol. 2, part 5: *Conventus Astigitanus.* Berlin.

Syme, R. 1958. *Tacitus.* 2 vols. Oxford.

———. 1969. "A Governor of Tarraconensis." *ES* 8:125-133.

———. 1977. "La richesse des aristocraties de Bétique et de Narbonnaise." *Ktema* 2:373-380.

———. 1983. "Antistius Rusticus: A Consular from Corduba." *Historia* 32:359-374.

Taglietti, F. 1994. "Un inedito bollo laterizio Ostiense ed il commercio dell'olio betico." In *Epigrafia della produzione e della distribuzione, Actes de la VIIe Rencontre franco-italienne sur l'épigraphie du monde romain*, 157-193. Rome.

Talbert, R.J.A. 1984. *The Senate of Imperial Rome.* Princeton.

Taylor, L. R. 1961. "Freedmen and Freeborn in the Epitaphs of Imperial Rome." *AJPh* 82:113-132.

Tchernia, A. 1980. "D. Caecilius Hospitalis et M. Iulius Hermesianus (CIL, VI, 1625b et 20742)." In *Producción y comercio del aceite en la antigüedad: I Congreso Internacional,* 155-160. Madrid.

————. 1986. *Le vin de l'Italie romaine.* Rome.

Tellería Sebastián, J. C., and F. J. Medianero Soto. 1995-1996. "Intervención arqueológica en Sierra de Yeguas: Materiales y cronología." *Mainake* 17-18:171-179.

Temin, P. 2001. "A Market Economy in the Early Roman Empire." *JRS* 91: 169-181.

Thevenot, E. 1952. "Una familia de negociantes en aceite establecida en la Baetica en el siglo II: Los Aelii Optati." *AEA* 25:225-231.

Thompson, L. A. 1982. "On 'Development' and 'Underdevelopment' in the Early Roman Empire." *Klio* 64:383-401.

Thouvenot, R. 1940. *Essai sur la province romaine de Bétique.* Paris.

Tovar, A. 1974. *Iberische Landeskunde.* Part 2, vol. 1: *Baetica.* Baden-Baden.

Tsirkin, J. B. 1981. "The South of Spain in the Civil War of 50-45." *AEA* 44: 91-100.

Van Nostrand, J. J. 1937. "Roman Spain." In T. Frank, ed., *An Economic Survey of Ancient Rome,* 119-224. Baltimore.

Vaquerizo Gil, D., and J. Carrillo Díaz-Pines. 1995. "The Roman Villa of El Ruedo (Almedinilla, Córdoba)." *JRA* 8:121-154.

Vaquerizo Gil, D., J. F. Murillo, J. R. Carillo, M. F. Moreno, A. León, M. D. Luna, and A. M. Zamorano. 1994. *Arqueología cordobesa: El Valle Alto del Guadiato (Fuenteobejuna, Córdoba).* Córdoba.

Vaquerizo Gil, D., J. F. Murillo Redondo, and F. Queseda Sanz. 1991. "Excavación arqueológica con sondeos estratigráficos en el Cerro de las Cabezas (Fuente Tójar, Córdoba). Campaña de 1991. Informe preliminar." In *AAA 1991. II* [publ. 1993], 120-126. Cádiz.

————. 1992. "Excavación arqueológica con sondeos estratigráficos en Cerro de las Cabezas (Fuente Tójar, Córdoba). Campaña de 1991. Avance a su estudio." *AAC* 3:171-197.

————. 1994. *Arqueología cordobesa: Fuente Tójar.* Córdoba.

Ventura Villanueva, A. 1993. "Susum ad montes s(ocietatis) S(isaponensis): Nueva inscripción tardorrepublicana de Corduba." *AAC* 4:49-61.

————. 1999. "El teatro en el contexto urbano de Colonia Patricia (Córdoba): Ambiente epigráfico, evergetas y culto imperial." *AEA* 72:57-72.

Veny, C. 1979. "Nuevos materiales de Moro Boti." *Trabajos de Prehistoria* 36: 465-488.

Veny, C., and D. Cerdá. 1972. "Materiales arqueológicos de dos pecios de la isla de Cabrera (Baleares)." *Trabajos de Prehistoria* 29:298-328.

Veyne, P. 1961. "Vie de Trimalcion." *Annales: Economies, sociétés, civilisations* 16: 213-247.

Villanueva Acuña, M. 1993. "Condicionantes de la economía rural romana: Aplicación al análisis de la economía de las *villae* peninsulares." In *II Congreso Peninsular de História Antiga*, 931–954. Coimbra.

Villaseca Díaz, F. 1997. "La producción anfórica de los hornos de la finca 'El Secretario' (Fuengirola)." In *Figlinae Malacitanae* 1997, 261–269.

Villaseca Díaz, F., and R. F. Hiraldo Aguilera. 1991. "Excavaciones de urgencia en el yacimiento romano de la finca 'El Secretario.' Fuengirola-Málaga." In *AAA 1991. III* [publ. 1993], 385–388. Seville.

Vittinghoff, F. 1952. *Römische Kolonisation und Bürgerrechtspolitik unter Caesar und Augustus.* Wiesbaden.

Vries, J. de. 1974. *The Dutch Rural Economy in the Golden Age, 1500–1700.* New Haven.

Wells, C. M. 1972. *The German Policy of Augustus.* Oxford.

Whittaker, C. R. 1985. "Trade and the Aristocracy in the Roman Empire." *Opus* 4:49–75.

———. 1993. "Do Theories of the Ancient City Matter?" In T. J. Cornell and H. K. Lomas, eds., *Urban Society in Roman Italy*, 1–20. London.

Wickham, C. 1988. Review of A. Giardina, ed., *Società Romana e Impero Tardoantico*, vol. 3, *Le Merci: Gli Insediamenti* (Rome and Bari, 1986). *JRS* 78: 183–193.

Wiegels, R. 1972. "Die römischen Senatoren und Ritter aus den Hispanischen Provinzen." Ph.D. diss., University of Freiburg.

———. 1985. *Die Tribusinschriften des römischen Hispanien.* Berlin.

Wierschowski, L. 1995. *Die regionale Mobilität in Gallien nach den Inschriften des 1. bis 3. Jahrhunderts n. Chr.* Stuttgart.

Will, E. L. 1983. "Exportation of Olive Oil from Baetica to the Eastern Mediterranean." In *Producción y comercio del aceite en la antigüedad: II Congreso Internacional*, 391–440. Madrid.

Wilson, A.J.N. 1966. *Emigration from Italy in the Republican Age of Rome.* Manchester.

Woolf, G. 1998. *Becoming Roman: The Origins of Provincial Civilization in Gaul.* Cambridge.

Yardley, J. C. 1994. *Justin: Epitome of the Philippic History of Pompeius Trogus.* Atlanta.

Zarzalejos Prieto, M., et al. 1994. "Excavaciones en la Bienvenida (Ciudad Real): Hacia una definición preliminar del horizonte histórico-arqueológico de la Sisapo antigua." In J. L. Sánchez Meseguer et al., eds., *Jornadas de arqueología de Ciudad Real en la Universidad Autónoma de Madrid*, 167–194. Madrid.

Zevi, F. 1966. "Appunti sulle anfore romane. I—La tavola tipologica del Dressel." *Archeologia Classica* 18:208–247.

———. 1989. "Introduction." In *Amphores romaines et histoire économique: Dix ans de recherche, Actes du colloque de Sienne (22–24 mai 1986)*, 3–19. Rome.

Index

kilns (or ovens), 42, 61, 84, 87, 91, 93,
96–101, 116, 210n.137
Kotinoussa (Gades), 27
Kouass ceramics, 21

La Alcazaba de Badajoz, 201n.40
labor: in Egypt, 127; in fish sauce production, 26; of independent persons,
170; in oleiculture, 45, 134; as productive factor, 171–172; productivity of, 2,
173; on small *fundi*, 216n.95; temporary, 129–130. *See also* Africa; *merce-
narii;* slaves; tenants
Lacernae Baeticae, 65
Lacilbula, 81
Lacimurga, 38, 55
Lacippo, 49, 104
Lacus Ligustinus, 25, 43, 56, 106, 139,
187
La Fuente del Río (Cabra), 29
Laguna Salada or de Fuente Piedra, 72,
94, 111
La Loma (Chipiona), 26
lamps, 30, 51, 54, 92, 110, 118, 120, 174
landholding, 33, 37, 69, 78, 80
La Rambla (Sabetum?), 19, 193n.5
La Serena, mining region, 48, 65
La Tabla de las Cañas (Capilla), 201n.40
Latium, 59, 194n.22
legions, 174; *Alaudae,* 17; X *Gemina,* 48;
IIII *Macedonica,* 48: *Prima,* 48;
Quinta, 17; XX *Valeria Victrix,* 139;
Vernacula, 17
legumes, 134, 216n.97
Lex: Irnitana, 5, 8–9, 82, 109, 177–179;
Trebonia, 16
Libertas Augusta, 166, 213n.18
Licinius Crassus, M., 18
limes, 189
limitatio, 78, 186
liturgies. *See munera*
locatio censoria, 27
locatio-conductio (leasing), 62, 87, 104,
113, 208n.92, 220n.76

locupletes, 90, 178, 182, 190
Loma del Juncal, 57
Lomba do Canho (Roman fort), 25–26
London, 148, 221n.111
loom weights, 42–43, 75, 97, 100
Los Castellares, 192n.30
Los Castillejos-2 (Fuente de Cantos),
201n.40
Los Pedroches, geology and soils of,
116–117
Los Villares (Andújar), 102–103
Lucena, 98, 104
Lucius Caesar, 46
Lucius Verus, 90, 92; rescript of, 182–183
Lugdunum, 71
Lusitania, 46, 55, 63, 67; boundaries of,
34; fish sauce producer from, 203n.83;
property of senatorial Tutilii in,
219n.57; *sigillata* from Isturgi in, 102

Mâcon, 157, 225n.178
magister navis, 182
magistrates, local, 5, 8, 18–19, 52–53, 56,
90, 109, 112–113, 136, 142, 144–146,
153, 155, 158, 163, 166–167, 178,
224n.163, 227n.234. *See also*
Singili(a?) Barba
Magnius Rufus Magonianus, P., 142
"maisons fortes" or *turres,* 48–49, 51,
110; chronology of, 199n.9; at Torremorana, 75
Malaca, 17, 28, 63, 102, 104, 125, 179;
minimum census of jurors at, 177; Pottery (*figlina*) in, 85; Syrian and
Asian(?) merchants at, 94
mancipatio, 131
marble, 54, 72–73, 100, 104–105, 112;
revetment plaques, 23, 75, 106
Marcus Aurelius, 90, 92, 128, 206n.40;
rescript of, 182–183
Marismas, 43, 107–108
Marius, Sextus, 65, 67, 143, 219n.62
Marius L.f. Gal. Vegetinus, L., 138, 218–
219n.46